RAVEN *and the* HUMMINGBIRD

Also by Renate F. Caldwell

No Key to Turn: A Documentary Film

RAVEN *and the*
HUMMINGBIRD

A Healing Path to Recovery from Multiple Personality Disorder

A True Account

RENATE F. CALDWELL

Raven and the Hummingbird:
A Healing Path to Recovery from Multiple Personality Disorder

For information about this title or to order other books and/or electronic media, contact the publisher:

M & M Publishing
http://www.ravenandthehummingbird.com
mandm_publishing@yahoo.com

ISBNs:
978-1-7379199-2-6 (hardcover)
978-1-7379199-0-2 (paperback)
978-1-7379199-1-9 (eBook)

Printed in the United States of America

Library of Congress Control Number: 2022903071

Publisher's Cataloging-In-Publication Data
(Prepared by The Donohue Group, Inc.)
Names: Caldwell, Renate F., author.
Title: Raven and the hummingbird : a healing path to recovery from multiple personality disorder : a true account / Renate F. Caldwell, LPC.
Description: [Norman, Oklahoma] : M & M Publishing, [2022] | Include bibliographical references.
Identifiers: ISBN 9781737919926 (hardcover) | ISBN 9781737919902 (paperback) | ISBN 9781737919919 (ebook)
Subjects: LCSH: Multiple personality--Patients--Treatment--Case studies. | Psychotherapist and patient--Case studies. | Psychotherapy--Case studies. | LCGFT: Case studies.
Classification: LCC RC569.5.M8 C35 2022 (print) | LCC RC569.5.M8 (ebook) | DDC 616.85236--dc23

Cover design: Robin Locke Monda
Interior design: 1106 Design

Photos of *Hide and Seek* used by permission. Tchelitchew, Pavel (1898-1957). *Hide and Seek*. Derby, Vermont and New York, June 1940—June 1942. Oil on canvas, 6'61/2" x 7'3/4" (199.3 x 215.3 cm.). Mrs. Simon Guggenheim Fund. Digital Image © The Museum of Modern Art/Licensed by SCALA/ Art Resource, New York.

Artwork by "Joan" whose true name is withheld by mutual agreement. Photos of Artwork by Gina Dittmer, Dittmer Photography. Author's Photo by Gina Dittmer, Dittmer Photography.

For Joan
A Woman of Substance and Faith

A Note of Caution

Raven and the Hummingbird includes some passages that describe child sexual abuse in graphic detail, a necessary depiction to fully understand the traumatic childhood experiences leading to multiple personality disorder. Should you, the reader, have a history of trauma and become emotionally overwhelmed, please put this book aside and, if appropriate, seek counseling.

TABLE OF CONTENTS

Introduction   xiii

Prologue: Women at the Well   xvii

I Unfolding

Chapter 1   Joan's Choice 3
Chapter 2   Emergence 8
Chapter 3   The Tree Girls. 18
Chapter 4   A Safety Plan 27
Chapter 5   Accidental Feelings 34
Chapter 6   Longings 42
Chapter 7   Establishing Communication 50
Chapter 8   Leslie 54
Chapter 9   Notes and Secrets 62
Chapter 10 The Pending Visit 68
Chapter 11 The Safe Place 76
Chapter 12 Out of Darkness 79
Chapter 13 The Sentinel 86
Chapter 14 Lamentations 93
Chapter 15 Unrest 96

II Telling Secrets

Chapter 16 The Rope 103

Chapter 17 See But Not Know Me 111

Chapter 18 Heartbreak 114

Chapter 19 Alcohol Is a Fickle Seducer 119

Chapter 20 A Blue Aura 122

Chapter 21 Night Falls 126

Chapter 22 The Barn 130

Chapter 23 The Mother's Bed 135

Chapter 24 JJ 138

Chapter 25 Educating Roger 141

Chapter 26 Shadowman 146

Chapter 27 Sophia 151

Chapter 28 Deliverance 157

Chapter 29 Setback 166

Chapter 30 The Internal Mother 168

Chapter 31 The Mischief-Maker 177

Chapter 32 Love Is Like a Flashlight 180

III Suffering Through

Chapter 33 The Wounded Rose 185

Chapter 34 Shadowman's Struggle 196

Chapter 35 Confessions 204

Chapter 36 Tickle Therapy 210

Chapter 37 B.G.G.I.Q.Q.I.S.S.I.I. 214

Chapter 38 A Test of Courage 217

Chapter 39 Bringing to Consciousness 220

Chapter 40 Patrolling the Forest Edge 225

Chapter 41 The Helpmate 230

Chapter 42 An Abhorrent Memory 237

Chapter 43 Love Hunger 240

Chapter 44 We Don't Want to Be Here Anymore 247

Chapter 45 Dispatches 252
Chapter 46 Roger's Concerns 258

IV   Soul Shattering

Chapter 47 Wrecked 267
Chapter 48 Leaf 272
Chapter 49 The Rescue 278
Chapter 50 The Seed of Knowing 289
Chapter 51 A Forest Girl 293
Chapter 52 Intimacy 296
Chapter 53 They've Crossed Over 300
Chapter 54 A Delicate Matter 305
Chapter 55 The Mother Wound 309
Chapter 56 Baby Donald 320
Chapter 57 A Letter of Truth 328
Chapter 58 Snapshot: Now and Then 331
Chapter 59 Sacrificial Lamb 336
Chapter 60 Fury 1 344
Chapter 61 Departure 348
Chapter 62 Updates 351
Chapter 63 The Black Spider 353
Chapter 64 The Lake 357
Chapter 65 The Truth Seeker 361
Chapter 66 Leaves and Knives 369
Chapter 67 Cleansing the Vagina 376
Chapter 68 The Only Medicine 381
Chapter 69 Living Is Too Hard without Love 389
Chapter 70 The Family 392
Chapter 71 The Furies 402
Chapter 72 I'm Done with All That 413

V   Transcending the Past

Chapter 73 Rapprochement 417

Chapter 74   Adversity Transforms Us 421
Chapter 75   Recommitment 426
Chapter 76   Many Voices 432
Chapter 77   The Dark Force 436
Chapter 78   The Visit 444
Chapter 79   Driving Out Anger 451
Chapter 80   The College Girl 456
Chapter 81   The Lifeline 463
Chapter 82   Aftermath 470
Chapter 83   Black Sacredness 473
Chapter 84   Empty 476

VI   A Vibrant Mandala

Chapter 85   The Very Best Medicine 483
Chapter 86   Toward Wholeness 493
Chapter 87   The Grandmother 497
Chapter 88   Doubts Put to Rest 501
Chapter 89   The Happy Drunk 505
Chapter 90   Hope 511
Chapter 91   Unhinged 514
Chapter 92   Over the Rainbow 517
Chapter 93   Jane 524
Chapter 94   A Second Chance 532
Chapter 95   A Promise Fulfilled 540

The Inhabitants of the Inner Realm   545

The Imaginary Landscape   549

In Gratitude   551

Resources   553

About the Author   559

INTRODUCTION

What you are about to read is the story of a forty-four-year-old woman of substance and faith, one with remarkable intelligence and creativity, who writes poetry, paints in the primitive style, and is a gourmet chocolatier. Her name is "Joan." At age thirty-two, her mind broke open and her life fell apart. She was diagnosed with multiple personality disorder (MPD), aka dissociative identity disorder (DID), the consequence of extreme childhood trauma. After eleven years of unsuccessful therapy, a fateful chance encounter brought Joan and me together. Hopeless and in despair, she asked, *"Will you take me?"*

In my care, Joan revealed that, from infancy through adolescence, she suffered unimaginable abuse: maternal neglect, sexual molestation, rape, and physical mutilation. Her only defense against the unrelenting torment had been to flee into a dissociative state, during which she created alternate personalities ("Parts") to endure the unbearable and protect her from remembering the unthinkable. These Parts found refuge in an imaginary realm in Joan's mind: an internal landscape of evocative features comprising the Dark and Haunted Forest, the Abyss, the River of Tears, the Cave, the Path of Crushed Lies, and much more—a world imbued with magical realism and inhabited by Raven the Light Bearer, Shadowman the Persecutor, Beth the Messenger, Elizabeth the Internal Mother, the Three Furies, the Tree Girls, and a host of others.

Raven and the Hummingbird chronicles Joan's harrowing survival, redemption, and ultimate transcendence. Treatment with me lasted five years. I distilled thousands of pages of handwritten progress notes, a great number of letters, and her insightful poetry and artwork into an illustrated narrative dialogue among the client, the therapist, and the Parts. With no formal training in treating a person with MPD, I learned from each session, worked my way out of the pitfalls, and immersed myself in the publications of leading practitioners. I avoided labels and judgments to foster a trusting, purposeful treatment approach, which included using various therapeutic methods, directed visualizations, trust in the Sacred, and, most importantly, a reliance on love—tough, demanding, compassionate love.

Joan's recovery took persistence, hard work, creativity, and courage. Sometimes slow and backsliding, sometimes heartbreaking and shocking, other times playful and joyous. Her quest for wholeness was arduous, littered with obstacles, and often smothered by exhaustion. What Joan revealed, while burdened with ailments, family strife, and addiction, was agonizing for her and taxing for me to hear firsthand. *Raven and the Hummingbird* may be just as challenging for you, the reader, as it lays bare the consequences of relentless sexual trauma on emotional, mental, physical, and spiritual well-being. Together, Joan and I struggled through. I encourage you to persevere, as we did, and find the universal value in Joan's efforts to transcend the past and achieve a singular, authentic life.

I am indebted to the generosity of this brave woman who gave permission to use her progress files in hopes of making a difference in the lives of others. I have strived to honor her truth, its mystery and grace. Names have been changed, physical features modified, and events conflated and juxtaposed for clarity, continuity, and especially confidentiality. Other books about MPD/ DID present the reader with scholarly research, historical narratives and memoirs, or professional expositions with anecdotal examples in support of a particular theory or treatment approach. In *Raven and the Hummingbird,* the reader will bear witness to the intimate process of treatment—the full experience, session by session, step by step, and as transparent as possible.

Joan and I trust that learning about her healing path will provide hope for those afflicted with MPD, their families, caregivers, friends, and service providers. While bringing to light Joan's particular story may add to the body of professional knowledge, my aim is to inspire more mental-health professionals to accept the challenge of treating those with MPD and to demonstrate a range of possibilities for finding a healing path to recovery. My further purpose in writing the book is to encourage understanding and empathy by expounding a broader, more holistic view of the disorder and its treatment. For the general audience, I hope *Raven and the Hummingbird* may shift misunderstanding and skepticism about MPD, and make more comprehensible the nature of healing practices that take place during psychotherapy.

~

Prologue

WOMEN AT THE WELL

Summer 2003

*S*itting with a circle of women in a meeting room in the basement of a local church, I introduce myself, reminding the group that I am the substitute therapist until their regular therapist returns. As my eyes touch each face, I sense their anxiety rising. A few of the participants look at me expectantly, while others appear suspicious, avert their eyes, and sit in silence. Against the far wall, a middle-aged woman with auburn hair sits alone in a straight-backed chair, her knees pressed together, her purse clutched to her body. She sits stone-still as tears track down her face.

A young woman speaks up, shyly at first. She has finally found a job, applied for food stamps, and says she's getting by since her husband left. Her eyes pool with sorrow. Her teenage son has run away.

The women listen, respond, understand. They need little of me. Talking is their solution.

~

Observing them takes me back to the farming village in Germany, where I lived as a child during and after World War II. Most mornings, a small cluster of women, three or four perhaps, would huddle together in the street. From their haggard faces, it was easy to surmise they were lamenting the latest irreversible loss, the difficulties of providing daily for the ones who depended on them, or some other heartache. A woman would blow her nose. Another would quickly touch her eyes with a handkerchief. But never did any of them cry out loud. Victims of forces they could not control, they murmured comforting words and patted one another on the arm before hurrying off to attend to what was left to care for. Their gestures of farewell held the promise of meeting the next day at the same time and place.

~

This ancient tradition of "gathering at the well" offers women, then and now, a lifeline of survival and hope. Among those around me today, an older woman speaks with grief etched on her face. Her husband is still gone. She hopes he never comes back. Last time, he asked for money. When she refused, he beat her.

My role is to listen, observe, empathize.

At some point, a feather-light touch on my shoulder distracts me. Absentmindedly, I brush at whatever it is. As I listen to these battered women tell their ages-old stories of hardship, sacrifice, desperation, and tragedy, I feel a presence behind me. When I turn to look, no one is there.

In time, the conversation comes to an end. The group disbands. Some chat in clusters. Others go for coffee. The woman who was sitting against the wall, silently weeping, walks toward me. She hands me a crumpled piece of paper, and without a word, turns and speaks to two women she knows. Together they leave the room. In a rush to meet my next appointment, I slip the note into a side pocket of my blazer.

Days later, I discover the forgotten note and call the phone number scribbled there. After several rings, a soft, melodic voice answers, "This is Joan."

Identifying myself, I apologize for having misplaced her phone number.

"I was afraid you wouldn't call," she says in a breathy voice.

I ask what had persuaded her to reach out to me. Her reticence is palpable. But she manages to convey a sense of urgency to connect with me—for reasons she is unprepared to talk about over the phone. Being a therapist, I understand her reluctance and ask if she wished to set up an appointment in early September. She agrees and then surprises me by saying, "I've been waiting for you a long time."

~

I

UNFOLDING

Late Summer 2003 to Spring 2004

Chapter 1

JOAN'S CHOICE

At *about six in the morning*, with my robe wrapped about me and a cup of tea in one hand, I stepped onto the deck attached to the modest clapboard house my husband and I call home. As I lowered myself onto an Adirondack chair, the sun slipped its brassy ring on the slender finger of the horizon. I treasure these moments when the night gives way. The stillness of first light invites me to examine my state of being and set things right within myself before starting the work I love. This morning, I thought about the day's appointment with Joan. *What stories will she bring into my treatment room?* Draining my cup of tea, I watched dawn's pewter sky turn a blush pink.

Returning inside, I quickly dressed for the day in navy-blue slacks and a white blouse and added pearl earrings. I slipped into black patent lace-ups and affixed a Timex to my wrist. As I flew out the back door, my husband called out, "What's your hurry?"

I retraced my steps, kissed his forehead, and said, "See you for lunch."

Sheer, lacy clouds drifted north as I made my way along the narrow stone path, a mere fifty paces through the garden to my office in the small white bungalow next door, where I practice psychotherapy. I rushed up the three steps onto the blue-painted concrete floor of the wraparound porch. I gave the old porch swing a playful push and then adjusted the placement of a plastic chair, where I often sit between appointments watching students hurrying past to the university a few blocks away. I unlocked the office door and crossed the threshold into my domain.

My professional library greeted me, the shelves overflowing with cherished books—my teachers for more than twenty years—a yellowed copy of *The Varieties of Religious Experience* penned by William James leaning against Viktor Frankl's *Man's Search for Meaning*. Freud's elegant prose in red paperbacks standing beside Jung's expansive volumes. *Darkness Visible* paired with *Night Falls Fast*. Evelyn Underhill's *Mysticism* side by side with Judith Herman's stark warning in *Trauma and Recovery*. Jean Houston's *The Search for the Beloved* and a hundred more of my beloved texts, each containing a world of ideas and wisdom. I checked my phone messages and, as I booted up the computer, briefly paid homage to a framed poster of Pavel Tchelitchew's masterpiece, *Hide and Seek,* which I use as a teaching tool to illustrate the struggle toward individuation. When I completed the usual morning tasks, I moved into the therapy room, where I placed a box of tissues with a bottle of water on a side table and lit a cluster of candles. Satisfied with these simple preparations, I waited for Joan's arrival.

Promptly at nine, my office door opened. A full-figured woman with wavy auburn hair stood at the threshold clutching a black vinyl purse, her knuckles white.

"Please come in," I said. "I've been expecting you." With a welcoming gesture, I led her into the therapy room. She moved stiffly to claim a place on the blue two-seater couch. I sat opposite her in my upholstered rocking chair.

"I'm sorry I'm late," she apologized in that breathy voice I remembered from our telephone conversation.

"You're right on time, Joan," I said.

She sat erect on the edge of the couch—knees clamped together, purse in her lap, and sandaled feet flat on the carpet. Long silver earrings dangled at her neck. Her brown eyes furtively glanced around the room, taking in three large pastel works of art that speak of family dynamics, before shifting her attention out the window to where the end-of-summer light reflected off the shrubbery in my husband's garden next door.

Joan took a deep breath. "I almost didn't come," she said, barely above a whisper.

"But you did," my tone gentle.

She spied a row of teddy bears, large and small cuddly things, atop the bookcase. Her lips parted slightly. Catching herself, she turned away, looked at my framed credentials on the wall, and let out a sigh. "You impressed me at the group meeting last month," she said. "You were kind and listened respectfully. That's why I found the courage to give you my phone number."

After a moment's hesitation, she continued, "A few months ago, my therapist—her name's Helen—told me she needed to take some time off. My phone calls day and night, she said, and my frequent crises had exhausted her and disrupted her family life. Then, a few days later, she let me know she could no longer provide the care I needed."

"How long have you been seeing this therapist?"

"Eleven years?" she replied as if the length of time was in question. "I had been in therapy for almost seven years when Helen gave me a brochure about MPD—you know, multiple personality disorder. She believed it described what was wrong with me."

"And what persuaded her to think that?"

"She said alters had been coming out."

"After you read the brochure, were you convinced?"

"I suppose so."

"Do you know anything about these alters that Helen observed?"

"There's one called Beth. She's a young girl. Helen told me she also met Samantha and Sarah and Rose. I believe there's one called Elizabeth. And according to Beth, there's another alter named Raven. Helen said he appeared once. She was moved to tears and thought she was in the presence of an angel."

"Did she speak to him?"

"Helen was too awestruck to say anything."

"So, you talk with Beth?"

"Sometimes."

"How about the others?"

"I can hear them in my head, talking. Sometimes I hear them cry." She looked at me with her soulful brown eyes as if I might not believe her.

"How did your therapist respond to these alters?"

"Beth said Helen was very kind to them when they came out." She paused. "Beth loved Helen. She was upset and very sad when we couldn't go back to see her."

"And how did *you* feel, Joan?"

"Betrayed. Abandoned. Despaired."

I empathized with her sense of rejection.

"Well, Joan," I cleared my throat, "what you've described does suggest you may indeed have multiple personality disorder. However, until I meet two or three alters, I can't be sure." I thought a moment before asking, "After you both agreed on this diagnosis, did your therapist change the treatment approach?"

"Not really. We continued to focus on my depression and anxiety, and when I felt suicidal. I did tell Helen about my stepfather—his name was Charles—and how he sexually abused me when I was a young girl. We also talked about my mother some."

"Eleven years ago, what persuaded you to seek out a therapist in the first place?"

She bit her lower lip. "That's a long, sad story, and I've already taken up too much of your time."

"We have time," I coaxed.

"Why I came to see you today . . ." she paused again. "Would you be willing—I mean, would you take me as your client? When I first saw you, I immediately knew that you were the one I'd been waiting for all my life. When you walked into that room, I felt a jolt, a sudden pressure in my head. It felt like everyone had rushed forward, pressing against the back of my eyes, jostling to peek out."

"Everyone?"

"My alters. It was like a crowd of children pressing their hands and noses against a windowpane to glimpse something miraculous. 'She's here,' I heard one announce. 'Do you see her silvery hair?' another said. 'See her blue eyes?'

a young voice lisped. 'Hear how softly she speaks.' Then a chorus of voices said, 'The Helper is here.' No words are adequate to describe our relief and joy and sense of hope. We knew God had fulfilled His promise."

Joan's revelation, stated with such conviction, rendered me speechless. She must have sensed my confusion and went on to explain, "One Easter Sunday morning, when I was very young, God spoke to me as I walked into church. He told me my life would get much, much worse, but that I should be patient, and one day He would send someone to help me."

When I found my voice, I asked how old she'd been.

"I was seven."

No matter how provocative her statement was, I chose to honor her reality as she saw it.

"Let's continue our talk one more afternoon. After that, I'm sure you and I will know what we should do next."

Her brows drew together in a frown of disappointment. I smiled encouragement. "Should we decide to work together, Joan, I'll need your consent to request a copy of the clinical notes from your former therapist."

The furrow between her brows deepened. "Helen never made a lot of notes."

Be that as it may, I thought. We agreed to meet the following week. She stood, her purse tight against her body, and walked to the office door. Pivoting to face me, she asked, "Do you believe in such a thing as multiple personality disorder?"

"Yes," I responded, "it can be a consequence of extreme childhood trauma."

The tension lines around her eyes smoothed as if she had been relieved of a burden. She nodded and eased the door shut behind her.

～

Chapter 2

EMERGENCE

September 24. Joan arrived early for her appointment. Again, she hesitated at my office door. And again, I invited her into the therapy room. With a faint smile, she acknowledged my invitation and then quickly claimed the same place on the blue couch. Her wavy hair was well-groomed, her makeup tastefully applied. She looked down at her delicate hands, carefully examining her manicured fingernails. I waited until she made eye contact and then suggested we continue our conversation about what had initially persuaded her to seek therapy.

She let out a deep sigh and flipped her long hair from one shoulder to the other. "My troubles began about a year before I started seeing Helen. My family and I went home to visit my mother. We weren't there thirty minutes when I found out something so horrific that I felt my brain or my mind—I don't know how to describe it—break into a million pieces."

"Can you tell me about the horrific thing?"

"My younger brother Sammy . . ." Her chin trembled. She turned her head toward the window and stared outside. "That's when it all started," she murmured as if to herself.

After taking a few moments to regain her composure, she turned her attention back to me.

"That's when the voices in my head started again—the voices I sometimes heard as a child. This time, though, they were too far away for me to understand what they were saying, but I heard them whimpering and whispering, even arguing. I thought I was going insane. After we got back home, I began to lose time, and when I came to, I had no idea where I had been or what I had done."

Again, she stared out the window without seeing. In a voice with no affect, she described how her husband had urged her to get professional help, if not for her own sanity, at least for the sake of the family. None of them knew what to do when she ran around the house screaming; or sat in a corner talking to herself, rocking and moaning; or hid in a closet or under a bed. So, they looked in the *Yellow Pages* for a therapist and found Helen.

"There were a lot of other changes in my life, too. I started to shut myself off from the world. I stopped seeing friends, or going to church, or attending PTA meetings. That was very painful. I had always been a homeroom mother at my children's school and loved to teach crafts and painting."

Joan stopped. Her lips compressed into a thin line of disappointment. She placed her right fist above her heart and said, "My poor children. All I ever wanted was to be the best mother I could be. And I *was* until my brain broke open and the alters began coming out. I'm sure it must have confused and upset my children. Megan was still in kindergarten, and Stephanie was barely ten. When my younger alters came out," Joan smiled at the memory, "Megan thought Mommy was pretending to be a little girl—a playmate. But, when some of the older and more aggressive ones came out, Stephanie remembered how my sweet Megan would get scared and cry." Joan flicked her hand as if she could fling away all that encumbered her. "I was disciplined. I did my work as a devoted wife and mother. I took care of our house. I cooked for my husband, and I always, *always* kept myself together."

"What do you mean by 'kept yourself together'?"

"When I finally left my mother's house, after I got married, I decided never to look back. I would do the best with whatever life gave me. But every once in a while, I felt there was something wrong. I'd have a strange humming in my head. I'd pay it no mind and will myself to go on with whatever I was doing."

"That must have taken a great deal of self-control."

Joan seemed not to hear me. There was a languid movement to her eyes. Her head did a subtle tilt to the right and a beguiling smile spread across her face. I held my breath. *Might an alter be coming forward?*

"Will you take us?" she lisped.

"Should I?"

"We waited for you a long time. We were so happy when we saw you. All of us pressed against Joan's eyes to get a look at you and hear your voice. We knew right away that you were the one God promised to send to us. He told us to be patient, and now you're here. Will you take us?" she repeated.

Confounded, I thought, *How can I defy Providence?*

In my next breath, I asked, "What is your name?"

"Beth," she said. "I sleep on a purple bed in a purple room. Purple's my favorite color."

"And where is your room?"

"In Elizabeth's House. She takes care of us."

"And how old are you?"

"I'm seven. And I like to be happy. I like to play and do stuff. Joan lets me come out sometimes to color, and she teaches me how to make things, and sometimes she lets me talk to the bird."

She smiled and disappeared as mysteriously as she had appeared.

Embarrassment flushed Joan's cheeks. "I heard you met Beth. I'm surprised she came out to see you so soon. After what happened with Helen, I expected Beth and the other alters would find it difficult to meet with a new therapist. They all must have felt betrayed by Helen's abrupt termination."

"Beth and the others are really parts of you, Joan. Instead of alternate personalities or alters, I like to call them 'Parts.' Beth's early appearance is a good sign. And even more promising than that is your resilience. After eleven years of therapy and family turmoil, I'm impressed with your tenacity and determination to get well."

A glittering realization filled Joan's eyes. "Does that mean you *will* accept me as a client? Or," she paused, "are you reluctant to work with someone like me who has alters—I mean *Parts?*"

"A couple of years ago, I heard Colin Ross speak. He's a leading psychiatrist in the treatment of MPD and maintains that recovery is possible, but treatment takes time and patience and endurance for both the client and the therapist. That means long hours in session and a willingness to work hard."

With no discernible reaction from Joan, I went on to explain that Ross posited the disorder was neither a mental illness nor some genetic defect. Instead, it was a brilliant coping strategy set in motion by the remarkable creativity and intellect of a child, usually a girl. To assure her survival when repeatedly abused, and with no one to come to her rescue, her only defense was to dissociate; that is, she retreated into the safety of her mind. And in that state, he said, the child imagined that another "little girl" was being hurt so she didn't have to endure the physical torment and emotional pain. If the abuse was extreme and continued unabated over a long time, her mind created "other girls" to take the anguish for her, thus ensuring she remained untouched.

Dissociation and the Creation of Parts, Joan 2004.

"Those imagined girls, Joan, are like Beth, whom I just met, and the others you hear talking in your head." I told her they were parts of her who had been "split off," a mysterious phenomenon about which we have little understanding. "I like to believe it's your Self—your life-preserving essence—that initiated the creation of your Parts to help you endure the unbearable and protect you from knowing the unthinkable."

Joan had moved to the edge of the couch, poised as if to capture and lock away every word I uttered.

"Ross counseled it's important to remember that the Parts are embodied in you. They are not separate people, Joan, even though they may present themselves with charm and assurance, like that sweet young Beth." He stated, I explained, Parts differ in age and sex and levels of cognition. They have individual ranges of memories, emotions, self-perceptions, attributes, and even desires. And Ross maintained each has a distinct role within a kind of internal structure or system organized to keep a semblance of order among the Parts. "Some Parts, Joan, might have relationships with other Parts and different people, and those associations could be supportive or conflictual."

Realizing I had slipped into lecture mode and had perhaps explained too much too soon, I proposed we bring our conversation to a close.

After Joan left, I sat at my desk and considered what accepting her as a client would mean for me. *As a sole practitioner in private practice without being associated with an inpatient treatment facility for people with MPD, I would have twenty-four-hour responsibility for crisis intervention. Although I had no formal training in this specific disorder, my experience with traumatized clients had taught me, and as Ross advised, treatment could be long-term and could require intensive therapy. Treating Joan would demand acquiring new knowledge and skills specifically responsive to her care. Questions flew into my mind: At what age did the abuse begin? How severe had it been? How long had it lasted? How many Parts did she have? Would I, at age sixty-five, be able to provide the continuity of care necessary to complete Joan's treatment?*

And yet . . . How could I refuse? Beth's plea, "Will you take us?" had touched a long-healed wound. I, too, had been a child in desperate need of being taken in—a child for whom loneliness and rejection had been a constant.

~

As the offspring of an unwed mother—a whisper child—I had been deposited from birth in a state-run facility for newborns. Years later, my foster mother described the events of that fateful day she took me in. A white-uniformed matron and a strawberry-blonde woman in silk stockings and high heels stood watching as "Mama" lifted my squirming sixteen-month-old body out of a urine-soiled crib. With sturdy hands, she tied a woolen cap under my chin. Stiff with fear, I stared into her plain face as she swaddled me in a warm blanket. All the while, the one in high heels—my birth mother—nervously explained in Hochdeutsch that working at night left her no time to raise a child. And now that the Brownshirts were on the march, her daughter would be safer in the village. "God willing," Mama had murmured in a soft southern dialect. Hurriedly, we passed among the rows of cribs, the matron's starched uniform swishing before us. Additional documents, she decreed over her shoulder, had to be signed before my release. Eventually, as we pushed through a heavy door that opened onto a noisy street, I started to wail. My birth mother hastily excused herself but promised to visit now and again. Mama held me tight against her bosom as we left behind the gray stone building.

We caught a yellow streetcar and later boarded a bus. From the last stop on the route, we walked through the village to a centuries-old house. We climbed a flight of wooden stairs and entered a warm kitchen. She sat me down, untied my cap, and offered me warm milk in a cup. I pushed her hand away and began to squall. She picked me up, cradled my head against her shoulder, and walked me back and forth, back and forth. I was home.

~

The following morning, I telephoned Joan to inform her I would take her case. The challenges and opportunities were too compelling to resist. We agreed to begin our work together the following week. At that moment, I reached for Ross' book to start my study of MPD in earnest. I thought I understood the challenges before me, but I did not foresee how my commitment to Joan's care would impact my marriage and my health, and dominate my professional life for the next five years.

October 2. I watched from my office window as Joan made her way from the parking area and up the steps to the front porch. She sat in one of the white plastic chairs, sheltered from passing cars by a low holly hedge. She surveyed the tree-lined street of bungalows as if the tranquility of the scene might wrap her in a protective coat, impervious to the tempest awaiting her behind my blue office door.

Was Joan having second thoughts about starting therapy with me?

When she finally took her place among the cushions on the couch, she had difficulty making eye contact. "I hope you aren't going to be upset with me," she began but kept her gaze on the intricate pattern of the small Persian rug between us. "For the last few days, I've been conflicted about working with you. I've been wondering if Helen would take me back when her health improves. After all she's done for me, working with you without telling her first makes me feel disloyal, even though I know you're the one to help me get well."

A shadow crossed her face. "You see," she said, "Helen and I were together for eleven years. We were friends. I thought she loved me. I certainly loved her. I miss her." Only then did Joan look up, her eyes pleading for understanding.

"It's painful to lose someone you've trusted," I declared. "Someone with whom you've felt safe. May I suggest you visit with Helen? Talk to her. Perhaps the two of you can come to an understanding that will preserve what you felt for each other and provide some kind of closure."

She pulled her purse close to her body. In an about-face, she said, "I couldn't. She hurt me too much. Dropping me like that." She pursed her lips. "In my opinion, letting me go like she did was unprofessional."

"I can see how hurt and angry you are."

"I'm not angry," she protested. "I feel like an object that's been discarded. But what else is new?" Bitterness etched deep lines at either side of her mouth. "I'm used to it. Let me tell you something," the words spit forth, "when someone treats me like that, I can turn my feelings off," her fingers snapped, "and walk away from them like they never existed. Besides, seeing Helen would upset the alters. They loved her, too. Seeing her again would start a commotion in my head. I'd dissociate, and who knows what would happen then. My husband and children would have to deal with the havoc. I wouldn't want that to happen."

Surprised by her mercurial mood, I let her simmer for a while and then redirected the conversation. "You seem to have a relationship with the Part called Beth. You talk to one another, and when she comes out, you do activities together."

"Sometimes. I do enjoy being with her."

"In therapeutic terms, you and Beth are co-present. Are there other Parts with which you have such a relationship?"

"Not really," Joan replied. "Usually, when I feel an alter come out—I mean a Part—I go away. You see, most of the time, I can hold myself together. I pretend to be normal. I keep the door locked (*metaphorically speaking*, I thought) to keep the Parts inside. It's exhausting. But I'll do anything to keep my husband and children from getting upset. Especially my husband. He doesn't deal with the Parts very well. He just gets angry."

Joan's expression softened. "My daughter, Megan, will be going to high school this year, and my oldest, Stephanie, is in college studying to become a lawyer. I'm so proud of her. She's always been my confidante and helps me when I'm not myself. Last year, she moved out of the house. But when things get out of hand, she comes home and quiets everyone down."

"How does Megan handle your condition?"

"Mostly, she gets confused and upset, like my husband. I do my best to keep her calm. After an episode, I try to set things right. You know, make up for my badness."

"What do you mean by your 'badness'?"

"I've always felt that I was bad. It was the only way I could explain to myself the terrible things that were happening to me."

"Abused children often feel that way. They can't believe that the parents they love would punish them—hurt them like that—if they weren't 'bad'."

Folding into herself, she sat brooding about feelings and thoughts she could not resolve. *In eleven years of therapy*, I thought, *had she not been given the tools to dismantle this faulty self-perception, a rationalization she had accepted all her life?* At that moment, I determined I would help Joan reframe her self-condemnation. Then, as I watched, her eyes moved rapidly from side to side, and the childlike Beth found her way out.

"I was bad, too." She hung her head. "That's why I was hurt."

"Do you want to tell me about being hurt?"

She shook her bowed head, eyes on the carpet. "Elizabeth knows already. She tells me I'll be all right. She helps me feel better. I know God loves me—Raven told me. Joan's always nice to me, too." Still looking down, she said, "I heard you and Joan talking about Helen. I miss her, too, but I hope Joan doesn't go to see her again. We all know you're supposed to be our real Helper and make us feel happy. But today, I'm not happy, and I want to go back now."

She disappeared, trailing a melancholy smile. I expected Joan to return. Instead, her body seemed to shrink as another Part came out. Like Beth, she hung her head and averted her eyes. She struggled to speak. After a few tries, she managed a soft, "Hi."

"Hi," I mirrored softly, not to frighten her.

"I was hurt, too," her voice desolate. "He took me to the forest and hurt me. Afterward, he gathered up lots of leaves and piled them all around me and lit a match. He said I had been bad—I told. That's why I needed to be punished. That's how we learned not to tell."

"What happened to you in that forest must have been very frightening. But I want you to know it will never happen again. You and Joan have moved far away from that place. No one can hurt you like that ever again."

She didn't respond.

"What's your name?"

In a fading whisper, she offered, "I'm Rose."

When Joan reappeared, I asked if she had heard Beth and Rose.

Her eyes went blank. "No, I went away."

"When you go away, Joan, where do you go?"

She pointed to her right temple. "I believe it's around here somewhere."

Noting our time was about up, Joan started to rise from her seat but abruptly sat back down. "I want to talk to you about integration and what I have to do to become . . . I don't know how to say it. I want to be whole."

From my bookcase, I retrieved a volume illustrated with exquisite mandalas. I handed Joan the book, and as she flipped through a dozen pages, I explained that a mandala symbolized the inherent wholeness in us all. This harmonious oneness, as Carl Jung proclaimed, is promoted by the Self—the unifying principle of the psyche—that strives for order and guards against fragmentation. "In other words, Joan, the Self fosters integration."

"Oh, my," she exhaled, "they are so beautiful. May I take the book home with me?"

"You certainly may." Almost as an afterthought, I mentioned that not all people with MPD have the goal of integration. Some simply want the Parts to learn how to cooperate better so that their lives are less disruptive.

Joan shook her head. "My goal is to integrate. I want to be a whole person."

I went to my outer office and brought back the print of Pavel Tchelitchew's *Hide and Seek* that depicts the individuation process required for healing a beleaguered psyche. I invited Joan to use her finger to trace the stages of suffering the painter endured before he could accept, and then transcend, his tragedy. I asked her to consider Tchelitchew's painting as a visual metaphor for the journey that she, too, sought to undertake.

~

Chapter 3

THE TREE GIRLS

October 9. Joan had decided to work with me if I was still prepared to have her. After affirming my willingness, we completed some necessary paperwork and recorded a brief overview of Joan's family. I explained we would gather more-detailed information as treatment progressed.

"Before each session, Joan, I like to start with a short meditation."

Joan nodded in agreement.

I invited her to sit comfortably and close her eyes.

"Take a deep breath. Let it out slowly. Mindfully breathe in and slowly breathe out . . . empty yourself of the noise that directs your daily life . . . let go of the anxiety . . . worries . . . or any discomfort you may be experiencing. As you sit relaxed in this quiet room, invite your mind and heart to open . . ."

We sat in silence a full minute.

"I'm not used to telling," Joan offered. "Not letting people know me, that's how I survived."

"I will not pressure you, Joan. You will determine when you are ready to talk. Your conflict with trust is understandable. Telling can be risky. Discriminating between who is and who isn't trustworthy is indeed necessary for survival. However, talking is the healing function of our work together." She nodded in what seemed like acceptance of my explication. "Every time you decide to take another step in the process of disclosure, be assured you will broaden your understanding that, despite what you suffered, your goodness and innocence have not been destroyed.

"Speaking of trust, Joan, I believe we are off to a good start. Beth and Rose came out to see me almost immediately. From what I've learned, Parts are usually slow to appear. They only come out when they feel safe in trusting the therapist."

"When I worked with Helen, I believe Beth came out after about a year."

"That sounds about right. It takes time to gain trust."

Joan seemed to listen inward. Lines of tension around her eyes softened. I recognized Beth's arrival by her disarming smile.

"I'm glad Joan finally listened to us. We told her that you were the one who could help us."

"I'm glad, too."

"I like to come Outside. Sometimes, I'm afraid I'll get stuck when I cross through the Outer Edge. But I come out anyway because I like Joan's house. Mr. Roger is nice, but," she whispered, "not always. The cat and the bird, they're always nice." Her smile faded. "I like to fill myself up with hugs and love, except today there's not that much room left in my heart. It's filled with hurt and sadness."

I gentled my voice to ask if she wanted to tell me about her "sadness."

"When I was very little, I was in the bathroom with a lady and a man. They pushed something hard and cold into my bottom. It really hurt. I tried to get away from them, but I couldn't reach the doorknob. It was too high . . . but I really don't want to talk about it. It's too scary, and when I get scared, I go back Inside to Elizabeth's House."

Her features brightened. She gave me an intriguing smile. "Do you know God is all glittery?" she asked. "He really is! Sometimes I see him all sparkly."

Before I could respond, another Part appeared. She turned her face to the wall as she spoke. "I live in a tree at the edge of the Forest. He cut me, and it hurt bad. But I never cried. I never told anyone. If I had, I would have been punished."

With a furtive glance my way, she revealed, "Rose always cleaned us up after we were hurt." She paused. "Most of the time, I don't want to live. I'm bad. I'm dirty. And I'm tired of it all." She sighed. "Raven tells me I have suffered enough. He says I need to look forward, not backward anymore."

Then, turning to face me, she said, "There are two others just like me. They are my sisters and live with me in the Tree. One is called Sarah. The other is Sebunome. Raven talks to them, too."

I noted the oddness of the name which the Part pronounced *see-buh-no-mee,* as in *see but no me.* "What are *you* called?"

Her head dipped. "I'm not supposed to tell. I'm not supposed to be here. I know a lot about what happened. I'm old enough to know." Then she was gone.

I called for Joan. There was no response. To bring her back, I cautiously touched her hand and called her name. Joan's eyelids fluttered. She opened her eyes and looked around, embarrassed. "I'm sorry," she apologized. "I must have lost time."

I asked if she had heard what Beth and the other Part disclosed.

"When a Part comes out, I go away. I don't hear or see or feel anything. I call it the White Zone."

"You mean you dissociate?"

"And that's what I want to unlearn—to stop going to the White Zone whenever I hear something that makes me feel uncomfortable or frightens me."

I vowed we would work on the challenge of changing her habitual method of coping. However, learning a new way, I cautioned, would take time and require patience.

She gave me a wan smile.

October 15. Since her husband's head injury in a car accident a few years ago, Joan complained Roger had difficulty remembering things and resolving problems. When she questioned his judgment, he would get mad. "I know I should be more patient with him. But he can be so annoying."

Joan's features softened. She had dissociated and I immediately recognized Beth.

"I'm scared." Her voice thinned to a whine. "He made me go to the basement with him." Her eyes glistened with tears. "Down there, he did grown-up stuff to me. You know, what people do to make babies. When he did that, I went to sleep." *Here I understood "going to sleep" meant Beth had withdrawn into a state of amnesia and inactivity.*

Without another word, she disappeared. My heart shuddered.

Joan re-emerged. She looked around as if unsure of her whereabouts. "I guess I must have gone away." *Meaning she temporarily dissociated,* I thought.

I quickly summarized Beth's disclosure and asked if she had any memories of what might have occurred in that basement.

"My grandmother's house had a basement with an incinerator that made horrible noises. Whenever we went to visit her, I avoided going down there. It frightened me."

"Do you know *why* it frightened you?"

She moaned softly. I asked her to breathe deeply, stay present, all the while reminding her that she was safe with me, but she seemed not to hear. Her head snapped back harshly, painfully, and she moaned again. This was alarming. I called her name repeatedly until she opened her eyes. She bent forward, cupping her forehead in both hands, and complained of a terrible headache.

"Do you know what just happened? Is there a Part that gets upset when you disclose certain events and punishes you for telling?"

She didn't answer my questions. Instead, she chose to recount some family history. *Perhaps a safer topic,* I thought. At age fifteen, she said, her mother was pregnant by a young man only two years her senior. A hasty marriage preceded his enlistment in the Navy and deployment at sea. In his absence, Joan's mother lived with her parents for a time, which proved to be one of the most difficult periods in her life. After the husband's discharge from the Navy, the young family moved into an attic apartment, where Joan's sister, Lillian, was born. Two years later, when Joan was four, her mother divorced her father.

"Do you know why?" I asked.

"My mother never said much about it to me. From what my grandmother told me, he was an alcoholic, verbally abusive, and physically violent. After the separation, my mother took us back to live with our grandparents. When I was six or so, she met my stepfather. I believe I was eight when they bought a house on the outskirts of town. We moved out of my grand-parents' home, which was in a working-class neighborhood of immigrant families. Everyone had well-kept houses with nice yards and tall trees. I fondly remember having friends and playing outdoors. Moving away was sad for me. I hated to leave."

"Last session," I said, "Beth revealed she had been hurt in a bathroom by a woman and a man. She tried to escape but couldn't reach the doorknob. My guess is she was two or two and a half years old then. But you know you were the one in that bathroom, very frightened, probably dissociated. Do you suppose Beth was created at that time to protect you from harm?"

Joan's response was vague, but she did affirm having always hated being in a bathroom. I presumed we would find out what happened in that bathroom if ever the memory surfaced. I noted important information had come to light and thought it time to end the session.

Before I left the office, I transcribed my notes. Thus far, I had met three Parts: Beth, the youngster; Rose, the sad one; and the "Tree Girl." Four others had been alluded to: Elizabeth, a mature Part with maternal attributes; Raven, another mature Part, who apparently gave advice; and two other "Tree Girls"—Sarah and Sebunome. Lastly, from what I had observed today, I surmised there might be a Part acting as a kind of persecutor.

That evening around eight o'clock, Joan telephoned to say that Rose needed to speak with me. The tenor of her voice softened as Rose came on the line. "I'm scared. I saw blood when I went to the bathroom."

Joan's voice came back on the line to explain she was experiencing menses, and this time of the month always brought internal unrest.

An hour or so later, a Part calling herself "Samantha" phoned. She alarmed me by saying she wanted to kill herself. She thought the abuser had returned and feared what he would do. She said Rose was also upset, had left her "Cave," and had come to "my Tree at the edge of the Forest." *Was this the Tree Girl who spoke with me in session?* I tried to calm her, saying we would talk about her fears next time Joan came to see me.

"That doesn't do me any good," she insisted. "If you don't help me now, I *will* hurt myself."

I asked to speak to Joan. When she came on the line, she stated she was "too tired" to cope with the situation. She was going to take "a couple Xanaxes" and go to bed. *I thought the Parts had reached out to voice their fear for a purpose, and the threat of self-harm was not to be disregarded.* I asked to speak with her husband, but she objected. "He just gets riled up and doesn't know how to help." For her safety and my peace of mind, I offered to call her eldest daughter to look in on her. Joan agreed to this, and in due course, Stephanie called to report her mother was now asleep. I noted Stephanie's voice had the melodic quality of her mother's.

The next morning, Joan telephoned to apologize for the previous night's disturbance. I accepted her apology and added that we needed to formulate a protocol—a safety plan—for when she was in crisis. After this brief conversation, Joan called another three times, seeking reassurance that I would continue working with her.

Around noon, the Part called Samantha telephoned to ask, "How do I know I can trust you?"

"To find out," I replied, "we have to enter into a relationship. That way, you can see if I keep my promises and don't lie. Then you can decide if I'm worthy of your trust."

October 21. "I don't want to think about anything today," Joan began at our next session. "Writing a safety plan isn't in me. It will upset me too much, and I'll end up in the hospital." She described having had an episode two years previously that resulted in being hospitalized. Joan's memories of her stay were vivid and unpleasant, including being forcefully medicated and confined in a bed. "Anyway, I don't think I could bear to hear what the Parts have to say, especially that one who lives in a tree."

"Her name is Samantha, I've been told, and she has two sisters, Sarah and Sebunome. I understand your trepidation, Joan, but listening to their memories is necessary. The healing process asks that you become aware of what happened to you and the Parts, including Samantha and her sisters— shall we call them the Tree Girls? Perhaps we can invite Beth and Rose to go to the place where the Tree Girl resides and tell her not to be afraid. Let her know she's welcome to come out to see me. Perhaps they may be able to persuade Samantha to bring the other two Tree Girls with her. You see, Joan, keeping them silent will not help you become a whole person."

Joan wrapped her arms around herself. "I'm afraid of them."

Her features relaxed. I heard a voice lisp, "I want to help." Beth was looking at me as she said, "But I don't think they're ready to climb down from their Tree."

"Would you be willing to go talk to them?"

"If Rose will come with me. Maybe we could bring them a bowl of warm water and a washcloth so they can clean up and won't look so scary. I don't think I want to go all the way to their Tree, though. Do you think leaving the bowl right at the edge of the Forest will be okay? I better ask Elizabeth if this is a good idea."

She tilted her head slightly as if listening to some inner voice. "Elizabeth thinks helping the Tree Girls is a kind thing to do, and Rose said she wants to help. And Lisa volunteered to go with us. She's older than me and lives in Elizabeth's House in the yellow room next to mine. She wants to hum a song for them. We decided that when we come close to the edge of the Forest, Rose and I will chant, 'Don't be afraid. We like you,' and Lisa will hum her most beautiful song."

"With your help, Beth, the Tree Girls might come forward in a way that doesn't scare any of you."

Her face contorted.

"You meddling bitch," a voice hissed.

I rocked back in my chair at this unexpected hostility.

"What do you think you're doing? We don't want those three dirty girls coming close. Let them stay where they belong. Two of them already know how to get out and cause trouble. The best thing would be for them to go back to sleep."

"I can see you're angry," I responded calmly to this aggressive Part. "May I ask who you are?"

"I'm one of the dangerous ones. We are the Furies. Can't you see how red I am? If you touch me, I will burn you. Don't come close."

"Who has made you so angry?"

"Him! And her!"

"Would you like to tell me what they've done?"

"Are you kidding? Telling gets you punished." She looked around the therapy room, her attention lingering on my framed diplomas. "You know that other one tried to put us to sleep."

"Who tried to put you to sleep?"

"Helen. She thought we upset everyone and caused too much trouble. She really didn't like us. She told us to go back to sleep."

"Did you?"

"Hell, no! We only pretended."

"And why did you pretend?"

"Because Joan and the other goody-goodies wanted to make Helen happy. So, we moved back into the Forest and kept quiet."

"And where do you live now?"

"Around. We don't have a real place."

Before I could pose another question, Joan re-emerged. I asked if she had heard.

"I heard Beth say she and Rose and Lisa wanted to help the Tree Girls get clean." *Did that mean she hadn't heard the hostile Part?*

"A moment ago, you made it quite clear that the Tree Girls may hold painful memories you don't wish to hear."

Joan pressed her lips together as if to trap words in her mouth.

I told Joan of my suspicion that the Tree Girls might be just as frightened to tell what they knew as she was to hear what they had to say. But despite this mutual fear, Samantha had come out to speak with me and also had made contact twice by phone. Reaching out like that suggested she might be receptive to Beth's brave offer. And thus, the Tree Girls could begin to overcome their distrust and venture out. Once that was achieved, my responsibility would be to convince them they were safe in my presence. Only then could I invite them to disclose their memories.

"The most important thing for you, Joan, is to learn to listen to what the Tree Girls have to say. To do this, I will help you enter a trance, during which you may create a place of safety—a refuge in your mind—where you can listen to what they have to tell without being afraid."

Her chest heaved, fear bloomed in her face. I leaned forward. "Joan, I promise I'll keep you safe."

"How can I be certain of that? I trusted Helen, and look what happened."

"I'm so sorry your relationship with Helen ended in disappointment. But I'm glad you and I are off to a promising start when it comes to trust." I pointed out she had trusted me with some of her family history, particularly about her parents' troubled marriage. In addition, the number of Parts who had spoken to me indicated some degree of trust already had been established. I was also aware of a few of the intriguing features of an imaginary landscape inside her mind—Elizabeth's house, a cave, a forest, and an "outer edge," which, I assumed, was the opening where the Parts exited that inner system.

"What you've called the *inner system* is called the Inner Realm." Joan's voice was almost inaudible.

"How do you know that?"

"I just do," she replied.

"Well, as you can see, some trust already has been established, and a great deal of information has been communicated. That's encouraging, right?"

"Everything is just going too fast. It's overwhelming."

"Simply tell yourself the time is finally here to do the work that eventually will lead you to become a whole person—a woman whose memory and identity are both 'cohesive and readily accessible.'"

Joan let out a long, soulful breath and gathered up her belongings. After she left, I added Fury and Lisa to the list of Parts and filed my notes.

Chapter 4

A SAFETY PLAN

October 26. Joan entered my office carefree, her purse dangling from the crook in her left arm. She announced a solemn commitment not to give up on herself or the Parts, and to learn to cope differently with the unwanted feelings that upended her peace of mind, the terrifying memories that exploded in her head, and the horrific images that flashed across her eyes. She wanted to learn how to stay in the present instead of dissociating. "That's why I've come up with my own safety plan." Unzipping her purse, she pulled out two sheets of paper.

"Would you please read it aloud, Joan?"

She swallowed hard and read with the earnestness of a beginning student. Her seven-point plan reflected her Christian faith and the power of prayer. It contained expressions like "ask God for His direction" and religious phrases like "seek to please God."

When she finished her recital, she looked at me expectantly.

"I'm touched by what you've written, Joan. It reflects your deep faith in God's help and guidance. I can see how uplifting reading this document would be when you are at an end."

"Growing up," she said, "I believed I deserved being abused. I felt I was flawed. So full of self-loathing that I wanted to die. But my faith in God kept me alive. Even as a very young girl, I knew God loved me and would protect me and save me."

"I, too, believe you're deserving of His grace, Joan. Trust your faith to sustain you when the memories of abuse come forward." I deeply appreciated Joan's reliance on God, yet I didn't want her to go without a plan she could devise and put into action herself. "I think you need some practical strategies to ensure your physical and psychological well-being."

With that said, I handed her paper and pen and suggested she write down what came to mind in response to my suggestion.

Ten minutes later, she put her pen down. "This is what I've written so far."

- *Practice avoiding being seduced by denial, illusion, and delusion.*
- *Become more mindful of harmful thoughts arising and do all I can to counteract them in a positive way.*
- *Practice being kind and compassionate to myself.*
- *Do something for another person—bake a cake, write a letter, make a phone call just to say hi.*
- *Improve my health and stamina by eating regularly and taking my meds religiously.*
- *No overdosing.*
- *Try going to bed earlier than 4 in the morning. Nights are bad times for me, always have been.*
- *Read inspirational books, or paint, or write about my feelings.*
- *Listen to classical music, which I love.*
- *Work in the garden or just take a walk.*

"I thought about adding '*Take a Shower*,' but that's a dangerous thing for me to do. It causes a real commotion on the Inside. Anyway, there's always prayer," Joan smiled sweetly, "and Lisa. Her songs are like celestial hymns, incomparable in their beauty. And if all else fails, I can call you," she ended brightly.

"Excellent, Joan. So, you see, you aren't helpless in the face of emotional challenges." I suggested she read what she had written whenever she felt overwhelmed. Then I offered another way to stay in the present. The moment she sensed she was about to lose time, she should take a deep breath, keep her eyes open, look around the room, and acknowledge where she was. Then go to a mirror and look at herself, and confirm her identity by saying aloud: "I am Joan. I'm forty-four years old. I have two children. I have a husband. I live in my own home. I'm safe. No one can harm me." Then she should take another deep breath and return to what she was doing before the episode.

"Responding like that will take lots of practice," she said.

"And practice we will," I replied. "Utilizing your breath and being mindful will become indispensable. We will use these techniques in many creative ways to achieve your objectives." I looked into her eyes. *Was there a veil of fear there?* "Before we close, Joan, is there something else on your mind?"

"I'm concerned about those Furies."

"The so-called 'Dangerous Ones'?"

"Often, I can sense their anger, and, as you know, I'm afraid of anger."

"In time, Joan, you will learn to share their anger and eventually accept that you are capable of expressing anger yourself."

She avoided responding to my comment.

Her mood shifted. "Rose is beginning to speak to me," Joan said with a hint of pride. "Yesterday, she asked me if she could see you today."

"Please tell Rose I look forward to seeing her next time."

Before Joan left, I reviewed her progress. Two Parts—Beth and Rose—were communicating with her. She had been able to overhear conversations among a few others. I advised she build on that success. "When you hear the Parts crying or arguing, listen to them, perhaps even speak to them. Assure them that you have heard and that you care. And just as important, let them know you're learning to accept that they are a part of you." I explained that doing so might help decrease their fear and anger, or their faulty perception of being unlovable. And I encouraged Joan to invite Beth to function as her messenger to bring words of comfort, for example, to a Part in need.

That evening, Beth called to announce that Joan and Elizabeth had given her permission to call.

"I'm happy the three of you are communicating, Beth. However, please call me at home only if there is an emergency."

"I just wanted to say hi," she whined, "and ask if you like me."

"I do, Beth."

"Rose wanted to call you, too. But I guess I'll just have to tell her to talk to you when Joan comes to see you next time."

"That's the right decision, Beth. So, allow me to say goodnight."

"Goodnight," her voice glum.

Without much of a greeting, Joan took her place on the couch. After a long while, she said, "Beth told me she wasn't allowed to call you unless she needed your help."

"That's right," I replied, "and that applies to you and all the Parts. Calls to my home should be made only when you are in a crisis and no family member is available to help you."

Joan bit her lip. "Beth and Rose want to know if . . . perhaps . . . once a week . . ."

A voice in my head told me not to allow this, but I reluctantly agreed they could call me on Wednesday evenings between six and seven. "Remember, Joan, you may leave a message on my office phone anytime. I shall return your call as soon as possible."

Joan's eyes glazed over. A wilting voice said, "It's me, Rose."

"Hello, Rose," I replied. "You want to talk with me?"

"A few nights ago," she said, "I just wanted to tell you that I was hurting. I was afraid he would come and hurt me some more."

"Who would come and hurt you?"

"I can't tell, or he'll punish me." Rose shuddered and moaned, "It hurts . . ."

I assured her she was with me and safe. "If you can hear me, Rose, please take a deep breath . . . breathe in and out . . . in and out . . . now, very slowly, allow the hurt to flow out of your body. What you are remembering and re-experiencing happened a long time ago."

Another Part emerged through Rose's features. With shoulders hunched, eyes distrusting, she studied my face and then disappeared as if some internal switch had been flipped.

Joan slowly re-emerged. "I didn't clearly understand what Rose was telling you, but I felt her shudder. This is a first. Usually, I never physically experience what a Part feels."

"Perhaps soon you may be able to co-experience Rose's pain."

"Maybe," her reply uncertain. "I hear Beth. She's asking if she can come out."

"Of course she can."

Beth exited and leaned forward to say, "Since we promised to help, me and Rose and Lisa have been bringing three bowls of warm water and three clean towels every day to the edge of the Forest for the Tree Girls. And guess what? I saw them sitting under their Tree. They didn't look so scary and weren't as dirty as they were when we saw them the first time."

"I'm glad the Tree Girls have started to climb down from their Tree and are using the water and towels to wash themselves."

I asked if Lisa was humming a tune for them. "Sometimes she does, sometimes she doesn't. I think Lisa is a little afraid of them because, you know, they're much bigger than we are. And besides, she doesn't like to get that close to the Forest. It's dark in there."

Beth's eyes took on a faraway look. She recalled living at her grandparents' house. A German lady lived on their street, with two little girls about Beth's age. Sometimes when they played together, the German lady invited her into their house. She was so kind and sweet that Beth wished to be her little girl. In a hushed voice, she confided, "When I was in the lady's house, I never told her about . . . you know. Staying quiet was good. Never complaining was good. If we told, we were punished—like I said."

Then to my surprise, Beth asked if I would allow her to sing and laugh and even "talk really loud" here in this room. I assured her she could if that made her happy.

"Then I'd like to stay here with you." And like the first time we met, she pleaded, "Will you take me?"

I said as kindly as I knew how, "Beth, you are part of Joan. You have to go home with her."

"Can I call you 'Oma'? The little girls who belonged to the nice German lady had a grandmother, and they called her Oma."

"Would you like that, Beth?"

"It would make me feel like I belong to you a little."

"Then you may."

When Joan came forward, I summarized what Beth had reported. Joan warmed to the memory of the German woman and her daughters. Then, in an offhand way, she said, "There's a Part named Ana—spelled with one 'n'—who's been a presence in my life ever since I can remember. What's strange is that I sense her helping me when times are hard."

"Do you know how many other Parts exist Inside?"

"Inside?" She sounded confused. "Oh, you mean where the Parts are when they aren't out? I told you, it's called the Inner Realm."

"Do you know how many Parts reside there?"

"Not really. But awhile back, Beth drew a picture for Helen of all the Parts Beth knew." Joan promised to find the drawing and bring it to our next session.

After she left, I added a new Part named "Ana" to Joan's system.

November 20. "I almost canceled today's session," a pale-faced Joan said and complained of having no energy to engage in any kind of conversation. But did say Beth had something important to tell me. She closed her eyes, and Beth immediately came forward whining about "icky stuff" in the back of her throat. "I feel like throwing up, Oma." Perspiration beaded her forehead.

After walking her to the bathroom, giving her a glass of water to rinse out her mouth, and wiping her face with a cool washcloth, I guided her back to the therapy room. As she sat down, she asked me to sit beside her and hold her hand.

After a few moments, she whispered, "I think there were other little girls in the bathroom when my daddy and his friends hurt me." *Was Beth now revealing an event which occurred in another bathroom?* "One of those little girls was Annie. And maybe," her chin quivered, "Rose and Joan."

Did the number of Parts present at this event suggest that Joan may have experienced other sexual molestations—perhaps a number of times—at a very early age? A disturbing thought.

I thanked her for being brave and overcoming her fear of telling. Beth smiled weakly and said she wanted to go back Inside.

Within moments, another Part exited. By her demeanor, I thought she must be younger than Beth and asked how old she was. She held up three fingers but then began slapping her face while saying, "Bad. Bad. Bad girl." With caution, I grasped her hands and suggested she hit a pillow if that would make her feel better. With both fists, she beat a cushion until exhausted, all the while repeating, "Annie bad. Annie bad." I asked if she knew a girl named Beth. She nodded, so I invited her to go play with Beth.

Joan's hands trembled while I summarized what Beth had shared. Joan claimed to have heard nothing because she had gone to the White Zone. I then proposed that she and I create a safe place in the Inner Realm, where she could go to observe and listen.

"Would you be willing to do that?" I asked.

"What choice do I have? You said our work requires that I hear, see, and feel the memories the Parts hold."

I ignored her petulance, smiled, and told her we had learned a great deal in this session. After she left, I added a new name, "Annie," to Joan's system.

～

Chapter 5

ACCIDENTAL FEELINGS

December 4. "I feel so much better," Joan said for having met with her former therapist. "But I do believe Beth, Rose, and maybe a few others continue to feel abandoned and need your assurance." She touched her brow. "I feel pressure behind my eyes."

Rose emerged. With her head bowed, she stammered, "I feel dirty. I'm so ashamed." She gave me a sidelong glance. "Sometimes he laid on us, and when he pushed himself into me, I felt something strange down there. It felt bad. It hurt, but kind of felt good. Ever since, I've been ashamed."

"Rose," I explained, "when someone touches your body, the nerves in your skin respond—it can't be helped. You see, the good feeling just happened, like an accident over which you had no control." Seeing her frown, I knew she was not convinced.

I redirected the conversation by asking if she had seen the Tree Girls recently.

"Beth, Lisa, and I still bring water to them every day. But I think they feel dirty and ashamed, like me. I heard one of them—her name is Sarah—she said she had the same good and bad feelings as I did when Charles laid on her. Samantha, too."

"Rose, if you're up to it, tell the Tree Girls about our talk today, especially about accidental feelings." The painful expression that crossed her face suggested the issue needed time to be resolved.

When Joan came back, I started to share Rose's disclosures, but she held up her hand, palm out, tucked her purse under her arm, and left without saying goodbye. *Her hasty departure suggested she had heard Rose and could not bear the betrayal of her body's reaction.*

About eleven that night, Rose called. Her voice quavered when she told me our conversation about "accidental feelings" had upset Joan. The Tree Girls also were crying.

"That's why we have to talk more about those feelings," I responded. "Talking always helps, Rose."

Then Beth came on the line. She, too, complained that everyone was upset. I repeated my comment to Rose and promised we would talk more about this another time. I noted it was late and reminded her of our agreement to call only when there was an emergency. She hung up abruptly. Within a few minutes, Joan called, her voice somewhat slurred. "I'm at a loss as to what is going on. Can I see you tomorrow? Please?"

The following day, Joan reported Rose was depressed. During the night, Rose had heard the Tree Girls crying about the shame they felt over the "dirty secret" she'd told.

"How do you feel about their secret, Joan?"

To my complete surprise, she admitted she once experienced "accidentally" some kind of pleasurable feelings when Charles abused her.

"I don't like to think about it because it makes me feel guilty. But it's strange—for some reason, I don't feel any shame."

I didn't let on that I knew the Parts—Sarah, Samantha, and Rose—carried the shame for her.

"Last night on the phone, you sounded like you'd been drinking."

"I hoped it would calm my nerves."

"Alcohol never keeps its promise, Joan. Once its haze dissipates, you will still feel the same anxiety. There is a positive way to calm your anxiety—meditation. May I demonstrate?"

Lowering my voice, I began: "Make yourself comfortable so your body feels well supported. Feel free to close your eyes. Now imagine a Golden Light warming the crown of your head. Feel the warmth as it flows down onto your forehead . . . over your temples . . . flowing into all the little muscles around your eyes . . . over your cheeks and jaw . . . your whole face becoming warm and soft. Now allow the warmth to flow down your neck . . . cascading over your shoulders and deep into the muscles of your back . . . linger in this state of complete relaxation and tranquility . . . and when you're ready, open your eyes."

"That was nice," her tone mellow. As I watched, the corners of her mouth turned down as an unfamiliar Part slipped out.

She looked at me with suspicion. "I want to end all this. The shame and the guilt and the anger. Yeah, especially the anger."

"Who are you?"

"I'm Sarah."

Cloaking my concern behind a neutral tone of voice, I asked how she would go about "ending" those painful emotions.

"I'll cut my body. I'll swallow a bottle of pills—that should do the trick. Or I'll drink all the alcohol I can find in the house."

"Any of those actions might numb your desperate feelings for a little while, Sarah, until the effects wear off. Then, you'll find yourself stuck in the same place, and the feelings will return."

"Not if I kill myself," she countered.

I pointed out the Body belonged to Joan. If she killed herself, Joan and all the others would die.

She looked perplexed.

"There's a better way. You could visit with me and tell me about all those feelings. Do you know what caused them?"

"I know plenty, believe me. I'm old enough. But you don't understand: Telling is out of the question."

"Another Part—I think it was Samantha—told me you will be punished if you tell secrets."

"And do you have any idea what 'being punished' means?"

"I imagine it means being scolded or demeaned, tormented, or sexually abused."

"Those are just words for you," resentment in her voice. "Anyway, I don't care anymore."

"But I care, Sarah. So I suggest you think seriously about what I've said and postpone killing yourself until you and I talk again. Can I trust you to do that?"

"I suppose so."

Joan came out. She looked thrilled to announce, "I heard snippets of what you and that Tree Girl talked about."

"That's real progress, Joan. By the way, the Tree Girl's name is Sarah."

"I know. Beth told me."

"Beth seems to be an irrepressible messenger."

Joan then revealed that my "reprimand" of Beth for last night's phone call had resulted in Beth leaving her purple bedroom to hide in Rose's Cave and she refused to come out. "Perhaps you can persuade her."

"I'll try, Joan, but if she won't come out, there's not much I can do. You see, I'm still unfamiliar with how information flows between the Inner Realm and the Outside." I told her I'd read that an internal communication structure could be fluid, and information might move back and forth readily. But some structures, I said, could be complex. When this was the case, the flow of information was usually jealously guarded by a gatekeeper, whose purpose was to preserve the status quo and shelter the system from harmful outside influences.

"You still could try."

I invited Joan to re-enter the meditative state she had achieved earlier. She took a deep breath. Her features went lax. I tentatively spoke through to the system for the first time. "Beth, I know why you moved into Rose's Cave. I know you feel upset with me. Won't you come out so we can talk?"

I waited.

Beth came forward, her brow knitted. She lisped, "Elizabeth said I should come to see you. She's upset with me, too. She said I needed to apologize. It wasn't polite to call you late at night."

"Please understand, Beth, evenings are my private time. That's when I rest and look after my own family."

Contrite, she said, "I'm sorry, Oma. Elizabeth explained it to me. I promise to call you only if there's a real emergency. Is that okay?"

"Yes, and I accept your promise, Beth." Hoping not to sound too much like a schoolmarm, I said, "I appreciate Elizabeth encouraging you to behave respectfully toward others. Next time you come to see me, let's talk about what a 'real' emergency is."

"Can I go back Inside now?"

"Of course, you can. But I trust, instead of going to Rose's Cave, you'll go to your purple room in Elizabeth's House. Please tell her I appreciate her support."

Beth looked relieved and hastily retreated. Again, I called for Joan. She thanked me for my patience with Beth and Sarah. Pulling a sheet of paper from her purse, she said, "This is addressed to you."

I read the note out loud.

December 2, 2003
A Message to the Helper, [Abridged]

I have never addressed you directly and hope you do not mind my doing so now. I do not speak in your world. I hope using written communication will not present a problem.

Things have been in upset. I am writing now because of my concerns involving Beth. She is worried still that you may abandon her [but she] is doing much better. I did ask her to make sure to apologize for infringing on your request to rest. She is deeply sorry. The one at the Outer Edge is agreeing to be more in contact and more helpful concerning the girls, even if it is painful. Denial of truth leads to great upset, as we have seen. Joan, [at the] Outer Edge, has been present most of the day. Everyone Inside needs a rest as I am sure you do also.

If you request communication with me, I will be as cooperative as possible. Your dedication and obvious caring for my girls are greatly appreciated.

Elizabeth

I turned my attention back to Joan, who smiled and said, "According to Beth, Elizabeth has no breasts but is always kind and good, even though she doesn't cuddle or comfort them." *Not having breasts,* I thought, *could be symbolic of a caretaker who doesn't extend emotional and physical endearments. Perhaps when Elizabeth and I have established a relationship, I can encourage her to express affection toward those in her care—to nurture them when they are troubled by memories and fears.*

December 17. Joan lamented her continued inability to stop dissociating. I reminded her how she had been able to stay present when Sarah entertained suicide. Her bleak smile indicated my praise had failed to ameliorate her concern.

"Unlearning the habit of losing time will be a difficult task, Joan. It will take time, mindfulness, and patience." Dissociation, I thought to explain, had served her well in childhood and adolescence as both a neurobiological response and a psychological defense to disconnect her from the incidents of abuse she suffered. She had compartmentalized and segregated her memories, feelings, and perceptions associated with the maltreatment, thus preventing them from being assimilated, as would normally occur with other knowledge. Over time, dissociation became an automatic protective response, which she had continued to use as an adult when she felt discomfort or was upset or threatened by something or someone reminiscent of her past. But "going away" was disruptive, prohibiting her from living life in full awareness and functioning in ways that were consistent and rational. "These are good reasons, Joan, for learning how to stop dissociating and will be an essential component of your therapy."

Without warning, Sarah replaced Joan. "I've been moving a pile of shit with a bulldozer, and I told 'em they can have their shit back."

"Who are 'they,' Sarah?"

Glaring at me, she spat out, "Charles and the Mother. I don't really know if I got rid of *her,* but I got rid of *him.* That's for damn sure."

She refused to talk further about Charles and "the Mother" even though I pledged to keep her safe. Instead, she expressed doubt about my sincerity.

I thanked her for keeping her promise not to harm herself last week and obtained another commitment for the upcoming week.

Joan re-emerged. Fidgeting in her seat, she confessed, "I tried to listen, but Sarah frightens me. She's so angry."

"And full of pain," I added.

She reached into her handbag. "I found this poem in my purse this morning."

To the Helper

I see you sitting there in your chair
You move across to me with tenderness and care
Here with you, the safest refuge in our world so bleak
A place to learn, a place to speak
Of how it's been, how this can be
To be trapped here, this person, me
Torn between self-hatred and shame
Knowing in truth I have no one to blame
For what I have done and what I do
I feel so ignorant that I haven't a clue
How do you change the bad to good?
To live in a life the way that I should
Now as I see the compassion in your eyes,
I try to sort the truth from the lies.
Will you teach me to live the way that I should?
I know you can't save me, I wish you could.
—Sarah

Joan said, "I guess this says it all. We want to trust. We want to tell. We want to let go of the self-hatred and shame but don't know how. We all depend on your compassion and commitment to teaching us how."

"We will do this together, Joan. You will find the courage to do the work, and I will offer you the guidance you need to make the changes, still your fears, and learn to embrace yourself with compassion. Healing will take time, tenacity, and commitment."

"God willing," she said under her breath.

"And trust your faith to sustain you."

~

Chapter 6

LONGINGS

January 6, 2004. The hubbub of the holidays had barely settled down when Joan telephoned. "We have sort of an emergency here. Beth wet the bed during the night and is inconsolable."

Beth came on the line. "Oma, I had a bad dream last night about Charles in the bathroom. He took off my clothes and pinched me all over and hurt me . . . down there. It made me wet the bed, and I woke up. Mr. Roger took me to the bathroom and helped me change into a dry nightgown. But, Oma," she said, "he didn't hurt me like Charles. He was nice. Now comes the bad part: I told him it wasn't me who peed in the bed, but Annie. But it *was* me, and now I'm really ashamed. I'm going back to Rose's Cave. That's where I belong."

I told Beth she could undo the white lie if she returned to Elizabeth's House and apologized to Annie. I assured her that would make her feel better.

"Okay, Oma. I'll tell Annie I'm sorry I fibbed."

Later that evening, Joan called to say Beth had made amends with Annie. Then somewhat hesitantly, she told me Beth's story had triggered her memory about the bathroom incident. She had been about eight years old and believed the incident occurred before Charles and her mother married. He had already started molesting her in minor ways, but she couldn't recall what transpired that evening in the bathroom. What she remembered was having wet herself and Charles telling her to ask her mother for a dry nightgown. When she did, her mother became angry and made her wear her soiled clothes for the rest of the night.

Two days later, Joan marched in, and without a word of greeting, opened her purse and pulled out a carefully folded, small, white square of paper. "This is what I found in my shoe this morning as I dressed."

She unfolded the square. Her eyes darted over the content. "It's a poem . . . by Sarah."

"Would you please read it?"

She shook her head.

I heard a voice say disgustedly, "It's just like her. Always the goody-goody. But she was there. I know she was. She cared for her, too. She hugged her. But now I'm the one stuck with these feelings."

"Is this what the poem is about?"

Sarah stared at me.

"Would you like to read it to me? You know you're safe here."

Sarah exhaled deeply and then read aloud:

Bad

How bad am I to kiss you?

To feel unafraid?

To be just a person

How a person feels

After being afraid for so long

How did I allow everyone else to be?

When I'm allowed nothing at all

Knowing how bad I am

How bad will I become?

—Sarah

"Do you want to talk about your poem?"

"Only if you don't judge me," she replied, her eyes awash with guilt. "I don't need criticism. I feel bad enough."

"Regardless of what you tell me, I will continue to accept you as you are."

With a tiny tremor in her voice, Sarah said, "We were about fourteen when I befriended a girl in our neighborhood. We became close, and my mother allowed me to spend the night with her. Sort of a sleepover. It was the first time I had any sense of freedom. I felt unafraid and just enjoyed myself being there. When it came time to go to bed, we slept together in her room. We laid there comfortable and sweet. Feelings I never had before. At first, my new friend and I held hands, and then she moved close and gently hugged me. To my surprise, it felt nice. I wasn't frightened. I wasn't being hurt."

She took a breath.

"This went on for about a year. My mother never objected to me spending the night, but for some reason, she became suspicious and accused me of being a lesbian. At first, I had no idea what she was talking about. I had to go to the library and look up the word. I was confused. My mother kept insisting that I wasn't normal. Why should I be normal when I never had a normal connection with anyone? Not to her and certainly not to the pervert she married."

She again took a breath before continuing.

"After that, my mother stopped me from visiting my friend. She told me she was not going to support my . . . sick inclinations. I didn't tell her that I wanted to be with my friend not because I was a lesbian, but because I felt safe and cared for by someone for the first time in my life."

Her shoulders slumped. "Now that you know what I am, you're probably disgusted, like my mother. But I don't care. When my friend hugged me, I never experienced any sexual feelings. I just enjoyed being held without being hurt."

"When we are lonely, Sarah, all of us yearn for a kind word, a gentle touch, and a caring embrace. What you and your friend did was simply an innocent exchange of affection."

"I just want you to believe that I'm not a lesbian. I'm afraid God will strike me down for having a special friendship with a girl. That's what Joan believes."

"Well, I believe God loves us all. No matter who we are, no matter what we do, He accepts us and holds us in His grace."

Sarah looked at me in disbelief. "Not me!"

Before I could respond, she was gone. I was left with the image of shadows clouding her eyes. *How difficult will it be*, I wondered, *to resurrect her belief in her innocence and goodness?*

I called for Joan. Instead, I found myself facing a new presence exuding dignity and grace. "I'm Raven," he announced. "I'm older than time. I perch atop the tallest tree in the Inner Realm. I am not like the others. I am unharmed and unburdened by mental and emotional travail. I fly close to God. My calling is to advise, protect, and guide. Presently, I am watching over the Tree Girls. Sarah has returned safely to her Tree and rejoined her two sisters. Thank you for extending your kindness to her. Before I take my leave, may I warn you that danger looms. Shame is crushing Sarah. For now, I am able to soothe her despair, but only the future can tell for how long. I do not know if I can fulfill my calling with what is to come. Now that you are here, though, I am more hopeful."

I sat in silent awe of this enigmatic figure as he continued his cautionary appeal.

"I'm aware you have been told that God promised to send you to help Joan and all the others. For that, I am thankful. Before I return to my Perch, may I be so forward as to advise you to talk to Joan about remembering that she, too, cared for Sarah's friend."

I heard my voice respond, "As soon as Joan returns, I shall talk with her."

"Thank you. Please allow me to withdraw." Raven bowed his head and disappeared.

Was this the "angelic presence" Helen had encountered? Did Raven's declaration of devotion to the Tree Girls imply he could be an "inner self-helper"? From what I had read on the subject, some clinicians perceive an inner self-helper (ISH) to be an angel, like Helen had. Others feel an ISH has "transcendental abilities, including healing and psychic powers." Ralph Allison defines an ISH as the manifestation of a child's Self that comes forward to "form" the Parts as surrogates to suffer the abuse and retain the memory. Other prominent psychiatrists posit an ISH as a "protector personality of a higher order." They contend that this manifestation is not the child's Self but agree with Allison that an ISH has superior intelligence and evolved spiritual qualities, possesses extensive biographical knowledge about the client, and makes an excellent co-therapist. All agree that the presence of an ISH indicates the child's trauma likely started before the age of seven or eight; the abuse may have been extreme, frequent, and long-term; and a high number of Parts could be present.

With all that running through my mind, I called for Joan. I summarized Sarah's disclosures and told her of actually meeting Raven, who advised me to remind her that she had shared a caring relationship with Sarah's friend.

Joan's brow creased as she replied, "I vaguely remember having had a friendship with that girl, but I prefer not to be reminded about it."

"Has Raven ever spoken to you?"

"About eighteen months ago, I heard him speak to Beth. His voice was deep and calm. At first, I thought it was God speaking. But Raven has never spoken directly to me. Looking back, I have a sense he's been a part of my life ever since God spoke to me when I was seven. Probably that's when Raven became my link to Him. But did I realize it then? No."

That evening, when I transcribed my notes, I repeatedly tapped my pen on Raven's name while deep in thought. *From what little I knew about him—his deportment, mystical statements, and professed calling—could Allison's declaration be correct? Or could Raven be something other than an extension of Joan's Self? Was he what Joan sensed—a conduit for God's wisdom and mercy? In practical terms, I hoped Raven did hold useful historical information and could be an insightful resource in the treatment process. If he was an ISH, then Joan's abuse may have begun at an early age and must have been extreme. Consequently, the number of her Parts could be greater than I had anticipated. At that moment, I didn't know enough about the nature and function of an inner self-helper and the complexity of Joan's case to draw any conclusions.*

My phone rang around half past ten that evening. I heard sobbing.

"Oma, it's me." I recognized Beth's lisp. "The Tree Girls are out. They're running around the house, screaming. I think it's Sarah and Samantha. We can't find Joan."

"Is Mr. Roger home, or Megan?"

"No. Please help, Oma," she said through tears.

"Try to stay calm, Beth, and do what you can to stay on the Outside."

"I don't think I can. They're pushing at me."

"I'll hang up the phone now and call Stephanie."

After introductions, I explained the situation. Stephanie said she'd be there in twenty minutes and promised to update me by phone. Ten minutes later, the phone rang again, too soon for Stephanie to be at Joan's house. No one spoke when I answered. I heard a thump and noises like furniture being pushed around. Then I heard a Part yell, "I must die! I must die!" followed by thrashing and screaming. I immediately hung up and called 911.

Some ten minutes later, Stephanie called back. She was vexed and told me I had no business calling the police. She maintained she could manage her mother, that she had done so since the age of ten and knew more about her condition than I did. I replied that her agitation was understandable but explained my responsibility as her mother's therapist was to assure her safety. She begrudgingly accepted my explanation, adding she would remain with her mother until her father came home from work about two in the morning. She said she knew how to "handle the alters." As soon as her mother "came out of it," she promised to administer her nightly medication. I requested that her father contact me first thing in the morning.

Roger called the next day to say everything had been calm since his arrival home. I suggested we needed to set up a protocol to follow whenever Joan threatened to harm herself. I explained that as a therapist in private practice, I had no facility to take care of Joan when she was suicidal. She would need hospitalization.

"Our health insurance will not pay for a hospital visit whenever Joan is in trouble," he replied sharply.

Accepting his contentiousness as a mask to conceal his embarrassment, I advised he bring the family to my office so we could formulate a life-preservation contract that would keep Joan safe. I even offered to make home visits to help in critical situations, but Roger declined.

When Joan came to therapy that afternoon, I observed a bruise on her forehead, a black eye, and a cut on her upper lip. I didn't comment. For a while, she just kneaded her purse. Eventually, she spoke. "I'm sure you've noticed the bruises on my face. It happened when havoc broke out at my house last night. I'm sorry for all the trouble I've caused. Do you still want to work with me? I won't blame you if you don't."

"Crises are part of the process," I said. "A crisis encourages one to explore what triggered it and then face working through that cause. So, ask yourself, what triggered your crisis?"

"After you told me what Sarah talked about," she stammered, "images started to crowd my mind. I saw myself with that girl, being happy and feeling free from all that was so terrible in my life. Being with her offered me an escape, at least for a few moments. It gave me comfort, and I was able to forget who I was. I'm not a lesbian and never have been, but my mother said what I did was immoral. She made me feel ashamed."

Joan's features hardened. Samantha was now sitting before me. "She's still a blabbermouth," she snapped. "She had no right to tell our secret."

"Who told a secret?"

"You know—Sarah. She should have told me she was going to tell what we'd never told anyone before."

I asked if she was upset because the secret was out or because Sarah told it without asking her first.

"We're supposed to stick together," she said, her voice edgy. "Not telling keeps us safe. But now that the blabbermouth has told you, you're probably as disgusted as the Mother. Are you going to send us away?"

"You mustn't worry, Samantha. I'm Joan's therapist. I'm here to help."

"Sure, you want to help *her*, but what about *us*—Sarah and me?"

"You and Sarah are part of Joan, which means I'm here to help all of you."

Before she returned Inside, I advised her to talk it over with Sarah without being angry. "I don't know how not to be angry," Samantha replied. "Sarah's the same. We're always angry. We're always afraid."

"Would you like to learn how to talk to one another without lashing out?"

She didn't respond. Instead, an unexpected serenity washed over her face, and Raven appeared. "Thank you, Helper. From now on, I shall take special care to fly closer to the Tree Girls so I can hear what they are angry about."

Before I could respond, he was gone.

A forlorn Beth slipped out to thank me for helping when they all were in "big trouble." Ever the informant, she added that Elizabeth and Raven had helped, too.

Joan listened to my account of Samantha's visit. I impressed on her that Sarah and Samantha shared her feelings of shame. From my library, I retrieved a recent journal article addressing relationships among sexually traumatized teenage girls. I suggested she read the article out loud for Samantha and Sarah to hear, which I hoped would shift their perspective on the matter.

Joan looked puzzled. She had never directly communicated with any Parts other than Beth. I encouraged her to try.

Before she left, Joan informed me that she and her family were willing to sign a life-preservation contract. I was relieved.

~

Chapter 7

ESTABLISHING COMMUNICATION

January 15. I knew Joan was a late-morning riser. She never went to bed before midnight. This morning, she had awakened at eleven with her usual headache and feeling depressed. "Before I even got out of bed," she said, "I wondered if it wouldn't be better to do away with myself and end the misery. But I heard a soft voice say, 'Not today. Today is not the time to end it all.' I didn't want to dissociate, so I started to breathe as you taught me. I thanked the voice for her advice and somehow found the courage to ask her name. 'I'm Rose. I'm the one who bleeds. I'm the one who hurts.' I kept very still, hoping she would continue. She said nothing more, so I repeated I was glad she spoke to me directly, and that I was willing to listen any time she needed to tell me something. But that wasn't the end of it." Excitement animated Joan's voice. "I heard another voice say, 'I'm Sarah. Samantha and I can hear you when you talk to the Helper. We know you are afraid of us because we're trouble and we know too much.' I told Sarah I was trying hard not to be afraid and was willing to listen. But she didn't say any more."

"That is encouraging, Joan. You have established communication with Rose and two of the Tree Girls—not accidentally, but consciously. That is one of the most important steps in the treatment of MPD. And equally important, Sarah and Samantha have started to talk between themselves. In therapeutic terms, that means they are becoming co-conscious. Soon they may begin to share more memories and feelings with each other. Plus, you utilized your breath and stayed in the present. Well done, Joan!"

Joan glowed, and then her shoulders sagged. Sad eyes looked at me. "I'm the one who bleeds. I'm the one who hurts. I killed a baby."

This must be Rose, I thought. "Would you like to tell me more?"

"We can't tell anyone. He would get mad. We never can speak about it. We have to be quiet and pretend we are fine."

"No one will punish you in this room, Rose. You will always be safe here with me."

She withdrew without responding, and Sarah came forward.

"If Rose is too afraid to tell you, then I will," she said. "Last Sunday at Joan's church, people erected crosses for babies who had been aborted. Samantha and Rose and I met yesterday at the Forest Edge and talked about the abortion. Rose was eleven when she started to bleed all the time. She thinks she killed the baby. And we think Joan heard what we were talking about."

She abruptly disappeared as if she'd been *pulled* back Inside.

Rose reappeared. "I heard what Sarah told you. Maybe I didn't kill the baby? Maybe there was no baby?"

"Rose, you were too young to have a baby. Perhaps that's when Joan began having her monthly period." *On the other hand,* I thought, *Rose might hold a memory of Joan possibly having had an abortion.*

"No one ever told me that before, Oma."

"Now you know and no longer need to fear you did something to cause the bleeding."

"But I'm still bleeding all the time down there. It hurts. Joan doesn't know. But I think she doesn't want to know, either." *I began to suspect there might be something sinister behind Rose's bleeding. Could she be having visual hallucinations of blood running down her legs after having been raped by Charles?*

"I want to tell you one more thing," she whispered. "Mama knew he was hurting us, but she never stopped him. She never wanted to hear what we tried to tell her. She always told us to hush."

"When I heard Rose talking about the bleeding," Joan said upon re-emerging, "I panicked and went to the White Zone. I'm sorry, Renate."

"But you stayed in the present long enough to hear *some* of what Rose talked about. And yesterday morning, you communicated with Rose and the Tree Girls for the first time without dissociating. You should be optimistic about the progress you're making."

"I want you to know, the other day I called my mother to tell her about Charles. I barely got out a couple of sentences before she cut me off. She said I should 'forget about it' and go on with my life. I guess she still wants to deny everything. Just pretend nothing ever happened," bitterness coating her words. She let out a deep sigh. "I'd better go now," she said and picked up her purse. "Before I leave, though, I have something for you. I found these poems in my nightstand this morning. They have your name on them."

I

I can

I can hate

I can hate men

I can hate men who hurt girls

I can hate mean men who hurt girls who will learn to hate men

I have learned how to hate them

I can hate me, not them

Just me

—Samantha

Questions

What will it be?

Are you, you, and I, me?

Pieces to a puzzle that will never seem to fit?

Eyes in the darkness that never has been lit

By the sunshine of peace from the heavens above

Questions of faith and questions of love

Who can answer to the pain that we feel?

How can we know what really is real?
Can you answer the questions that burn in our eyes?
Can you give us an answer to the tangled up lies?
—Sarah

My Name
See me, but don't know me
Why?
Because I have to hide
Why?
Because I can't live in a world of so much pain
With all in mind
All which I have seen so clearly
I see, just don't see me
—Sebunome

The existence of the poems indicated the three Tree Girls were beginning to risk revealing themselves. This development suggested they were in the process of establishing trust, meaning they were starting to share memories among themselves and with me.

Chapter 8

LESLIE

January 20. Joan's bruises and abrasions from the night of chaos had not completely healed, although she attempted to mask them with makeup. With a subtle transformation of her features, Sarah was now sitting before me. She spoke in a hushed voice. "Joan and I met Leslie at her house."

"Leslie?"

"She's Joan's best friend. At first, Joan was there, but when I hugged Leslie, she went away. Leslie told me she loved me. All I've ever wanted was someone to love me, and someone loves me now. That's all that matters."

"How old is Joan's friend?"

"Same as Joan."

"Then Leslie must be old enough to be your mother."

For a moment she looked confused.

"Do you want Leslie to love you like your mother never did?"

"No, I just want her to love *me*."

"What if Joan objects?"

"She doesn't know." Sarah gave me a withering look. "You're just like my mother. You can't stand it when I'm happy. And I almost trusted you." She squinted to push back the tears. "I'm done here," and was gone.

Within seconds, Samantha exited, her eyes blazing as she told me how angry she was about Sarah's behavior. I told her Sarah was confused and encouraged her to be tolerant of the situation until a solution could be found. At my urging, Samantha promised not to lash out at Sarah, at least for the time being.

I asked Joan to return. As I briefly recapped what Sarah told me, Joan looked puzzled. "It's true," she said. "Yesterday afternoon, I went to see my friend Leslie. I've known her for many years."

"Sarah seems to want a special friendship with Leslie. Are you aware of that?"

"Sarah must be confused. We're just good friends."

Joan commenced to rummage through her purse. "Here's the drawing I promised you awhile back."

"Is this the one Beth made of all the Parts that reside Inside?"

Beth popped out. "Hi, Oma. I heard Joan brought you my drawing. I made it for Helen after I woke up. I couldn't draw very good back then."

I studied Beth's crayon sketch. It featured a cave and a big house with flowers in front. At the top of the drawing, she had drawn a tree and written *Lots of tree people. Not girls, not boys.* "I see you labeled some of the Parts with their names." I pointed to the figures I recognized. "I know of Lisa and Rose and even Fury 1. But there are new ones, too. Annie, Mean Fury 2, Tiny Baby and Biger [sic] Baby, and Maria. Who is the 'Pome [sic] Maker,' Beth?"

"That's Elizabeth," she lisped.

"At the bottom, you wrote down *tree people* and Sebunome's name, but you didn't draw a picture of her. Nor do I see Sarah and Samantha."

"Oma, when I drew the picture, I didn't know what the Tree Girls looked like."

"But now you do?"

"I don't really know what Sebunome looks like, but Samantha is really tall and has long black hair and blue eyes. I think she's eighteen, and Sarah is sixteen. She's not as tall as Samantha, and she has brown hair and brown eyes."

"I see Rose has lots of long blonde hair and green eyes. And Lisa over here has straight red hair. You've drawn Elizabeth in a black dress with black hair done up in a bun. And that's you," my finger tapping the drawing, "with a red ponytail and wearing a purple dress."

The Parts, Beth 2002.

"Purple is my favorite color," she said with a proud smile.

"Here at the bottom edge of the paper is Fury 1, with lots of black, curly hair."

"She's not too nice, Oma."

"There's this other Part beside her you labeled 'Fury 2,' the one with wild orange hair."

"Helen put her to sleep because she was really, really mean. I don't know where she is now, but I'm glad she's not around. She is too scary, Oma."

"Who is this black figure here in the middle of the picture? You labeled him 'Shadowman.'"

Beth put a forefinger to her lips. "Shhhh, Oma. He's the meanest of all. He hides behind a big tree close to the edge of the Forest. He's dirty and slimy and covered with bark."

"How do you know what Shadowman looks like?"

"Upstairs in my purple room, I can see him through the window. Sometimes Maria and Lisa come to my room, and we peek at him. But not for long because he scares us. He has red eyes and gets really, really mad when we tell secrets. Right now, he's mad at Sarah. Remember when Joan got in trouble? Shadowman hit her in the face and gave her a black eye."

Aha, I thought. *That explains Joan's black eyes and cuts. He must be a persecutor Part. From what I've read, they are usually angry adolescents. They engage in malicious harassment directed toward the client and other Parts. They hold rage and experience themselves as outsiders. Over time, however, if treated with respect and compassion, persecutors can be persuaded to become allies in the healing process.*

"Why did he do that, Beth?"

"I don't know, Oma. I think he probably thought he was punishing Sarah for telling a secret—you know, about her special friend." She lowered her voice, "Oma, don't ever talk to him and tell him what we tell you 'cause he will hurt you really bad."

"I'll be careful, Beth. Who protects you from Shadowman when he gets angry?"

"Raven warns Elizabeth, and she tells everyone that lives in the House to come inside, and then she locks the door. We stay with her downstairs in the big room, and she reads us stories and tells us everything will be okay."

"Who protects those who don't live in the House?"

"Raven, I guess. I know Rose hides in her Cave, and the Tree Girls climb back up in their Tree."

"May I ask you something else, Beth? Who can hear me on the Inside when Joan and I talk?"

"Sometimes I can," she replied. "And I think Elizabeth and Raven listen sometimes, but not always. And you already know Sarah and Samantha and Rose can hear you. Sometimes they come out even without asking permission. That's when Shadowman gets mad. Oh, I almost forgot. When Elizabeth asks me to tell you things, that's when I come out."

"So, you're Elizabeth's helper?"

"Oma, you know I like to help. Raven told Elizabeth that's my job."

Joan came back. "I didn't know all of this was going on in my head," she said with a crooked smile. *I was impressed by her willingness to listen instead of retreating to the White Zone.*

"I have something else for you. It's a letter from Many Voices."

"Who is Many Voices?" I asked as she handed over a sheet of paper.

"I don't have a clue. Almost every day, I find writings like this hidden around my house."

A hopeful sign, I thought, *that the Parts wanted to communicate.*

January 18, 2004
To The Helper, [Abridged]

And in a moment the words of reality [have been] finally and truthfully spoken aloud. The foundations of the fortress of denial begin to shake. Not that reality had been altered, but hearing, really hearing, for the first time with open ears what denial, time, and living far removed from it all could not change. It does not matter—guilt or innocence, knowledge or ignorance. When truth is glimpsed, reality digs into awareness, steadily chipping away pieces of denial. There comes a place of no turning back. She, the Mother, might not be able to turn away completely ever again, [or] deny the identity of her child, the reality of its life, and the lives within her.

This is not a story of blame, although if told [in a] spirit of bitterness, despair, anger, and vengefulness, it could have been. In the beginning and now nearer to the end, there is only one way to look at it: She did the best she knew how to do. Pitiful [are those who] have never known compassion, love, and truth. The fortress shakes, and the wall of denial starts to crumble. All of us wish she learns to walk in the light of truth.

—Many Voices

Before I closed the office for the night, I studied Many Voices' communiqué. *Could she be something more than another Part? Her knowledge of Joan's past and her philosophical erudition suggested she might be another inner self-helper. She was aware of Joan's attempt to speak to her mother about Charles' sexual abuse. The possibility of a second inner self-helper made me wonder if there might be a second system harboring Parts I knew nothing about.*

Throughout that evening, the phone rang incessantly. Sarah called first to assure me she would not harm the Body or create a crisis for the next six days. Then Samantha called to tell me she would inform Raven of Sarah's decision, so Raven could inform Elizabeth, who could ask Beth to tell Joan. After that, Rose called to complain she was bleeding and experiencing pain in her lower abdomen. Between moans, she said she had been violated and that Charles had pushed her into a "grave" and threatened to "burn her alive."

"I'm praying," she whimpered, "but I can't breathe. I'm choking. I think I'll die."

"Keep praying, Rose. You are remembering a terrible thing Charles did to you a long time ago. Find Samantha, and tell her what you're re-experiencing. Talking with her will help."

Shortly after that, Samantha called to confirm she had comforted Rose. "She's safe in her Cave now. What Rose told you is true," she added hoarsely. "Many of us were there."

I thanked her for being kind to Rose.

"I guess I'm changing," she said. "Perhaps I can become a helper."

"You already are, Samantha."

59

February 17. Joan had not been to therapy for almost a month. Today, I hoped to learn why. As soon as she sat down, I realized she had dissociated. Samantha moved Joan's purse aside, sat up straight, tilted her head slightly upward, and announced, "I want to be like Athena."

Some time ago, I had given Joan a book about Greek goddesses. I asked her to carefully study the descriptions of each deity and ask herself with which one she most identified. While Joan read the stories about the Greek goddesses, Samantha explained, she had read along and decided she wanted to be strong and fearless like Athena, with a breastplate and sword. She wanted to protect the younger Parts and keep them safe when in danger. She could roam the Inner Realm like a sentinel, always on the lookout, and protect everyone from Shadowman and the Dangerous Ones if they ever came back. Samantha chewed at her lower lip and frowned. "I'm not sure if I can always be brave and protect the younger ones. I still don't know if I can overcome my anger and stop drinking. Sometimes I'll be scared, but I'll pray for courage. And I hope you and Raven will watch out for me."

I praised her for the transformation she was contemplating and assured her of my support. Samantha's expression became grave. She told me of glimpsing other Parts roaming the Dark Forest. They looked worse off than she and her sisters.

"The Dark Forest?"

"Yes, in Many Voices' Realm."

So, there is a second system with Parts, I thought, *and Many Voices must be another inner self-helper.*

Later, as Joan prepared to leave, she hugged her purse to her bosom and said, "There's something I want to tell you, but I don't know how to start."

I smiled and waited.

She let out a long sigh and lifted her eyes toward the ceiling. "My husband doesn't see me when we're intimate. All he wants is to satisfy himself." Tears pooled at the corners of her eyes. "As you might imagine, having sex traumatizes me. I try to stay in the present and not dissociate. I don't want a Part taking my place." Another sigh leaked out. "I'm not sure, but I suspect

Roger likes to upset me on purpose, so I'll go away. I think he might be having sex with some of the Parts."

"Have you mentioned this to Roger?"

"I've tried to explain that if a Part is out, it isn't me, but he gets upset and insists it *is* me. Maybe he's just confused and thinks it's okay."

"Perhaps he *is* confused," I echoed and asked if she knew which Parts her husband had sex with. As far as she knew, the only ones old enough would be Samantha, Sarah, and possibly Rose.

"Have you pointed out that they are adolescents?"

"No . . . but it bothers me, Renate."

"Do you want to bring Roger here to discuss your concern?"

"I doubt he'd come."

~

Chapter 9

NOTES AND SECRETS

February 20. I inquired if Joan was willing to start keeping a journal of her childhood memories that she and the Parts recovered. *In due course, her effort would yield an autobiographical timeline affirming the events of her life. In my experience, this type of journal-keeping had therapeutic benefits that would contribute significantly to her healing.*

Joan squirmed as if she were sitting on a prickly cushion. "I'm not sure I'm ready to put on paper what you're asking. Besides, for some time now, I've been uncomfortable with you taking notes. I'm told the ones Inside don't like it either and have decided to stop writing letters and poetry for you to read. There's a question of confidentiality."

I masked my disappointment and asked what had created this distrust.

Sarah hurried out. She pointed a finger at me and said, "You have to stop writing on your clipboard what we say to you. What do you think will happen to us if your notes fall into the wrong hands? Believe me," she warned, "there would be serious consequences."

With a stern look, she went back.

Joan frowned in annoyance. "Can you believe she just pushed me aside?"

"Her appearance did seem abrupt. Perhaps we can figure out some way the Parts can let us know when they want to exit. I suggest we ask them to signal in some way before they take over your body and come out."

Joan looked both perplexed and amused. "We can try."

I stood and gestured for Joan to follow. We walked to the cabinet, where I keep my clients' progress notes. I selected a key from the ring clipped to my waistband and unlocked the file cabinet. I invited Joan to look inside at the tabbed folders with coded labels. Then for emphasis, I shut and re-locked the drawer. "As you can see, my notes and the poetry and letters are locked up safely. I'm the only one who has a key."

After we were reseated, I explained why I took notes. Our sessions were long—often about three hours. And during that time, much information was disclosed. Details I jotted down allowed me to piece together the memories and emotions the Parts held and shared about specific events. Studying my notes, I could detect relationships among the Parts, which gave me insight as to what functions they served within the system. I gave Joan a couple of examples of what I had deduced from my notes: Beth functioned as a messenger between the Inside and Outside, and Rose's frequent complaints suggested she held much of the physical pain of the sexual abuse. I told her I also wrote down what the Parts said about the features and their locations within the Inner Realm. I now knew that the Tree Girls lived close to the edge of the Forest not far from Shadowman and his Tree. And that Rose hid in a Cave close to Elizabeth's House, where Beth and some young Parts resided. From my notes, I gleaned that Raven's Perch was atop the tallest tree in the Inner Realm. In addition to my notes, the poetry and letters provided valuable insight into the Parts' suffering—their longings, fears, and anger. "I study all this," I concluded, "to uncover connections between the Parts and events which I hadn't noticed before and to help me prepare for upcoming sessions. Does this help you understand how invaluable my notes are?"

Joan didn't comment. I interpreted her silence to mean more trust needed to be established before Joan and the Parts felt their disclosures were safe with me. Consequently, I pledged to refrain from taking further notes. And in doing so, I hoped to provide peace of mind for her and the ones Inside.

Samantha called that evening to assure me of her trust. She wanted to continue our work even if I wrote notes. From now on, she wanted to be more supportive, and express empathy for what Joan and the others had endured. I thanked her for trusting me and for wanting to show compassion for Joan and the Parts.

A flurry of phone calls ensued over the next two weeks. One came from Beth, whispering that Shadowman was mad about something, and now everyone was filled with dread. Rose called to inform me that fear had driven her out of the Cave, and she was presently sleeping in front of Elizabeth's House with a "green blanket" and a "pink pillow." Another time, Samantha called to tell me she was trying to be a helper "like Athena" and protect Joan and the others from Shadowman. One afternoon, Roger phoned to say Joan was not herself and had begged to speak with me. Instead of Joan coming on the line, an unfamiliar voice whimpered, "Make it stop!" When I inquired who was speaking, the Part replied, "I don't know," and dropped the phone. Roger picked up the receiver. I advised him to watch over his wife and call me should her condition worsen.

The following day I called to check on Joan. I spoke with Megan, who confirmed that Joan indeed was not herself, but promised to look after her mother until her father came home from work. Sometime after midnight, he called, sounding frantic, and implored me to speak with Joan. I heard her whimper, "I hear loud voices." Then that unfamiliar voice again wailed, "Make it stop!" In response to this confusion, I told Roger I would contact Stephanie, and if need be, the two of them could take Joan to the hospital. Stephanie called an hour later to report her mother continued to be distraught. She had not taken her antidepressants for days. Stephanie agreed to stay overnight, and near seven the next morning informed me her mother had walked around the house all night. Joan came on the line to apologize for having been "such a bother." I encouraged her to see me as soon as possible. She demurred, saying she hadn't slept in days and felt too weak to come to my office.

March 10. The dark circles under Joan's eyes spoke of her misery over the last month. She moved with care, as if each step was painful. She held a painting in one hand. Settling on the couch, she let out a low moan and laid the artwork facedown on the cushion beside her.

"I can't tell you how relieved I am to be here. My days and nights have been filled with voices crying out in pain and calling for help. Once, a menacing voice tried to seduce me into committing suicide. The only one who would suggest such a horrible thing, Renate, is Shadowman. He's been on a rampage the whole time. He keeps threatening that if the Parts and I don't stop telling secrets, he will inflict unspeakable pain on all of us. He's been chanting over and over, 'Be quiet. Don't talk. Don't feel. Or else.' And insisting we can't have feelings for Leslie or you or anyone else on the Outside. He kept screaming, 'People on the Outside cannot be trusted! They hurt! They punish! They lie!'"

She lowered her voice. "I don't know how I coped, but somehow I stayed in the present. I held on because I was afraid if I lost time, Parts might come out and create havoc, and who knows what would've come of that. So, I held on. I didn't have a choice."

"How difficult it must have been to stay present through such an ordeal," I said without revealing I knew other Parts had been out during this distressing time. "And by doing so, you managed to keep yourself and the Parts safe. What an accomplishment! Now think back and recall who else has threatened to punish you if you dared divulge what you suffered."

"That's not hard," Joan replied, an edge to her voice. "My mother. Usually, with screams and threats before I could tell her anything. And Charles, of course, constantly threatened me to keep my mouth shut."

"So, you learned to keep quiet. You thought not telling kept you safe, kept you from being punished. I wonder if Shadowman might also believe his cruel tactics are his only way to keep you and the Parts safe from outsiders."

"If he wants to keep us safe," Joan queried, "why does he try to lure me into killing myself?"

"That's hard to say. We don't know much about him. If we are patient, I'm hopeful he will exit and reveal his true purpose. Just remember, whenever he threatens you, you do not have to act on his terrifying suggestions. As soon as you become aware that Shadowman is going on another rampage, please call me immediately."

She drew a deep breath, her eyes veiled. *Perhaps my attempt to reframe her perception of Shadowman had been premature. I hoped at least I'd planted a seed.*

Joan picked up the painting she had brought with her. "I have something for you. I didn't do it alone. Several Parts must have worked on it at different

The Tree Girls, Joan and the Parts 2004.

times over several weeks. I'd get up every morning and find new features added. I was amazed when I finally saw the finished product."

She handed me the picture. What I saw was completely unexpected. It depicted the three Tree Girls as branches growing out of a barren tree, blood from an open wound flowing down the trunk, pooling at its base. Behind them was a leafless forest with a multitude of beleaguered young faces staring out at me. In the upper left corner was written the word "EVIL," and below that was an ominous gray figure of a man casting a long shadow. At the top right was a raven, from which a golden radiance emanated. On the lower right, the figure of a little girl without arms leaned against a tree, her legs spread wide. At the bottom center of the composition was a rose with its severed stem dripping blood. Nearby were three golden stars—the Trinity.

I started to hand it back, but she said, "Oh, no—this is for you."

I thought her painting was remarkably insightful: Its barrenness spoke of a grim, loveless childhood, yet sacred symbols promised survival.

She placed a trembling finger on the figure of the armless girl. "This must be me."

~

Chapter 10

THE PENDING VISIT

April 16. Joan rushed to her seat. She apologized for being late. Her mother had called out of the blue to announce her decision to pay Joan a visit in two weeks and stay until the middle of May.

"Are you ready for that?" I asked.

"I believe I am. The last few days, I haven't lost time. The Parts have been less restless, less agitated. And what a blessing that has been. It gave me time to be alone with my thoughts and do the things I wanted. Not dissociating for this long has given me the confidence that I can get through my mother's visit without a major incident. Besides, I still have two more weeks to get myself ready mentally. I want to make her feel welcome. I hope she and I can begin to have serious conversations about the past and, possibly, start having a meaningful relationship."

"You seem very confident, Joan."

Samantha emerged.

"Sarah, Sebunome, and I know the Mother is coming. We heard Joan talking to her. We got on the phone and told her we wouldn't take any shit from her and that she couldn't scare us with those yellow eyes," anger dripping off her words.

"I'm sure you have good reasons to be angry. But for now, please return to the Inner Realm, and inform Sarah and Sebunome that at our next therapy session, Joan and I will start preparing for the Mother's visit, and, by the time she arrives, I'm sure Joan will know what to do. I'm hoping the three of you will help Joan make the visit a pleasant one, at least one without arguments."

Her eyes continued to hold the heat of anger as she faded.

"I had no idea," Joan said, confidence shaken, "that I had gone away during the phone call. Now I'm worried. What would happen if the Tree Girls come out and start an argument? Or tell her how she failed us? This would make the visit much more complicated. I had hoped to resolve some things between us. You know, at times, I feel compassion for my mother. I've seen her other side. To be fair, she could be kind and charitable toward *others*. But never toward me. What would my life have been like had she loved me?"

She shook the thought from her mind and said that, despite how the Parts felt, she wanted to be kind and accepting of her mother. I reminded Joan that expressing compassion is a privilege she has as an adult and didn't mean she must approve of her mother's failures.

In session three days later, Joan said she was not the only one troubled by her mother's pending visit. She had heard that Beth and Rose were hiding in the Cave. She also had felt Samantha and Sarah's anger.

"Last night, the Parts you just mentioned telephoned. They needed assurance that you'll be supportive during your mother's visit."

Uncertainty clouded her eyes. "How can I be supportive?"

"You might listen inward. Connect with the Parts emotionally, and share their anxieties."

"That will be difficult," she said. "My confidence has gone out the window. I already feel my tongue freezing in my mouth. I see myself shrinking into that obedient girl—the plastic doll who expects to be tongue-whipped into a blob. I have to remind myself that *I* choose what to think and feel and do. Otherwise, I'll be pulled into that nest of snakes that slither around in my mother's head."

"Just remember," I urged, "she's coming to *your* house, where she is a guest and should be on her best behavior."

Suddenly, Joan broke out in uncontrollable laughter. Spit-bubbles accumulated in the corners of her mouth. Struggling for breath, she pushed out, "The day after she arrives, I'm scheduled to have an operation on my ankle. Nothing serious, but I'll be unable to get around for a couple of days. There *is* some justice in this world. She'll have to wait on me for a change. And while she does, she'll have to play nice in front of my husband and kids, right? Won't that be a switch."

Joan's merriment was interrupted by Beth's appearance. She said in a timorous voice that she was afraid and knew Rose and Sarah were, too. She needed a hug, and my assurance that all of them would be safe during the Mother's visit. I sat beside her. She laid her head on my shoulder and held my hand.

"Beth," I softly said, "could you ask Elizabeth to comfort you if I'm not available?"

"Oma, Elizabeth doesn't hug. She doesn't even pat me on my head. She's always kind and takes good care of us, but she never hugs. She teaches us how to read and how to behave. But in her black dress and apron and her keys rattling at her waist, she doesn't look like a mama. She doesn't look like you," she whispered into my shoulder. I felt her slip away.

I sat in my rocking chair, expecting Joan to come back. Her body shuddered as Samantha made her way to the Outside.

"How can I support Joan during the Mother's visit if I'm still covered in slime and filth? Before I can help her, I have to wash off this stinky stuff. I can't cross the Forest Edge to be close to Raven and the other Parts if I'm unclean."

"I hear the urgency in your voice. There may still be time to arrange a cleansing ritual. Have you sought Raven's advice?"

"Yes, he knows, but I can't understand why he's letting me wait so long."

"I imagine he and Elizabeth are discussing how your new purpose as a helper will benefit the Parts and Joan. I'm confident that, as soon as they come to an understanding, Elizabeth will send Beth to tell us to proceed with your cleansing ritual. So please, be patient."

"When the moment comes, will you be at my side?"

"You have my word."

After dinner that evening, the phone rang. An unfamiliar voice with an Irish lilt stated matter-of-factly, "Elizabeth here."

"I'm pleased to hear from you, Elizabeth."

"This is the first time I have addressed you. Yesterday, I overheard your conversation with Beth. When she returned to the House, I asked if the care I provided was enough for her. The brave wee girl admitted she needed more. She yearns for emotional and physical affection, which I have not provided. I have refrained from doing so because expressing affection has, since I can remember, brought nothing but heartache and disappointment. You see, the Parts and Joan live in a conflicted reality. They yearn for love yet have no love for themselves, nor can they accept love from others. Love represents a danger to their welfare within both the Inner and Outer Realms. Long ago, when Raven and I recognized that fact, rules were established that discouraged anyone from experiencing such feelings—I mean to say Joan on the Outside and the Parts on the Inside. And let me further mention, these rules are fiercely defended and enforced by Shadowman. At this very moment, he is demanding the Tree Girls inhibit their feelings—in particular, for you—and insists they not move beyond the Forest Edge."

"Thank you for this insight," I responded. "I understand the purpose of the 'rules' is to assure the Parts' safety and keep further pain and betrayal at bay. As you are aware, Beth, Rose, Samantha, and Sarah are reaching out to me—if only tentatively. For our work on the Outside to succeed requires your approval of their behavior and your *affection* to foster their self-assurance. That means expressing physical and emotional appreciation for who they are. So, if not you, Elizabeth, who then, on the Inside, can extend those gifts to them?"

"I will consider what you have said," Elizabeth replied. "But for now, may I ask *you* to provide extra time and care for Beth, so she will have her needs met? Perhaps this will lessen her fear about the Mother's visit."

Then, almost as an aside, she announced, "Raven and I are cognizant of Samantha's wish to be cleansed and leave the Darkness of the Forest. As soon as we agree on how to proceed, you will receive written suggestions. I have noted that some of the Parts are aware of this impending occasion and are prepared to contribute. I shall now say goodnight."

April 20. In response to Elizabeth's counsel, I arranged a tea party for Beth. Joan arrived with a gleam of mischief in her eyes. "Here we are. Beth can hardly contain herself. She's been chattering away since we left home," Joan said as she seated herself.

"If you wish," I said encouragingly, "you may silently take part in the fun Beth and I are going to have this afternoon."

"Oh, no—she's all yours," Joan replied with a wave of her hand. "Beth has looked forward to spending time with you without me eavesdropping."

"You know, Joan, the goal this afternoon is not only to help Beth feel more secure and less afraid about your mother's visit but also to help you and the Parts feel less anxious as well. In fact, the process may have already started. When you walked through the door, I noted your high spirits. Beth's joyful anticipation of having fun today has probably activated the neurotransmitters in your brain to produce what I call the 'feel-good' hormones. And when Beth and I start playing or reading or listening to music, those feel-good hormones will increase your sense of mental and emotional well-being."

"Even though I'm dissociated?" Joan asked, clearly puzzled.

"Yes, indeed."

She closed her eyes, and Beth leaped out, beaming.

"Hi, Oma," she said, stretching out the three syllables. Surveying the room, she clapped her hands with glee when she spied the small table I had set for tea. "I love tea parties!"

"Where would you like to sit?" Beth chose her place, and I sat facing her. "Miss Beth, would you be so kind as to pour the tea?"

"I will be happy to," she said, and then added with an impish smile, "Miss Oma."

I held out a plate of cookies. She hesitantly reached for one and delicately laid it on her napkin. When she saw me putting milk and honey in my tea, she commented that Joan put only sugar in her tea, never milk.

"The English drink their tea with milk," I explained. "My husband lived in London for a while, and he taught me."

"Okay," she said, "then I'll try it."

As I added milk to her tea, she asked, "Is your husband nice?"

"Yes."

"What color are his eyes?"

"Blue."

For a split second, her eyes veiled, but she quickly wrung the allusion from her mind. She picked up her teacup and took a tiny sip. She held the tea in her mouth without swallowing. She must have let the liquid trickle down her throat before she said, "Mmm. Oma, I like English tea." She picked up her cookie and took the tiniest bite. She was careful not to let the cookie touch her lips. She held the crumbs in her mouth as if she had an aversion to swallowing. Eventually, she did, though. And with a forced smile said, "This cookie is delicious."

"Our tea party, Oma, reminds me of Alice having tea with the White Rabbit, the Dormouse, and the Mad Hatter."

"So, you've read about Alice's adventures in Wonderland?"

"Elizabeth reads it to us. Usually before we go to bed."

"After we have our tea, would you like to sit on the couch and read the story again?"

Instead of responding to my invitation, she chatted on. "When Alice fell down the rabbit hole, it was very, very dark in there. It reminds me of when I decided to go away. I didn't fall down a hole like Alice. I just closed my eyes and went to sleep. I slept for a long time. When I woke up, Elizabeth found me and took me to the House, which was much smaller than it is now. When Maria and Lisa woke up, we had to build on two more bedrooms."

"Shall I get the book so we can read the story?"

Again, she didn't respond directly. "Did you know, Oma, Alice fell into a pool of salty tears?"

"Do you think Alice filled that pool with her tears?"

"I don't know, Oma. We don't have a pool. We have a river. It's called the River of Tears."

"Was your river created by Joan's tears and yours and the others?"

"You'd have to ask Elizabeth and Raven. I was only eight when I went to sleep."

She returned to Alice's tale. "The Queen of Hearts, who yelled 'Off with their heads!' reminds me of my grandmother. She yelled and was mean like the Queen. I hope when the Mother comes, she doesn't get mad and yell at us."

"Let's hope she won't. It isn't nice when one gets yelled at for no reason. What did you think about Alice going through the Looking Glass?"

"That part of the story made me sad, Oma."

"And why is that?"

"It reminded me of the Girl in the Mirror. I saw her when I was in the bathroom with my daddy. She looked so sad, Oma, before she disappeared." *I wondered if the Girl in the Mirror was a fragment Part that had splintered off Beth to help her endure.* "Do you think someday we can find her and help her get out of the mirror?"

"I think she'll come out when she's ready, Beth."

"I hope so, Oma. I don't want to talk about Alice anymore. Let's do something else."

"How about reading *Snow White and the Seven Dwarfs*?"

She rolled her eyes. "Oma, that's for babies," she lisped.

"Then what do you want to do, Miss Beth?"

"Can we listen to 'Over the Rainbow'? It's my favorite song."

"I'll put the disc in the boombox and we can sit on the couch while we listen."

She rested her hand in mine and sat as close to me as she could. "Maybe someday, Oma," she said wistfully, "I hope I can fly like a bird over the rainbow. And when I do, maybe I can see God, or He can see me."

As the melody filled the room, Beth became dreamy-eyed. After listening to the recording several times, she gave me a sidelong look. "I guess when the song is over this time, I'll have to go back."

"Did you have a nice tea party, Beth?"

"Oh, yes, Oma. But I'm still scared about the Mother visiting us. Maybe not as much as before. If she gets mad and starts yelling at everyone, I think

I'll just go to my purple room, close the door, and put my purple pillow over my head. Rose said I could hide in her Cave if I got really scared. And Joan promised to help us stay safe."

"It's good you have several options to help you cope with the Mother's visit, but now I think it *is* time for you to go back Inside so I can speak with Joan."

When Joan came back, she looked relaxed. "What time is it?"

"It's time for you and me to go home," I teased.

"Oh, my goodness—yes," she said, glancing at her wristwatch. "I've lost track of time."

As she gathered her things, I said, "It was good of you to tell Beth and Rose that you would help them stay safe during your mother's visit."

"I have to help myself first before I can help them, but I'll try."

"And you will, Joan. I'm confident about that."

Privately, I promised myself that, at a more appropriate time, I would inquire about the impact of her grandmother's anger on Joan's life as a child, and about my suspicion that Beth's aversion to swallowing could be a consequence of having endured oral sodomy.

"Perhaps next time we might review the safety plan that you and the Parts put together awhile back."

"That's a good idea," she said and left.

~

Chapter 11

THE SAFE PLACE

April 21. "What a morning!" Joan said with a crooked smile. Yesterday she had left my office feeling rested and peaceful. But while she slept last night, something in her mind shifted. "I woke up full of anxiety. Harsh memories flashed across my eyes. I'd laugh hysterically while tears ran down my cheeks—and you know how afraid I am of crying. I had to struggle not to spiral downward. It's amazing I didn't lose time. I know some Parts were fearful and close to going back to sleep, especially Beth, but I was able to calm them down. I'm terribly proud of that, Renate. But Lord, I'm bone-weary."

"I can see how tired you are." I paused a beat. "Would you like to talk about those 'harsh' memories?"

Joan sidestepped. "You know, everyone in my family was a superb liar. Early on, I learned to hide inside their lies to keep from getting punished. But I lied to everyone, just like they did. Worst of all, I lied to myself so convincingly that I came to believe I had escaped unscathed from that house of horrors. I fashioned a mask of deceit to cover my pain and anger, and the sense of betrayal I felt toward my mother. And even now, I have a hard time admitting to myself how great the damage has been."

She rummaged in her purse. "Here, this letter's written to you. There are some notes on the back. I found it in my dresser drawer when I was getting dressed."

I quickly read the letter aloud. Elizabeth and Raven agreed to honor Samantha's wishes. They approved of her emergence from the "Forest" and sanctioned her cleansing ritual. The notes on the back pledged additional support from Beth, Sebunome, Lisa, and Maria.

Joan feared Samantha's cleansing would elicit horrid memories and painful emotions. She was unsure of her ability to remain in the present throughout the ritual. I suggested this might be the right time to add a safe place within her imaginary landscape. A place of refuge and contemplation, where she could find solace and security when feeling overwhelmed. A perfect place where she could listen to and observe the Parts in the Inner Realm without being frightened.

"How do I go about creating such a place?" she asked.

"I'll guide you into a meditative trance that will enable you to enter the Inner Realm without having to dissociate."

With her consent, I began.

"Make yourself comfortable . . . and as you sit here with your eyes closed . . . aware of the sound of my voice . . . you begin to breathe in and breathe out . . . in and out—that's right . . . as you sit here breathing in comfort . . . and breathing out disquiet . . . you begin to drift into a light trance . . . in your own way . . . in your own time—that's right . . . as you continue breathing in comfort . . . breathing out discomfort . . . taking in what you need . . . letting go of what you do not need . . . in a way that is just right for you—that's right . . . breathing in safety . . . you begin to float toward your Safe Place . . . wherever you wish it to be . . . a place of security and calmness and serenity . . . a place within the Inner Realm . . . your Safe Place . . . experience its shape . . . its color . . . its furnishings . . . you may wish to linger awhile . . . and promise yourself to come back to the Safe Place you created . . . created to sustain body—mind—heart—and soul . . . the place that is yours . . . yours alone . . . and so now as you begin drifting back . . . becoming more aware of the sound of my voice . . . your conscious thoughts and feelings returning . . . up nearly to the surface . . . of wakeful awareness . . . allow your eyes to open . . . and mindful awareness to return . . . quite completely now—refreshed."

Joan's eyelids fluttered open. "That was amazing," she said. "When I surrendered to your voice, I allowed myself to float through the Outer Edge and into the Inner Realm. I stopped midway between the Edge and Elizabeth's House—the perfect location to create a safe place."

She built her Safe Place out of stone, she said. It was small, with two windows and shutters. After installing two doors—one accessible from the Outer Realm—she added locks and bolts on all the openings. That way, she told me, anyone seeking refuge there would feel protected and safe from unwelcome intruders. The interior walls she painted green and furnished the room with one overstuffed chair, a table, and a pair of stools. For a few moments, she had rested in the armchair, examining her handiwork. Smiling, she told me about possibly putting some of her paintings on the walls next time she went there.

"I wanted to stay longer, but I heard your voice inviting me to return. So, I made my journey back to this room. I'm astounded by what I've just experienced. When your voice guided me to the Inner Realm, I was in a trance, but at the same time completely conscious. Imagine that, Renate. What a revelation. To be able to stay in the present and yet find myself in that imaginary landscape, where I can see and hear the Parts."

"Remember, Joan, you may seek out the security of your Safe Place whenever you feel the need to get away. Simply allow yourself to 'float through' the Outer Edge and find your way there."

With mischief playing in her eyes, Joan quipped, "I can go there during my mother's visit, or even when my husband gets on my nerves."

～

Chapter 12

OUT OF DARKNESS

W*ithin the space of eight days,* Joan and I met four times to prepare her and the Parts for both her mother's visit and Samantha's cleansing. Today her face looked pinched, her breathing shallow, her apprehension palpable.

"Since yesterday afternoon, when I left your office, my emotions have fluctuated between hopeful excitement and fearful anxiety. I pray that after Samantha leaves the Forest and is cleansed, she'll stop drinking and fighting with my husband. But I'm afraid of the memories she'll disclose."

Joan's voice wavered. "What will happen if I or Rose or Sarah or Sebunome or any of the others can't cope with what Samantha reveals? What will happen if what she says triggers a flashback in me? I just don't know if I'm strong enough or have the kind of courage it takes to witness what's about to happen."

"It's true," I cautioned, "that the cleansing process Samantha has chosen to undergo may arouse painful memories in some who are in attendance. However, I'll be present to guide the process. And let me assure you, as soon as I become aware that you or any of the Parts are becoming overly distraught, I will intervene before the suffering becomes all-consuming. I promise to keep you safe. All of you."

I paused briefly to allow my pledge to resonate.

"Under my guidance, Joan, re-remembering and re-experiencing a memory of abuse will not create the same physical and psychological torment that you, Samantha, or any of the other Parts experienced during the actual maltreatment. Understand that once you are in the Safe Place, you may choose to open the shutters and unlock the windows so you can see and hear what is taking place. You may choose to use the breathing exercise to decrease the intensity of your emotional response and help you stay in the present. But you also have the choice to keep the windows and shutters closed and sit in your overstuffed chair without observing anything. Remember, you are in a protected place—safe and secure. When all is done, you will hear my voice guiding you back to this room."

I paused again, hoping my explanation would help her find the emotional strength to be attentive. The silence grew between us. I could see her struggle, and then, with quiet resolve, Joan said, "I guess I'm ready."

I asked her to close her eyes, relax, and take a deep breath . . . I guided Joan to the Safe Place and asked Samantha to exit. "Samantha, this is a significant day for you and the Parts that reside in the Inner Realm. Before you walk out of 'Darkness,' allow me to read the letter I received yesterday from Elizabeth. It includes comments from Raven and several Parts.

April 23, 2004
Dear Healer, [Abridged]

Raven and I have agreed to allow any or all of the Girls to have a voice in the anticipated Emergence of Samantha from the Forest, the first to leave the misery of the Darkness into a place of more light, [and]to be cleansed in the River of Tears. This is an occasion Raven and I have long awaited. To bear witness I will, for the first time, go beyond the boundaries of the House and Yard. After the Ritual, Samantha has free will to choose where she wishes to reside in the Inner Realm.

Congratulations to you for the progress you have encouraged. It has been a short time with great results because of your unwavering support and compassion for my Girls and all the others who reside in the Inner Realm. Raven and I are grateful.

Respectfully, Elizabeth
P.S. The Girls were encouraged to write notes of support.

~

Dear Helper, you are encouraged to remind Samantha of how courageous she is to be the first to walk out of the Darkness. Those in the Forest will be asked to bear witness. God be with you.
Raven

~

Please don't leave us forever! You are very brave, Samantha. I don't think I could be that brave. Don't get hurt in the water.
Sebunome

~

Oma, I will give Samantha one of the clay vessels I made for her to put her sadness in. I will watch from my Cave.
Love, Rose (the one with thorns)

~

Oma, I will pick flowers for Samantha and leave them in the pot from Rose.
Love, Beth

~

Maybe I will sing. Samantha can decide. We will still bring water to Sarah and Sebunome.
Lisa

While I read, Samantha sat before me, wide-eyed and attentive, her cheeks flushed. Perhaps she finally realized the implications of her decision.

"Let me prepare you for what will take place during this special event. It will begin with you leaving your Tree, your safe haven. Once you lower

81

yourself to the ground," I cautioned, "painful memories will rush into your awareness. With each step you take, the memories will multiply, and the severity of your emotional suffering will increase. At some point, you will hear my voice asking you to disclose aloud the abuse you endured, suffer through the anguish of those memories, and accept what hurt and demeaned you many years ago. Throughout, know that what happened to you, Samantha, was not your fault. After you complete this difficult task, you will have the opportunity to grow into a helper. I now invite you to return to the Inner Realm so we may begin."

"Will you be at my side?" she asked. "I trust you."

"When you hear my voice guiding the cleansing ritual, know I will be with you in spirit."

"But I need you to be there."

"I wish I could be. The only way I can is if you and I *imagine* that I'm there, so to speak. You will feel my presence encouraging you, comforting you."

She raised a nervous smile.

"Now please move aside, Samantha. I would like to speak with Raven."

"Move aside how?" she asked, befuddled.

"Just move aside, Samantha. Try it. You can do it. Then listen to what is said."

Raven emerged.

"Before we begin, Raven, will you please be so kind as to draw a map locating the features of the Inner Realm so I can visualize the path Samantha will take to the River of Tears?" Within minutes, he handed me a simple line drawing mapping the imaginary landscape.

"Samantha and I will now return to the Inner Realm and await your instructions."

After assuring myself that Joan was in a trance, I spoke through to the system to address the Tree Girls—Sarah and Sebunome—and the other Parts who chose to bear witness. "I invite you to become aware of a Golden Light above you. Experience its warmth and radiating energy. Ask for its blessings. Let go of whatever binds you. Free yourselves of any apprehension. Be assured that you are safe." Leaning back in my chair, I took a deep breath, entered a meditative state, and visualized my presence floating through the Outer Edge into the Inner Realm.

What happened next I can only describe as a composite retelling of Raven's observations, my directives to Samantha, her responses and disclosures, and my vivified suppositions and visual imaginings. Using the iterative method of directive-and-response created a mental construct of the abreactive ritual taking place in my treatment room.

In my mind's eye, my presence passed Joan's Safe Place and Elizabeth's House, turned left and crossed the Forest Edge to arrive at the foot of Samantha's Tree. Seeing Samantha sitting on a large branch, I encouraged her to find within herself the fortitude to leave the "misery of the Darkness" and assure her sisters, Sarah and Sebunome, that she would not forget them.

Samantha climbed down and for an instant faltered, but then took her first step. When she crossed the Forest Edge, she acknowledged Raven's presence flying ahead to guide her. As she made her way, she sighted Rose's Cave, Rose and Beth peeking out as she passed. Far off on her left, she saw Elizabeth standing in front of the House. Farther along, she walked past the Meadow on her right, turned left onto a path that led to the River of Tears, and made her way down its embankment. Sharp-edged stones cut her feet, but the stones became round and smooth as she neared the water's edge.

Sensing her diffidence, I spoke aloud and directed her to take off the dirty rags clinging to her body and wade into the River. I envisioned her taking a step into the water despite her trepidation, then a second, and another, and another until she reached the middle of the River. She bent over, cupped water in her hands, poured it over her head, and began to frantically wash her hair. Through clenched teeth, she hissed, "You used my hair to wipe yourself after you were done with me." Her breath shuddered when she poured water over her upper body. Her face scrunched in pain. "You bit me and dug your fingernails into my breasts before I was old enough to have any." Her hands scrubbed at her chest. Rage bloomed in her eyes as her hands slid down to her pelvis. Her breath became ragged. Primal sounds escaped her throat. "You ripped me open," she moaned.

"You made me bleed. You stole my innocence and shamed me." She cupped another handful of water to rinse out her mouth and throat. She gagged and retched, her knees almost buckling as she struggled for air. "You with your foul breath," she wailed. "Your stinking sweat." She doubled over, her hands clasping her knees.

"Stay with your feelings, Samantha," I directed. "Let your feelings rise. Feel them through. Take a deep breath and let go of the pain. Now, wash off the blood. Wash off the shame. Cleanse yourself."

I imagined Samantha reaching for the clay vessel Rose had so lovingly created. She filled it to the rim and slowly poured the water over her head, allowing it to flow down her body. She placed her hands above her heart and turned in the direction of her Tree, a gesture of devotion to Sarah and Sebunome for bearing witness to her transformation. She carried Rose's vessel back to the water's edge, stepped out of the River, and there, near its bank, discovered a golden comb, a white dress with tiny red roses at its hem, and a narrow red belt. She proceeded to comb out the tangles in her long black hair and then slipped the dress over her shoulders and fastened the belt. At that moment, I pictured Raven flying from his Perch and placing a wreath woven of pink and white primroses on Samantha's head.

"Well done, Samantha," he praised.

With tired limbs, she walked to the Meadow and lay down to rest. That was when I withdrew my visualized presence.

Before I called for Joan, I allowed a few quiet moments to pass. When she emerged, Joan struggled to be in the present. After regaining a semblance of composure, she said, "I couldn't reach the Safe Place. So, I hid behind a tree. From there, I could see Elizabeth in front of her House. She looked exactly as Beth had described, sort of like a schoolmarm. I heard you speak to Samantha, but when your voice guided her to the River of Tears, all I could make out was a shadowy figure. I heard Samantha begin to rage at Charles. That's when I went away. I guess I wasn't ready to hear more. I'm sorry if I failed you."

I praised her for staying present long enough to see Elizabeth and hear the first of Samantha's accusations. "Only when you couldn't bear to hear her anguish, that's when you went away."

"Perhaps I did accomplish more than I think. Right now, though, I have a terrific headache and I'm bone-tired."

When she regained strength enough to drive, I escorted Joan to her car and requested she telephone me when she arrived home.

Back in my office, I thought I could have summarized for Joan what else occurred during the time she had been dissociated. However, I recognized she was too vulnerable to hear it, so I chose not to take that approach. As treatment progressed, I assumed other opportunities would be forthcoming for Joan to re-remember or even re-experience what Samantha suffered through today. Plus, I hoped Samantha's transformative act might inspire other Parts to leave the Darkness.

I recorded Samantha's disclosures in my progress notes. Writing of her outrage and despair chilled my heart. Fatigue washed over me. I struggled out of my rocking chair, blew out the candles, locked the office door, and, with heavy steps, walked home.

~

Chapter 13

THE SENTINEL

April 28. "My God," Joan exclaimed, "you can't imagine how thankful I am to sit in this peaceful room with you. I've been having the worst nightmares. Like from hell, pure evil. If anything could push me over the edge . . . I've tried to drive the images out of my mind. I thought about calling your office, but I was too afraid even to get out of bed. The only thing I could do was pray. I also thought that listening to the meditation tape you made for me would help, but I was even too terrified to open my nightstand drawer to get it. I've experienced the terrors of sleep paralysis many times in my life, but this was the worst."

I saw a pulse of fear in the hollow of her throat as she began recounting her nightmares.

"In the first dream, I found myself in Hell, where naked, evil creatures crawled all over me, scratching me with their claw-like fingernails and screeching out of toothless mouths. Sharp bones protruded through their decaying flesh. I struggled to get away, but there were too many of them. I woke up screaming.

"In another dream, I was locked inside a cathedral crammed full of drunken people and unshaven old men. Priests were raping young boys right on the steps of the altar. Loud, jarring sounds spewed out of the organ. I was enveloped by the evil spirit of the place. I saw myself crawl to the door of the cathedral and claw to get out, but it was locked. I woke up paralyzed, not knowing if the evil I saw was inside me or outside. I prayed to God to help me stay awake."

Joan looked spent and asked if we could go for a walk and get some fresh air. I offered her my hand, and we strolled through the neighborhood while she puzzled over her dreams. "I've asked myself if God wanted me to see what was in store for Charles. Or was I shown that Hell is my destiny because I tolerated Charles' evil? What do you think?"

"In time, I believe you'll make sense of it, Joan. As for your destiny, ask yourself if God would send an innocent girl to Hell because she was the target of evil."

"How about being locked up in the cathedral? Is Charles' evil still inside me? Aren't I trying to free myself of all that disgusting stuff? That's what we're working on, right?"

"Exactly," I replied. "Samantha has taken the lead in washing away the foulness Charles inflicted."

She said nothing more while we made our way back to my office and resumed our conversation.

"Since Samantha's cleansing ritual, have you experienced any physical discomfort?"

"I've had migraines, and my body has ached more than usual," Joan replied. "So have my breasts. And I've some discomfort . . . around my pelvis," a blush of embarrassment coloring her cheeks as she rushed on. "There's a lot of unrest on the Inside. Beth and Rose asked to call you on the phone, but I told them they could speak to you when I saw you."

Before we did that, I wanted to guide her to the Safe Place so she could listen to what was being said. Good-naturedly, I asked her to be sure not to end up hiding behind a tree again. To indicate when she had arrived, I suggested she lift her right forefinger once. When she wished to return, do the same twice, and my voice would guide her back. She closed her eyes and took a deep breath. And then my voice directed her Inside.

"Hi, Oma. I'm really glad to see you," Beth lisped. "Me and Rose have been worried. Ever since Samantha washed herself in the River of Tears, we're afraid Shadowman is going to come out from behind his big Tree and hurt Samantha for leaving the Forest and telling about Charles. We're scared he'll hurt us, too. But so far, he hasn't. And there's another thing I want to tell you. After Samantha rested in the Meadow, she put a metal thing over her chest. It was all gold and shiny, Oma. And she picked up a sword in a holder and tied it around her waist. I think she wants to protect us from Shadowman."

"That's exactly what she wants to do, Beth. To be a helper."

"That's good, isn't it, Oma? Can Rose talk to you now?"

Rose exited, her head down, eyes on the carpet. "When Samantha went into the River of Tears," her voice just above a whisper, "and washed off the blood down there, it made me feel better. But now we have a new pain down there, and it's not from what Charles did. It's from what Mr. Roger has been doing. Sometimes when Joan's not there, he has sex with the Body. I thought I should tell you."

She receded. Samantha appeared, wrapped in an aura of confidence.

"See how much longer my hair is? I've grown up. I'm twenty now. Can you see my golden breastplate and sword?"

Accepting the magical realism of her self-perception, I said, "I can see your splendor, Samantha. You truly look like a Sentinel—golden breastplate, sword, and scabbard."

"My calling now is to assist the Parts that need help," she said with unexpected formality. I smiled at her endearing emulation of my tone of voice. "And protect them from Shadowman's wrath. Plus, I'll patrol the Forest Edge and warn everyone in Raven's Realm when Parts try to enter that don't belong there."

"Who are those other Parts, Samantha?"

"They belong in Many Voices' Dark and Haunted Forest and not with us."

Changing focus, she said, "I know about what Rose told you. Ever since my cleansing, I have refused to give in to Roger. I've tried to dissuade Rose from giving in, too. So far, I don't think she's been brave enough to say no."

Her eyes filled with longing. "Sarah continues to hide in our Tree. Even though she yearns to walk into the Light, she's too ashamed and too afraid. But I'll keep encouraging my sister."

88

"I'm grateful, Samantha, for the help and protection you'll provide."

I called for Joan, who said she had heard what Rose told me about Roger.

"Haven't you suspected this for some time?" I asked.

"But only with Samantha and Sarah, as I've told you."

"Could you speak to your husband about this? Help him understand he's upsetting the Parts."

"I will as soon as I have the nerve." Joan examined her fingernails. "My husband isn't like Charles."

"But isn't it up to you to put a stop to this kind of behavior?"

Joan looked like she had been scolded.

Had I been too direct?

Joan phoned, sounding frantic. She said unrest on the Inside had increased, and she needed to see me right away. As soon as she opened my office door, she blurted out, "You know my mother's coming tomorrow. I can't handle the turmoil. Maybe you can settle things down."

Joan took her seat and closed her eyes. Samantha immediately appeared.

"It's Sarah causing the trouble," she said.

"Does Sarah need our help?"

"She believes she's too dirty to be helped. I told her she should do what I did—leave the Forest and cleanse herself in the River of Tears. But Sarah's not ready to leave the Forest. She's ashamed of her feelings for Leslie. And she feels bad about letting Roger have his way. I told her I would protect her from Roger by showing him my red-hot anger and using Joan's voice to make him stop."

"As the Sentinel, Samantha, do you really want to use anger and deception?"

Her cheeks flushed. "I guess I should use cold anger and speak in my own voice."

"That's right—but use reason. And allow Joan to speak to Roger."

"I told Sarah I'm not angry anymore about Leslie."

"I'm sure she appreciated your empathy."

"But now I'm afraid Sarah's going to lash out at the Mother as soon as she walks through the door. Tell her how much she hates her for failing to love and protect us. If Sarah starts screaming at her, the young Parts in Many Voices' Realm will wake up."

"They're young?"

"Most are younger than us and are upset with the Mother, too."

A kind of radiance filtered through Samantha's features that told me Raven had appeared. "Teacher, I'm aware of Sarah's dilemma. She yearns to walk toward the Light but feels unworthy. Elizabeth and I have met about this matter. We have decided Beth and Rose will carry two large buckets of soothing water from the River of Tears and set them at the foot of Sarah's Tree. Samantha will accompany the two girls and bring clean garments. Elizabeth and I pray that Sarah can be persuaded to wash herself clean. It is our fervent hope that the healing power of the water may diminish her feelings of shame and cool the rage she holds for the Mother. I am aware that this is only a temporary solution to restore a sense of calm within the Inner Realm and encourage Sarah to shift her negative self-perceptions. I shall fly above the Parts and provide guidance if needed. So that all goes well, Samantha will provide protection."

"Protection from whom?"

"From Shadowman. The changes taking place within the Inner Realm have aroused his wrath. Samantha will attempt to keep him from erupting."

"Would you like me to speak with him?"

"Shadowman despises you. He will not come to see you, nor will he negotiate."

"Perhaps in time, Raven, I can persuade him to think otherwise. In the meantime, I shall await the outcome of your efforts on Sarah's behalf."

Raven bowed and withdrew.

Beth slipped out. "I told Rose instead of carrying those heavy buckets of water into the Forest, we could ask God to install a shower like Joan has. Rose told me it was a silly idea. My feelings got hurt, Oma, but I guess she's right. She's older and smarter than me."

Upon her return, Joan confirmed she had heard everything because she had dared to open the windows in the Safe Place. She was relieved the Parts were helping Sarah contain her rage until her mother left. "I can't imagine my mother's reaction if Sarah came out screaming insults. I'm afraid she'd think it was me."

Joan and I communicated a few times by phone during her mother's visit. A hectic round of activities with no time alone left Joan emotionally on edge, with depression never far away. On the twentieth of May, she called to request a short meeting to reconnect.

"I can't tell you how glad I am to be here," she said, once more seated in my therapy room. "I finally can breathe again. Two weeks was a long time to be around my mother without any arguments erupting. But it didn't take long for her to start doing what she does best, meddling and stirring up stink. I can't tell you how she grated on my nerves. But I told myself, 'Don't think, don't feel, just exist.' Mostly I worried that how I was feeling would affect the Parts on the Inside. I talked to them often to keep them from getting upset—especially Sarah. I prayed she wouldn't come out and cause a scene."

Whenever she had a moment alone, Joan told me, she used her breathing skill to cope. Occasionally, she was able to get away to meditate and paint, which carried her to a faraway place, a calming place. Nevertheless, the whole time Joan felt like she was sitting on a powder keg waiting for the explosion. That had been a disappointment. Joan had hoped she could be around her mother without so much tension. "Thank God we got through it without a confrontation. We survived, and what a relief when my mother finally went home."

She looked around the room and then out the window at the spring foliage in the garden next door. "Aside from Beth, don't be surprised if the Parts don't come out for a while. After not seeing you for two weeks, I believe they may feel you've abandoned them."

"Be patient, Joan. When they realize I haven't, they will reach out so we can continue our work."

"Can Beth come out just for a few moments? I know she missed you the most."

Joan closed her eyes, and, within seconds, Beth appeared. "Hi, Oma. I missed you so much. I was scared I wouldn't see you again. Rose was sad, too. Elizabeth and Raven watched over us so we wouldn't get too upset. And I think Samantha talked with Sarah a lot to help her not get mad. Please," her lisp pronounced, "don't leave us, Oma."

"I promise I won't."

"Good. I'll go back now and tell Rose."

When Joan came back, she said, "I guess it will take us a little while to get back on track and continue our work."

"Let's agree then to see one another in about a week." *I was gratified by how well our preparations had served Joan and the Parts. Perhaps Samantha's newly acquired self-assurance had bolstered Joan's resolve.*

〜

Chapter 14

Lamentations

ay 26. Previously, Joan had told me of her conviction that God spoke directly to her when she was about seven. While driving to my office this morning, Joan decided to trust me with other mystical experiences she'd had as a child. "When I was little—maybe three—I recall sitting in church, wrapped in a merciful embrace of Light, which I remember as the only time in my young life that I felt loved. Later, at about the age of nine, angels came to cradle me in their arms after Charles abused me. They made me feel that someone cared, that I wasn't so alone."

I held back from explaining that traumatized children often experience audio and visual hallucinations. Instead, I said, "What a comfort these experiences must have been."

"But when I got older, all that stopped."

Raven surfaced in a rush. "I apologize for interrupting your conversation, but I believe it is urgent to inform you that Sarah is thinking of harming herself. Would you be so kind as to speak with her?"

Without any encouragement, Sarah appeared. "What's the use for me to keep on going when all I think about is how disgusting I look and how bad I've been? I might as well do away with myself."

"Would you like to talk about what makes you 'disgusting and bad,' and why the only choice you have is to do away with yourself?"

"We've talked about it enough. It's about everything—Leslie, Roger, Charles. And me being stuck in that Tree at the Forest Edge."

"Have you done anything to resolve '*everything*'?"

"I want Joan to go with me to see Leslie, but she refuses."

"Perhaps next time you ask, she'll give in and go. And isn't Samantha helping you with Roger?"

"But I'll always be stuck in that dark place."

"You saw how Samantha left the Darkness. You can do the same. Samantha, Raven, and I will help."

"I'd rather just do away with myself."

"All right, Sarah. Then tell me how you want to do it."

"Turn on the gas stove. Or get in the bathtub and cut my wrists. Or get drunk and wreck the car. I also could hang myself."

I felt my pulse racing. "Have you decided specifically when?"

She told me she hadn't figured out the exact timing yet. I asked her to promise not to do away with herself for one week.

"But only for one week," she said, wagging a finger at me.

"Then you won't mind writing down your promise, right? And just so we understand one another, please list all the harmful things you will *not* do during the next seven days."

Disgruntled, Sarah took the pen and paper I offered and wrote:

I promise to be good, not hang, cut, burn, poison, or hurt myself in any way. Even though I want to, I won't. I also will tell myself that I'm not bad. That is a lie because I'm good. That is why I promise not to kill myself until next week. I will also listen to Samantha and ask her to visit me in the Forest so I'm not so alone.

"That's very good," I said, and we signed the contract together.

A Part appeared I didn't recognize.

"Where is he?" she asked. "Is he gone?"

"Is who gone?"

"Grandmother's boyfriend, the one with black hair. He hurt me in the attic, where I was dancing."

"You don't have to worry about him. He's not here. The man with the black hair is gone and never again will come back to hurt you. What's your name?"

"I'm Charlotte. I used to be four, but now I'm ten. I love ballet, but she took me out of class and stopped my lessons."

"Who is 'she,' Charlotte?"

"My mother."

She looked around the room. "Where am I? And who are you?"

"I'm a therapist helping Joan and other Parts like you."

Charlotte looked confused, uncomprehending. Before I could explain further, she got up from the couch and walked over to my chair. She tentatively touched my hand, then my hair, and finally, my cheek.

"I guess you *are* real."

"Let me help you go someplace where you will be safe and cared for." I called for Beth and asked her to speak with Elizabeth about taking in the new Part. Moments later, she informed me that Elizabeth was willing, but only after Charlotte washed her face and feet. She lowered her voice and whispered, "Oma, I know her. She was with us when I was four but ran away to Many Voices' Dark and Haunted Forest after Charles came." In her whispered lisp, she added, "She must have escaped, Oma. But now she will be with us in Elizabeth's House in the blue room next to mine. I promise I'll be really nice to her."

"Thanks for telling me, Beth," I whispered back.

"That's my job, Oma."

When Joan reappeared, I summarized Sarah's agreement not to harm herself and reported my conversation with the new Part named Charlotte. Joan remembered having ballet lessons when she was four. But for some obscure reason, her mother had stopped her from continuing.

"Do you recall dancing in your grandmother's attic? And her boyfriend molesting you there?"

"No . . ."

Was that the occasion when Charlotte was created to endure Joan's sexual traumatization at age four?

~

Chapter 15

UNREST

For roughly ten days, I received numerous phone calls. Roger's continued emotional indifference hurt Joan. Memories of drowning plagued Rose. Sarah confessed she'd given in to Roger again and felt "filthy." She had been drinking and still contemplated killing herself—but she promised to abide by her contract even though she accused me of being incompetent, disloyal, and uncaring, like the Mother. With uncharacteristic detachment, Raven reported that Sarah's despair, her loss of faith, and suicidal ideation, disturbed the system. Beth whined that she heard crying all around her. Raven confirmed that "wailing" Parts residing in Many Voices' Dark Forest were beginning to make their way to the Forest Edge with intentions to infiltrate his system. He told me Samantha was nowhere to be found and might have lost her resolve to patrol the Forest Edge.

By the evening of June fifth, I had become alarmed by all the turmoil. I phoned Joan, urging her to see me. Reluctant at first, she eventually agreed. The next afternoon, I summarized for her the many phone calls the Parts had made. She remembered calling a few times but hadn't been aware the Parts had phoned. She apologized for having been detached from what had gone on Inside. I asked to speak with Raven and Elizabeth.

Raven appeared. He, too, apologized for being what he called "inattentive" to Sarah and assured me that, in the future, he would be there to "advise and guide." I explained that, during the last few days and nights,

Sarah had needed more than his advice. She needed him to listen to her concerns and empathize with her despair. I urged him to express compassion and convey caring.

His reply was terse. "As an essence, I'm incapable of such human emotions. You're asking me to be more than I am."

He bowed stiffly and withdrew.

I spoke through to Elizabeth and asked her to lift the right forefinger to indicate she could hear me. When she obliged, I told her that Beth and Rose had been distressed and had frequently contacted me by phone to seek comfort. I explained I needed her help and once again asked if she would consider expanding her role from caretaker to the internal mother, who could be both emotionally and physically demonstrative toward her young charges.

Moments later, Raven reappeared to report that Elizabeth had heard my request and wanted a few days to ponder the implications. Once she arrived at a decision, she would write to inform me of her intentions. He smiled politely and was gone.

Several days later, I received the following letters:

June 8, 2004
Dear Healer and Helper, [Abridged]

It is with humble and solemn hearts that we write to you. We have greatly desired to be Essences of purity either in the Light above as Raven or grounded in the House as Elizabeth.

Thank you for opening our eyes to what is best for the system and for allowing us to ponder our motives for wishing to remain removed from feelings. Your suggestions pointing out where changes are needed are well received.

We are accountable for our own wishful thinking and hopeful illusions. We have learned from you that we must dwell in the reality between the world of the spirit and the routines of human existence. We have done what has been necessary to preserve and protect. We are learning that what was needed may now no longer be what is best for the system.

I, Elizabeth, have been known to some of the girls for most of their lives as their caretaker. Alone, without guidance or direction, there was no way to function and allow myself attachments and feelings. It is far easier and efficient to care for wounded children from an emotional distance, to view the pain from afar without being touched by it personally, and not letting heart get in the way of the work needing to be done. I have agreed to do as you suggest, to become less rigid. You are the first I have trusted.

Elizabeth

~

I, Raven, promise to fly closer to the Forest Edge and all those who need my help. [But] what a comfort it is to remain up high, close to the Light. Like Elizabeth, I have chosen to hold myself back from feelings. [But] for me to selfishly [continue to] avoid feelings would only help to keep all within the Inner Realm tucked away Inside forever. I have seen how tormented they have truly been, and how frightened they still are. In the Forests are those that are mute from pain; blind from looking into those yellow eyes; unconscious from fear of suffocation; and [there are] those too fragile, too damaged to emerge into the Light. So, dear Healer, I will do my best to take your guidance and pray may God's will be done.

Raven

June 16. Joan came through the door smiling. She said Beth could not contain herself and had something "pretty wonderful" to tell me.

Beth popped out. "Guess what, Oma?" she bubbled. "Last night, Elizabeth let us have a slumber party. Me and the babies and the younger ones, and

Charlotte and Lisa, and even Samantha and Rose. We had popcorn and green Kool-Aid while we played games and sang songs. We had so much fun, Oma. One time, Elizabeth gave me a pat on the head and even gave me a hug, which she has never, ever done before. She also held one of the babies in her arms and talked to her in a soft voice. While we all sat around the table, Elizabeth explained that she is working hard on learning how to be sweet to us.

"Sarah wants you to know that Raven is keeping his word. He flies down low to be close to her when she's in her Tree. She said he has started listening to her, even though what she has to say is very sad. Sarah told me and Samantha that sometimes she has no feelings at all, just a big empty place on the inside. That's more horrible than feeling sad and being upset. I don't like it, Oma, when someone has no feelings inside."

"You have a warm heart, Beth."

I got up from my chair. "Let me show you something that will give you joy." I offered her my hand, and we walked through my husband's garden next door. Under the wooden deck, my Siamese cat had recently given birth to five kittens. I whispered, "Shhhh. Let's wait here and watch." Shortly, Fernanda and her brood peeked out. "Oh, how cute," Beth murmured, squeezing my hand in delight.

Back in the therapy room, I asked Joan to return from the Safe Place. She empathized with Sarah's emptiness. "I know how that feels," she confided. I told her I was pleased Elizabeth and Raven had become less detached and were offering more demonstrative support and compassion for the Parts.

Joan shifted focus. The spark in her eyes telegraphed its importance. "Roger and I had a long conversation—no, not a fight, a conversation. I made it clear he wasn't showing me the kind of affection I need. Also, I explained that the Parts and I had begun to communicate, and they had told me about him taking advantage of Sarah and Rose when I'm away. At first, he didn't want to take me seriously, but I insisted he needed to change his ways."

"That took some nerve, Joan."

She held up her palm. "There's more. Roger has already started to adjust his behavior toward the Parts. You know he's always treated Beth sweetly, and now, believe it or not, he's talking more kindly to Sarah, even though I have it on good authority that she recently threw a beer bottle at him for yelling at her."

I couldn't restrain my amusement at the image of her husband ducking the beer bottle. "Sounds like your home life has taken a positive turn, Joan."

II

TELLING SECRETS

Summer 2004 to Spring 2005

Chapter 16

THE ROPE

June 30. After she took her seat, Joan's eyes immediately glazed over. Rose exited. She jerked up and whirled around to face the sofa. She fell to her knees as if pushed from behind by an invisible hand. With her face buried in the cushions, she flung her arms wide and held them motionless as if bound at the wrists to the sides of the couch. She let out a muffled yowl as her spine arched back.

I scrambled to my feet and kneeled beside her. "Who is hurting you?"

Rocking back and forth, she moaned, "Charles. His hands are gripping me. He's pushing himself into me." She let out an agonizing scream.

I called through her agony, "Rose, you're having a flashback. Take a deep breath, and let it out slowly. That's right. Take another deep breath. Exhale slowly, and release the pain you're experiencing. Tell yourself it's a memory. It's not happening right now. Continue to breathe in and breathe out. Listen to my voice. Allow it to guide you safely back to this room."

She turned her head to me, the terror slowly leaching from her eyes. Dry-lipped, she whimpered, "Help me. Untie my wrists from the bedpost." Before I could respond, Rose's right hand pulled free from where she seemed to have been tied. She slumped to the floor, her left arm outstretched, her legs folded under her. I started to reach out but stopped midway, reminding myself a touch, any touch, could take her back into the flashback. Compassion had to wait. I continued to verbally assure her that she was with me, that she was safe.

"I know," she uttered, closed her eyes, and was gone.

In an instant, Sarah emerged trembling, ashen. She pushed herself up onto the couch.

"I saw and heard what Rose endured for all of us, but when it happened that night, I wasn't there. As soon as I heard his footsteps, I went away—what a coward. I'm so ashamed. Poor Rose, all alone with that bastard. You keep saying that remembering this stuff will heal us, but who wants to?" she bristled. "What's the use of remembering? I can't change what happened. I'd rather be dead."

"I trust you remember your promise, Sarah."

"I know, I know. If I kill myself, all the others would be dead, too. I'll just go back to my Tree and fume."

"That would be sensible. I have a feeling Samantha is waiting for you."

Raven appeared. He thanked me for helping Rose. He confirmed that Samantha had guided Rose and Sarah to Elizabeth's House, where Beth and Charlotte had prepared a room for them. However, both had refused to sleep in a bed. Sleeping on the floor *under* the bed had seemed less terrifying. All were resting now, exhausted and understandably disturbed by what Rose had revealed.

"Please thank Samantha for her assistance."

"I am encouraged she is maturing into a true helper," he said and withdrew.

Joan's eyes clouded as she admitted to having shut out Rose's retelling. When she heard Rose scream, she had closed and bolted all the windows in the Safe Place, sat in her chair, and envisioned how to make it more comfortable for the Parts should they ever need to go there. She had added a couch and another overstuffed chair. And reinforced the walls with another layer of stone.

"What persuaded you to add more stone?"

"I felt an ominous presence filter through the walls, which is odd because I thought I had built the Safe Place in such a way that nothing could penetrate it."

"In time, Joan, we will know whatever it was."

"That's what I'm afraid of."

July 8. Joan complained the previous week had been difficult. Unrest on the Inside had started immediately after our last session. Every day she woke up with a splitting headache and couldn't think or do anything. "Roger told me the Parts came out willy-nilly. I couldn't stop them."

"Perhaps," I said, "what Rose disclosed may have horrified or even re-traumatized some of the Parts."

"That could be," Joan replied. "I haven't heard from Rose. Nor has Beth asked to come out. The only Part I've heard clearly was Sarah talking with Samantha, telling her how sad and guilty she felt for not having rescued Rose. Said she felt bad enough to kill herself. I couldn't understand Samantha's reply but sensed they were comforting words. This afternoon, before leaving the house, Samantha told me Sarah had written two poems last night and urged me to share them with you."

Joan reached into her purse, withdrew Sarah's poems, and volunteered to read them aloud.

I'M SORRY TO EVERYONE
So sorry to be broken, Rose,
With thorns that pierce your soul.
It's not your fault how crushed you are.
It's not you that made it so.
Cruel words and crueler flames
Of wicked pain plunged deep inside.
No one was there to help or care,
Nor even asked to hear the silent cries.
You have withered, it's true, low and alone
In a Cave of darkness where nothing can thrive.
We will wait for you. Wait for us, too,
While we all learn to be alive.
Sorry to the broken Rose.
We know just how much he stole.
Hopes, dreams, and innocence
All shattered now.
We struggle to be made whole.
—Sarah

Joan's voice broke. She blinked back her tears, swallowed hard, and then continued with the second poem.

I CAN'T
I can't stay here anymore.
Though the Forest is filled with
Pieces and parts of shattered souls,
I can't stay pushed back in a place
That's become my own personal hell.

Without Samantha by my side
The shadows loom large, and strong.
I say I want to die, not be here anymore,
Not mostly, I mean, but sometimes.
I'm scared to feel put away and so alone.
When you are not loved, nowhere is your home.
—Sarah

"Can you help her, Renate?" she asked with hope in her eyes. "I'll go to the Safe Place."

Raven emerged. "Elizabeth and I agree that Sarah should leave her Tree before the feelings that have wrapped her in such anguish plunge all of us into a place from which we cannot return."

"As always, Raven, I respect your wisdom. How do you wish to proceed?"

"I shall fly ahead, leading Sarah to the Waterfall at the head of the River of Tears. Rose will join the procession. Once there, Sarah will discard her defiled garment into what I have come to call Rose's Vessels of Sorrow. She will stand beneath the Waterfall to cleanse herself. After that, she will be offered a white gown with yellow flowers at its hem, and I will place a wreath of wildflowers upon her head. Then we will escort her to Rose's Cave, where she may stay, at least for now."

"Where will Samantha be?"

Raven paused before answering. "Samantha will be in attendance. However, she will position herself so she can observe Shadowman. He is poised to disrupt our efforts. Now," Raven smiled graciously, "I have to attend to my duties."

I felt a sense of accomplishment. Elizabeth, Raven, Rose, and Samantha had taken the initiative to rescue Sarah. They had formulated a solution to a dire concern and were implementing their plan to assure the well-being of the system. I thought their self-determination signaled significant progress.

After a long while, Sarah emerged to tell me she had cleansed herself of Charles' filth. She had washed away her guilt and shame, her sadness and regret for not being there to help Rose endure the pain. Then she let out a woeful sigh. "I couldn't wash off one feeling, though. It has nothing to do with Rose. But before I tell you, I need to know you won't throw me away."

"No matter what you tell me, Sarah, I will accept you as you are."

"I'm . . . I'm ashamed about something I did," she stammered. "I don't think any of the others know, but I learned how to move my hips in a certain way that made Charles leave us alone much faster. That kind of badness can never be washed off. That shame will never go away." She hid her face in her hands. "Now you know."

"What you did wasn't shameful, Sarah. It was smart and justified. Cutting short the torment benefited Joan and the others. At least that's how I view it."

"I want to believe what you're saying, but right now I can't."

"In time, I hope you will. Today, know you have been very brave."

Joan reappeared. After raising the windows and opening the shutters in the Safe Place, she had heard and seen it all. An imposing figure watched the cleansing ritual from behind a tree near the edge of the Forest, emanating the same ominous feeling she had felt days before. "I was relieved when Samantha took charge to guide Sarah and Rose away from that intimidating presence. What Sarah confessed a moment ago about . . . you know. I never suspected one of my Parts could do such a thing. I'll probably struggle with that for some time."

At seven the next morning, Joan called, her voice sounding tinny. I was alarmed. Phoning that early was unusual for her. She told me she'd gone to bed about three in the morning like she usually does but couldn't sleep.

She felt Sarah's anger pounding in her head and heard Rose whimpering. Samantha's voice had told her Rose needed help and urged Joan to call me. We made an appointment for later that afternoon.

Joan arrived promptly and volunteered to go to the Safe Place so I could speak with Rose and Sarah. She promised to listen in.

Within seconds, Rose appeared. "Blood is running down my thighs. I can't stop it with a tissue." She slid to the floor, kneeled, and faced the couch like before. She stretched out her left arm and, with her right hand, pulled and tugged at her wrist as if a rope was encircling it. "I'm still tied to the bedpost. Will you untie me?"

"I'm sorry I didn't do it yesterday," I replied.

Before I could help, though, her frantic efforts freed her. She spoke as if to Charles, "You told me I was bad. That I deserved to be punished. I'm older now—fifteen. You can never tie me up again and hurt me."

Seemingly exhausted, she leaned her head against the seat cushion and then crawled onto the couch, sat upright, and massaged her wrist. She bent over and, as if picking up an object from the floor, said, "I want to get rid of this rope."

Rose's facial features distorted as Sarah pushed out. "I'll help get rid of that damn rope. Maybe burn it or bury it someplace." She listened inward and then, in a desultory voice, said, "Samantha wants to speak with you. I guess she wants to be in charge."

Samantha emerged through Sarah's frown. "I want to help get rid of the rope, too. I was there when Charles tortured Rose. I didn't feel the pain he inflicted, only her rage. Sarah needs to be there, too. She can barely contain her indignation. Raven suggested we take the rope to a far-away corner in the Forest and bury it. Be rid of it forever. Even then, he made it clear that the three of us still have to suffer through the memory and come to terms with what happened." She hesitated a moment and then asked, "Helper, would you invite the Golden Light to illuminate the path we must follow to find a suitable place for burying the rope?"

I leaned back in my chair, invited the Golden Light to guide the trio into the Forest, and waited. Outside my office window, the shadows beneath the trees grew long before Samantha finally re-emerged.

"It's done," she said tonelessly. "We did as planned. Raven flew above us, and the Golden Light lit our path. Some distance into the Forest, it illuminated a small clearing. The three of us gathered around as Rose handed me the rope. I pulled my sword from its scabbard and hacked the rope into small pieces. We threw them into a hole Sarah dug with her bare hands. We filled the hole with dirt and patted it down into a small, hard mound. Sarah's anger exploded as she stomped on the mound, calling Charles names I prefer not to repeat. Sarah tried to entice Rose to join her, but she refused, saying she was incapable of feeling that kind of rage."

"And you, Samantha? What did you experience?"

"Like Sarah, I wanted to scream and hurl ugly words at him. But I didn't allow my feelings to overwhelm me. I'm learning a different way to come to terms with my anger. But I had help. Raven told me expressing my feelings in an undignified way would be unfitting for a Sentinel. When Sarah realized I wouldn't participate, she stepped off the mound, embarrassed. She asked if I'd help her become like me. I told her I could be her example but that changing was up to her. She said from now on she wanted to be called 'Sarah Christine.' The name would remind her of Jesus, who never sought vengeance or lashed out at his enemies." *I thought not to set right this innocent perception.* "Raven must have been listening," Samantha continued, "because he flew down and made the sign of the cross on Sarah Christine's forehead. I left them standing in front of Rose's Cave and came to see you."

"Samantha, how much you have matured. You are truly becoming a helper. May I ask you for a favor? Would you go to the Safe Place and tell Joan about the ordeal Rose endured? Tell her that you, too, were present. Tell her your feelings about it. And if you will, please inform her of the changes Sarah—I mean, Sarah Christine—wants to make."

"I'll do as you wish." She bowed with dignity. I smiled at her Raven-like formality.

After some moments, Joan returned. "How can anyone torture a young girl like that?" she said, bitterness framing her words. "I never wanted to say this about anyone, but I'm convinced Charles was *evil*. He must not have had a conscience."

109

"I believe he was empty of *all* feelings, Joan. A vacuum at his core. What we know of pedophiles is they want to feel something—*anything*—and the only way Charles could was to torture and rape you. Then, after his orgasm, he plunged back into that hellish void and set the cycle of victimization in motion again."

"And I was his victim," Joan said. "Poor me. Poor Rose. Poor all of us." Sorrow haunted her eyes. "Coming face-to-face with such ugliness is hard, but I know there will be much more that the Parts and I have to confront to get well."

Healing her mind would require just that, I thought. *But she and the Parts should be hopeful. Our work went well today. Rose had closure. Sarah Christine was making changes. Samantha was maturing and proving to be of great help—an example for the others. And Joan had chosen to listen to Samantha, chosen to stay present, chosen to hear the truth.* That was real progress, and I told her so.

"Earlier," Joan said, "I forgot to tell you that while Samantha, Sarah Christine, and Rose were in the Forest burying the rope, I felt that ominous presence again."

"Someday, we'll meet that 'presence.' Let's be grateful it didn't interfere today."

⌒

Chapter 17

SEE BUT NOT KNOW ME

July 29. Midmorning, I received a long-distance emergency phone call requiring me to travel. I informed Joan and her family that I would be absent for about one week. I suggested they could call me if a crisis arose and reminded Joan she could reach out to my colleague if need be.

Around noon, Raven telephoned. He apologized for the intrusion.

"I'm pressed for time, Raven."

"I understand," he replied, "but the Tree Girls . . ."

In resignation, I sighed, "Tell Joan I can meet her briefly this afternoon."

As she walked through the door, Joan said, "Something's going on Inside."

Raven exited immediately. "I have wonderful news. Samantha and Sarah Christine have persuaded their sister to climb down from her Tree. Sebunome is standing at the edge of the Forest waiting for you to invite her to come out to see you. If she does, please be your most gentle self. Now, I must take my leave and fly to the Forest Edge to lend my support before her courage falters."

Moments later, a figure cowered before me like a wingless bird poised to scurry back to the protection of her Tree should I make an unexpected sound or gesture. She sat motionless in fearful silence, her eyes downcast. The only thing I knew to do was to mirror her silence. I began to breathe softly in and out, hoping she would become attuned to my rhythm and let go of her frozen affect. Still avoiding my eyes, she made writing motions with her hand. Keeping my movements to a minimum, I offered her paper and pen. Bent over, nose to the paper, she wrote with intensity. When finished, she held out the sheet of paper for me to read. But what I saw I couldn't decipher. Upon closer scrutiny, I realized she had written the words backward. I reached for my purse and took out a small hand mirror.

"I have to use the mirror to read what you've written. I'll read out loud so both of us can hear what you want me to know."

I'm Sebunome. I'm scared to death to be seen. Scared to get hurt. Women hurt with their eyes and so do men. That is why I try to be invisible, so no one can see me or know me. One woman hurt me the most and so did Charles. He always saw me. He always could find me under the bed, in the closet, [and] then he hurt me. That is why I am invisible, but sometimes I'm not.

"Perhaps next time," and I remembered to pronounce her name phonetically ('See-buh-no-mee'), "you will allow me to see you," I said in a soothing voice, mirroring her self-perception of invisibility.

"Maybe," she said softly. "But it will hurt your eyes when you see how dirty I am." *Having heard this word used by other Parts, I had come to believe "dirty" symbolized having been defiled, a consequence of the abuses they suffered.*

"I can see that your dress is dirty, but because you tell me you're invisible, I can't see if *you* are dirty."

"Believe me, I'm dirty. Don't touch me. My dirtiness will burn you. It's hot. Red-hot." *I thought "red-hot" might represent hidden anger and rage, a result of the feeling of helplessness in the face of wanton abuse.*

"And what makes your dirtiness 'red-hot'?"

Silence.

"Perhaps next time, you'll tell me."

"Maybe, but promise not to hurt me."

"I promise, Sebunome."

She gave me a furtive glance and, without another word, withdrew to her Tree, or so I assumed.

"I'm amazed," Joan said upon her return, "that Sebunome trusted you enough to come out. I guess she wants you to know her."

~

Chapter 18

HEARTBREAK

August 12. "Since we last met," Joan began, "I've felt a lot of discomfort. But I've been able to paint some. That always helps."

Before I could comment, Joan's features sharpened, and Sarah Christine pushed through.

"I still yearn for Leslie." She looked hollow-eyed with longing. "We hug sometimes, and that makes me feel loved. Before I went away, I dreamed of having a small house with a yard and children. And a place to paint and write. But since I'm awake, those dreams have come to nothing. My only chance for a life is with Leslie."

"I believe you're confused, Sarah Christine. After all, you are a Part that split off from Joan. She already has a home with a yard and children. *And* she's married to a man."

"I didn't wake up and leave the Forest to be a fat, old gray-haired woman married to some man," she scoffed. "Roger is not like Charles, but he's still a man, and I despise men."

"It is a delicate and improbable situation you find yourself in. Why not ask Raven for his guidance?"

With a sullen look, she left.

Summing up my brief exchange with Sarah Christine for Joan, I suggested we talk with Leslie to clear up the confusion.

"When would we do that? Next session? Leslie is a sweet, gentle, and loving soul. She has always been there for me when no one else was. Aside from you, Renate, I've never known anyone else who accepted my past without judgment and just loved me. I don't want her to be hurt. I don't want to be hurt, either. But I don't see anything but hurt coming from any of this."

Two lonely tears made their way down her face.

Raven spoke: "Helper, I have listened, and so have Elizabeth, Samantha, and Sebunome. All of us are concerned for Sarah Christine. She holds a powerful human emotion that seeks to be fulfilled. If she were to lose hope, she might descend into a deep depression, which will spread darkness throughout the system. But allowing Sarah Christine to pursue what she desires will create dire consequences. And may I remind you of Shadowman? He holds the strongest opposition. We cannot disregard his malevolent powers and the harm he will inflict if Sarah Christine cannot be dissuaded. Therefore, it is vital for Joan on the Outer Edge to stay strong. She is the body and mind that houses us all."

Love and reason, I told him, would best equip everyone for what may lie ahead. And caution and patience, Raven added, before volunteering with Elizabeth to formulate a plan of action addressing Sarah Christine's unrealistic longings. He stressed that Sebunome also needed my help since she was the one who most feared Sarah Christine's yearnings that had reawakened her painful memories of betrayal. A somber Raven withdrew.

Sebunome emerged, shoulders hunched, eyes averted.

"I'm against Sarah Christine's feelings for Leslie coming Inside," she lamented. "When I was eleven, I was hurt by a woman who I thought loved me. But she deceived me."

Softening my voice, I advised her to talk to Sarah Christine and tell her how she felt and why. Sebunome feared her sister might get angry, so I suggested she tell her in a note.

Sebunome gave me a shy glance. "Would it be okay if I come to see you again?"

Over the next four nights, my phone rang nonstop, awakening me at all hours. Beth complained about being confined in Elizabeth's House until

Sarah Christine's issues were resolved, and Rose let me know she was hiding in her Cave, scared. But Sarah Christine made the most calls. She sounded intoxicated and again accused me of being just like her mother—disallowing whatever made her happy. She insisted I had betrayed her by taking sides with Raven, Elizabeth, and Samantha. Joan made the last call, and like Sarah Christine, slurred her words, "I have to see you."

When Joan walked through my office door, her face was puffy. She was wearing no makeup, and her hair was uncombed. "I'm worried. Leslie told Sarah Christine she wanted to end our friendship because it created too many misunderstandings."

"When did that happen, Joan?"

"Yesterday afternoon. Then Sarah Christine went to the liquor store, bought a bottle, and got drunk."

"Would you like Sarah Christine to tell you what happened?"

Joan closed her eyes, and Sarah Christine came out. I encouraged her to meet with Joan at the Safe Place and share what had happened between her and Leslie yesterday afternoon.

"I won't go without Samantha. She's still on my side—sort of. But before I go, I want you to know that, when I met with Leslie, she acted strange. I sensed she was going to tell me something I didn't want to hear. Something that would really hurt. That's why I went to the liquor store, and I've been drinking ever since."

Joan came back, trembling. "As soon as I got to the Safe Place, Shadowman started a rampage. I shuttered the windows and bolted the doors. He yelled, 'No more talk about outsiders. All they do is hurt and lie.' Then he began reciting the old litany we used to chant when we got scared. 'Don't talk. Don't tell. Quiet is good. Quiet is safe. Don't feel. Be invisible.'"

"So, because Shadowman frightened you, you didn't have a chance to talk with Sarah Christine and Samantha about Leslie?"

"All I saw were two shadowy figures approaching before I closed the shutters."

"Could you have urged them to hurry up and find safety with you instead of leaving them at the mercy of Shadowman?"

Her temper flared. "I don't know what I could have done or should have done."

Was there another reason why Joan bolted the door as fast as she did? Did she not want to hear about the ending of Sarah Christine's friendship with Leslie? Did she experience that ending as a loss or as a relief? Or was she not yet ready to acknowledge Sarah Christine shared her yearning to be loved—that fervent yearning for affection Joan must have felt as an abused fourteen-year-old girl?

"I wonder, Joan, if you could talk to Shadowman, perhaps explain that his behavior is stifling your efforts to heal."

"Not me. After what I just heard, I couldn't do it. Why don't *you* talk to him?"

"I'm prepared to help, but I still think you, or someone from Inside, should talk to him. Maybe Samantha can."

"I know Samantha is brave, but asking her to approach Shadowman?"

Joan's resistance to reaching out to Shadowman and persuading him to become a positive force instead of a hindrance in the treatment process made me think my overtures were premature. So, for the next few sessions, I proposed avoiding any subject that might arouse Shadowman's wrath.

At this juncture, I thought to end our discussion, but Beth ducked out.

"Hi, Oma," she said, a smile in her voice. "I know it's time to go home, but Elizabeth wants me to tell you some things. Sarah Christine is with Raven. He wants to make sure she doesn't drink and upset everyone about Leslie again. And guess what? The babies are getting bigger! One is walking around the House, and the other one stands up in her crib and bounces.

"And Maria, Lisa, and Charlotte have moved in together. They're staying in the yellow room next to mine and I hear them talking a lot. I think they want to be together forever." *Perhaps they're talking about merging,* I thought. "There's one more thing," she said, her expression growing more serious. "I'm eight now. Getting older helps me remember things—you know, stuff that happened," her lisp more pronounced.

Beth's features froze. Her eyes glazed over, trance-like. She began to recite, "Down three steps, turn. Down seven steps. One more step, turn right. Up on the dryer. Pinching. Ow! Panties off. Two fingers, no, three, push into my peenee. Hurts. Burns. His voice, 'You like this, don't you?' Shake head. No kiss, no kiss!" She shuddered. "Door opens. Scared! His voice, 'Quick, hide.' Under basement steps. Lots of spider webs. Big hand over mouth. Can't breathe. His voice, 'Don't make a sound.'"

Beth's eyes lost their faraway look. "Oma," her voice fell to a whisper, "there's more to tell, much more than I want to. Sarah Christine and Samantha and Rose, and even Fury 1, came to help so I could get away. That was when God told me things would get worse, but He said He would make me strong. And He did."

She paused. "Being eight makes me sad, Oma. I just want to be happy. Do you think I can go back to being seven again?"

"I don't see why not, Beth," echoing the Part's magical thinking.

The brightness in her eyes returned. "Thank you, Oma."

As she departed, I imagined her red ponytail bobbing jauntily toward Elizabeth's House.

I chose to avoid upsetting Joan further with a description of Beth's flashback and ended the session.

～

Chapter 19

ALCOHOL IS A FICKLE SEDUCER

September 17. Since last December, I had become aware that Joan, or a Part, was abusing alcohol. In our last session, I selected several articles from my library on alcohol addiction and advised she read them. Today when I inquired, Joan admitted she hadn't read even one.

"Do you know the reasons why you drink?" I probed. "Are you aware of the toll alcohol takes on your health and your family, not to mention the disruption to our work?" My remark was uncharacteristically direct.

Her lips crimped. "I don't consider myself an alcoholic."

"When you married and moved away at twenty, you did your best to have a normal life, at least, what you thought was normal. You shut off the past and put on a mask. When the Parts woke up, you heard voices in your head, whispering and crying. And when you couldn't quiet those voices, or the flashes of memory of physical and psychological abuse, what did you do?"

Silence.

"And there's your mother. She insists all this is a fabrication. But since you and I have been working together, you have become more aware of her denial and neglect. Who could blame you for wanting to numb out for a day or two? But what happens when the effects have worn off and nothing has changed? What then?" She shifted in her seat. "Alcohol is a fickle seducer, Joan. It's not your friend. Please, reconsider reading those articles."

"*I'm* not the alcoholic. It's Sarah Christine who drinks."

"However, Joan," gentling my voice, "be aware there are times when the *need* originates with you."

Through her defiance, Raven emerged.

"Please be patient, Teacher. When Joan is ready, she will arrive at the necessary insight. With your permission, I'd like to convey some good news. Celestial music is being heard more and more throughout the Inner Realm. Also, I have something extraordinary to report. Samantha wants to be an essence, like me," he said, one eyebrow arched.

I assured him I would honor his advice about Joan's drinking and also thanked him for his "good news."

"My energy is depleting," he said in apology. "Being out of the Inner Realm is still a new experience. In the past, I rarely came out to converse with anyone. I find it exhausting. Before I withdraw, may I impress upon you Sebunome's need for your attention."

Sebunome came forward. She looked down at the well-worn Turkish rug beneath her shoes, unable to bring herself to look directly at me.

"I'm afraid if people touch me, I will burn them."

Cautiously sitting beside her, I proposed she touch my index finger. She timidly extended her hand and touched me.

"Look, Sebunome. Does my finger look burned?"

She shook her head, her hair swirling about her face. She raised her eyes to mine but quickly looked away. "Eyes scare me."

Taking a chance, I encouraged her to recall what had destroyed her trust—particularly in women.

A tremor shook her body.

Seeing her distress, I realized my encouragement had been hasty. More trust would need to be established. I asked her to breathe deeply until she calmed. She again lifted her eyes to mine. "Will you be my friend?"

"I will be your friend, and I promise not to deceive you." I paused to let my meaning register and hoped my promise comforted her. A fleeting smile parted her lips before she shrank back into herself and vanished.

Beth jumped out, sparkles dancing in her eyes. "I'm so excited, Oma. We're making something special for your birthday. It will be a surprise."

Joan re-emerged. "I heard Sebunome ask you to be her friend. As distrusting as she is, that's real progress, isn't it? So much is happening, Renate. I'm impressed with what we've accomplished in this first year of treatment. I feel so hopeful."

I, too, felt hopeful, with one reservation—her excessive drinking.

The next day, I found this letter from Sebunome in my mailbox:

September 18, 2004 [Abridged]
Dear Ms. Renata [sic],

I have wanted to write to you. I am still a bit afraid, but I think I'm trusting you a little bit now. I don't think your [sic] going to hurt me on purpose. I just am afraid of both men and women—everybody. I don't take chances much and I don't think I'm to [sic] brave.

I am glad I didn't hurt you when we touched fingers. I haven't been touched in a very, very long time. You touch the others a lot, Raven said, and it really helps them. I don't know anything about love, especially. Just that love hurts to [sic] much. Touching hurts your body or your heart or both.

But thank you for being so nice to me and acting like you like me and are happy to see me.

I'm cleaner now but not all the way. I do whisper thank you to the girls that bring the warm water and towels, but I don't talk much to anyone really. I am good at listening. I know all about quiet.

I am afraid sometimes. A lot sometimes. Thank you.

  Sebunome

Chapter 20

A BLUE AURA

In session, Joan presented a disturbing dream, one that portrayed me as cruel and disloyal. When I asked what she thought the dream meant, Joan replied it was telling her to stop treatment and return to being her "old distrustful self." She complained of her inability to set aside her mistrust. "I wish I had Samantha's courage."

"But she is a part of you, Joan."

"Sometimes I forget."

"Let me ask Samantha if she would be willing to help you overcome your misgivings."

I guided Joan to the Safe Place and then called for Samantha. Instead, Sarah Christine appeared. I inquired if she knew of Samantha's whereabouts. She shook her head.

Puzzled by this response, I sought Raven's counsel.

"I don't know where she is either, Helper. Will your presence join me Inside to search for her?"

"If you think it helpful." I leaned back in my chair, entered a meditative state, and, in much the same way as I recorded Samantha's cleansing ritual, I visualized my presence actively participating in the magical realism of the Inner Realm.

Directing our search beyond the Forest Edge, Raven spoke in hushed tones. "We are now in Many Voices' Realm. I have never ventured this far into the Dark Forest. Do you see the many young Parts peeking out from behind those barren trees?"

Suddenly, he hovered and whispered, "Behold, I hear a muffled voice. Could it be Samantha's? Do you see a blue aura emanating from that mound of earth? Isn't that Shadowman looming there?" He reflected a moment. "Aha! Now I understand. Samantha has made it her mission to transform Shadowman's malevolence. He knows Samantha has become a helper, so to maintain his dominance, Shadowman has buried her there beneath his massive foot."

Raven addressed the mound and asked Samantha to tunnel out to safety.

"I'm staying here to cleanse Shadowman of his malice with the fire of my blue essence," came her faint reply.

The Blue Aura, Samantha 2004

"Attempting to cleanse Shadowman of his darkness is commendable," I said. "However, Samantha, it's Shadowman's responsibility to change himself."

Raven urged Shadowman to surrender Samantha into our care.

"I will consider it if treatment is discontinued," he demanded.

"Joan and the Parts have asked me to help them, and I have promised to do so," I interjected, determined to engage him.

He turned his menacing gaze to me. "I might surrender Samantha," he said, taking another tack, "if I'm allowed to cut the Body and bleed out the changes Joan has made."

"Change occurs in the mind and heart, not in the blood."

"Then I have another proposition to make. I might let Samantha go in exchange for Beth. She poses the greater threat with her mingling on the Outside."

Raven and I refused in one voice.

Shadowman began to growl. "Do you see the redness in my eyes? You underestimate my powers. I can destroy all of you."

I acknowledged being fully aware of his abilities. But instead of keeping Joan and the Parts hostage to the past, I invited him to utilize his formidable "powers" to aid us in our efforts to create changes that would eventually heal all—including him. Shadowman laughed derisively.

After my visualized presence withdrew, Raven mused, "Samantha may perceive herself as another St. George."

"Unlike St. George," I responded, half-amused, "our goal is not to slay Shadowman but to pacify his animosity by convincing him he has value and that he belongs. Instead of rejecting him, we should befriend him."

A Part I had not yet encountered appeared. She leaned in close. A loving radiance enveloped us. She looked deeply into my eyes, clasped my hand, and bestowed the sign of three crosses on my palm. *Who was this gentle presence?*

Joan reappeared from the Safe Place. Samantha, I explained, had chosen to defuse Shadowman's distrust and domination with her blue essence, which was symbolic of her newfound mission as a helper. I told Joan I hoped others would emulate Samantha's use of reason and emotional restraint to promote reconciliation and change. Healing the past, I told her, could not be achieved without a shift in the power structure within the system. Joan listened intently, a furrow between her brows, but made no comment.

I thought the internal struggle between Shadowman and Samantha was reflective of Joan's inner conflict between opening up to new ways of dealing with the past or remaining bound by the security of old defenses. In time, I wanted Joan to understand Shadowman's domination and intimidation had been formulated as a method of protection against parental abuse. I thought it imperative for her to recognize that Shadowman, the persecutor, must not be shunned, but rather recruited to serve as Shadowman, the helper, who could then cooperate in the therapeutic process.

~

Chapter 21

NIGHT FALLS

During the evening of the following day, Joan telephoned, a tremor in her voice. "I hear fearful moaning and crying on the Inside."

Sarah Christine immediately came on the line. "I fear night falling. I'm worried about Samantha's welfare and what Shadowman might do to her. It's my fault—I'm the one who brought the feelings of an outsider Inside. I hear Shadowman raging. It's about me and Leslie. I won't survive the night."

I advised her to go to the Safe Place. She reluctantly agreed.

Raven came on the phone. "I will watch over Sarah Christine and the others. I suspect Shadowman will follow through on his dark intentions. He may be the devil himself, with his red eyes and hideous appearance."

"His fierceness may be frightening," I agreed, "but I don't believe he's evil. Instead, may I propose that, early on, he observed that threats and punishments meted out by the adults worked well to keep Joan quiet and docile. He may have internalized their abusive behavior as a way of protecting Joan from harm."

"I will consider your supposition another time," Raven interjected, "but at this moment, we need to formulate a plan, so no one gets hurt." He proposed Rose seek shelter in Elizabeth's House with the younger Parts; advised Sebunome to move away from the Forest Edge and hide behind Rose's Cave until the danger passed; instructed others to erect crosses all along the border that separated Many Voices' Dark Forest from his Realm;

and asked the Blessing Lady to consecrate each cross. "These create a sacred barrier that Shadowman will dare not violate."

"Are such precautions necessary?"

"Teacher," impatience in his voice, "these are our *only* defenses."

"You mentioned a Blessing Lady—who is she?"

"She embodies gratitude and comfort." Raven paused, and then, in warning, said, "Sarah Christine is lingering around the entrance to the Safe Place but has not entered. Please urge her to do so."

I did as he requested and told Sarah Christine to lock all the doors, shutter the windows, and remain there. I heard her express delight upon entering the refuge. Through its glass ceiling, she could see the stars. And was surprised to find a small fountain in the middle. She thought the bed with a green blanket and pillow was just right and was confident she'd be safe there.

The next evening, Sarah Christine telephoned. "Night has fallen again. Shadowman hasn't stopped raging. He wants me to harm the Body. It takes all my strength to say no to him." I encouraged her to stay strong, find her resolve, breathe in the Golden Light, and exhale her fears. And then I again guided her to the Safe Place.

Another phone call woke me near midnight. Raven apologized for the late hour and asked for my assistance. Sarah Christine had left the Safe Place and was wandering around, terrorized by Shadowman's demands. Raven said he couldn't watch over her any longer. He had to protect Sebunome now.

Sarah Christine came on the line, her teeth chattering. "I'm lost and can't find my way back to the Safe Place. His constant screaming has me completely turned around. I can't think."

"Listen carefully, Sarah Christine," my imagination racing. "Look down at the ground. You will discover at your feet two white pebbles. You have the choice to continue to be lost and victimized by Shadowman *or* to silence his ranting by putting a pebble in each ear. Then you can think more clearly and find your way back to the Safe Place."

There was a moment's pause.

"It worked! I can find my way now."

September 27. "I've had it," Joan exclaimed while hanging up her jacket.

"What's going on?" I asked.

At home, Joan complained, she felt unappreciated. Seemed like all she ever did was stand at the stove. And for the last week, she'd had to put up with Roger's "rotten moods." As soon as he came home from work, he would turn on the TV so loud she needed earplugs. Every time she asked him to turn down the volume, he would throw a fit. "And he's always after me for you-know-what. I could just scream. And my daughter, Megan? Drives me up the wall." She flicked her long hair off her neck. "You should see her room. It's full of stuff—clothes, shoes, makeup, CDs—scattered around. And when she can't find something in all that clutter, she accuses me of misplacing it. From now on, she can pick up her own mess. But I've complained enough," she said with a weary wave of her hand.

Looking out the window at the firestorm of color in the maple trees, Joan said, "It's the worst time of year for me. Come October, that's when the voices in my head are loudest. I hear crying and shouting. Flashing images intrude into whatever I'm doing. Memories surface, and it's difficult to push them away. I try not to lose time. I'm afraid of what would happen. It's a struggle to get through the day. The nights are even harder. I hope this fall I'll not be swallowed up, at least not without resisting."

An expression of serenity transformed Joan's features. Raven appeared. "We are all aware of the ominous feelings that fall brings," he said. "Let me assure you, Joan and the ones on the Inside will survive, but not without drinking from the bitter cup of this season. This, too, shall pass, Teacher," and faded.

Joan immediately bent over, pressing her fingers against her temples. She slid off the couch onto the floor and lay there, wiping at her mouth and coughing as if trying to spit out something.

I knelt beside her. "Where are you?"

Her eyes were dilated in terror. "I'm in a grave covered with dried leaves," came the strangled reply. I realized Sebunome was the one speaking.

"You're having a flashback, Sebunome." I saw a flicker of recognition. "Feel through what you are experiencing, but know you are safe here with me in the therapy room."

"Samantha and Sarah Christine are with me," she spluttered.

I held out my hand. "I will help you climb out of the grave." She grasped my hand, and I pulled her upright. "You see, you're here with me. You're safe. Now you can return to your place at the Forest Edge."

Joan came out of the episode looking perplexed. I encouraged her to walk around the room to reorient to place and time before she left for home.

More ominous hints were to surface about that long-ago autumn. But I would have to wait three more years for Sebunome to disclose the monstrous story of Charles' worst deeds.

~

Chapter 22

THE BARN

My sixty-sixth birthday on October second marked the completion of my first year of working with Joan. On that special day, I found a gift-wrapped, oblong package leaning against the front door of my home, addressed to "The Healer." I suspected it was my birthday present from Joan and the Parts. I lugged the heavy package with its yellow ribbon into the house and tore away the wrappings. Inside was a ceramic tray containing a hundred or more small, highly polished stones of varying sizes and colors. Each rock was imprinted with a single word—some written in black ink, some in white, and some in blood-red. The words expressed different sentiments: love, secrets, healer, tell, tears, etc. Some had only symbols: a cross, a teardrop, a heart, a drop of blood, etc. For many reasons, this remarkable gift remains my most treasured birthday present.

A letter accompanied this enchanting gift:

October 1, 2004 [Abridged]
Dear Healer,

    This has been a whole-system project, and hopefully one that will convey to you all you are to us. A list of words was made, by all Parts known to you, months ago. These words were written on stones . . .

to show you our devotion, our gratitude—and yes, our love.

It has been a full year now since we were blessed with you in our lives, the promise made so long ago. You have been a wonderful and sweet presence in our lives, a gift long awaited. An Oma to Beth [and] others who need a loving presence. A teacher, healer, mentor, and guide for those of us, the elders of the system, who seek your wisdom . . .

Truly, words cannot convey the impact you've had upon us. For many years we've waited, and now . . . we are seen. The faith and hope you give [and] carry for us is astounding. That you believe we will overcome is precious . . . invaluable.

So . . . happy birthday from all of us. You are a gift and a voice to penetrate the Darkness. You soar with us to the Light—an Earth Mother to those lost, who with gentle patience await.

Happy Birthday
with love from All

Elizabeth and Raven

Early one morning in the middle of October, Rose telephoned. "I need to tell you something terrible," she stammered. "When I was about nine, Charles took us all out to a barn somewhere. I'm not sure, but I think it belonged to his dad. He made me pull on a boy-sheep's penis. I didn't want to do it, but Charles and his dad made me. It's a secret," she said, her voice conspiratorial, "but I wanted you to know."

Sarah Christine called at two a.m. My husband grumbled in his sleep as I tiptoed out of the bedroom.

"I want to cut myself," Sarah Christine screamed into the phone. "I feel like I'm trapped back there in the barn."

I reminded her that she wasn't in the barn and elicited her promise to remain safely near Elizabeth's House for the rest of the night.

The next morning, Roger called to report Joan had dissociated. The Parts were causing chaos. He was hesitant to take her to the hospital. I reluctantly agreed he could bring her to my office. She arrived dazed and disheveled. I guided her to the couch and placed a heart-shaped, maroon pillow in her lap, the one she often held for comfort when we talked. I asked her husband to wait in my outer office.

To avoid frightening her, I lowered my voice. "Joan, you're here with me," I said softly. The sound of my voice brought her back. She looked around the room, bewildered. "Roger thought you needed my help."

"I couldn't cope with what Rose told you." She pressed the pillow tight against her abdomen. "It made me nauseous. I have only a vague memory about a sheep, but I do recall Charles took Lillian and me in his car and drove us somewhere out in the country. I had never met his father or brother before. Unlike Charles, they both were tall but had his sickly white skin. The idea of grown men forcing a young girl to do such a thing . . . it's . . . it's wicked."

"Yes, Joan, it was wicked. I'm sure Rose's disclosure also upset some of the other Parts. Do you mind if I speak with them?"

She leaned into the cushions with a sigh and closed her eyes. I turned my attention to the Parts and spoke through to the system. "Sarah Christine called last night to tell me she had been with Rose in the barn. I wonder who else among you were there and are upset. Talking to me might help you cope with those feelings. So, I propose that each of you come out, one at a time, and tell me what you remember."

I could not identify the first Part to appear. "I was nine," was all she said. The second Part to exit was Rose. "You already know I was there. Lillie, Joan's little sister, was there, too. She was crying. The men got mad and told me to shut her up. Then they told me to make Lillie pet the sheep's thing, too. That's when I went away."

Sarah Christine came forward next. "I took over after Rose. I put my hand under Lillie's little hand to save her from having to touch it. Charles' brother told me to pull down my underwear and bend over. I held on to a wood railing and heard his dad yell, 'Bring that sheep over here.' I don't remember much after that, just the men laughing and jeering . . ." She took an anguished breath. "Then, there was a loud noise. Charles' dad told me to get dressed quick. We were dazed and scared. When we stumbled out of the barn, Charles' dad grabbed us and took us to a chicken coop. He picked one up and cut off its head with a knife. Blood squirted everywhere. He said, 'If you two girls tell anyone what happened here, I'll cut off your heads just like this chicken.'"

Sarah Christine said she grabbed Lilly's hand and they ran toward Charles' car, their legs pumping like pistons. When they got home, their mother scolded them and demanded to know where they had been. "None of us ever told."

My heart raged against my ribs. The stench of the men's depravity hung in the air like a fog of corruption. I could barely breathe as I thanked the Parts for having the fortitude to tell this barbaric story.

I invited the Parts who had been present throughout the telling to walk to the River of Tears to bathe in its soothing waters. Within moments, a hysterical Sarah Christine came out, unmollified. "I can't bear this. I can't get rid of those awful images. And the disgusting sounds those perverts made . . . give me a knife—no, a razor blade. I have to cut myself. Help me!"

This was not the time to worry about traditional therapeutic principle— better to respond creatively to Sarah Christine's desperate need.

"Let me see what I can find." I walked hastily to my adjacent office and rummaged through a desk drawer until I found a small sewing kit.

"You know cutting the Body hurts everyone," I said, standing before Sarah Christine with a needle, "but I can help you release the tension another way."

She grabbed for the needle.

"Shhhh. Relax, Sarah Christine. Let me do this. Hold out your hand. I'll prick your forefinger. When you see the first drop of blood, take a deep breath. And as you slowly exhale, let go of those ugly images and disgusting sounds." The pinprick released a droplet of blood, and Sarah Christine collapsed. I gathered her in my arms and held her until she disentangled herself.

"I heard," Joan uttered from someplace deep in her throat as she re-emerged. "I think I'm going to be sick." I escorted her to the bathroom, supported her head as she vomited, and afterward wiped her face with a cool washcloth. When I was confident she was sufficiently stabilized, I called in her long-waiting husband and apprised him of her condition. I suggested he keep a watchful eye on her.

~

Chapter 23

THE MOTHER'S BED

October 22. Joan sprawled on the couch. Her purse slid off her lap to the floor. She complained of having been bombarded over the last few days with gruesome images and disgusting talk that made her feel ashamed and dirty. She had tried to hold on, stay in the present, but didn't dare go to sleep.

"As a little girl," she recalled, "I listened for his footsteps, hoping he wouldn't come for me. I'd make myself stiff as a board and pull the covers up to my chin. When he pulled back the covers, I felt like I was being stripped of myself. I thought I wouldn't survive the night."

Joan's eyes danced back and forth. Sebunome came out, cowering, her small voice tremulous. "At night when my mother was at work or visiting a friend, that's when Charles came for us. Once, he told me to get out of bed and took me to the room where he and my mother slept. He told me to climb up onto the bed. He pinned me down and pushed into me hard." Her eyes vacant, her spine arched, she called out, "Mama. Mama, help me. It hurts."

"Sebunome, you are not with Charles," I said gently. "Take a deep breath. What I want you to do is climb out of your mother's bed . . . and walk back to me."

She returned to the present, dazed.

"See, you are right here with me in the therapy room. What you just experienced was a flashback."

Her eyes blinked as if reality had suddenly come back into focus. She reached for my hand and, with shame in each word, said, "Every time he did that to me, he whispered in my ear, 'Tell me it feels good.' So I made myself say it. I was too afraid not to. He made me promise never to tell my mother, or next time he would hurt me worse. Once I did try to tell her, but she got angry and told me, 'If you don't behave, I'll send you away. You should be grateful for what you have.'"

"When Charles took you to your mother's bedroom, could you have refused to go?"

"How could I? When he told me what to do and looked at me with those dead eyes, I couldn't say no. Does that make me bad?"

"The shameful thing Charles did was not your fault. You were an innocent victim. Always remember that."

Sebunome's features nuanced back to Joan. "How could my mother leave us alone with that monster? She didn't give it a second thought. She just left." Her chin quivered. "I can't begin to forgive her."

"Forgiving her, or not, is your choice, Joan."

Looking at me askance, she snatched up her purse from the floor. "I think we've done enough for today," she snapped and stormed out.

After her abrupt departure, I reflected on Sebunome's progress. *She was daring to meet my eyes, touch my hand, and trust me enough to disclose a disturbing memory. I hoped she might soon consider abandoning her isolated existence at the Forest Edge and reunite with her sisters, Samantha and Sarah Christine.*

Her mouth an unhappy crescent, Joan said, "I have some bad news. I've found empty bottles everywhere—drawers, closets, under my bed. I assume it was Sarah Christine's doing. I'm concerned about my health. My body can't continue to endure this. It's poison for me."

The lines around Joan's eyes lost their tension, and her brow smoothed as a Mona Lisa smile touched her lips. "The excessive drinking has become a deterrent to progress," announced Raven. He recounted Sarah Christine's struggles to feel loved, Shadowman's exploitation of her vulnerability, and how the use of alcohol diminished the Parts' ability to think coherently. Raven also warned me about Marjorie, the most dangerous of the Furies, who harbors rage against the abusers. "She is active again," he said, "and I pray Sarah Christine does not come under her vengeful influence."

I asked Raven how we could persuade her to resist Marjorie's influence.

"The only thing that comes to mind, Helper, is to ask Samantha if she would be willing to accept Sarah Christine as her apprentice. If Samantha agrees, that may provide Sarah Christine with a sense of purpose. Then she might be able to resist drinking and withstand Shadowman's and Marjorie's wicked intentions."

Raven withdrew. Sarah Christine quickly took his place.

"Why would Samantha have me as her assistant? Everyone knows I'm the troublemaker who drinks. Anyway, I already have a purpose. I'm supporting Shadowman. He's convinced me it's safer to stay quiet, don't feel, don't expect, and don't change. He told me if I drink, the Body will get sick, and everyone will be too weak to oppose him. That's my purpose now," she said, cocksure.

"But Shadowman is just using you," I countered. "He's afraid to change. But Samantha isn't. She's the brave one. She wants you to change, like she has, so you can become a helper instead of a troublemaker."

"Well . . ." She paused, as if weighing the alternatives. "If she will have me . . . I guess I would have to stop listening to Shadowman."

"And what about listening to Marjorie?"

"I never listen to her. She's too mean. She turns on you like *that*"—she snapped her fingers—"if you don't do exactly what she wants." She thought a moment and then said, "I'd better go find Samantha."

"I hope this works," was Joan's comment when she came back. "I hate to admit it, but I understand why Sarah Christine drinks. It's what we've always done—numb out and go away."

"Could there be something more to it than that?" I probed. "Has Sarah Christine accepted that her youthful yearning for affection can never be fulfilled? And has that left her bereft of hope to ever be loved?"

Joan's nod was almost imperceptible.

～

Chapter 24

JJ

I *think Sarah Christine and Samantha* working together is going well," Joan stated ten days later. "And I'm staying sober—even though I still have the shakes, you know, withdrawal symptoms." She let the moment hang. "I feel someone would like to speak with you."

In the sibilant voice of a young child, Beth said, "I'm in the attic dancing. Like a ballerina. I look pretty." Holding up her fingers, she said, "I'm almost four. I hear the man with black hair coming up the stairs. He smiles at me. He's touching me and wants to do what Daddy did, but Mama's calling, and I have to go." Then she said as if in an aside, "When he put his fingers down there—in my peenee—he calls me 'little Joan.' But I'm not Joan. I'm Beth."

Her head bowed as if the memory pressed down on her. "I don't feel so good, Oma. I want to go back to Elizabeth's House."

Beth was barely gone when an unknown Part jumped up from the couch.

"A door opened and I ran out and it slammed shut behind me. Where am I?"

"You're with me. I'm Joan's helper. What's your name?"

"I'm J-J," she said, carefully sounding out the two letters. "Do I have to go back? I don't want to go back there. If I tell, it's wrong. And if I don't tell, it's just as wrong. Will you take me?"

"I wish I could, JJ. Let me speak to someone who can find you a good place to stay."

Raven emerged to report he had consulted with Many Voices. JJ had been created at a time when Joan became exhausted and unable to maneuver in her mother's world of contradictions. JJ split off to prevent Joan from having a nervous breakdown. For a long time after that, Joan rarely spoke and did what she was told. JJ later found refuge in Many Voices' Dark Forest.

"Thank you, Raven, and please thank Many Voices for this information. You and Samantha have on occasion mentioned her. However, I'm still unclear as to her role within the Inner Realm."

"She is the protector of the young Parts that reside in the Dark and Haunted Forest."

"Is she a . . . a second inner self-helper?"

"Yes," Raven confirmed. "She is the observer and the scribe. She holds the history of all that has transpired."

Quite a difference from my earlier understanding of Raven's function, I thought. *What a remarkable division of responsibility.*

Joan reappeared. "I heard a door suddenly slam shut. What was that?"

"A new Part came out," I explained. "She calls herself JJ." I recounted Raven's description of JJ's function, the existence of a second system, and the role of Many Voices. "Perhaps," I speculated, "JJ's escape has opened a new path from Many Voices' system, making it possible for other Parts to find their way into Raven's realm."

"Well," she said, "remodeling my brain makes for a terrific headache."

I asked if she could manage one last question. Could she remember how her mother's conflicting demands affected her? She answered that getting through an ordinary day was like walking in a minefield. If she disobeyed one rule, she was in trouble. If she complained about anything, she was called ungrateful. When she cried, she was sent to her room. If someone asked her a question and she just smiled and pretended not to know, then she'd get scolded for acting dumb on purpose. No matter what she did, it was wrong. "I thought I would lose my mind."

"Was there no relief?"

"There were moments when I felt free. At night, after everyone was asleep, that was my time. I would read and write poetry and draw. That's when I started hearing the celestial music in my head."

"That must have been a comfort."

"Yes . . . and so was school," Joan mused. "I was shy and afraid to go at first. That's when Samantha came to help. In time, I learned to love school. It became the only place I felt safe. Once, a teacher told me I was very smart and gave me some books to take home. But I couldn't read them in front of my mother, or I'd be called a show-off. She never liked anything I ever did in school."

I was relieved to know that as a child Joan had a place to be that she loved. A place where she felt safe.

~

My own memories of school are almost non-existent. I can't recall if I loved or hated school. Or if I did any schoolwork. Or if my teachers ever addressed me. I have only one indelible memory: the day I entered first grade. I remember a nun's habit flapping like a blackbird's wings as she led us—a bedraggled group of young girls—through the streets of an unfamiliar village toward a small schoolhouse. Local women, arms folded across their chests, with young children hanging onto the folds of their skirts, scrutinized us with suspicion. During the tumultuous days after Germany surrendered, the nuns had opened the doors of their cloister to the likes of us—refugees and displaced children, or like me, an abandoned child.

A hush fell over the classroom when we stood at its threshold. Elbows bumped elbows. Snickers sounded from behind hands cupped over mouths. A thrust of the teacher's chin directed us to the far wall. As we passed the rows of desks, faces turned away. Whispers stuck to our backs as we scurried to our assigned bench. With a slate tablet balanced on my knees, I sat in rigid attention. The teacher's lips moved but I could not comprehend the meaning of his words. I studied the backs of the children's heads before me. I wondered if they, too, were hungry and lost. Or lived in a house with a good Mama—a Mama like I once had.

~

Chapter 25

ʻEDUCATING ROGER

November 17. Although angry about her husband's lack of affection and his constant demands for sex, Joan was more upset by his continued misguided behavior toward Sarah Christine and Rose.

"Have you confronted him again?"

"What's the use? He just denies it and gets mad."

Sarah Christine came out, hot. "She's such a coward. She doesn't have the guts to confront anyone. It's me that does the yelling."

She jumped up from the couch and snatched paper and pen from my side table. She drew a stick figure. With a vicious stroke of the pen, she drew a horizontal line to separate the head from the body. She repeatedly tapped the line with the nib of the pen. "This is where it's stuck. The anger in my heart gets stuck right here—cut off from my head. I'm always angry but can't put words to it. I just yell."

In frustration, she grabbed the plastic scissors from the toy box nearby and cut the figure across its neck.

"So, your heart can't talk to your mind about the anger you hold, and your mind can't explain to your heart why that is so."

I braced myself for an outburst, but Sarah Christine leaned back, deflated. "Oh, what's the use," she said dispiritedly. "I'm tired of screaming and acting out. I'm tired of holding the anger. As soon as I let it out, it just fills right back up again."

"You're right," I said. "When the heart and mind can't communicate, nothing gets resolved. So, the vicious cycle continues, fueled by irrational thinking and inappropriately expressed emotions."

She sighed, tears welled up, and, for the first time, I saw Sarah Christine weep.

I knew the violence against her sketch represented not only her sense of frustration but also Joan's unexpressed, deep-seated anger. It would take time and patience to undo the affective and cognitive disconnect. To rationally externalize unexpressed emotions requires hard work.

December 10. During the early-morning hours, Joan learned that Roger had again seduced Sarah Christine and Rose. She challenged him and again explained how his behavior upset the Parts and triggered flashbacks. When she rejected his excuses, Roger had stormed out of the house. That afternoon in therapy, Joan told me of the morning's events. I thought the time had come to address this issue directly with Roger and encouraged her to persuade him to attend our next session.

Joan's eyes emptied. Her head tilted slightly forward and to the right. Sebunome looked out from under her eyebrows and confided she and JJ had fused, and she was now the "guardian of the door."

"I have to make sure the door will never close again," Sebunome said. "With it open, the Parts who live in Many Voices' Dark Forest can flee to Raven's Realm."

As she spoke, questions tumbled through my mind. *Had JJ been the first Part to escape through that "door"? Would there be others? How many? Would they come all at once or one at a time? What memories would they hold? What would this mean for our work? All this uncertainty made me uneasy.*

Late that afternoon, Joan informed me Roger had agreed to attend our next session.

I greeted the couple warmly, shook Roger's moist hand, and invited them to sit across from one another. After removing his black leather jacket, Roger lowered his lanky frame into an upholstered chair. Joan, wrapped in a bulky green sweater, sat in her usual place on the couch, her purse tight against her body. I gave her an approving look. Her brown eyes reflected my silent praise with a mixture of determination and anxiety. I thanked both for coming and acknowledged our goal was to examine their intimate relationship. Roger studied the stitching on the tips of his black cowboy boots. Joan's eyes pleaded for me to take the lead. I purposely waited.

Roger cleared his throat. "What relationship?" he asked with a hint of sarcasm. "There is none," his gray eyes flashed. "Whenever I approach her, she goes away, and one of them comes out. What am I supposed to do?"

I looked at Joan for a response. She swallowed hard and addressed the wall behind me. "When he approaches me . . ." With a subtle movement of my head toward Roger, I indicated she should address him directly. She fiddled with the top button of her cardigan. "When you want sex," she began again, "you do things on purpose to make me lose time."

The muscle in Roger's jaw knotted.

"You sneak up behind me and push yourself against me without warning. A jolt goes through my body, and I'm gone. That's what Charles used to do. I would tremble because I knew what he would do as soon as he had the chance."

"But I'm not him," Roger's voice rising in defense, his eyes imploring.

"No, you're not," I validated.

"How many times have I told you? If you want to be intimate, ask me to my face with some kindness in your voice. Don't *demand* like I'm your personal property."

"Don't I have *some* rights? I'm your husband."

With arms folded across his red-checkered shirt, Roger again focused on the tips of his boots. With some discomfort, he said, "If I have to put up with all the crazy stuff going on, why shouldn't I satisfy my needs the way I want to? Joan's other therapist said it was okay to have sex with the alters 'cause they're really Joan."

"It's true," I replied, "they *are* part of Joan. However, sex for them is a frightening imposition."

"Then why do they come out in the first place?"

"To rescue Joan when she perceives your advances are unloving or frightening. They submit to your 'needs' to protect your wife from experiencing emotional and physical distress. Please understand: If you satisfy your sexual needs with the Parts, you will retraumatize them as well as Joan."

Joan's lips quivered. "That's what I've been trying to tell you, but you don't hear anything I say."

They lapsed into silence.

Then Joan quietly said, "I know what you think of me."

"And what's that?" Roger asked.

"You said I'm damaged goods."

He dropped his head and knitted his large hands between his knees. "I didn't mean it." He again cleared his throat. "I'm sorry for saying that."

Joan's shoulders relaxed. She gazed out the window at the bare branches tossing in the December wind. Roger turned to me and asked, "What now?"

"I believe apologizing to the Parts you took advantage of would be beneficial."

"How?"

"Joan, would you feel comfortable if I ask the Parts who hold grievances against Roger to come out?" She consented and closed her eyes.

Sarah Christine came forward and accused Roger of seducing her. Embarrassment flushed his cheeks as he struggled to apologize for his misguided behavior. Meek Rose came out to complain that Roger had "hurt" her, too. Shamefaced, he apologized and explained he had not meant to harm her. Next, a confident Samantha confronted him. Since she had matured and now understood how harmful his advances were, she no longer would allow herself to be used. Her assertiveness left Roger at a loss for words.

Joan returned to confirm she had witnessed her husband apologizing. She expressed hope that their sexual relationship would improve—*if* he stopped taking advantage of the Parts and showed her genuine affection.

I thanked Roger for sitting through this trying session. I praised his willingness to examine his actions and sincerely apologize. He assured me he would do everything he could to help Joan get better.

"I'm sure Joan appreciates you saying that. To develop true intimacy, give yourselves time. Discover what you both enjoy and appreciate. Be kind and treat one another with respect. In the meantime," I smiled, "perhaps a bit of abstinence might not hurt."

Days later, I found this letter and a box of homemade chocolate truffles leaning against my office door. I accepted Joan's gift as a tangible way to validate her growing sense of personhood.

December 18, 2004
Dear Renate, [Abridged]

I think that up until [this] week I felt little hope of having an authentic relationship with my husband.

You have done so very much for 'all of me' that I can hardly find the words to express my heartfelt gratitude. You gave us the gifts of being validated, defended. [I]t touched me to the core of my being. "Thank you" seems not enough.

It's been only four days since that session, [but] I feel like a weight has been lifted. I can see a speck of light at the end of the tunnel. I hold no illusions of "happily ever after," but to sum it up, things are going well though I do feel as if I've done battle—emotionally and physically. I know [Roger and I] have a lot of work yet to do.

God Bless you, Renate. Last session helped set me/us free so that we may know what [married] life is truly meant to feel like. It is the beginning.

With much gratitude, Joan and All

Chapter 26

SHADOWMAN

January 19, 2005. In our first session after the holidays, Joan questioned my assumption that Shadowman saw himself as "the protector."

"I'm not sure who Shadowman really is," she said, "and what he represents for the system. I think he might be a diabolical spirit."

"What persuades you to think that?"

"Well . . . he terrifies us with his threats and the inhuman noises he makes. He manipulates Sarah Christine to drink and cut herself. He even tried to convince me to commit suicide. Thank God I came to in time. Another time, he got me to hit my thighs with a hammer until I was black and blue. Remember? I showed you the bruises."

"No doubt Shadowman has hurt you. But the question arises in my mind: What motivates him to be violent and then withdraw before there's a fatality?" Contemporary psychiatrists pioneering the treatment of MPD—those I had studied, I told Joan—encountered similar persecutor Parts among their patients. They puzzled over such behavior and in time concluded that these Parts became enraged by their inability to protect the victim and her Parts from abuse. Like misguided teenagers, they thought that they could mitigate the abuse by imitating the threats and physical harm that the abusers had used to keep their victims subjugated. "As I've mentioned before, Joan, I believe instilling fear, even going as far as inflicting physical injury, is Shadowman's 'misguided' way of protecting you from outside harm and betrayal."

146

I allowed Joan to absorb my reasoning, and then I proposed that, instead of condemning Shadowman as an evil spirit, we should reach out and help him understand that his methods, regardless of how well-intended, were no longer necessary. Once he comprehended that his ways were counterproductive, she and the Parts might engage him as a helper, a positive force in the service of what Joan wished to achieve.

"I still believe I'd be better off if we could get rid of him somehow. All he does is disrupt and try to undo everything we've worked for."

Suddenly, Joan winced in pain.

"Stop explaining!" Shadowman ordered as we came face-to-face. "Stop tricking Joan and the Parts. All people betray. That is the rule." He puffed out his chest, posturing to intimidate me. "I have a net of Puppets to do my bidding. They can overpower Joan when she enters the Inner Realm and keep her imprisoned forever. And believe me," he growled, "I can hurt you, too."

"You might, but do you truly want to? What has persuaded you to visit me? Are you curious about the lady who helps the others?"

"Leave Joan alone. Leave the Parts alone. I warn you!"

"I promised to help them. I will not betray Joan and the others. Allow me to help you, too. Join us.

Shadowman and His Puppets,
Joan and the Parts 2005.

I'd like to hear all about you and your Puppets."

"I'm not interested in your help. Why should I tell you anything?" he scoffed.

I hoped Shadowman's Puppets somehow were listening, possibly watching from behind his eyes. I called out to the Puppets, "Cut yourselves loose from Shadowman, and run toward the Light."

A look of uncertainty crossed Shadowman's face. His unguarded expression changed to a malevolent mask as he retreated to the Inner Realm.

Sarah Christine rushed out. "Maybe I can cut the Puppets loose."

"That might be possible," I said. "Shadowman might be less powerful than all of you think."

We explored who else could assist her in this perilous task. "I'll ask Raven," she said, "if he can send Feather to help."

"Who is Feather?"

"One of Raven's little helpers."

Her chest heaved, and she abruptly changed the subject. "I only came out to talk about Leslie. The other day I heard her say to Joan that she has a new girlfriend. I guess it's really over now." Her attention drifted. She divulged her fear of becoming an empty nothing should she surrender her job of holding the anger Joan couldn't express. I suggested that, if she were considering surrendering her job, then this might be the right time to think about integrating with Joan.

"If I integrate, does that mean I'll lose your affection?"

"My dear Sarah Christine, after you become one with Joan, I believe somehow you will continue to feel my affection."

She faded without comment.

Raven exited. "I am aware the hour is late, but before we say goodbye, I want you to know that I rarely doubt the wisdom of your guidance. However, I must voice my opposition to your advice to Joan and Sarah Christine. It is futile for a Part to approach Shadowman and extend understanding and kindness. Nothing will persuade him to change. Nothing will transform his malevolence. As you have been told, he is a diabolical spirit, which I do not consider a part of the system."

"Because the hour *is* late, Raven, instead of attempting to reframe your conviction about Shadowman, let me tell you a mythic tale recorded by Joseph Campbell in his book *The Hero with a Thousand Faces*. The Sumerian goddess, Inanna of the Upperworld, had a sister, Ereshkigal, goddess of the Underworld. After great misfortune befell her realm, Inanna descended into the shadowy Underworld to confront her sister, whom she believed was responsible. In the myth, the proud goddess of the sky eventually comes to the stunning realization that she and her sister were 'one goddess in two aspects.' In that sense, she encountered the mirror-side of herself, that part which she had denied."

I asked him to consider how the myth might relate to his feelings about Shadowman. Inanna had to put aside her lofty self-perception and submit to the intolerable fact that she and her opposite were one. Could he possibly see himself as Inanna and Shadowman as Ereshkigal? Could he accept that the negativity embodied in Shadowman might be the mirror-side of himself?

Raven sat pondering this. "Teacher, I must confess, this paradoxical proposition causes me great discomfort. If I may be honest, I'm not completely convinced."

"Please allow yourself time to contemplate the meaning of the myth. In time, you may recognize how contradictory attributes can work in concert for the welfare of the system."

Raven bowed and retreated.

A few days later, I received the following mailings:

January 21, 2005 [Abridged]
From the Inner Realm to the Outer Edge [Joan] *and Blessings to our Healer,*

You, on the Outer Edge, as we have not continued to live outwardly, are as tightly bound as we to what was. Lack of cooperation in any area can only slow the process. To move ahead despite fear must be the goal. Fear, as well as anger, can be a great motivator. We have never been without God, as you well know. With and through the Healer He promised and provided, we may all continue on into the miracle of life, of living for the first time in many, many years in the full awareness of total being. It will serve no purpose for any to be dragged back and remain in the darkness. Past and present must reconcile, or there will never be a contented, wisdom-filled future. God has kept his promises and has never deviated in his plan for you. Make a promise now to preserve yourself in a healthy, complete life. Do not turn away out of fear of the unknown. In time you will know. Elizabeth and I have good purpose in being the encouragement and bearer of messages from the Inner Realm. For more than a year in your time, you have come to know love, caring intuition, great dedication, wisdom, and an extremely hard-working advocate that far exceeds any expectations ever held. God's promise is to be fulfilled. Work hard, and do not let this opportunity for healing to be in vain.

Blessings, Raven

~

Dear Helper,

For any person holding onto old, unexamined feelings, emotions, ways of thinking, illusions, and being held in the ice-cold grasp of the past, a prison is created. A self-built, well maintained, and invisible prison. And for a person divided, it becomes a prison within a prison. The acceptance and examination of long-held beliefs lead to a newness of being. Hard work, yes, to face reality with honesty and courage, to let go of what once served so well. Hard work must be done on both sides. For, in order to complete the Outer Realm, the Inner Realm must let go of all it has known and exist in a new way, the way life was intended to be lived. The acceptance of the truth will lead to transformation.

With Respect, Elizabeth

~

Chapter 27

SOPHIA

February 9. On this day, Joan's upbeat mood was contagious. We shared amusing life experiences, which generated much laughter. I contributed to the merriment by recounting how my husband recently helped a woman chase down a man who had grabbed her purse and ran. "Imagine my sixty-two-year-old husband, dressed in a suit and tie, running down an alley shouting, 'Stop, thief, stop!'"

Joan covered her mouth with her hand and giggled. "Did the thief get away?"

"No. Thanks to my hero, the police eventually took the purse-snatcher into custody."

Our high spirits ended abruptly when a Part came out, panting. Her eyes darted around the room, coming to rest on my face. With frantic gestures, she indicated she could not speak. I encouraged her to write down what she wished to say. When I handed her paper and pen, we inadvertently touched. She jerked back her hand as if scalded.

"It's all right," I said. "I won't hurt you."

She gave me a furtive glance and then, with bold letters, printed:

TOUCH—HURTS. HURTS BODY TOO—BITE HURTS—
   NO VOICE—THROAT HURTS—SEX—BODY—HURTS TOO
      BODY—BITE HARD—BLOOD—MORE HURT—LIKE FIRE-
STILL HURTS

She lifted her head and, with large, brown eyes, searched mine. I read aloud what she had written. She moved her head vigorously up and down.

Then she drew a female form and viciously marked its breasts, pelvis, and vagina with three large X's. Next to the figure, she printed: PAIN. She slashed thick, black horizontal lines across its throat and mouth. She proceeded to draw a circle around the figure and wrote SECRET above it. Below she wrote:

ME US SCARED TO TALK
We All r Secrets
Many little [and] Big -> 7 8 9 10 11 12 13 14 15 16 17 18

I wondered if the numbers might indicate Joan's ages during the time of Charles' abuse. Impatiently, her hand reached for a second sheet of paper. In the middle of the page, she drew a large oval, within which she drew a smaller oval filled with fourteen tiny circles. One near the center, she blackened with the tip of her pencil and labeled it "me." Above the oval, she wrote:

We are many
All are Secrets
me little in big secret Place

Below the oval, she sketched a rectangle, a house, and a small stick figure on a path. Her hand moved quickly to the upper-left corner, where she drew a stick figure entering another rectangle, which she labeled: SCHOOL. Bending her head over a third sheet of paper, she wrote:

At school—no talk—Look blank—sleep on desk—not act ok—
THEY NOTICED.
TEACHER Go [to] Nurse—We shake—WE GO TO SMALL ROOM—
[nurse] WITH US—INSIDE WE SCREAM—NO CALL MOTHER—
no one
Cry inside—will BURN EYES out—blind CRYING

Counselor lady comes in with us—Mother comes—TROUBLE
  I TRY TO RUN OUT
    GET AWAY
    HER EYES
  MOTHER SLAMMED BODY INTO [the door]
   Held us inside the room—YELLING screaming at us!!!
WHAT IS WRONG
  NOTHING
   ACT RIGHT
FRAID OF MOTHER—NOT TALK FOR DAYS—Mother very
SCARY
   SHE VERY ANGRY—wants to make eat
  NOT EAT
    BAD VOICES AT NIGHT—THING[S] FALL OFF WALL
    CURTAINS BLOW—WINDOW IS CLOSED
POWER—EVIL—IT COMES—IT REALLY HAPPENED—HE
NOT THERE—
  WE ARE TOO
    SCARED.

"Would you like me to help you find your voice so you can tell me more? You will be safe. I will be gentle and patient."

She took the paper out of my hand and wrote: [When I was] 14 one nice lady [at] church [noticed that] we were many—She afraid [and] goes away [because] I will not speak—[I] am waste of time—Have become Total Silence.

"I won't go away," I said.

She wrote: Why you want to help bad girls?

"Because I care for you and the other ones who are afraid."

U can write That on clean paper for us—loving words.

"Yes."

She lifted up her pencil again and wrote: Saving broken pieces to put back.

153

"I would like to help you do that."

To get sunshine—want sunshine
    to walk with you and be not stuck here and afraid
        not hit not yell not force
           and i be real
please not ever hurt
    they can't hear me
    no one can hear me

"I can hear you. I will not hurt you. And I won't yell at you. Will you come back to see me?"

Terror fled across her face. She anxiously touched her throat, followed by ragged inhalations. Then she was gone as if pulled back Inside by an invisible hand.

Had she escaped from Many Voices' domain? Had this Part with no voice fled through the door Sebunome vowed to keep open?

I laid the sheets of paper aside and called for Joan. Rubbing her temples with both hands, she grumbled, "What happened? All I remember is laughing—then nothing."

After a brief account of the Part that had suddenly appeared but could not speak, I told Joan she'd written in a kind of stream-of-consciousness, filling four sheets of paper with random phrases and drawings that revealed she held secrets about abuses similar to what Samantha brought to light during her disclosures at the River of Tears. To avoid burdening Joan, I refrained from telling her "no voice" revealed that there were many more like her in a "big secret place," which I thought must be a reference to Many Voices' system. "The phrases and drawings also suggested an incident at school," I concluded.

Continuing to massage her temples, Joan said, "I vaguely recall my mother coming to school one day. I believe I was eleven or twelve. She created a big scene—she was furious with me because I had brought attention to myself. I had felt sick and was hurting—you know where—so the teacher sent me to the nurse, and the nurse called my mother. As soon as she entered the nurse's office, she grabbed my arm and pulled me out into the hallway, slamming the nurse's door behind us. She called me names which I won't repeat. I had violated the family rule to act right and not bring attention to myself. To my mother, appearances mattered more than anything else."

She momentarily closed her eyes, as if to steady her mind after relating this painful event. "On our way home, my mother screamed, 'What are you trying to do? Ruin my life? What an ingrate! Blah, blah, blah . . .' So guess what she did? She took me and my sister out of school, and the whole family went out to the country for a few days to let the dust settle. Everyone slept in the same room, even Charles. Yuck."

"Once your mother was made aware of the school's concern, did she take you to a doctor to find out what was ailing you?"

"Like I said, my mother would never do anything to bring attention to what was happening at our house. She desperately wanted to believe that our family was normal. If I revealed anything, she threatened that Social Services would have to investigate, and me and my sister would be taken away."

"Do you know if the school counselor or the principal notified the local Department of Human Services?"

"Not that I know of."

How sad, I told myself, but not surprising. Such is often the case. And then tragedy strikes.

~

The plight of my half-sister, Herta, came to mind. Our birth mother had chosen an unconventional life and found taking care of a young child to be a tiresome inconvenience. She had placed Herta in the care of strangers, exposing her to their negligence, and worse. And when the teachers and authorities reported Herta's unruliness, neither my mother nor anyone else made an effort to find out why or how to correct her misbehavior. Instead, my mother clung to the delusion that, by taking Herta back home, indulging her with food, and lavishing her with verbal and physical endearments, she could save her daughter. Until, inevitably, the child's presence again cramped her lifestyle. Then she would place my sister in the care of new strangers, and the cycle of abuse resumed.

I remember one night many years later, my mother telephoned to plead for me to come to Germany. Something terrible had happened to Herta. Upon my arrival, I found my sister sitting in a prison cell, hollowed out, skeletal. She had stabbed her son in the heart. His last words had been, "Mama, what are you doing?" An act of love, she told me, to save him. She couldn't stand by and watch him become, at fourteen, a petty thief, alcoholic, drug-addicted, and sexually exploited—as she had been.

~

Chapter 28

DELIVERANCE

*J*oan arrived disoriented. Her unbuttoned coat hung haphazardly over a faded house dress. I helped her out of her wrap and guided her to the couch. A Part immediately appeared. Her skittishness made me suspect it was No Voice, who had frantically written down her story at our last session. I again offered her a pen and sheet of paper. She printed: **The Puppets tried to catch me. They tried to stop me from coming out.** The pen fell out of her hand. The Body began to shake as if in the grip of a seizure.

Alarmed, I called for Raven. He came out quickly. "My system is under siege. Shadowman's Puppets are preparing an assault. They intend to plunge the Parts back into Darkness."

"What can you do to defend yourselves?"

"I have instructed Samantha to don her breastplate and sword, and lead Sarah Christine, Sebunome, Rose, Maria, Lisa, Charlotte, even Beth, to the Forest Edge. I told them to hold hands and form a chain the Puppets cannot cross. I asked them to repeatedly chant 'love,' which I pray will create enough discomfort in the Puppets to weaken their resolve. Excuse my haste, but I must return to guide the Parts. Before I take my leave, may I ask you to watch over us?"

"Of course—that's my job. However, if Joan and the Parts become too distraught, I shall have to call for an ambulance and notify her family."

"That is your responsibility, Helper. But for now, allow us the opportunity to face the challenge at hand with all the courage we can muster."

With Raven's departure, Joan's body again began to convulse. Her eyes rolled back in her head. I cradled her in my arms, which took all my physical strength. I encouraged her to breathe deeply. In a soothing voice, I repeatedly said, "You are with me. You are safe. I'm watching over you until the chaos has passed." Joan's body continued to spasm. I managed to slide her off the couch and onto the floor. I surrounded her with pillows to assure her safety and create a symbolic bulwark to keep back the Puppets. I sat beside her on the floor.

Joan momentarily regained consciousness. "It's Shadowman! He's behind it all."

I pondered Shadowman's motives for staging an attack on Raven's system. Was it fear of losing control? Fear of being unable to silence the Parts? Did he believe the Parts now emerging from Many Voices' system posed a threat?

No Voice came back and sat up. Retrieving the pen, she wrote: The Puppets are coming now like a wave. They are trying to trap us. Only love can hold them back. Or when we say a prayer. That stops them, too. She murmured a prayer and then wrote: The Puppets are retreating now. They are afraid of love.

She drew a straight line across the page and printed: They think like that. Then she drew the symbol for infinity and wrote: They can't think like this. Shadowman will not let them. That's the rule! Then somewhat cryptically, she added: Love heals all for all.

No Voice offered to communicate in sign language. I told her I didn't have that skill. She wrote: I can teach you. I smiled and admitted I couldn't memorize the symbols. Because I was dyslexic, I couldn't even recite the ABCs. She laughed at that and wrote: We could practice.

"I'd rather help you find your voice so you can tell me your name."

No Voice cleared her throat and rasped, "I have no name."

"No name?"

She shook her head.

"What name would you like?"

She shrugged.

I told her I always had loved the name Sophia. In mythology, I explained, she was an ancient goddess that embodied wisdom. No Voice seemed delighted. In a thin, hoarse voice, she proudly proclaimed, "So I shall be known as Sophia." After a moment's reflection, she confided, "I know a lot about the bad things that happened."

"I believe you, Sophia," and gave her a light pat on the shoulder. This time she didn't recoil.

"Many in the Haunted Forest are listening. Please don't turn them away."

Sophia's face reddened. Her nose flared. An angry Sarah Christine pushed out. "I want to cut the Body!"

I reached for her hands. She leaned away.

"If you touch me, I'll cut you, too,."

"I'm here to listen. Remember, I care for you." My words seemed to give her pause. "Can't we work through your anguish?"

"No, I can't go on. I want to die."

"If you do, all the others will die, too. Isn't there another way?"

"No, I'm all anger and hatred and pain inside. I can't bear the memory of Charles' brutality any longer. Or my mother's betrayal. She never loved me. No one ever loved me. And that's all I ever wanted. Now, I just want to die."

When I heard the despair in her plea, I decided then and there to embrace her wish. But how? It was plain to me that Sarah Christine's "solution" could not be achieved by an "exorcism" or the futility of putting her to sleep, as Helen had attempted. Rather, some kind of deliverance from her despair was called for. I could envisage how her memories would be a gift to Joan, who then would have the opportunity to work through the hatred and anger and yearning for love that Sarah Christine had held these many years.

"If that is truly what you want, Sarah Christine, then I will help."

She awkwardly hugged me in relief. "Thank you for understanding," she said through bitter tears. "Thank you for caring."

I sat quietly to allow my mind to float to a place of "not knowing" and waited for an appropriate solution to manifest itself. "What if . . ." I began and then paused to *see* the "idea" more clearly. "Sarah Christine, what if you choose to surrender your anguish and despair by dissolving in the River of Tears?"

The tension left her face as Raven came forward. "I agree with what you are proposing, Helper. It is the merciful thing to do."

Taking a moment to prepare myself, I visualized how to proceed and then asked Sarah Christine to lay flat on her back on the floor. Lying beside her, I reached for her hand and suggested she close her eyes and breathe deeply. My voice guided her through the Outer Edge back into the Inner Realm to the River of Tears. I invited the Parts who loved and feared her to assemble along the riverbank. I imagined Samantha in breastplate and sword, Sebunome dressed in shy lavender, Elizabeth in black, and Beth and Rose in their finest, holding bouquets of wildflowers. My voice encouraged Sarah Christine to wade into the water and ever so gently slip beneath its surface. I felt her body shudder, then relax. I visualized her slowly dissolving as her essence entered a higher level of consciousness. In my mind's eye, the Blessing Lady appeared and erected a cross on the riverbank. Beth and Rose placed their flowers on the cross, and I thought I heard Lisa comforting all present with a celestial hymn.

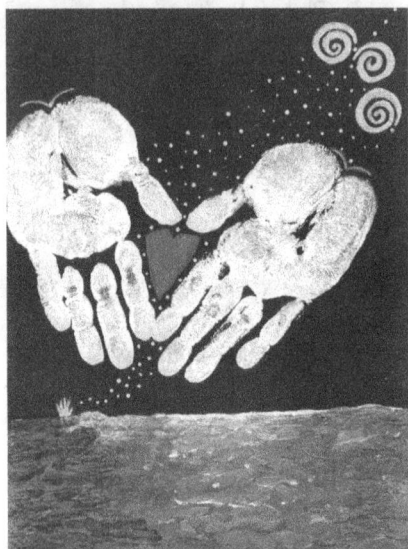

Deliverance of Sarah Christine,
Joan 2006.

I sat up and, feeling my age, rested a moment. Rising from the floor, I called for Joan. Ashen, she struggled to re-enter the present. I helped her stand, put my arm around her shoulder, and guided her into the guest bedroom adjacent to my office. As she bedded down, Joan held my hand before falling into instant sleep. It was midnight.

Stiff with fatigue but gratified by having had a role in helping Sophia and Sarah Christine resolve their plight through the magical realism of our

DELIVERANCE

intertwining imaginations, I telephoned my husband that a client was in a crisis and that I planned to stay with her all night. I made myself a cup of strong tea and ate a protein bar. Throughout the hours before dawn, I sat at Joan's bedside, wrote my record of the nine hours of turbulence and resolution, and kept vigil over my charge as she slept, the Parts fitfully switching—appearing and re-appearing—in a kind of intermittent delirium.

When Joan finally came to, she said, "I have the strangest feeling in my head. Am I having a breakup or a breakdown?"

"I think it's a breakup, Joan. I suspect Sarah Christine's dissolving has caused the Inner Realm—I mean your brain and mind—to shift in some tectonic way. To absorb all that she was into your consciousness and regain your equilibrium will take time. Be patient."

Joan stayed with me until noon, when I felt she was sufficiently self-aware to go home. I had kept the family informed, and when Stephanie picked up her mother, she assured me she would look after her and keep me updated. Although resembling her mother in voice and stature, her shock of curly red hair and fair skin took me by surprise.

A few days later, I found a letter from Raven and a poem by Many Voices in my mailbox.

February 13, 2005
Dear Helper, [Abridged]

Your love, devotion, and compassion have reached far inside the one made of many parts. The trust you have won by keeping your word . . . and by being there when . . . needed is truly a blessing. There is much work yet to be done but may be easier now without Sarah Christine's influence and domination . . . She truly would not have allowed survival for all in the long run. [Hers] was a destructive anger . . . Your decision to allow her a way out was wise. She did indeed get what she desired and has been absorbed . . . I can feel what her misery was like, but [I] can move above it.

Elizabeth and I thank you for all the work you did to support and save the system.

Blessings and love, Raven

PS. Much is happening in the Inner Realm: One of the infants in Elizabeth's care has fused with Annie; Sebunome is thinking about leaving her hiding place to be close to Rose; and Rose is debating whether to leave her Cave and move into Elizabeth's House. Three little ones have fled from Many Voices' Forest and moved into Elizabeth's House. Since the Door is being kept open by Sebunome, I surmise there will be more. I have enclosed a poem by Many Voices.

EXPOSURE [Abridged]
In the whispers can you hear
The voices that tremble [and] shake with fear.
The voices long silenced inside
We're many voices, many voices forced to hide.
Waiting for a way to be set free
Away from the tortured pain of life's decree.
Imprisoned beyond the confines of time
Can you tell us what was our crime?
Now in our darkness we are heard and seen
Standing in line to become clean.
Humbled, knowing we're absolved of our sins
Yet wondering if always the predator wins.
Please hear us and see us—we've waited so long.

Written for the Healer by Many Voices, for Many

Ten tumultuous days followed the Puppets' siege and Sarah Christine's dissolution. I had not anticipated how much these events would traumatize Joan. She found herself incapable of driving her car, exhibited no sense of direction, had to cancel work, and even forgot how to cook favorite meals. At times, she seemed to have regressed to the level of a seven-year-old, unable to read well or tell time. Throughout this ordeal, her husband and daughter acted as caregivers. I counseled that Joan's regression and forgetfulness would cease, I believed, when the process of assimilation was complete, emphasizing that the brain, in conjunction with the mind, makes every effort to reconnect and retrieve what appears to have been lost.

However, her difficulty in regaining homeostasis was a concern. I thought it prudent to take Joan to seek counsel with her psychiatrist. After evaluating Joan's mental state, she determined Joan was experiencing an extremely elevated mood and agreed with me that her age-regression would be only temporary. To address her condition, the psychiatrist adjusted Joan's medications. As we drove away, I could tell Joan felt relieved. I advised her to be mindful of her body, her feelings, and thoughts; and to use her breath to minimize any discomforts. Together, we agreed the stressful events of the past few weeks had exhausted us both.

That night, I suffered a grand mal seizure. I informed my clients of my condition and assured them that counseling services would resume as soon as I regained my health.

February 26, 2005
Dear Renate, [Abridged]

> *I hope you will be feeling better soon . . .*
> *I know that Sarah Christine truly wanted to get away from . . . all that she carried for me . . . and [from] living a life that felt "not hers." Right now, losing her strength has left me feeling quite exposed and vulnerable . . . In "losing" Sarah Christine, I think the others are freer in giving me more information in the form of memories, both good and bad . . . I have tried to reassure all inside that Sarah Christine made*

a good choice. [What she did] is not something any of them will be forced to do . . .

Thank you for all you did during that time and for going with me to see Dr. [W.] It was really helpful . . .

There is light, there is hope. I believe in us working together. I trust in the strength and love in our relationship so that, with you walking beside me, I will get where I don't just want to go but need to go. I am praying for your health. The Parts miss you very much.

With much love always, Joan

On the first day of March, Joan stepped through my office door after three weeks without therapy. During that time, Roger reported that his wife's cognitive function was improving, although she continued to exhibit symptoms of hyperactivity. I could see her ordeal had left dark half-moons under her eyes, which she had camouflaged with makeup. As we embraced, I noted her trembling. I led her to the place on the couch she had made her own.

"I feel shaky," her voice weak.

"Then let's sit here for a moment and just breathe . . . and reconnect with the strength . . . and faith . . . that has brought you through this recent crisis."

Her words came slowly. "Roger has been remarkably kind and caring during this whole ordeal. I can tell I'm getting better. I can read a bit, but my comprehension is slow. Sometimes, I feel so ignorant, kinda retarded. I have waves of sadness and feelings of loss, but thank God I don't feel her despair or hear her threats of suicide." She glanced out the window and then back to me. "Since Sarah Christine's deliverance, Raven has confided that her torment has been transformed into positive, loving energy. He's written a poem in commemoration. May I read it to you?"

SOAR

Come fly with me
Breathe in the sparkle of a clear blue sky
In the light of life let Him touch your face
His presence all fears will erase

And the warmth of His glowing
Will envelop your soul

Come fly with me
Up, down, all around to what will be
Home, beyond this earthly life, is what you'll see
Where the purest Love resides
There's no reason to hide
Let this truth set you free

Come fly with me
With confidence take hold of my wings
And discover the glory, such miraculous, splendid things
Of joy, and light, and truth so pure
Have faith in what is sure
Let the knowledge ignite your mind

Come fly with me
Up way beyond the stars
Where finally He can remove the scars
Of the past that lives inside your mind
Healing by love beyond our dreams, love divine
Let the light heal all within

Come fly with me
Become a free spirit, truly alive
And soar.

—Raven

Inspiring, I thought, *how Joan's creativity could blunt the sharp edges of torment and anguish that had cut at her heart these last four months. In my relief, I gave no thought to the tenacity with which feelings of grief and despair cling to the soul.*

~

Chapter 29

SETBACK

Within forty-eight hours, Joan descended into an alcoholic fog. This news came from her husband, who came home from work to find Joan passed out on her bed. Since then, Joan had been under "house arrest" with her husband and daughter, Megan, acting as guardians. Roger confiscated Joan's car keys and all the cash in her purse. Once when she attempted to leave, Roger blocked the door, and, in the ensuing scuffle, a pint bottle of vodka fell out of her coat pocket. He had immediately poured the contents down the sink. Roger suggested Joan was addicted to alcohol, and no matter what he did, Joan would find a way to obtain another bottle.

In the days that followed, Joan refused to leave her bedroom and entered a deep depression. Fearing for her safety, I advised her husband to take control of her medications and keep me apprised of the situation. Mid-March, when Joan came to session, I didn't comment on her recent setback. I hoped she would take the initiative. Instead, she said Rose wished to speak with me.

"I'm sad, Oma. I've been staying all alone in my Cave since Sarah Christine went away. Beth came by and suggested we should build a room onto Elizabeth's house for me so I won't be lonely. Charlotte and Maria are going to help, too. We'll make it out of mud to look like my Cave. We'll put branches and moss on the floor for me to sleep on. I'm going to paint flowers and birds on the walls. And the vessel which holds Samantha and Sarah Christine's sorrow will stand in one corner."

Rose confided that, although the pain in her vagina continued, her fear of water prevented her from seeking relief in a warm bath.

Why, I asked myself, *did Joan and several Parts fear water?*

Rose's features transformed into Sophia's.

"Shadowman's Puppets look like demons," she said and paused as if to gather courage. She reported many others like her lived in the Haunted Forest, and since the night of the Puppets' siege, three had escaped and fused with her. "What they remembered hurt a lot."

"Do you want to tell me about what they remembered?"

"The Mother . . . She never held them close. Never spoke sweetly to them. Never read a story to them at bedtime. They felt she never loved them." Sophia's face scrunched up to suppress her tears. "I wanted her to love me, too."

"I understand, sweet Sophia. Being loved is what all children need."

Later, as Joan prepared to leave, she remarked that Roger and Megan had been trying to control her every move. I asked what persuaded them to do that. Avoiding my eyes, she exhaled loudly and left. The door had barely closed before she was back. "You've known all along that I've been drinking. Why didn't you say so?"

"Because I hoped you would take the lead."

"I know I have to face the fact that I drink too much. Not the Parts—me. The only excuse I have is the loss of Sarah Christine. And after I read *Becoming One,* which you gave me to read awhile back, I got frightened because the book made clear that, after I integrate, I have to cope on my own without being able to dissociate. I think it'll feel like I'm in a straitjacket."

~

Chapter 30

THE INTERNAL MOTHER

Treatment was again at a standstill. Roger reported that Joan had no initiative, behaved mechanically, and was visibly depressed. Near the end of April, she finally returned to therapy. Her movements were lethargic, and, without much of a greeting, she sank into her seat.

"I'm not quite sure I'm up to doing serious work," she began. "All I want is to sit here in this peaceful room and soak up its stillness. I've been sleeping and eating better and taking my meds conscientiously, but the best news is I'm working to stay sober. During the day, it's pretty easy, but after dark, my resolve wanes. The shame I feel about . . . my drinking is demoralizing.

"I've been reading some more in Caroline Myss' book. It's made me think about how 'biography is biology.' With all my illnesses, I'm certainly proof of that. She talks about taking responsibility for becoming one's own healer. I feel I've done the exact opposite for more than thirteen years. I know my family longs for peace, and so do I. Myss also writes God created all of us in his image, which I believe is a fact. If I become disconnected from what I've known all my life—that I'm part of God and He's part of me—then I'm truly lost."

With a wave of her hand, she said, "I'd better stop talking. Beth wants to visit with you."

"Hi, Oma. I've missed you. Guess what? Rose has started to sleep in her new room. But you know what? She sleeps on the floor on branches and moss. But when she hurts really, really bad, she goes back to her Cave. A couple of times, Sebunome walked over to Rose's Cave, and when she did, Rose came out and talked to her."

Sebunome ending her isolation by reaching out to Rose was a welcome development.

"We've all been sad, Oma, even Elizabeth, 'cause Joan didn't keep her promise to stay sober. None of us trust her anymore. Lisa hasn't been singing. And Raven hasn't flown down from the top of his Tree, either. Sometimes when I look up there, I can see right through him. And sometimes, I see only silvery sparkles up there. Why is that, Oma?"

"He might be weary, Beth," I offered. "Perhaps he yearns to be close to God, to be restored by His love and grace."

From my library, I selected a book of Pavel Tchelitchew's art to find an image I thought could depict Raven's see-through gestalt. I showed Beth a drawing of what the author called the "purified oneness" of the painter's soul and spirit.

"Perhaps what you see here is like Raven's essence."

"His *essence*, Oma?"

"His spirit."

"Oh, you mean his silvery sparkles."

What an appropriate description of an essence, I thought.

She studied the drawing with the earnestness of a child. "I want to go back Inside now, Oma, and tell everyone what I saw in your book.

"Oh, before I forget, Oma, there's one more thing I want to tell you. Remember little Amber? The Forest girl? Well, she has started to sleep at night on the ground in front of Elizabeth's House. So, I cover her up with a green blanket." She smiled and faded. In her place now huddled Amber, sucking her thumb. I sat close beside her.

"Mama's yellow eyes are scary," she murmured around the plug of her thumb as she pressed herself against me. "She sees us even when her face is turned away."

"Mama's eyes can't hurt you anymore, little one. You are safe now. Please go back Inside and find Beth. She will take care of you."

The pressure against my side eased. An unfamiliar Part emerged. She seemed in anguish.

"Hands are burning. Don't touch my hands. They burn like fire."

For some time now, I was certain that the red-hot burning to which so many of the Parts alluded represented the unexpressed rage they held against the abusers.

I placed my hands between hers to demonstrate that I would *not* be burned. I asked her to breathe deeply and press the flame-like sensation into my hands. In apparent surprise at my immunity, her eyes met mine for a split second. She immediately turned away and exclaimed, "Eyes are dangerous! But yours aren't like Charles'. His are cold and mean."

"What is your name?"

"Cannotlook."

"It is such a lovely afternoon. Would you like to go outside with me?"

As we sat on my porch enjoying the sunshine, she seemed delighted with the bright yellow of the daffodils my husband had planted around the base of the trees. When she finally turned to face me, her eyes were those of a matronly woman. She adjusted her posture, sat more erect, knees primly together, feet firmly on the blue-painted concrete floor.

"I have not been outside the Inner Realm, on the plane of your conscious-ness, in ages," she said in a proper English accent colored with an Irish lilt. "But today I allowed myself this treat. I have instructed Beth, Rose, and Charlotte to take care of the wee ones."

This must be Elizabeth, I thought.

She looked out at the spring-green foliage of the neighborhood. "Oh, how I love a tree-lined street. And listen to those songbirds. I wonder if I shouldn't have birds in the House for the wee ones to enjoy. I deeply regret that they have missed the miracles of nature. They have lived in Darkness for so long . . . But I do enjoy the positive stillness of the Inner Realm. I do, indeed."

"You are Elizabeth, I gather."

She nodded in a formal, glad-to-make-your-acquaintance kind of way. She asked how I was able to recognize the Parts, create an intimate connection with them, and know what they were feeling. She marveled at my ability to visualize the features of the imaginary landscape and inquired how my imagined presence was able to interact within the Inner Realm.

"Recognizing a Part is not as remarkable as you might believe," I replied after some thought. I explained that, from the first moment of meeting a Part, I carefully observed her posture and body language—how she held her head, her hand gestures, and facial expressions. I studied the light in her eyes, the tone of her voice, and her speech pattern. I estimated her age from her verbal and reasoning skills. To intuit her feelings, I listened with my heart to sense her mood and empathized with what she was experiencing. "I've had a good many years to practice this, Elizabeth—a lifetime, actually."

And there was no real mystery either, I told her, about how I was able to visualize the features of the imaginary landscape. Raven and Beth had been kind enough to draw maps for me, and other Parts had provided verbal descriptions with specific details.

"You asked how my presence can interact within the Inner Realm. What a challenging question, Elizabeth. I must admit, the transition is somewhat mystical." I attempted to put into words how directed visualization served that purpose. "I sit still and breathe rhythmically to enter a meditative state. I then consciously unburden my being of what Raven calls 'intense emotions, faulty perceptions, and human travails' of any kind. Once free of the concrete plane of consciousness, which you have been admiring from this front porch, my imagination ascends to that mysterious domain that embraces all that is known and ever will be known." It was at that level of consciousness, I told her, that my imagination entertained the magical reality of the Inner Realm and became interactive with Joan, the inner self-helpers, and the Parts to serve the therapeutic processes that hastened healing.

She rewarded my explanation with a knowing smile, and then tentatively expressed a wish to touch my face. I moved closer. She reached out and placed her right hand along my cheek. I cautiously touched her hand. Being touched by someone other than her girls was a new experience and a surprisingly pleasant one to her. She asked if I experienced her as being a bit stuffy. I smiled as I said Beth and some of the others had told me she was a bit formal in her black dress and starched apron. They thought she was strict but fair and continued to be somewhat cool and distant with her affection.

"I will consider what you have said and what I have learned and experienced today about touch. I believe it may have a positive effect on my girls if I can soften a bit and touch them in a more caring manner."

Elizabeth's tone of voice became somber. "I am not afraid of the events to come. In the other system, that of Many Voices, changes are taking place." She described that system as being made up of a few older Parts, but mostly younger ones—more than thirty of them, she thought. They had slowly awakened and were beginning to remember verbal and physical mistreatment, neglect, and an existence without love and hope. Some of the young ones were like JJ and Amber. The older ones were like Charlotte, Sophia, and Cannotlook. Elizabeth said she would not be put off by them should they leave Many Voices' Forest—even if they were "unclean."

Then, in an offhanded way, Elizabeth announced, "You may not know, Helper, that I am not a Part but an essence: I am that I am."

This rather biblical remark puzzled me. I promised myself that as soon as I returned to my office, I would look up the passage in the Old Testament that recounts the Hebrew God announcing to Moses, "I am that I am."

I asked Joan to come out, but she had difficulty returning to the present. So, I shifted to a practical activity with the hope this would help her regain awareness. For about twenty minutes, Joan and I swept the sidewalk to my office and pulled weeds in the garden until I heard her say, "I'm back."

We went inside to my library and found the passage in the Bible. I made a copy for Elizabeth and handed it to Joan to take home. Just about suppertime, Elizabeth called and, in her matter-of-fact fashion, apologized for the intrusion and then thanked me for the passage. She explained that she did not believe herself to be divine. "I am not like God, who is pure existence at the center of all being. I do not want you to think I am so grandiose in my self-perception."

I had accepted the suppositions of the distinguished clinicians, Krakauer and Putnam, that having more than one inner self-helper—Raven and Many Voices—was a possibility. Now Elizabeth proclaimed she, too, was

*an essence, not a protector Part, as I had assumed. Was she a third inner
self-helper—an internal mother come to care for the young Joan? Had a
loveless childhood crippled Joan's mother's capacity to nurture her young
daughter? Had the marriage to a violent alcoholic left Joan's mother psychologically barren, which further diminished her ability to provide for her
child's emotional needs?*

"So, you finally met her," Joan said, eyes wide with amazement two weeks later,
as I told her of my conversation with Elizabeth. "I wish I had listened in."

"Elizabeth commented about the increasing number of Parts awakening
in Many Voices' system."

"I'm worried," Joan said, "about the unrest they may cause Inside should
they come forward."

"How do you feel about hearing what they may have to say?"

Joan's eyes filmed over. She abruptly changed the subject. "Before I forget,
Sebunome sent you a note." The words were written in her backward script.
"We'll have to read it reflected in the bathroom mirror."

May 12, 2005
Dear Oma R, [Abridged]
    I know I don't talk much, it's an easy lesson to learn.
Our message has always been "be good, good is quiet, quiet
is safe, safe is invisible." The ones in front [Raven's sys-
tem] are learning that doesn't have to be the truth. Not with
you. I want sometimes for you to see me, to hear me. I'm
still scared to believe. Not because of you. I can hear you
and know you will always be safe. I still don't know how to
trust, maybe being so close to the forest and hearing all the
reasons not to trust truly doesn't help.
    I really just wanted to tell you [that] once you can get
the ones to look at you who are afraid of eyes, [and then
get] the ones to speak who've had no voice, and when you
can reach them all it will be better for the whole forest.

Sometimes looking at one may be looking at many, just so you know.

　　If you see me sometime I hope you'll remember me.
　　　　　　Sebunome

"She has such a sweet spirit," Joan said.

Yes, I thought, *she is scared and distrusting but pleads for those who exist in fearful desperation. Perhaps it was time I reached out to them in earnest.*

I wondered aloud at what age Sebunome began writing backward. Joan thought it must have been when Charles' abuse escalated—around the age of ten or eleven. She believed Sebunome probably kept a diary and acquired this skill to keep her entries secret.

May 13. Joan pulled up her sleeve and held out her arm for my inspection. "I don't know how I got these scratches. I got up today, and they were there. All I recall is dreaming about my grandmother spanking me with a belt." Joan's eyes moved rapidly from side to side, a sign a Part was about to exit.

"I scratched her," a new Part confessed, "to wake her up. I don't like getting spanked."

She walked to the window and admired the view of the garden. As if talking to herself, she said, "No one listened. No one cared."

She turned to face me. "I'm Angelina. Are you the shining lady God promised would come to help us?"

"I'm not sure I'm *that* shining lady," I smiled, "but I *am* here to help you."

"I'm ashamed of being too afraid to stop him. That's why I went into the Forest and fell asleep in a cold, dark place."

Her features shifted subtly, lips tightening.

"I'm not ashamed, like her," another Part scoffed. "I always said to the pervert, 'Get it over with.'"

"And who are you?"

"I'm the slut Charles used. It didn't bother me much," she smirked, "as long as he provided the booze." She crossed her legs, attempting a provocative pose. When I didn't respond, she tossed her head with indifference. "Why do you just sit there? Say something. You think I'm trash."

"I don't think you're trash, but I'd like to know what motivated you to tell the pervert to get it over with."

"Are you kidding me? I wanted to get rid of him as fast as I could."

"That was smart," I said, "and I'm glad you did—get rid of him, I mean."

A half-smile pulled at a corner of her mouth. Slut disappeared, and Joan came back.

"How is it possible that one like that is part of me? How shameful."

"You heard what motivated her to think like that?"

"It's still immoral."

"I see it more as an act of self-preservation, Joan. Remember, Sarah Christine had a certain way to get rid of Charles, too. This one stopped the abuse as fast as she could. I think she's a realist." Then, against my better judgment, I added, "Do you remember what Sarah Christine said when you insisted on taking the moral high ground? She told you to get off your high horse. You might want to consider what made her say that, Joan. And when you do, you may see the attitude and behavior of the so-called slut in a different light."

A few hours later, Beth called to tell me Angelina had not gone back to that "cold, dark place." Instead, Samantha took her to stay with Sebunome at the Forest Edge for the time being. Beth and Charlotte had seen four or five new ones sneak out of Many Voices' Realm. And, from their bedroom window, they watched as Slut ran back into the Dark Forest.

This latter observation suggested that Joan was in a state of self-denial, not ready to acknowledge that one of her Parts had used alcohol-induced indifference to minimize the impact of the physical pain as well as the emotional distress associated with Charles' abuse.

Two days later, Joan, sounding intoxicated, called to let me know she had left work due to losing time. Over the following nine days, I received at least twenty phone calls. The caller didn't identify herself but hinted she had influenced Joan to drink. She mocked our work, suggesting we were wasting our time and that talking wouldn't stop the hurt or the fear. Throughout that period, Joan telephoned to repeatedly cancel her scheduled appointments, again sounding under the influence. Once, her husband rang to inform me of finding several empty bottles in the usual hiding places. Also, he reported Joan's employer had warned him that she made comments about wanting to commit suicide.

"Frankly, Renate," Roger complained, "I don't like coming home anymore. I've had it with the drinking and the never-ending melodrama."

~

Chapter 31

THE MISCHIEF-MAKER

June 1. Her face was a puffy mask as Joan sat stiffly on the couch, avoiding my eyes. I told her of the many phone calls and asked if she had been having flashbacks. Or if a memory had surfaced, causing emotional distress, which she squelched with alcohol. Perhaps my tone of voice sounded accusatory. Discernible dread froze her features. *Chastened, I promised myself to be more considerate of her fragility.*

Joan stuttered, "I can't explain why I fell back into the pit and started to drink again. All I know is sometimes I heard a voice telling me getting drunk is the only way to cope with the stress and forget the past."

"Could that voice be your own?"

"Or perhaps," Joan sidestepped, "it belongs to the Part that made all those aggravating phone calls."

"Perhaps we should find out," I suggested.

Joan closed her eyes. Her head tipped to one side.

"I'm the one you want to see," a Part volunteered jauntily as she came out. "I'm like the fallen angel in my old catechism book. I like to trick Joan into drinking so she can forget. I've been trying to annoy you with my phone calls. I hoped they'd exhaust you and make you frustrated enough to stop helping. My name is Evilette."

"Evilette? That's a most unusual name. I appreciate you trying to help Joan, but drinking doesn't work. As soon as the alcohol wears off, her

177

stress and pain return. Believe me, your phone calls were frustrating, but your mischief will not keep me from working with Joan and the Parts."

Evilette fastened her eyes on me as if assessing my resolve and then said, with a note of swagger in her voice, "Someday I'll introduce you to my twin. Her name is Drunkette. She can masquerade as a drunk without touching a drop." *I wondered if her "twin" was an imagined sister. However, I knew twin Parts or even triplets had been encountered in other cases of MPD.*

"Let me get this straight," I said, amused despite myself. "You trick Joan into drinking and your twin sister plays at being drunk, right? I must admit, you two are quite a pair."

I guess my nonjudgmental attitude and sense of humor disarmed her. Her bravado fell away, replaced with a childlike vulnerability. Her posture as the "fallen angel" dissolved in a fit of giggles.

Before this light-spirited moment passed, I asked if she would be willing to stop her pranks for just seven days. "All right," Evilette hiccuped as she regained her composure.

"Would you be willing to put your promise in writing?"

"Okay, but my handwriting's not so good. Would you write it for me?"

"I will, but you have to tell me in your own words what you promise to do."

With several false starts and some coaching, Evilette made the following pledge:

I promise not to trick Joan into drinking alcohol so she can forget what can't be forgotten because I was told drinking does not work. I also promise not to frustrate the Helper with phone calls because no matter how often I call, she will not stop helping Joan and the others.

After she signed, her features softened, and Beth slipped out.

"Hi, Oma. When you talked with Evilette, we all went to the Meadow and listened. Everyone, even Elizabeth and Raven, thinks it's a good promise. All of us voted on it, and we all said a big YES and cheered." With a twinkle in her eyes, she confessed, "Oma, when we voted, I raised both hands just to make sure."

Her brow tensed, and then Beth admitted she and Rose also had made several of those anonymous phone calls during the three weeks of "troubles." She said they broke the rule in desperation, Beth out of longing and Rose because of extreme discomfort in her vaginal area. She apologized for both and asked to be forgiven.

"Would you be willing to make a contract, like Evilette did?"

"Okay, Oma. That way we won't forget."

We agree never to call Oma Therapist's house late at night because we honor, respect, love and care with all our hearts for Oma. In an emergency (TRUE EMERGENCY!!) we can call Oma's house anytime. Not keeping this promise will mean no calls allowed (ever!) until the rules are respected.

Signed by Beth and Rose

Witnessed by Oma

When Joan reappeared, I handed over the "contracts" and asked her to review the terms to which Evilette, Beth, and Rose had agreed. With tongue-in-cheek seriousness, I quipped, "I hope this might restore some late-night peace in *both* our households."

Chapter 32

LOVE IS LIKE A FLASHLIGHT

June 8. With the hope of restoring her self-respect and that of our relationship, Joan stayed sober all week, recommitted to attending AA meetings, and found a sponsor. I asked her if she knew anything more about the mischievous twins. At that point, Evilette emerged through Joan's features and announced that she and her twin sister, Drunkette, had vowed not to make mischief that impeded Joan's goals in therapy. At her request, we took a short walk through the neighborhood, during which she revealed that Raven had been teaching her how to change. Returning to the office, I gave her a bracelet of small white and green beads to help her keep her promise and to remind her that someone cares.

"My goodness," Joan said upon her return. "I must have gone away for a moment." She looked quizzically at the band of beads wrapped about her wrist.

"That's a gift to remind you of the commitments you've made."

Without explanation, Joan made ready to leave early. Looking down at the car keys in her hand, she took a deep breath and said, "I think I should consider stopping therapy—like right now."

As an experienced therapist, I knew to remain neutral to ascertain the motivation behind Joan's melodramatic statement.

"Not because of anything you've said or done," she rationalized. "You've been more than patient. It's me. I can't bear constantly intruding on your life anymore. All we do is exhaust you."

"What do you think will happen to you and the Parts if you stop therapy?"

She sighed. "Inner chaos and despair. And slow death, probably."

"Is that what you want, Joan? Or do you want to accept responsibility for your life, apply what you're learning, and eventually integrate?"

"But what's the use? If you stop loving me because of all the trouble we cause, I don't want to go on."

"Joan, my love—or anyone else's, for that matter—cannot save you. I wish it could. Please understand that the love I have for you is a gesture of devotion and unconditional regard. The aim of my devotion is not to infantilize you or to make you dependent on me as a substitute for the love your mother was unable to provide. My love is like a flashlight to illuminate your innate goodness, your capacity to love others, and your intellectual and artistic talents. My love is meant to encourage you to hold dear all that you are. Even more to inspire you to marshal your resilience and faith so you can accomplish the work before you."

A ponderous silence lay between us as if her mind had to weigh my affirmation. When she finally spoke, she apologized, "I'm sorry, Renate, my mind got all tangled up with crooked thinking. Sometimes my emotions and guilt distort my perceptions. I do that even though I know it's self-defeating."

She stood, slipped her purse under her arm, and moved toward the door. "I'll see you next time . . . if you'll still have me."

I rolled my eyes in mock exasperation.

～

III

SUFFERING THROUGH

Summer 2005 to Spring 2006

Chapter 33

THE WOUNDED ROSE

July 27. "From what Beth tells me, Rose's pain is not getting better," Joan lamented. "In fact, it's getting worse. She needs your attention."

Round-shouldered Rose sat rocking back and forth, holding her genitals. "Oma, I'm still hurting."

"Would you like to talk about your hurt? That may help some."

A deep sigh escaped her. I suggested talking about this might be easier with Samantha, or perhaps even Joan. She could ask them to help her endure her pain.

"I can't. If I shared my pain with them, I would lose my purpose. And I'd probably die. Being with you, Oma—that's what helps."

When I reminded her that healing can happen if she shared with me and the others what she had suffered, Rose seemed unmoved.

Raven emerged through her silence. "I support your idea of encouraging Rose to share what she has endured."

"You've witnessed how unwavering she is about sharing her pain, Raven. Nevertheless, I want to respond to her frequent pleas for help. So, I propose using a technique that would encourage her to re-remember and hopefully work through the cause of her physical and emotional distress."

"And what would that be, Teacher?"

"I'll guide Rose into a trance and regress her to the events that caused her torment."

I called for Joan. Before I could inform her of my intentions, Joan's head jerked back painfully. She screamed as a Part roughly pushed her aside. I recognized Shadowman by the fury in his eyes and his menacing posture.

"No good will come of this," he sneered, then faded.

Joan struggled to come forward. "My neck hurts. I heard those frightening noises again. They sound inhuman. Was that Shadowman?"

"Yes. He's opposed to my efforts to help Rose disclose her misery."

After Joan left, I sat on the front porch outside my office sipping a cup of tea in the fading summer light, and contemplated what I had to do. *First, persuade Rose to allow me to regress her. Because we had been able to establish a trusting and caring relationship, I thought she would agree. Although Rose had verbalized some of what she had endured and the subsequent vaginal pain, I suspected she held much more. To bring Rose's full story to light, I wondered to what age the regression might take her. I had read the professional literature on regression/progression, taking particular note of how to avoid the pitfalls. From the descriptions of experienced clinicians, I understood the delicate nature of this process. But I could not foresee how severe Rose's pain might become, and this thought gave me pause.*

I had to anticipate how best to safely guide her while putting all my "book learning" to the test in a creative but sparing way. How other Parts might react made me uneasy. Rose's disclosures might reverberate throughout the system with unpredictable consequences. Some Parts might have been co-present with Rose and force their way forward to share what they saw or heard or smelled or felt. On the other hand, some might be further traumatized by these events unfolding before them. In any case, I knew regressing Rose presented my greatest challenge to date. As I closed down the office, I reminded myself of my professional duty: "First, do no harm."

August 3. Joan arrived as hesitantly as the first time she visited my office two years before. I reminded her I was not only responding to Rose's plea for help, but also to her and Raven's. Regressing Rose, I hoped, would reveal the causes of her suffering.

"I'm not sure I want to know."

"I understand your trepidation, but you know how important recovering memories is to healing."

Joan agreed to proceed. I guided her to the Safe Place, and with a reassuring smile, encouraged her to stay present and to keep the shutters and windows open so she could observe and listen throughout the process. Then I spoke through to the system. I addressed Raven to ask for his support and guidance. I needed him to talk for Rose should she regress to an age too young to verbalize. Should events trigger some other Parts to offer cognitive, emotional, and sensory memories they had co-experienced with Rose, his help would be required to keep their reactions from becoming disruptive.

Next, I called on Elizabeth to sequester the youngest Parts in her care. Turning my attention to Samantha, I asked her to keep Shadowman at bay and then invited the Blessing Lady to support the Sentinel in this demanding task. I requested Many Voices to contribute to the process by relating knowledge of the past only she possessed as observer and scribe.

Lastly, addressing all the Parts, I advised they discuss my proposal among themselves. "If you decide to support my plan to help Rose, then lift Joan's right forefinger once. If you do not, then raise her finger twice." I watched for a response. After some moments, Joan's forefinger gave me their sign of approval.

I invited Rose to exit and sat beside her on the couch. "I'm sure you've heard how we are planning to help you. Please sit comfortably, relax, and I will guide you into a trance. You will hear my voice counting backward from your present age of fourteen. Each time I voice a number, you will be a year younger. I will continue counting until you arrive at an age when you first experienced vaginal pain or any other kind of torment. I promise to protect you throughout, sweet Rose. Please trust me to bring you back safely. Are you ready?"

She squeezed my hand.

"Please close your eyes and take a deep breath . . . that's right . . . slowly breathe in and breathe out . . . you will now hear my voice say your present age—fourteen . . . now you're a year younger—thirteen . . . twelve . . .

breathe in and breathe out slowly, that's right . . . now you are eleven . . . ten . . . nine . . . eight . . . remember, Rose, you are safe." I paused here to encourage a disclosure, but when none came forth, I continued to count. "Seven . . . six . . . five . . ." I paused a second time and waited. Again, nothing came forth. This was totally unexpected. Much younger and Rose would be less able to communicate coherently. Keeping the anxiety out of my voice, I ventured further. "Four . . . three . . . two . . . one." A coherent response at this age would be unlikely. I thought the regression had failed and contemplated beginning her progression back to age fourteen.

As I prepared to reverse the process, a wail pierced the silence. Rose slumped off the cushions and tipped over to assume a prone position on her back, arms and legs flailing the air. Raven spoke: "Many Voices says the infant is ten months old. She's being molested and violated by a young man who is her babysitter. The grandfather hears her crying and discovers her lying in her crib with her diaper undone. Her little body is shaking and covered in feces. The grandfather weeps as he washes and dresses the infant."

Rose whimpered. Cautiously, I gathered her in my arms. I thought this must have been the moment when Rose was created, the very first Part to help the infant Joan endure. Now, I assumed, was the time to progress Rose back to the present. I gently laid her back on the cushions and began to count. When I said "Two . . ." Rose screamed. She curled into a fetal position. Raven again spoke: "Joan's father is drunk. As she toddles toward him, arms outstretched, he kicks her in the stomach. She flies across the room and hits a wall."

Rose continued to whimper. I gently caressed her back until her state of shock and the whimpering subsided.

I began to count again. "Three . . ." Beth lisped: "I have to go weewee." She sounded much younger than seven, certainly not more than three. "I in bat'room," she said. "Three men, too. I not see their faces. One pulls down my undies. Tha's bad, and I'm real scared. I want my Mama. He picks me up and moves me up and down against his tummy. It hurts my peenee. It hurts bad. Annie comes to help, and Rose takes the pain."

A terrible chill went through me. Only a toddler . . . had Joan been gang raped? A year of therapy would pass, however, and many more disclosures revealed before I would understand the momentous consequences of all that had transpired in that bathroom.

I restarted the progression. As soon as I said, "Four . . ." Rose bolted upright and shouted, "Mama crying! Mama hurt!" and clamped her hands over her ears. Raven spoke a third time to say that Joan and Rose heard arguing. They got out of bed, walked down the hall, and stopped at the kitchen doorway. They saw the Father in a drunken rage. He is shouting and physically attacking the Mother. He hit her hand with something sharp, drawing blood. Joan and Rose were terrified as their mother collapsed to the floor. The Father lunged toward her and shouted, "I'll kill you." But he stumbled. His knife fell to the floor. The Mother was weeping as Joan and Rose retreated. They pressed themselves against the hallway wall and slid to the floor, covering their ears with their hands. They were mute with shock.

Rose, rocking back and forth, gradually calmed. I thought, *Joan and Rose must have been co-present during this event.*

When I restarted the progression, counting "Five . . . six . . ." Rose began to writhe beside me. Beth spoke again, but with more maturity: "I'm in the kitchen sitting on Charles' lap. He's putting his fingers in my peenee. It hurts. Something hard is in his pants. I'm scared. But I don't cry. Rose is here, too, and she takes the hurt."

I continued counting. "Seven . . . eight . . . nine . . . ten . . . eleven . . ." Rose cried out, "Charles has a knife!" She sucked in her breath. "He's cutting . . ." Her eyes rolled back in her head as if she might faint.

I called her name and asked her to breathe in and out steadily. "Feel through the pain, Rose. That's right. Take another deep breath. You are safe with me. What you are feeling happened in the past. What you are experiencing is a memory . . . slowly exhale the pain."

I repeated this several times, but Rose remained agitated and groped at her neck. Although my heart raced, I asked in the most soothing voice I could muster, "Tell me what's happening now, Rose."

She struggled for breath—agonized gasps. She couldn't speak. I heard Joan say, "Rose is choking. I will speak for her." Joan recounted when she was almost twelve, her mother went to the hospital to give birth to her baby brother. Charles took her to her mother's bed and raped her. Joan thought it shameful and asked how he could betray her mother while she was having his child. He ignored her, and, when she struggled, he pressed his arm across her throat, choking her. "I couldn't speak. I couldn't breathe. I passed out, but Rose was there for me."

I advised Joan to stay in the Safe Place, intending to continue the progression, but Shadowman emerged, uninvited. "Helper, do not do this again," his voice emanating from deep within his chest. "Telling secrets is dangerous," he warned. "They will be punished if you continue." When I acknowledged his warning, he abruptly disappeared.

I meant to resume the progression, but that was not to be. Instead, a mature Part—that's what I took her to be—made an appearance, her facial expression an inscrutable mask.

"Healer at the Outer Realm, I am Many Voices, the one who speaks for many," she announced in a tone devoid of affect. "I have witnessed all that has transpired. May I offer you additional information? When the infant Joanna—that is her given name—was victimized that very first time, her innermost core changed. What you have referred to as Joan's 'Self' is Joanna's life-preserving essence, which initiated the fragmentation process of splitting off the first Part. That was Rose. At that same time, Raven and I came forward. He was called to be the advisor and guide, the one who protects. I was called to be the observer and scribe, the one who remembers." Without another word, she disappeared like a vapor.

Many Voices' recitation jogged my memory that Ralph Allison had concluded that inner self-helpers might materialize when a child is developmentally too young and too fragile to "metabolize" the sexual violence committed against her. What I just heard seemed to affirm Allison's observations.

Regaining my composure after this unexpected first encounter with a second inner self-helper, I attended to the task at hand and resumed the progression. "Twelve . . . thirteen . . . fourteen . . ."

Sweet-voiced, Rose said, "I'm back, Oma."

"So I see." I sighed with relief.

"I heard your voice, Oma, and felt your hand."

"I was with you all the while. To keep you safe."

"I'm very tired now. I want to go back Inside."

"I'm sure Raven, Elizabeth, and the others are waiting for you." I held her innocent face in both hands. She gradually faded.

Raven emerged, exhaustion reflected in his smile. "Dear Healer, permit me to extend my gratitude. Much has been revealed. Much more needs to be made known, but for now we are planning a gathering at the Meadow to share the knowledge of all that has been revealed. Together, we will mourn what Rose and the others endured." His shoulders sagged with weariness as he withdrew.

When Joan came forth, she sat quietly for some time, gazing out the window at the green of high summer as her mind drifted to the past. "It's true my mother named me Joanna . . ." She turned her attention back to me. "I now know much more than I did before," her voice sandpapered with emotion. "I need some time alone with what I've found out . . . When I feel stronger, I'll be able to talk about it."

I, too, was staggered by what had come to light. My body quaked as a surge of anger went through me, gratefully tempered by an immense sadness. I was sure the disclosures made today would be told and retold in more detail and then abreacted by Joan, Rose, and the others sometime in the future. Among the many poems I received throughout Joan's treatment, I believe these two poems best expressed her desperate plea after a calamitous early encounter with villainy.

DADDY
Daddy, did you see us, or were you in a fog?
Did we mean less than even an animal, a dog?
A piece of you created to be used?
Or are these things we remember somehow wrongly fused
Inside a brain where all might be wrongly accused?
Are we too twisted inside to know what is true?

Are we twisted because we're of you?
Daddy, could you see us, or were you in a fog?

MAMA
Mama, Mama, can you hold her?
Can you see her alone and so small?
Mama, Mama, why don't you come,
Can't you hear her call?
A tiny one, no voice to speak, so innocent and pure,
Just trusting so sweetly,
When there's pain but no cure.
Ignored yet seen by eyes that see nothing, just the past
A bloody-mouthed, wide-eyed baby.
How much longer will she last?
Mama, Mama, we know you can't see
That your baby was broken.
That baby was me.

August 23. Joan had not been to therapy for several weeks. Nor had she or a Part telephoned, which was unusual. As her silence stretched, I felt a pinch of worry. I feared our work with Rose may have reached too far back in time and touched too many wounds. When she eventually walked through my door, she had the haggard look of a woman bereft of her faith in humanity.

"I'm sorry I haven't come to therapy for a while," Joan said, her voice without affect. "There's been too much going on in my head, and I just didn't have the energy. But I've been talking to Rose. I told her I was grateful for what she had endured for me and the others. I promised her I'd share her pain whenever I could. Rose doesn't talk to me, but I know she can hear me."

What Rose's regression revealed had triggered Joan's memory. She now recalled the incident in her grandmother's kitchen where Charles first molested her. Her mother and Lillian had been there. Joan also remembered what had happened in her mother's bed, but about being cut, she had no knowledge.

"That kind of depravity is hard to understand," she said. "But the hardest thing for me was hearing about my grandfather having to clean me up after being molested as an infant. I can't imagine how sad he must have felt. I know he loved me even though he never said it."

"And what do *you* feel for little Joan lying there defenseless in her crib?"

She brought her hand up to her mouth, fingers tapping her lips. "There aren't enough tears . . ." was her muffled reply.

"Yes, there aren't enough tears."

Emotionally wrung out, she uttered, "I think Beth wants to talk to you."

"Oma, some of us are now sharing Rose's pain, but it doesn't feel so good. What will happen to us when everyone has shared all their pain? Then will we be grown up? Will I look like Joan?" She frowned, insisting that she didn't look like Joan and hoped that I could see her as she saw herself.

"I can see your upturned nose, your dancing blue eyes, and your bouncing red ponytail. But most of all, I recognize you by your sweetness and your desire to make everyone happy."

Beth admitted Elizabeth had explained that only on the Inside did she look like the girl she perceived herself to be. *I thought this was not unusual for Parts to have a unique self-image. From what I'd read, I understood they often adopted the physical likeness of a child or an adult they related to or admired.*

After Beth, Joan returned. Before she could speak, her body stiffened. Her head jerked back like someone had grabbed her by the hair. Her fingers splayed wide atop her knees as she moaned. Joan's soft brown eyes changed to hate-filled embers. I found myself face-to-face with Shadowman. I took a deep breath and leaned forward.

"I recognize you. You are welcome in this room."

An ugly grimace was his response.

"Thank you for protecting the Parts for such a long time," I said in praise. "I can't imagine how tired you must be."

He continued to stare defiantly, his fists clenched.

"You do look imposing, I must admit. But I know you don't wish to harm me." I smiled. He sat up straighter, chin jutting forward as if bracing for combat. I slowly pulled back.

"I acknowledge your power and strength, Shadowman. Your devotion to protecting Joan and the Parts is commendable. However, your frequent appearances suggest that you're ready to give up your lonely existence."

I leaned forward again.

"After so many years of faithfully shielding Joan and the Parts from the misdeeds of outsiders, I sense you may want to lay down your heavy burden."

Ever so lightly, I reached out to touch his hand. He tensed at my daring.

"If you so desire, Shadowman, I can guide you to become a non-violent helper, one that protects the Parts without threats or meting out punishment."

The lines of concentration at the corners of his eyes deepened. Uncertainty flickered in his "red" eyes. His defiant posture seemed to wilt. He looked conflicted and disappeared hastily.

Raven came forward. "Dear Healer," he stated, "thank you for your compassionate spirit and courage. When you spoke with Shadowman, we all heard what you said. We prayed you would come to no harm."

"Instead of fearing him, Raven, you and the others might consider reaching out to him."

"I will give your proposition serious thought, Teacher. Samantha would be the only one brave enough to approach him."

Joan struggled to come back. In a hushed tone, she finally was able to say, "Did you hear him roar? Shadowman is the most revolting creature I've ever seen. How can that filthy thing be a part of me?" She paused a moment. "But I guess I can't change the fact that he *is* part of me."

His abhorrent appearance, I explained, reflected the abusers' callous and mean-spirited methods, which Shadowman had observed to be effective in controlling her and the Parts' behavior. As contradictory as it might sound, I again told Joan I was convinced he used these techniques to protect her and the Parts from revealing secrets, which he feared would result in further abuse.

"I can't believe he has had such an important function in my survival."

"I get the sense, Joan, that Shadowman now wishes to be released from his burdensome role as the persecutor. I believe the roar you heard was not intended to scare you but rather was an expression of his anguish over the changes he knows he must make."

∼

Chapter 34

SHADOWMAN'S STRUGGLE

August 30. After complaining of a throbbing headache, Joan looked relieved when I suggested she go to the Safe Place. As she withdrew, Joan's features took on a youthfulness. An unfamiliar Part came out, her hands trembling as if she were frightened. When I produced a sheet of paper and a pen in response to her gestures, she jotted down in a girlish hand, "My name is Alice." With painstaking care, she recorded hiding under a bed to avoid being "bad." *I interpreted this as perceiving herself responsible for initiating the abuse.* But "they" always had found her, she noted, so now she "hides" in mirrors and windowpanes where she could never do "bad things."

While she wrote, Alice murmured as if in conversation with two others. *Was she speaking with imaginary playmates, which are sometimes created by children who have been isolated and victimized?* Once Alice lapsed into silence, I asked if she wished to return Inside.

"Inside where?" she asked.

"Inside, where the others are."

"They can't see me." She lifted a glass of water from the side table. "I'm as clear as this water."

Alice then vanished as mysteriously as she had appeared. *Perhaps back to invisibility where she could "hide" as a reflection in a mirror or a windowpane.*

When I mentioned this strange encounter, Joan remembered once seeing her reflection in a shop window that didn't resemble her at all and concluded that must have been Alice.

Rose slipped out.

"Oma, I want to tell you about Jolene. She's Charles' niece. She'd babysit us when my mother and Charles wanted to go someplace. One time, she asked Joan if Charles was doing something bad to her. She was suspicious because Charles had molested her when she was young. Joan was too afraid to say anything, so she just nodded her head. Jolene went and told my mother, who became so mad that she pushed Charles against the wall and slapped his face."

"There's more to Rose's story," Joan added, her affect flat. When she came home from school a few days after that incident, she discovered her mother had arranged for her to stay with Jolene's parents, Aunt Marcy and Uncle David. While there, Uncle David—Charles' brother—repeatedly molested her. Years later, Joan learned he was a known pedophile who had sexually abused his own daughter. "That's when I realized how much my mother had betrayed me. She took me there when she knew very well what might happen. How can any mother do that?"

Within twenty-four hours, Roger called asking to bring Joan to my office. She hadn't talked, eaten, or even changed her clothes since she got home after last seeing me. Roger's green truck pulled into my driveway within the hour. He coaxed his apparently dissociated wife out of the passenger seat. With an arm around her waist for support, Roger and Joan shambled one step at a time to the front door. I helped him seat Joan on the couch and said I'd telephone when his wife was ready to return home.

Raven immediately exited to ask for my assistance in locating Joan. He had searched for her unsuccessfully in all the areas of his Realm. Elizabeth also didn't know of her whereabouts, and neither did Samantha. Even Ana, Joan's helpmate, did not know where she was. I speculated that the revelations of the last few sessions must have left her devastated. Her heart remembered what her mind refused to acknowledge. And so, she had dissociated to insulate herself from the unbearable. Raven wearily agreed.

I lowered my voice and called for Joan. Instead, Shadowman appeared.

"Leave Joan and the Parts alone," he ordered. "They are under my control. I will never let them go. It is my job to protect them. You know too much, and you know too well who we are. They are not safe from the likes of you. Your so-called help has changed the system. Memories are being shared, and feelings are being felt. You know that is not allowed. It puts all of us in danger. Nobody and nothing is safe now."

"Please understand, Shadowman, the dangers of the past have been over for many years. Joan is an adult, and no Part, including you, will ever be abused again. Your methods of protection have become ineffective and counterproductive. You are working against your true purpose—your calling as the protector. That's why I invite you to let me help you change."

Black, scalding rage disfigured his features. "Why should I trust you?" he spewed. "You called me 'archaic' and 'inflexible' when you and Joan talked about me."

Even though I was aware of Shadowman's propensity for violence, I didn't shrink away. Instead, I leaned forward and apologized for my careless remarks. "What I meant was you are blinded by hatred and fear that prohibits you from adapting to the new reality. Your refusal to evolve impedes the healing process. Joan and the Parts are struggling toward the Light. Should you wish to do the same, I'm prepared to support you. Under all your pretense, you are like a beautiful blue diamond. I care for you as much as I care for Joan and the others."

Shadowman took my measure and shook his head in disbelief. He disappeared without another word. But to my surprise, he returned immediately. "I need a smoke." Visibly embarrassed by this show of weakness, he rummaged through Joan's purse until he found a pack of cigarettes and a lighter. We went outside and sat on the porch swing, where he lit a cigarette and inhaled greedily. As his eyes roamed the neighborhood, he spat out his contempt and disgust for the Parts. They were weak and couldn't defend themselves.

He even had to hold their rage for them. At times, their dependency was more than he could shoulder. They were exhausting.

"Then free yourself," I urged. I tentatively reached out my hand. He didn't pull away.

"You're touching me again," he said, looking down at my hand resting on his.

"What motivated your behavior, Shadowman, was wishing to protect those who were too young and too frightened to defend themselves. This is why I'm confident you can become a positive force within the Inner Realm. You need not terrorize the Parts any longer or hate me. I am not an abuser. I am a Helper."

He looked thoughtful. I moved closer and held his hand more firmly.

"I'm tired of being vile and cruel," his voice faltering, "feared by everyone and all alone."

He leaned against my shoulder. His tears came faster than he could wipe them away. I praised him for wanting to surrender his old ways.

In a rasping voice, he asked, "If I surrender my powers and become a helper, will you teach me how?"

"I will teach you how to protect the Parts with love and how to inspire their trust."

We sat quietly to allow the importance of my commitment to sink in.

"What about the Puppets?" I asked.

Uncertainty filled his eyes, and he disappeared.

Raven then emerged. "Many Voices informed me Joan is in the White Zone. I believe if you now call for her, she can hear you."

Joan did respond to my call but looked befuddled. "Where am I?"

"You are with me, Joan. Your husband brought you here a couple of hours ago. You had us all worried. Where did you go?"

"I went as far away as I could. All those memories rushing back . . . I just didn't have the will to go on."

"While you were gone, Joan, Shadowman and I had a serious conversation. He has finally consented to give up his role as villain."

"That's hard to believe."

"Not without a struggle, of course."

"A life without threats and growls?"

"Well, we shouldn't be surprised if it takes him some time to change."

In less than a day, Joan called to announce she was leaving home. Her daughter had called her a "psychopath." She asked if she could come to see me. I awaited her arrival standing outside my office. She sprang from her car with the air of a young person. A kind of innocence had smoothed the lines around her eyes and mouth. She bounced up the three steps onto the porch, saw a broom leaning in the corner, grabbed it, and started vigorously sweeping. She dropped the broom as if something or someone had frightened her. She ran off the porch, around the corner of the building, and out of sight. I searched and found her next door in the carport, pressed between the sidewall of the house and my old Ford. With eyes unblinking, she gazed at her reflection in the passenger-side window.

Could this be Alice? I cautiously approached and said, "There you are. I've been looking for you." The faint, silvery sheen that glazed her eyes dimmed as Joan came forward. "How did I get here? Why am I leaning against your car? All I remember is phoning you and flying out the door . . ."

Once settled in the therapy room, Joan told me that she'd had a particularly violent argument with Megan, who kept insisting that Joan was crazy and that her mother's illness had ruined all their lives. When Megan said she wished her mother were dead, one of Joan's Parts had jumped out to confront the daughter. They'd ended up in a wrestling match on the living room floor. In the melee, Megan bit the Part's wrist, and Joan came out screaming. She had then grabbed her purse and car keys, and left the house. Unable to continue, Joan bent forward at the waist and buried her face in both hands.

I telephoned Stephanie, and, after I explained the situation, she agreed to let Joan stay at her apartment until the strife with Megan settled down.

In session the week after this upheaval, Joan told me she'd stayed with Stephanie for two full days and then went to a motel for another day to pull herself together.

"Since I've been home, Roger has had anger fits over this constant fighting. Megan has threatened to move out. Says she's embarrassed to bring her school friends home, never knowing if I'll act weird or switch and attack her. She refuses to believe that sometimes I can't contain the behavior of the aggressive Parts."

Evilette suddenly appeared. "My sister, Drunkette, is here right behind me. We are the ones who fight with Joan's daughter. We're mad at her because Megan tells Joan she's ashamed of her because of us. When we come out, she belittles us and orders us to go back Inside. That pisses us off. She's very pretty and dresses up real fancy—sexy-like—when she goes on a date. When Joan comments, she becomes defensive and yells and tells Joan how she dresses is none of her business. That's when we come out, and the fight is on. She doesn't understand all we're trying to do is protect her from getting hurt."

"I know you two mean well, but Joan is the mother. It's her responsibility to look after Megan's welfare. Don't you agree?"

Evilette hung her head. "Megan reminds us that we were never young, like her. Charles stole our youth. We'll never get it back." She sighed wistfully and changed the subject.

Shadowman's barren Tree at the Forest Edge, she marveled, had begun to sprout green leaves. I thought, *Green leaves are the promise of a new beginning—life without threats.* The mischief-maker then surprised me by announcing that she and her sister had taken new names. Drunkette chose to be called "Jasmine," and Evilette chose "Eve" after the "first girl-name in the Bible." When I applauded their choices, Eve confessed, "You know, I'm not really bad. I just pretend."

"I've always thought so," I said, smiling.

After Eve withdrew, I asked Joan how she felt when Megan went out on a date.

"It worries me. She's only sixteen. Knowing what I know about men, my heart would break if someone took advantage of her."

"Have you spoken to Megan about your concern?"

"I don't think I could. She'd just brush me off. I can't deal with that."

I reminded her of the grounding skills we had practiced since the first weeks in treatment. "You could use them to stay calm while you talk to Megan about being careful out on a date."

"All I want is to keep her safe." She brushed her hand across her brow as if to wipe away the melancholy there.

I told Joan her concern for Megan's safety and her resentment at Megan's dismissive attitude certainly contributed to her despondency today. Her feelings of loss and regret—and even envy—at never having had a carefree youth like Megan's were factors as well. However, I suggested her interaction with Megan was but one aspect of a complex family dynamic. When one member of a family experienced severe trauma, I explained, other members were systemically affected, displaying specific, symptomatic behavior. "For example, Megan is confused, resentful, and angry about your psychological circumstance. Roger is exhausted, frustrated, and angry about his challenges as your caregiver. Stephanie is hyper-vigilant and overburdened by her obligatory role as intermediary." I advised Joan that her family might well benefit from counseling—an experienced professional with whom to talk about their feelings and the challenges they faced at home.

In the garden beyond the window, the fading summer light seemed reflective of Joan's cheerless mood. Almost to herself, she admitted being aware of what her family was going through. "I'm such a burden. I wish it weren't so."

September 13. Yellow and orange leaves swirled around my shoes as I walked to my office an hour early to review Joan's progress notes. *Despite the turmoil of July and August, trust was increasing in the therapeutic relationship, as were feelings of safety and stability. Joan had become conscious of more Parts and was directly communicating with a few. More and more Parts were exiting, memories were being disclosed, and the pain in those recollections was being suffered through, reframed, and accepted. Shared memories had begun to shape a chronological history of Joan's trauma. Moreover, Joan had started to accept the Parts as components of her fragmented mind and, on occasion, took responsibility for their actions. She did not yet embrace the*

Parts' behavior as an indirect expression of her own needs, thoughts, and feelings. But at times, she did acknowledge engaging in "crooked thinking."

Sitting before me now, Joan angled her head from side to side as if she were experiencing some internal discomfort. She dissociated, and Shadowman exited. His eyes were hooded, but they were more sad than aggressive. "I'm sitting on the edge between evil and good, between the old and the new. Old habits die hard. I doubt I can ever change. The Puppets are hanging lifelessly on my tree. I assure you I have not instructed them to capture any Parts or harm them in any way. Without my commands, they are in limbo."

"There is no need to doubt yourself, Shadowman."

He studied my face solemnly. "It is hard to change."

"Change is difficult," I agreed, "but I will guide you. Remember, I was privileged to see that precious blue diamond at the core of your being. It is a testament to your goodness. Embrace that goodness. Use it to transform yourself and build trusting relationships with Joan and the Parts."

He blurted out, "But must I endure all the horrors that the Parts disclose? And keep that knowledge inside me, remembering everything?" In a voice shrill with agitation, he said, "Must I suffer their hurt?"

"I empathize with your apprehension. I will be at your side when the acts of cruelty are disclosed. The truth is, Shadowman, revealing secrets is the only path to healing. And healing will not be without suffering, but you are brave and strong."

I observed his energies waning and suggested he return to his Tree. "Turn to the Light," I said to hearten his resolve. "Darkness holds no promise."

⌒

Chapter 35

CONFESSIONS

September 20. I received a lengthy, erudite "epistle" from Many Voices. Her "declaration of commitment" promised cooperation and support for change in the system. She announced that more and more Parts in her Realm had awakened and were wanting to be heard. The "observer and scribe" urged Joan, "the Outer Edge," to listen and acknowledge what the "voices whisper in the wind." I appreciated Many Voices' communique. However, at our next session, I did not share the content of her writing with Joan. I chose instead to focus on Shadowman's struggle.

"Shadowman needs our support," I told Joan. "His transition to helper is ongoing."

Before she could respond, Shadowman appeared, his features drawn.

"Do you know why I have eighteen Puppets? I saw a picture of the devil once. His mark is 666. That number, 6+6+6, inspired me to create eighteen puppets to be my minions. They carried out the many defenses I constructed to suppress internal upheavals and keep everyone safe from outside dangers. During our childhood, we could not express any kind of emotion. If we were sad, upset, frightened, or angry, our feelings were ignored. Offering an opinion or voicing dissatisfaction was put down by the ones on the Outside. If we misbehaved, we were rebuked, burdened with more chores, or placed under house arrest. The worst punishment for Joan and the ones on the Inside was confiscation of her art supplies or her small transistor radio. They would disregard her poetry and scoff at her artwork. To avoid this kind of mistreatment, I demanded absolute obedience from the Parts and used any means necessary to prevent forbidden words from escaping Joan and the Parts' lips."

Shadowman looked at me, aggrieved. "I was created to protect Joan and the others from the cruel behaviors of Charles and all the abusers, so the ones on the Inside could hold the Light. You said I could become a helper, but I can never be like the others. I internalized the dark ways of the abusers and used those to keep Joan and the Parts safe. Safe by cutting the Body. Safe by terrifying them. Safe—but with excruciating headaches and stomach cramps. Safe—but with a sharp pencil point into the palm. Any painful reminder to keep the words in."

Shadowman's mouth clamped shut. He lifted both hands, palms out. "The fire of my hatred and rage could burn down the Inner Realm if I let it go."

I suggested the heat of his emotions could be let out in small bursts and do no harm. Shadowman pinched the bridge of his nose. Heaving a sigh, he told me safety throughout the whole system was paramount before he would dare release his ire. The Parts would need to go somewhere safe, he thought, and Joan would need to be sent to the Safe Place. We debated how he could safely externalize his intense emotions. Shadowman offered to write down all the forbidden words in blood. He thought the Parts could help him with this task. I pointed out there wasn't enough blood in the Body for such a grand gesture.

"I will tell the Parts to write the forbidden words in ink," he said. "I will not threaten them, like I usually do. I will be humble. I shall whisper. Yes, I shall whisper as I tell them what to do."

"You mean, you'll *encourage* the Parts to write down the words that reveal their unspoken suffering and self-perceptions."

He looked as if in deep thought. "If I do this, will the redness in my eyes go away? You know everyone says they look like the devil's."

"We can hope," I replied in support of his magical thinking.

He crossed his arms atop his chest. "The list will be long. But one word *must* be written in blood. That one will be mine. Just one word made of seven letters—the number seven is a spiritual number."

"Writing this one word with your blood may indeed drain some of the redness out of your eyes."

"Once the list is complete, may I give it to you for safekeeping?"

"Behind lock and key?" I could see he liked this idea.

Shadowman nodded. "It appears to be a plausible proposition."

In aspiring to become a helper, Shadowman, I observed, had adopted Raven's mannered formality. "Then let's implement what you've planned."

"No one has ever supported me like this before," Shadowman said. "I thank you."

"We will face the challenges to come, side by side," I promised.

"I am sorry I terrified Joan and the others. I am ashamed of my punitive methods that provoked them to endanger the Body. I am craven, undeserving of their forgiveness." He shrank into himself, looking young and vulnerable.

"You have taken the first step, Shadowman, in the process of changing." Like before, I praised his long-standing commitment and tireless efforts to keep the Parts safe. I got up and shook his hand to seal our partnership.

"I am tired," Shadowman said and retreated Inside.

Then, unexpectedly, shy, introverted Sebunome came out. Unable to speak, she reached for paper and pen. She wrote a note in her unique way and handed it to me. I read her message aloud from its reflection in my hand mirror.

I Loved the library! [Abridged]
I have not been to see you because I'm scared of your books—many books. Like a library! Men hurt and ladies can hurt you too. I really am invisible and Rose told me she knows. We all try to be good—good is safe, safe is invisible. Our chant! Don't want to be afraid of you—but it's been a long time. Too alone.

The text continued in random phrases scattered around the edges of the paper:

. . . She wanted to hurt us . . . [the] librarian—
lost safe place. Will you? Hurt us? Touch in a bad way? I
am afraid . . . She wanted to take me to her home after
school . . . Sophia tested you. I need to test you. I am
afraid. [But]I will do it.

    Sebunome

I led Sebunome away from the "many books," out of the therapy
room into the adjacent office. There, she took my hand and placed it on
the left side of her chest. I was reluctant to engage in this intimate gesture but allowed her to re-enact the scene with the librarian as it made
sense to her.

"She kissed me on the mouth with her mouth open," Sebunome whispered.

"The librarian made a terrible mistake," I said as I removed my hand
from her chest. She nodded vigorously. "What she did to you was wrong.
She was a grown woman, and you were a young girl. You trusted her, but
she frightened and confused you."

Sebunome took a small step forward, leaned her head against my shoulder,
and uttered a muffled confession. "I wanted to kill myself, but I went Inside
instead and became invisible. When you had your hand on my chest, it was
a good touch. I was testing you, and you passed. Now I can be visible. I can
be like Sophia and Rose."

"You certainly can," I said as I guided her back into the therapy room.
By the time I sat her down on the couch, she was gone. In my mind's eye, I
saw Sebunome, Sophia, and Rose sitting in the Meadow chanting: "Being
visible is good. Being unafraid is good. Not being hurt is good . . ."

Joan's eyes roamed around the room. Her attention lingered on my
books without any apparent adverse effect. "I loved the library. I loved the
librarian, too. It was one of the few places I felt accepted and safe. I worked
there as a student assistant. Leaving was a great loss. I thought I would die of
loneliness." She smiled sadly. "I believe we really did want to kill ourselves."

Compiling my notes after Joan left, I gave importance to her claim not
to have heard my conversation with Shadowman. *This indicated Joan feared*

bringing to light the words that held the forbidden feelings and perceptions condemned to absolute silence.

Shadowman called about eleven that evening.

"Who I've been and what I've done is despicable. Dying is preferable to living with this shame."

"Taking an honest assessment of yourself may result in feelings like you're experiencing," I said.

"I'm scared. I don't know if there is any goodness in me."

"Your commitment to keeping the Parts safe all these years is evidence of your goodness."

"Talking to the Parts kindly, without malice in my voice, is hard."

"You'll have to practice."

"Will I ever become lovable?"

"You'll have to make some changes."

"What should I do?"

"You might begin by wiping off the slime and bark you cover yourself with."

"Making myself look less like an ogre will make me lovable?"

"That, combined with changes in your behavior. The Parts may even begin to trust you. And best of all," I said, "you may even begin to love yourself."

Silence. And then a sigh. "If I can accomplish all this, could I become a helper?"

"Yes, just like Samantha."

"Like Elizabeth and Raven, too?"

"No, they are helpers of a different kind."

Shortly after Shadowman hung up, the phone rang again. This time it was Beth.

"Oma, Joan has cut herself," she lisped in a whisper, "but I think it was an accident."

Immediately Rose came on the phone. "The cutting was not accidental," she corrected in a hushed tone, "but the bleeding stopped after I put a Band-Aid on."

"Do you know what persuaded her to cut?"

"We think she's afraid of Shadowman. We all are. We don't trust him. And now, he wants us to write down those words. That scares us. And maybe Joan, too."

"Give Shadowman a chance to prove his intentions are genuine. I'll talk about this with Joan in our next session. I promise."

Although both Parts sounded frightened, I was relieved the cutting had been superficial. I thought Joan's self-mutilation was due, in part, to the uncertainty surrounding Shadowman's intentions. More importantly, I believed the cutting occurred to rid the mind and body of the psychological tension created by the terror associated with "those words" and the consequent suffering that had to be worked through.

~

Chapter 36

TICKLE THERAPY

September 27. Joan had difficulty making eye contact and initiating conversation. I waited, but nothing was forthcoming. So, I repeated what Beth and Rose had reported on the phone. I quickly learned Joan's attention was on another matter. Leslie had called her again and wanted to renew their friendship. She had declined after she remembered the heartache Sarah Christine suffered. "Now Leslie is upset, and I'm sad to have lost my only true friend. After Leslie's call, I fell into a deep hole."

"Was that what persuaded you to cut yourself?"

"I don't remember cutting myself."

Joan's jaw muscles flexed. Shadowman emerged and confessed to being the one who cut Joan's thigh. His intention was not to harm the Body but only to warn Joan that caring for outsiders brought nothing but upset and betrayal. He couldn't allow the melodrama with "that woman" to start all over again.

"So, after you cut Joan, you encouraged Beth and Rose to call me?"

"I wanted you to know something was wrong."

I wondered if there was another reason. "Is there something else you'd like to tell me?"

"I'm tired," he admitted. "And always scared," his invincibility seemingly in the balance.

Rather than comfort him, I sat quietly for several minutes while Shadowman contemplated this crack in his persona. Then, to encourage a positive self-assessment, I praised him for wanting to protect Joan and the Parts from the perils of intimacy associated with all outsiders. I pointed out, "We are working diligently to overcome this faulty perception and learn to accept that most human beings can be trusted. I'm depending on your help to realize this goal."

I proposed writing a contract not to harm the Body. He shook his head. "I do not wish to write such a contract on paper. Someone who can't be trusted may find it, and we'll be punished. I'll write the contract on my palm. Elizabeth can be my scribe. I prefer her to Raven. He writes too fancy."

His right forefinger began to write on his left palm while he mouthed the words: *I, Shadowman, solemnly promise to do no harm to the Body.* To seal the commitment, we ceremoniously pressed our palms firmly together to imprint his agreement permanently on our hearts and minds.

The Body gave a jolt, and a young Part hurtled out. She looked startled, as if she just had been rudely awakened.

"Hello," I said softly.

Rigid as a wooden plank, she pushed back defensively into the cushions on the couch.

"Where do you think you are?"

"Shhhh," she whispered. "I'm looking for the closet to hide in so he won't find me—but he always does."

"Who?"

She pursed her lips and said nothing. I assured her she was safe here and asked her name. She shook her head and stammered that she had no name.

"I don't talk to anyone. I'm too dirty." She tilted up her face, pleading, "Will you take me? I have nowhere to go."

"But you do," I said. "You live in a special place Inside, with others just like you." From the quizzical look in her eyes, I realized she didn't comprehend what I was saying, so I asked her age.

"I'm almost seven. I protect my little sister, Lillie," she ventured. "She's a lot younger than me."

211

"Who are you protecting her from?"

"My grandmother. Sometimes she gets mad and screams at Lillian and spanks her with a belt. One time, we played doctor, and Grandmother thought Lillie touched our cousin where Grandmother said not to. She said Lillie was being bad and went to get the belt. Grandmother made me watch. I cried and cried and begged her to hit me instead. Lillie didn't do anything bad."

"So you tried to protect your little sister?"

She nodded.

"Then I shall call you the Protectress of Lillie. I'm curious about why you want to hide in a closet."

She told me of hiding in a closet hoping to avoid being molested, but Charles always found her. "Sometimes, he put his fingers in my private parts. That is a bad thing to do. Grandmother said so. 'Don't ever touch yourself down there or let anyone else touch you. Not ever!'"

"So, you thought you were bad when he touched your private parts?"

"Yes, it made me shiver. He said I liked it, but I told him, 'No! No, I don't like it.' But maybe I did. That makes me bad."

Like with Rose two years prior, I explained "shivering" was an involuntary response, like accidental feelings.

She looked up at me, her eyes full of questions.

I thought perhaps I should demonstrate. "May I sit beside you? And hold your hand? Now I'm going to brush my fingers ever so lightly across your palm. Okay? Tell me what you feel."

"It tickles a little."

"You see? My fingertips tickled your palm without you doing anything. The same thing happened when he touched your private parts. You shivered without doing anything bad. It just happened, all by itself."

"Maybe I wasn't bad?"

"You weren't bad. You are a good girl," I said, hoping to absolve her of the faulty perception.

Samantha came out, her eyes aglitter with amusement. "Who would have thought Shadowman has a sense of humor," she marveled. "He and I have been giggling about the tickle therapy you did with the Protectress. Such a forbidden topic usually arouses his disapproval."

"I'm encouraged that Shadowman is developing a tolerance for such things."

A trace of sadness eclipsed her face, and I realized I was looking at Joan again. In a melancholy voice, she said, "It's true about my grandmother. I was always overly protective of my sister. When my grandmother was on the warpath, we would hide in a closet. Once, she beat Lillian so terribly, I couldn't bear watching. I must have dissociated."

That probably was when the Protectress was split off. It's not unusual for older siblings to protect younger ones from harm, I thought. *The Protectress' disclosure about Charles suggested she, too, had taken her turn enduring his sexual assaults.*

Joan went on to tell me she heard my explanation of involuntary reflexes. My "tickle therapy" changed her childlike misperception. She finally understood her involuntary "shivers" did not mean she had enjoyed being sexually molested. This revelation relieved her sense of shame and left her euphoric.

Joan departed with a bounce in her step. At the car, she turned, smiled, and waved goodbye.

~

Chapter 37

B.G.G.I.Q.Q.I.S.S.I.I.

October 4. Joan told me of going on an outing with two ladies from her church. Their good times together reminded Joan of her life before the Parts awakened. Their re-emergence had robbed her of living a normal existence. She bemoaned her isolation of the past fifteen years.

Shadowman exited. He described how the drunken Father's violent assault on the two-year-old Joan had precipitated his creation. Before he could finish his account, Shadowman's mouth opened wide. A primal scream filled the room. I held my breath. His disclosure, I realized, had triggered a flashback. Whimpering, he curled into a fetal position on the sofa. I crouched beside him and, without touching, called out, "Shadowman, what you just told me catapulted you back to when that traumatic experience occurred. Take a deep breath. Listen to my voice, so I can guide you back to the present, where you are safe." As I continued speaking, Shadowman opened his eyes, slowly sat up, and resumed his disclosure.

Many Voices had been the one who told him that he came into being at the moment the Father assailed little Joan. Young and immature in his thinking, Shadowman began his existence as the protector but had been powerless to stop the abuses. So, he demanded that the Parts avoid bringing attention to themselves: be good, good is quiet, quiet is safe, safe is invisible—b.g.g.i.q.q.i.s.s.i.i.—became their absolute rule. Instead of being kind and compassionate, though, he expressed his protection in the same primitive and hurtful ways of the abusive adults in the family. He became the persecutor—but never like the abusers. When Parts disobeyed the rules, he punished them with threats and bodily harm. His methods turned increasingly harsh and merciless. Now, he thought his misdeeds had made him unworthy of forgiveness.

"I think your original motivation to protect Joan and the Parts was good, Shadowman, even noble, I grant you. However, your harshness has had unintended consequences. The Parts are fearful of revealing secrets, even to me. They are just now learning to overcome this inhibition."

"Is there any hope for my redemption?"

I reminded him of our contract and the faith I had in him. In a gesture of affirmation, he again firmly pressed his palm to mine. And returned to the Inner Realm.

Then, to my surprise, Rose exited.

"For as long as I can remember, Oma," she said, "looking into a man's eyes has terrified me. Charles had the coldest, deadest eyes. We became invisible, hoping he wouldn't see us, and *we* wouldn't have to see those eyes. Now Sebunome and me, and Sophia, think it's time we dared to look into a man's eyes. If we can, maybe we won't be so afraid to stay visible around men."

Rose's wish was easier said than done. Could I conduct such an experiment? And with whom? A directed visualization with an imaginary man seemed to lack agency, and I couldn't call on a colleague because mine were all women. Finding a man who would be kind and nonthreatening and open to such an unusual invitation was improbable. What then? Perhaps . . . the answer was right next door.

"Would you like me to arrange a visit with my husband? He's kind and won't frighten you. If Joan gives her consent, I'll ask him if he'd be willing to let you practice looking into *his* eyes."

"What color are his eyes, Oma?"

"Blue."

She paled and was gone.

Immediately, Beth rushed out with the news that the Part I had named the Protectress of Lillie now wished to be called Maggie. "She's very quiet and sleeps with me in my purple room. But Maggie pees in the bed, Oma. I'm trying to teach her to go to the bathroom instead. But I don't think she understands yet."

"Be patient with her, Beth. Remember, everything is new and unfamiliar to Maggie. I'm sure she will learn quickly."

Her features sharpened, smile-creases around her mouth deepened. A new Part leaned forward, fixing me with a penetrating stare, but did not speak. I blinked, and Beth was back. "It's not nice for someone to push me out of the way and not even say, 'Excuse me.'"

I agreed that everyone should practice good manners if they wished to come out and speak with me. As an excuse for the Part's impoliteness, I offered that perhaps she had only recently fled the Dark Forest and had accidentally slipped through the opening to the Outer Edge.

Beth shrugged, "Well, I pushed her right back. Anyway, all I wanted to tell you, Oma, is we all love to see your presence Inside. You look like golden sparkles."

Next, Samantha came forward. "Raven and I are all over the system trying to contain the chaos caused by the Forest Girls rushing in from Many Voices' Realm. Sometimes I regret not having wings."

I praised her for diligently performing her duties as Sentinel.

Rose slipped out to report back that she, Sebunome, and Sophia had agreed to my proposal and wished to proceed with the experiment on Joan's next visit.

~

Chapter 38

A TEST OF COURAGE

October 11. The pewter clouds, heavy with rain, reflected my mood as I walked to my office. Roger had informed me that Joan was drinking again. Professionally, I knew that without taking steps to address her dependency on alcohol, Joan's drinking eventually could derail the treatment process. My quandary was how to send a woman with MPD to rehab: Who would be present to receive treatment—Joan or a Part? And which Part?

After Joan settled in, I told her I had received incoherent phone messages over the past several evenings. She denied her husband's accusation and claimed she had been numbed out on Xanax and knew nothing about drinking or phone calls. Eve came forward to admit she and Jasmine had broken their promise not to drink. Fear of Charles was their excuse.

"So, when you drink, you feel less afraid?"

"For a little while."

Trying to hide my exasperation, I asked, "Can you think of another way to cope with your fear?"

She thought a moment. "Next time we get scared, me and Jasmine could talk to you on the phone instead of going to the liquor store."

"That's right. Just remember Charles can't hurt you anymore," I said, "and recommit to your sobriety contract."

Rose emerged through Eve's features. "We are ready to test our courage to look into Mr. Caldwell's eyes."

Joan had consented to Rose's experiment. My husband had agreed to participate and signed a confidentiality agreement. Having responded to my call to join us, he now sat on a folding chair directly across from Rose. I observed her body tremble, assured her she was safe, and asked Sebunome and Sophia to watch. Slowly, Rose lifted her head to look squarely into my husband's blue eyes.

"Your eyes are not dead like his," she sighed in relief and moved aside.

Sebunome came forward. At first, she kept her eyes fastened on the carpet. Then, she took a furtive glance at his face. Totally out of character, Sebunome motioned for him to sit beside her. She stretched out her hand, palm up. They touched briefly. Picking up pencil and paper, Sebunome wrote in her backward script: Your touch does not hurt.

Rose came back. "Sophia doesn't dare show herself. But she peeked out to get a glimpse of Mr. Caldwell. She thinks his eyes aren't scary—well, maybe just a little."

My husband smiled at that, and then excused himself and left.

I asked of the three, "What did you discover when you looked into Mr. Caldwell's eyes?"

"Not every man's eyes are dead and scary," Rose declared.

"Maybe I don't have to be invisible around every man," Sebunome contributed, meekly.

Sophia remained silent.

I invited the Parts to go to Elizabeth's House. "Perhaps you can persuade her to host a tea party to celebrate your newfound courage."

Unexpectedly, Elizabeth made a rare appearance. "Helper, the teakettle is already on. The lassies and I can sip our tea out front of the House and delight in the celestial music. We can admire the new leaves unfolding on one of the barren trees and welcome the wee bird, which seems to have come from nowhere to nest there." Elizabeth smiled politely and withdrew.

Raven exited, and in his usual dignified manner, complimented me on the work that had been accomplished. He admired the three Parts' courage and appreciated giving Eve and Jasmine another chance.

"I am gratified to report, Helper, the walls of secrecy between the Parts have *indeed* grown thin. Now they rarely wrap themselves in what you call a 'bubble of amnesia.' They are communicating with one another. Some are becoming more aware of their inter-relatedness and have begun to cooperate in addressing mutual concerns, as you have just witnessed."

"And let's not ignore Shadowman's efforts to abandon his punitive measures," I added. "This has opened the way for sharing additional memories and speaking the truth."

After Raven withdrew, Joan assured me she had heard and seen everything. "So, it wasn't me who drank after all."

"Even though Eve and Jasmine did the drinking, Joan, they are a part of you and you are responsible for their behavior."

"I'm trying," she insisted, a slight annoyance in her tone, "to come to terms with that."

∼

Chapter 39

BRINGING TO CONSCIOUSNESS

O ctober 25. Working through the night, Joan and the Parts compiled a list of words expressing what they thought and felt about the abuse and betrayal which had marked every aspect of Joan's life. I learned of their efforts at the beginning of our morning session when a gray-faced Joan handed over the list that Shadowman had promised weeks before.

Shadowman came forward and with gravity said, "The list contains sixty words. One word has been left off because we feel it holds the deepest meaning. It must be written in blood. I'll prick my finger with a needle and use the blood to write the word on the document."

"May I guide you in drawing the blood?"

He took my hand and held it to his cheek. "Trust me."

With some apprehension, I took a needle from my office sewing kit and held my breath as he pricked his forefinger. At the bottom of the list, he formed in blood the letters that spelled ENRAGED.

"*This*," he seethed, "is how we felt when we were abused, and *this* is how we feel now."

I asked what he wanted to do with the list.

"The Parts have chosen me to read the words out loud. May I begin?" He squared his shoulders, took a deep breath, and read aloud:

AFRAID SAD ALONE/LONELY CONFUSED INVISIBLE
HOPELESS HELPLESS DIRTY HURT WORTHLESS AN OBJECT
DISPOSABLE TIRED ASHAMED EMBARRASSED EXPOSED A
LIVING SACRIFICE HUMILIATED IMPURE DISTANT LIKE PREY
A BAD GIRL SICK + ROTTEN INSIDE NON-HUMAN NO SELF
MARKED SCARRED DIFFERENT THAN OTHERS NOT NORMAL
HIDDEN KEEPER OF SECRETS AN INGRATE SUICIDAL
NERVOUS ANXIOUS CRAZY/CRAZED UNTOUCHABLE
DEFILED INNOCENCE RIPPED AWAY LOST DISLOYAL
DISTRUSTFUL NOT "GOOD ENOUGH" CONTROLLED
SHY/TIMID "LESS THAN OTHERS" HOMELESS/HOME NOT
SAFE USED HATING MYSELF DECEIVED BETRAYED
UNLOVED/UNLOVABLE ANGRY GUILTY UNWORTHY OF REAL
LOVE VIOLATED HAVE(HAD) NO DIGNITY ISOLATED MUTE
DEPRESSED REPRESSED . . .

Shadowman gathered all his strength, and, from the depths of his being, shouted the last word, *"ENRAGED!"*

When his emotions cooled, he declared, "The Parts and I wish to burn the list to purge the torment these words hold."

"In mythology, Shadowman, the gods used fire to purify. They believed burning would release the malignant substances in matter and banish the darkness to some faraway corner of their world. Once your words are purged of their poison, healing the torment may begin."

With meticulous care, he tore each word from the list and placed the strips of paper into an aluminum ashtray I had retrieved from the porch. We left my office and proceeded to look for an appropriate place to hold the burning ritual. Shadowman and I sat beneath a maple tree turned gloriously amber and scarlet.

"Fall," he remarked, "is the best time to do this. That's when we always feel the most helpless and terrified."

I offered him a match, but he pushed my hand away. "They hold bad memories. One autumn Charles threatened to set us on fire. I want to use Joan's lighter instead."

Rushing to my office, I fished out Joan's cigarette lighter from her purse. When I handed it to Shadowman, he formally asked me to bear witness. He ignited each strip of paper, one after the other, and watched as each burning word curled and quickly turned to ash. Shadowman and I sat in silence as fire consumed the last word—*ENRAGED*.

As the ashes cooled, he proposed preserving the remains as evidence of their misery. We returned to the therapy room, where I presented him with a small, cobalt-blue and gold porcelain container. "You may put the ashes in here for safekeeping. They will serve as a reminder of your determination today."

I called for Joan, who said she had witnessed the ritual. I gave her the porcelain container. "This is an invaluable gift," she exclaimed. "So many tears and so much pain. I shall treasure it forever. Someday, perhaps after integration, we can scatter the ashes as the gods of antiquity did."

A week later, Joan said, "I don't know what's happening to me." Her pallid complexion and sunken eyes spoke of days and nights buried in a desolate avalanche of emotion. Her lips a sharp line, she confessed to having been consumed with shame and rage and mean thoughts. But now she was feeling like a nothing, hopeless and worthless. Wringing her hands, she said, "I'm tempted to swallow a bottle of pills."

Alarmed, I suggested she sit a moment quietly, close her eyes, and take a couple of deep breaths. I waited while she struggled to find her equilibrium.

"Can you remember when you started having those feelings and thoughts?"

"Out of the blue, snippets of the cruelest and most demeaning images would race through my head. I tried to ignore them but couldn't. They were like mini-flashbacks, if that's possible."

"What do you suppose brought them on?"

"I have a sense they started right after the Parts and I wrote down those words, and Shadowman read them out loud. I wish it had never happened."

"You mean you wish you could stay unaware of those unspoken thoughts and feelings?"

"Being aware is frightening. But having my perfectly constructed self-image crumble is terrifying. I've lost all sense of who I was."

"The loss of a false self can be an excruciating experience, Joan. We feel helpless and naked when stripped of our old way of being."

"I understand that the Parts and Shadowman were protecting me during all those years of being bullied into silence. But now that the words have been brought into the light of consciousness, must I embrace their meaning?"

"Or flee back into not knowing?" I countered.

A hopeless shrug was her response. Then, as if she had delved more deeply into my question, she said, "I guess that is the choice I have."

Joan fiddled with a button on her blouse. "I can't go on about all this anymore," she sighed and volunteered to go to the Safe Place. I invited her to keep the windows open so she could hear what was said while I spoke with Raven to find out how her state of mind was affecting the Parts.

Instead of Raven, Shadowman exited, his eyes hooded.

"Joan is not the only one feeling suicidal," his voice despondent. "Before I read those words out loud, Joan was innocently unaware. Now her innocence has been corrupted. I want to pull out my tongue so nothing threatening and foul can come out of my mouth ever again."

"My dear Shadowman, bringing to awareness what was hidden is of great importance to our work. Now Joan has the choice to accept or reject what has remained unfelt and unconsidered for much too long."

"And if she can't? She'll be damaged forever," his voice shrill.

"Trust in her resilience. And be assured I'll be there to help."

"I heard," Joan said upon returning, "but I'm not sure I have the strength or desire to do what you expect of me. The meaning in those words is intolerable."

"Do you recall your goal at the beginning of therapy?"

"To become a whole person."

"What is asked of you to become whole?"

"Become conscious of my past."

"And . . . ?"

"Accept what happened no matter how hard that is."

"And . . . ?"

"And suffer it through."

"Yes. And that means . . . ?"

"I have to acknowledge that I was capable—*am* capable—of thinking and feeling what all those words stand for."

"And my hope, Joan, is that, in time, you can accept what you thought and felt were justified responses to what you were forced to endure."

She sat in silence as if mulling over my words. Joan motioned for me to sit beside her. She put her head on my shoulder and whispered, "Thank you for accepting me as I am. Promise not to abandon me in my struggle."

"I will not abandon you, Joan. At the same time, trust in your strength, and lean on your faith."

I felt a tug on my silk scarf. A young girl's voice said, "I no cry so much anymore. I happy. Lizbeth sez I can see you cause you nice. You don't hurt. I not afraid."

"What's your name?" I asked, without looking to see who now was leaning against me.

"Annie. I no cry. Babies cry. I know Bethy. We play at Lizbeth's house. I see Samantha. She big." She stroked the scarf around my neck and snuggled against me. Looking up, she asked, "Are you my mama?"

"No, I'm not your mama, but I know you are a sweet little girl. Beth has told me about you. How old are you?"

She held up three fingers. After a few contented moments, she volunteered to go to Elizabeth's house to play with "Bethy" and withdrew holding onto my scarf.

"I thought I heard a little girl," Joan said, pulling away.

"I just met Annie. She came to visit me and played with my scarf."

"Beth has mentioned her, I think. Isn't she the one that's always crying?"

"All I can say is she was in good spirits today."

"My spirits are better now, too," Joan said, "but I'm tired beyond exhaustion."

I placed my scarf affectionately around her neck. "Take care driving home."

Near bedtime, Joan telephoned to say she had regained some hope. "I've been holding on to your scarf. It's like a lifeline back to you. Thank you, Renate."

～

Chapter 40

PATROLLING THE FOREST EDGE

November 15. Deep lines incised her forehead and the corners of her mouth as Joan forced an uncertain smile. "Staying present all the time wears me out. Keeping the Parts from coming out so my family doesn't get upset drains me."

"I'll put a disc in the boombox. The music might prove soothing."

As the first notes filled the air, Joan dissociated, and young Parts hurtled out over the next several minutes. Gradually, the music in the background seemed to still the agitation.

Raven appeared. "Helper, I am aware of the appearance of the young Parts. They belong to Many Voices' system. I tried unsuccessfully to catch them, but they ran back into the Dark Forest. I am very respectful not to cross the boundary into Many Voices' Realm, where a great number of Forest Girls reside. They hold fragments of memories of the Grandmother's physical cruelty and the Mother's negligence. Plus, the countless molestations by family members and others. They are leaving Many Voices' system in increasing numbers. I advise we make a plan for them to move forward in an orderly fashion. Otherwise, they will flood my Realm. Their secrets may endanger the welfare of the Parts in my care, and possibly undermine the healing achieved so far."

I impressed on Raven the importance of allowing these young Parts to tell their painful memories. Otherwise, integration might never come about. He fervently concurred but prudently advised making Many Voices aware of the Forest Girls' yearnings to move into his Realm and to persuade her to become actively involved in guiding the exodus. Should she be unreceptive, he feared the failure of her young charges to bring the Darkness of the past to Light would result in unpredictable consequences for both systems.

"In the meantime, what can be done?" I asked.

Raven drew a rough sketch of the imaginary landscape denoting specific features and marking the boundary between the two systems. "Shadowman resides closest to the border," Raven pointed out, "and he has volunteered to reactivate and guide his eighteen Puppets to function as lookouts and messengers. They will sound the alarm as soon as a Forest Girl is sighted. Samantha, in her formal capacity as Sentinel, outfitted in golden breastplate and sword, will also patrol the boundary between the two systems. She will discourage any Forest Girl from attempting to cross. Rose, and maybe Sophia, have offered to assist Samantha in her task."

"What a brilliant plan, Raven."

Rose emerged to tell me Sebunome was scared of the Forest Girls. All who lived in Elizabeth's House were trying to convince Sebunome to leave her hiding place at the edge of the Forest and sleep with them in the House.

"There's something else, Helper. It's very strange. The distance between Elizabeth's House and the Outer Edge is getting shorter."

"Why do you think that's happening, Rose?"

She gave me a blank stare.

I thought the shorter distance was symbolic of the Parts becoming less afraid, more trusting of people, and needn't be as far removed from Joan's world.

Beth slipped out. "I'm worried about the Forest Girls, too, Oma. And so are Lisa and Charlotte and Maria. I hear whispering and crying coming from the Dark Forest. It makes me feel like I've been bad."

"What makes you think that?"

She tilted her head to one shoulder. "Because . . ."

I encouraged her to make a list of all the positive and admirable things that made her a *good* girl. Beth looked relieved and promised to work "really hard" on her list.

"Oma, why do I always need refills of your love? I don't know where it goes. It just runs out of me."

How characteristic of victims of childhood abuse. The "hole where the love runs out" requires constant positive reinforcement to mend. I assured Beth that once she made her list and believed she was lovable, the love she was given would not run out.

She asked for hugs. "I need lots, Oma. Some are for me, and some I take Inside for the others." In my mind's eye, I saw her red ponytail bouncing as she went back Inside to dole out secondhand hugs.

I then briefly addressed the Parts in Raven's system and asked all to stay calm and support one another. I told them Raven had a plan for the Forest Girls to come forward in such a way that their arrival would work out well for all.

The Blessing Lady appeared and traced three crosses on my palm. I was grateful for her assurance.

November 21. Today, Joan seemed compelled to reminisce about her grandparents. Her grandmother was Italian, her grandfather Irish. Like many immigrants, they insisted on old-country values and believed girls should be ladylike and practice good manners. As a child, Joan loved them both. Still, she had been afraid of her grandmother's temper. She was hot-blooded, quick to scold and spank. On the other hand, her grandfather had been a quiet presence in the house. He was kind and never unfair. He and Joan shared a special bond. He always called her his "good girl" and encouraged her to do well in school. Growing up, she assured me, he had been a blessing.

"How fortunate for you, Joan. Child victims of extreme trauma have difficulty thriving—both psychologically and physically—without at least one person in their lives who loves and values them."

"Oh, I believe he loved me. And I adored him. However, my mother always found ways to belittle him, which I never understood."

"What do you think persuaded her to do that?"

"Maybe she was jealous. Perhaps my mother felt her father didn't love her like he loved me. You know, my mother didn't have an easy childhood. She claimed my grandmother never cared much for her, was demanding and unkind, even demeaning. They fought constantly.

"When my grandfather died at sixty-four, my heart broke. Grandmother lived on to be eighty. After I got married, my mother told me my grandmother cheated on my grandfather. She had an affair with a man for thirty years. I remember him." Her voice cracked. "He was a bad man. Whenever my grandparents were away, he'd take me to the attic and molest me."

Had Charlotte and Beth's previous disclosures finally brought to Joan's consciousness the memory of the man with black hair? I waited for Joan to return from that dark reverie.

She cleared her throat. "Grandfather never confronted my grandmother about her infidelity. In hindsight, I know he knew. He always made a point of telling me to be a good girl. And not too long before he died, he asked me if I'd *been* a good girl. What could I say?"

Joan looked stricken. "How should I feel about my grandmother? Was she good, or was she bad? Was my grandfather strong or weak? And my mother? How should I feel about her? And what about me? I never know if I'm good or bad."

Joan's eyes glittered with unwept tears. *To a therapist, Joan's mistreatment by her mother came as no surprise. Often the abused become the abusers. Joan's remarkable intelligence, resilience, and faith made her the exception.*

Before Joan left, she gave me a poem written by Rose. My heart swelled as I read it, particularly these last three stanzas.

WAITED FOREVER [ABRIDGED]
We held out in hope for as long as we could
and we waded in the truth and the lies.
Now in the midst of impossible hope
you have come to show us that we can survive.

You have been so deep within us to see sparkles
that no one could see, not a lover as it sounds.
Just pure love that abounds and frees
us from all the bad dreams.

So, we've waited forever to feel such sweet love
yes, we've waited with faith in our hearts.
The time has come for the changes to start
and to believe that we truly belong.
—Rose

Her words spoke of the hope and faith the Parts held for me. But could I meet their expectations? Would compassion and love be good enough to lead them out of their morass? Were my skills and knowledge adequate to pave the path leading eventually to their permanent place of belonging after becoming one with Joan?

~

As a young child, I had a place of belonging. My foster mother—Mama— had taken me in and made me one of her own until one day, my birth mother stole me from her arms. I remember my little suitcase stood waiting at the kitchen door. Its contents damp with tears. A taxi idled in front of Mama's house. The staccato of my biological mother's high heels climbed the wooden stairs. "The war is coming closer," she said to Mama. "It's not safe here anymore. I must take my daughter with me now," her hands reaching for me. Mama held me tighter, her tears lost in my hair. My heart numbed, the shutters of my memory closing as the taxi pulled away, my little suitcase at my feet. For me, waiting forever started when I was four.

~

Chapter 41

THE HELPMATE

November 29. At breakfast, I had promised my husband to close the office early so we could meet with friends and catch a movie. The moment I finished writing my last progress notes for the day, my office phone rang. "I'm scared," Joan slurred. She sounded over-medicated. "I can't stay here. It's too dangerous."

Raven's voice immediately came on the line. "Joan is indeed not safe here, Helper. There are knives and other dangerous objects around. She may harm herself."

"Is Roger home?"

"No one's home," Joan's voice again. "I don't know what to do."

My plans for the evening evaporated. "Hold on, Joan. I'll call Stephanie to bring you to my office."

They arrived about thirty minutes later. Joan's matted hair fell across her face as she struggled to get out of the car. Once standing, her legs faltered. I rushed out to help. Stephanie and I walked her to my office and settled her on the couch. With a weak smile of relief, she slumped back against the cushions, her rumpled housedress loose about her calves. As Stephanie eased herself out of the therapy room to return to work, I mouthed a silent *Thank you.*

"Tell me what's troubling you, Joan."

She gave me a vacant look and then unexpectedly sat forward and furiously pummeled her thighs with both fists.

I grasped her hands. "I can see you're upset."

Disjointed sentences spilled from her mouth. I gathered she hadn't slept, was losing time, and couldn't perform at work. Worst of all, she said Ana was not at her side to help her get through the day. I recalled Joan speaking about Ana once before when she was feeling healthy and full of energy. She and Ana enjoyed a special bond and had been together for as long as Joan could remember. She always felt stronger and more confident to face life when Ana was at her side. *Co-present,* I assumed. Raven called Ana Joan's "helpmate" and had pointed out how they complemented each other perfectly: Joan was sensitive and intuitive, while Ana was pragmatic and a realist; Joan was emotional, but Ana couldn't be bothered with feelings; and Joan liked to help friends and neighbors in need, while Ana focused solely on the family. Ana did the chores and got things done, and because of that, Joan could afford to paint and write.

From her growing sluggishness and the dullness in her eyes, I knew Joan was unable to engage in effective therapy that might bring to light what had frightened her. I suggested she go home and rest, and promised we'd address her concerns first thing in the morning. From the pocket of her housedress, she fished out her cell phone and called Roger at work to pick her up. When he arrived, I advised he watch over his wife until I could see her the next day.

Watching Roger and Joan drive away, I considered the value of merging Ana and Joan. *As I saw it, integrating Ana would stabilize Joan's affect and give her the strength and groundedness she needed to cope more adequately with her life's circumstances, past and present. Following through on this idea,* I thought, *would have to wait until an appropriate opportunity presented itself.*

"I knew this would happen," Joan said the following morning. She looked better groomed and seemed to have gathered herself enough to speak coherently, but she remained emotionally distraught. "Ana used to do it, but now I have to. And I did. I endured it. But I hardly felt anything."

Joan's features firmed. The mature Part now facing me said, "All these years I've been the one having sex with the Husband. At least most of the time. It never bothered me. In fact, I enjoyed it . . . sometimes. And if I didn't, I knew how to get it over with quickly. Know what I mean? But from now on, Joan has to put up with him on her own."

"You must be Ana. I don't think we've met before."

"You just didn't realize it was me. Joan and I can take turns being out without anyone noticing. We're the same age, and our voices and how we express ourselves are alike. So are our facial expressions and body movements. Otherwise," she said with a critical edge to her voice, "we are opposites."

"I guess I'm not as observant as I thought," I said ruefully.

"I came out to tell you some things you should know. I'm the one who found Roger. He was good-looking and seemed nice enough, polite, even kind. And Joan liked him. His parents were religious and had been married for a long time. They appeared so normal next to the Mother who married that pedophile. And the fact was that Joan and I had to get out of that house.

"After they married, I helped give birth to the children. I helped raise them, too. I took care of what needed to be done—I cooked and cleaned and everything else. Now, I'm ready to leave this marriage, and let me tell you, I could do it, too. But she loves him and wants to keep her vows—her promise. She believes, despite his faults, Roger has his good sides. And he has been loyal—I give you that.

"I also came out to tell you," her eyes never leaving mine, "I refuse to continue to function as Joan's caretaker. I'm too weary of being pulled back into that turmoil of endless ups and downs. I need to rest. God has to help Joan now."

"If what you need is rest," I said with empathy, "then that's what you must do. Once you've rested, I hope you'll consider returning to share Joan's responsibilities."

"I don't think that will happen. Joan and I are total opposites. And even if I did return, nothing would change."

"Perhaps you're right," I conceded. "But what if you and Joan merged? That might change your incompatibilities into positives. By merging, I simply mean you and Joan would function as one, combining your and

Joan's attributes and character traits. Imagine, Ana, your pragmatism would strengthen Joan's ability to cope. Your no-nonsense attitude and task-oriented focus would ground Joan's sensitivity."

She said she had no interest in merging with Joan or any of the Parts. "I don't belong to the system. I can live without them." I pointed out that would be difficult, since she was a Part, like the rest. "I just told you," impatient now, "I don't live Inside with the others. I live on the Outside. I *know of* the Parts—I'm just not one of them."

Joan came through her helpmate's features. "I heard Ana say she's too exhausted to continue and wants me to cope on my own. She's fed up with having to be responsible for me. Especially having to take care of Roger, dealing with his temper and meeting his sexual demands. I'm grateful for what Ana does, for propping me up when I'm unable to do for myself."

"I think Ana wants you to become more self-reliant and assertive," I offered. "And with guidance, you might find a way to be more proactive about implementing the changes you wish to make. Taking on more responsibilities to ease Ana's burden might persuade her to recommit to your long-standing partnership."

Then I questioned Joan about Ana's status within the Inner Realm. Joan said that Ana lived in the White Zone—the place where Joan had often gone before she and I created the Safe Place. I asked if she and Ana were aware of one another when they were both there. Joan rolled her eyes and, in mock reprimand, said, "As my therapist, you should *know* that when I'm in the White Zone, I'm dissociated."

Over the following week, Ana occupied my thoughts. I assumed she had been split off from Joan to take care of specific responsibilities for which Joan was unsuited. Would her withdrawal destabilize Joan and consequently the system? Could I convince Ana she was a Part like the others?

During the next session, Ana reminded me that her purpose included looking after Joan's health. She made sure Joan took her antidepressants and did what she could to bring her weight under control. "She's what I care about. I don't care about the Parts. Anyway, they're all too damaged.

You can't reverse any of that. They're all tired of trying. So why don't you just give it up?"

"Your concern for Joan is commendable, Ana, but your choice not to care for the others may have unintended consequences."

"I've experienced plenty of unintended consequences," Ana responded heatedly. She recalled the time when Joan and two-year-old Stephanie had gone to visit her mother. From the start, Ana knew they had made a mistake. She swore never to return to that house and consequently withdrew to the White Zone. Joan became depressed: She despaired, had thoughts of suicide, and was so despondent that she doubted her ability to raise her daughter. Even after returning home, Joan's continued despondency left her incapable of coping and unable to function. That was when Ana first realized Joan's dependency and the consequences of her choice to withdraw.

I thanked Ana for supporting Joan then and now, for sharing details about the past, and for providing further insights about their relationship. I recounted all the ways her character traits contributed to Joan's survival. As I spoke, the tension ebbed from her features. *Perhaps my words of praise had appeased her.* I then invited Ana to visit with me again in the hope of establishing a trusting relationship and exploring how to end her estrangement from the other Parts. I encouraged her to consider entering the Inner Realm to get acquainted with those who resided there.

She looked incredulous. "I don't know how to enter the Inner Realm. I've never been Inside where they are."

This revelation confounded me. "Perhaps another time I can help you find a way in," I said, choosing my words carefully. "Or at the very least, allow me to introduce you to some of the Parts."

After our session ended, I pondered Ana's statement. *If she did not know the way into the Inner Realm and had no relationship with the Parts, who or what was she—aside from being Joan's helpmate? What did Joan and Ana's complementary personalities and inter-relatedness suggest? I was completely baffled.*

December 20. Joan began by stating she had been deeply depressed over Ana's withdrawal. So much so that she could barely hear the Parts but sensed a kind of apathy—a dark mood—had spread over the Inner Realm. When Joan went to the Safe Place, Sebunome exited with eyes downcast, shoulders hunched.

"It's my doing," she admitted. "I'm tired of carrying the sadness and mistrust for everyone. I've been having thoughts of doing away with myself. The others all want to die, too."

"How do you know?"

"They look so tired and sad."

"*Looking* tired and sad doesn't necessarily mean they want to die, Sebunome. Shall we talk with the others and find out what makes them feel that way?"

She shook her head. "I'm just too tired to bother."

Rose emerged immediately. "It's sad, Oma. Sebunome has gone back to her old hiding place at the Forest Edge. And I've gone back to my Cave."

"Why is that, sweet Rose?"

She told me Joan and Beth had previously volunteered to share her vaginal pain, but after a while, they had stopped. And Rose felt dejected.

Samantha came forward. Her eyes had lost their sparkle. She had been comforting Sebunome and Rose, and mentoring some of the Parts, especially Eve and Jasmine. It had sapped her energy. Plus, she'd been busy patrolling the border. Although the Blessing Lady had been helping her contain the Forest Girls, keeping them behind the edge of Many Voices' Realm had been a big chore. Even though she had remained vigilant, Samantha explained, some had slipped out anyway—Angelina, JJ, Maggie, Alice, Cannotlook, and even little Amber all got through.

"Perhaps they wanted to leave the Darkness, like you did, and longed to share the ache in their hearts. We've learned a lot from them. That's a good thing, right?"

"But I'm supposed to keep them from crossing over. I'm the one in charge . . ." Samantha's shoulders sagged. "I need a rest. I'm worried that I'm not a good helper. Maybe I'll go stay with my sister for a while if she doesn't mind."

"I think Sebunome will welcome your company."

Instead of withdrawing, Samantha lingered as if something else was on her mind. "I'm scared."

"What brought on your fear?"

"I . . . We have shared too many memories among ourselves and with Joan. But our *job* was not to tell."

"That was true in the past. But your new purpose *is* to tell so all can heal."

Her chest heaved. "But after we've told everything we know, what then?"

"Have you spoken with Raven about your concern?"

"All he ever says is 'Everything will be as it is meant to be.'"

"Trust in his wisdom, Samantha. Be assured that all you do and all you tell contributes to the process of healing."

Joan's features firmed as Samantha receded. We talked about how those on the Inside mirrored her fatigue and depression. She wondered if the Parts were preparing to go back to sleep. I told her some Parts believed the consequence of telling all they knew would threaten their existence. I suspected this fear was one of the sources of the dark mood spreading across the Inner Realm.

"I heard Samantha tell you about that," Joan said. "I know Rose felt the same way. She was so reluctant to share her memories, so afraid she'd lose her reason for being. I'm devastated by the thought of the Parts infusing me more and more with what they know. Like I told you before, I'm apprehensive about the torment and pain. It's all too overwhelming. I want to go home and just sleep."

～

Chapter 42

AN ABHORRENT MEMORY

December 22. My two o'clock appointment had canceled, freeing me for an hour before Joan came to a special session. My legs needed stretching, and the rest of my body grumbled from too much sitting. Plus, my mind needed a good airing out. I zipped up my down coat and pulled a fleece cap over my ears. Breathing out white puffs of air, I strolled through the neighborhood, delighting in the red and green bejeweled windows and doors. As I passed lawns peopled with reindeer, Santa Clauses, and angels, I felt a dread building. *Joan had seen me just two days before. What was the urgency? Her apprehension at taking in more of what the Parts knew? Or was there another crisis at home? I wished Ana would return to help Joan cope.*

Soon the cold drove me back to my warm office, where Joan was waiting for me in her car. I sensed her despair as she took her seat on the couch and folded her arms across her purse. "Some days, it would be best not to wake up," she said, addressing the wintry gardenscape beyond the window. A memory had come up that she hoped had been forgotten. "It's about . . . terror."

"Terror?"

She shook her head and turned to face me. "It's difficult to talk about it. It's too shameful. I don't want my family to know or anyone else. Not even you."

"You know whatever you say in this room is confidential. No one will ever know. Would it be easier for you if I swivel my chair around?" With my back turned, I waited.

Her voice fraught with emotion, she began: "One afternoon—I think I was about three—my father gathered me up in his arms and carried me to his car. I vaguely remember feeling happy going someplace with him. Turned out we went to a bar, where two of his friends were waiting. He sat me on the counter and ordered something. He let me have a sip. It was white and foamy and tickled my nose. I liked it. I remember my father and his two friends drank and laughed a lot. After a while, my father had to go to the bathroom, and he took me with him. I watched him pull something out of his pants and asked what it was for. After he finished urinating, he said, 'Let me show you what it's for.'"

In the quiet that filled the therapy room, I felt Joan's revulsion. She cleared her throat. "The next thing I remember, I was back at the bar, where my father continued drinking and joking with his friends as if nothing had happened. I don't remember much after that." Joan paused. "Ever since, though, I have this aversion . . . to swallowing."

I turned my chair around to face Joan. She looked at me for several long moments.

"My father violated me, didn't he?" she said, already knowing the answer. "I was so young. How could he? Oh, God," she moaned.

What could I possibly say? No words of comfort would suffice. When she regained a semblance of composure, I thanked her for trusting me with her long-kept secret and gently added, "Recalling your father's appalling behavior was courageous, Joan. You said out loud what you could not consciously disclose before."

"I did, didn't I?" Joan said, just shy of a smile. Telling her story without losing time, without relying on a Part to help her avoid recalling this abhorrent event, was a tremendous step forward. And I told her so.

"The shame doesn't belong to me, does it? It rests on my father's shoulders."

"That's right, Joan. What he did was not your fault. Always remember that."

We sat for a few minutes draped in comforting silence.

Beth came out uninvited. "Oma, I heard Joan tell you about the bad thing my daddy did in the bathroom." She lowered her voice and confided, "Me and Rose and Joan were there. And Annie, too. But Annie went away."

Leaning forward, I whispered, "I remember when you told me about the 'icky stuff.'" *That had been two years ago,* I thought, *yet Joan, till now, had protected herself from this terrible knowledge.*

"A lot of other bad things happened when Mama married Charles and we moved to our new house." She reached for my hand. "I think I'm ready to tell you more about those bad things. And I think the others are ready to tell you, too."

"Anytime you and the others want to tell me more, I'm ready to listen."

"I love you, Oma." She hugged me and planted a kiss on my cheek and went Inside. But she immediately came back. "Oops. Sorry, Oma. I'm supposed to give you your Christmas present."

Beth reached into Joan's purse. With a dazzling smile, she presented me with a small gift-wrapped box and a card, which she read to me. With pride, she pointed out, "All of us wrote the words and signed the card, and we all picked out your gift." Together we unwrapped my present and marveled at the three chrome-plated figures nestled on red tissue paper inside the box.

"Oma, we got you the angels because some of us think you are one."

I expressed my delight for their sweet words and the ornaments, which I promised to hang on my Christmas tree as soon as I got home.

After she hugged me again, Beth faded and the Blessing Lady slipped out to make the sign of three crosses on my palm.

～

Chapter 43

LOVE HUNGER

January 16, 2006. Joan's eyes had a fiery sheen as she walked through my office door. *Had she come to rail against her father's betrayal? A healthy reaction,* I thought.

"I'm at the end of my rope. I can't tell you how aggravated I am with Roger." I hid my surprise at this unanticipated complaint. Since her husband had lost his job, she told me, he didn't know what to do with himself. Like a child, he would follow Joan and Megan around the house, peppering them with inane questions. Or he just sat in front of the TV with the sound blaring. He had no friends. He overate and was cranky, loud, and demanding. And, most bothersome, he blamed her for all his problems.

She blew out a puff of air in frustration. "I can't go on like this. I'd rather live under a bridge."

"Joan, it's difficult to think clearly when one is weighed down with emotion. Let's take a moment just to breathe. Relax, roll your shoulders, and exhale slowly."

After a few repetitions, she said, "Thank you, Renate. I don't know why I forget to breathe when I'm stressed."

"Have you talked to Roger about his behavior?"

"I don't dare. The slightest remark sets him off. I believe there might be something physically wrong with him. Like I told you some time ago, he was in a bad car accident and injured his head and back. Since then, he has become increasingly difficult to live with. Everything confuses him. He forgets to take his meds for his high blood pressure. When he goes to the grocery store, he comes home with half the items. He may have had a concussion. Stephanie thinks he should have an MRI, but Roger refuses. Whether or not he has anything physically wrong, I believe he should see a therapist who could at least help him manage his anger. If he doesn't get help, I'm afraid he'll have a heart attack or a stroke.

"You know, now that I think about it, he's a lot like his mother. She's self-centered and demanding, just like Roger can be. She seems to have a hard time genuinely loving her son—or her timid husband, for that matter. And on top of everything else, his mother is a religious fanatic. When Roger was a boy, she insisted he go to Mass with her every day after school. He had no time to play with friends. I think that left him lonely and insecure."

"How do you know these things about Roger's upbringing?"

"After we got married, he began to let things slip out. And when we visited his family, I would see how he was treated. Sometimes his mother ignored him; other times, she would boss him around like a little boy. 'Get me this, get me that,' without a single thank-you."

"As you have suggested, your husband may very well benefit from seeing someone he could speak with about his childhood and the consequences of his rearing. The next time Roger's anger spills over, keep in mind it's not about you. His outbursts and demands are more likely about his feelings of loneliness and insecurity." I softened my voice to say, "If you get frustrated with Roger, try conjuring up some compassion for that lonely little boy he used to be?"

A somberness filled Joan's brown eyes. When she spoke again, she said, "That's good advice, Renate. I guess when he's venting, I have to be mindful not to take it personally." She stood to leave. "That's something I'll have to work on."

Winter had deepened before Joan returned to therapy in mid-February. "I apologize for canceling the last few sessions," she said, unbundling from her down coat. "I just wasn't up to it." She lifted her auburn hair from the nape of her neck and swept it to one side. Without Ana in attendance, Joan confessed to having been lethargic, incapable of getting anything done. This past week, she hadn't felt well. Sick with nausea and diarrhea. She hadn't eaten at all, and her heart had been acting up again. The cardiologist had told her that her weight was part of the problem. Looking down at her midriff, she could hardly believe she had once been "thin as a rail" when Roger married her.

"I hate being overweight. It mystifies me because I hardly eat."

Joan's brow furrowed. A Part emerged, her head bowed as if having been scolded. "I'm the one who eats," she pouted. "I like lots of butter and cheese on my bread, and mushrooms, and chocolate ice cream. I come out when Joan is mad at that man who lives in her house. That's when I need to fill myself up. My name is Fat-And-Ugly. I live in the Dark Forest and sleep in a casket. I'm eight years old. I have a twin sister. She sleeps in the casket, too. Her name is Thin-And-Bad. When Joan is sad and lonely, my sister comes out and drinks vinegar and takes pills—lots of pills. The other night she came out and drank two whole bottles of pink stuff. It made her sick, and she threw up. She does that a lot." She lowered her voice. "We first came out when Mama married Charles. I hate him."

"What did he do that makes you feel that way?"

"He scared us and hurt us. He pushed stuff down my sister's throat that made her gag. She thinks Charles hurt her because she was bad. And that made her sad, so she stopped eating and got skinny. I got mad cause Mama didn't help us. I guess she didn't love us. So, I filled myself up with food." She lowered her voice again. "My sister threw it all up because she wanted to die. But," her tone back to normal, "when they kept hurting us, we went into the closet and got in the casket and slammed the lid with a loud bang," clapping her hands for effect, "and we went to sleep."

I wasn't surprised by what Fat-And-Ugly revealed. Victims of extreme sexual abuse often develop eating disorders—in Joan's case, alternating between bulimia and anorexia it would seem.

Joan's eyes opened slowly. I could see she was not fully present. When the opacity in her eyes cleared and she became cognizant, I told her I had met a Part named Fat-And-Ugly who cleared up the mystery of her weight gain. I told her what I had just learned and speculated Fat-And-Ugly must have reawakened in Joan's twenties, when she realized Roger couldn't love her as she had hoped.

"It's true, at twenty I was unhappy," a wisp of bitterness coloring her words. "Roger and I had just moved here. I was lonely and lost and realized my husband didn't know how to give me what I needed most—kindness and understanding and companionship. Turns out, we had little in common." Tears welled in her eyes. She reached for a tissue. "I didn't want to leave him. I cared deeply for Roger and couldn't bear to hurt him." She dabbed at her eyes. "After all, Renate, he was the man I had hoped to share my life with." She dabbed her eyes some more and blew her nose.

"So, when the kind of love and companionship you desired from Roger was not forthcoming, that must have filled you with disappointment. Fat-And-Ugly came out to still your disillusionment by filling your void with food. Just as she had when you were eight—to fill the emptiness caused by your mother's inability to love you."

A childhood marred by emotional privation, I thought.

"Fat-And-Ugly also told me she has a twin sister named Thin-And-Bad. When you're depressed, Joan, she comes out and takes laxatives and pills—enough to make you sick."

Joan's head dropped, her eyes focused on her fingers shredding the tear-dampened tissue in her lap. When she was first married at twenty, she recalled being full of romantic ideas, and had not known one thing about the realities of marriage. And how could she, she asked rhetorically, having grown up with people who knew absolutely nothing about love and kindness? And to be fair to Roger, she acknowledged he hadn't known anything, either, with the unfortunate childhood he'd had.

She continued her assessment of their relationship. "I've done a lot of thinking since our conversation last week. I now have more compassion for why Roger is the man he is and what makes him do what he does. Despite our differences, I'm beginning to appreciate how committed he's been to me and our children. I'm grateful for the many times he's protected me from myself. What he's put up with all these years . . . I think most men would have left long ago. But not Roger—he stayed. Maybe, I need to take a step back. Take my blinders off and appreciate his many kindnesses. Accept that compromise and tolerance are necessary to make a marriage work." In mock seriousness, Joan added, "That doesn't mean I have to like him turning up the volume on the TV till the windows rattle." Then with renewed conviction, she said, "I'm not fooling myself, though. Years of resentment won't evaporate overnight. But as I said before, I care deeply for my husband in spite of the years of frustration and misunderstandings."

To celebrate her insight, I invited Joan to have a cup of tea. She took a tiny sip. When she looked up, her eyes were filled with furtive longing. I realized Sophia, the outsider I had not seen in more than a year, had made her way through the Outer Edge.

"Hello, Sophia," I said, holding back my surprise.

The shy Part seemed not entirely present. "I've been hiding," she confided, barely audible, "in the dark, under the basement stairs, where the spiders and cobwebs are. I want to scream, but I can't. His hand is pressing hard against my mouth." She cupped one hand over her mouth and the other over her genitals. "He's pounding himself into me." She rocked back and forth in quiet agony, her eyes unseeing.

"Take a deep breath, Sophia. It's all right to cry out. I'm right here."

Her eyelids fluttered. The flashback faded, and Sophia was with me now, fully in the present.

"I want to tell you about being in the basement with Charles," she said hesitantly. "When something got broken, Mother would make me help Charles fix it. And we always ended up in the basement. Bad things would happen downstairs. I'd try to get away, crawl out the little window high up, but he'd grab me by the hair and pull me back down . . ."

She began to weep. "My heart aches awful."

"It's good to cry, Sophia. It's how we express our sorrow. Telling your hurt is what we practice here in this room."

She dried her eyes with a tissue in the silence of her grief.

Motioning for me to sit beside her, I moved to the couch. Sophia reached for my hand and laid it above her heart. "This is where it aches."

I removed my hand and, in a soft voice, said, "Close your eyes, and breathe in the Golden Light. Feel it envelop your ache. With its help, slowly breathe out the hurt that lies on your heart."

Sophia followed my instructions, but in the middle of the exercise, her eyes snapped open. She placed her forefinger across my lips. "Don't breathe in what made my heart ache. Or your heart will hurt like mine." I turned my head away to assure her I was not taking in the toxins from Charles' misdeeds.

When she completed the breathing exercise, she asked, "Am I ugly? Do I stink?"

I assured her neither was true. If she felt unclean, I suggested she go to Elizabeth's House and ask to take a bath. She politely refused, preferring to go back to Sebunome's place at the Forest Edge. Before leaving and with longing in her voice, Sophia said, "I wish I could have been your little girl instead of my mother's."

My heart surged with compassion for this lonely Part.

～

Growing up, I, too, had wished to belong to a mother other than my own. But a taxi had whisked me away from my foster mother, Mama, whom I loved, to a remote farmhouse that smelled of cows and pigs. This is how I came to live in two rooms with my birth mother for almost a year. I would sit on a wooden bench in the front room, mute, while she paced endlessly. Her volatility paralyzed me with fear. I ate little of the food she offered. When angry words rained down around my head, I cowered in a corner. If she tried to comfort me, I shrank away. At night, I slept at the edge of the family bed, careful to keep distance between us. Late one afternoon, I remember an ominous knock on the door. Two men in black leather coats and wide-brimmed hats stepped into the front room. One crooked his finger at my mother to come along. She took her fur coat off the hook by the door, picked up her purse, kissed my forehead, and was gone. After the sound of their footsteps faded, a neighbor lady rushed in, gathered me up, and hurriedly carried me away.

Time collapsed. I found myself in a small attic space with a tiny window, my little suitcase beneath a narrow cot. Standing at the door, my rescuer put her finger to her lips and said, "Don't make a sound." Then she turned and locked the door behind her. I tiptoed to the tiny window and peeked out over the village rooftops. I pressed my forehead against the glass pane and hoped Mama could see me. I was locked in that attic for nine months, frightened of my captors. In reality, they were protecting me from the Nazi secret police, who were rounding up the children of suspected dissidents.

~

Chapter 44

WE DON'T WANT TO
BE HERE ANYMORE

March 1. Over the last month, the Inner Realm had been in turmoil. Raven sent Beth to report that Eve and Jasmine, formerly known as Evilette and Drunkette, were causing all the trouble. They were "sneaking around and confusing Joan . . . and don't care about us." I spoke through to the system, assuring all that I was aware of their concerns. I advised them to assemble in the Meadow, sit in a circle, and talk about Eve and Jasmine's disruptive behavior. I suggested Eve and Jasmine be offered the opportunity to share their reasons for their discontent, and then, after all opinions had been voiced, those assembled could formulate a solution to appease the twins and restore calm and order Inside.

But the group process proved ineffective. Beth came back to report that the Parts had tried to follow my instructions, but everyone spoke at once. Eve and Jasmine had been uncooperative and ran around the circle the whole time "yelling and saying mean things."

Joan expressed amazement at my endeavor to create a group inside the Inner Realm for resolving the problem. I had thought the Parts had learned to share and cooperate sufficiently and now were ready collectively to find solutions without my guidance. Clearly, I had been too optimistic.

During the week that followed, Eve and Jasmine continued to create chaos Inside and out. They detested Joan's husband and were heard chanting at the top of their lungs, "We do not want to be here anymore!"

At our next session, I decided to give the group process another chance. This time, I asked the Parts to meet in the Safe Place, where they could be sheltered from any distractions staged by the twins. To maintain order, I asked Samantha to be in charge of the group discussion. Although Joan had never gathered with the Parts in the Safe Place, with my encouragement, she acquiesced.

Shadowman exited, offering his assistance to prevent disruption of the gathering by vigilantly supervising Eve and Jasmine but in a "kindly manner."

"If they disregard my good intentions and run amok, I shall instruct my eighteen Puppets to create a net with their bodies and capture them. Once they are contained, the Puppets will form a web-like dome from which the twins cannot escape. This, I trust, will allow those assembled to carry on a discussion without disturbances."

This was Shadowman's first attempt to function as a helper. I thanked him for his service and commitment. Raven, despite his skepticism about the success of this venture, offered to advise the Parts, if needed. Unfortunately, their second effort to find a solution as a group also failed, leaving Joan and the Parts discouraged. I, on the other hand, continued to feel hopeful the Parts eventually would learn to act in concert to resolve their conflicts.

March 21. "I'm sorry for what happened last week," Joan said meekly. "The Parts and I have tried hard to find a solution as a group."

"Don't be discouraged, Joan. Group work requires listening and cooperation to be successful. For now, I suggest I keep working with the twins. So if it's all right with you, I'd like to visit with them today." Joan agreed.

To my surprise, instead of Eve, who is the more talkative of the two, Jasmine appeared.

"Hello, Jasmine. Good to see you. From what I'm hearing, you and your sister seem to continue to be discontented. Are you willing to share with me your reasons?"

"Mostly it's that man in Joan's house. He's a lot like Charles."

"Let me assure you that Roger is not like Charles. He doesn't mean to hurt any of you."

"But Charles did!"

"Would you like to tell me how Charles hurt you?"

"The rule is not to tell."

"But you're safe here with me."

Jasmine looked straight ahead, the light dying in her eyes. "It's nighttime. I hear the floor creak and see the doorknob turn. We make our body stiff. You-know-who comes into our room. Sometimes he comes early in the morning before my mother is awake. He fondles me and takes off our clothes. Before we went to bed, we put on lots of clothes—three panties, two jeans, several tops, and a belt pulled real tight—hoping that would make it too hard to get to us. But it doesn't help. He takes off one piece after the other. It takes him a long time. Then he lays on top of me. He's heavy. What he does to me always hurts, and sometimes I bleed. When he's finished with us, he leaves without saying a word."

She dropped her head, as if drained of all energy. "I think I was fourteen the last time he did this," her voice low, flat.

"How did you endure the pain?"

"Eve and I took turns. We shared it. We also shared our disgust. One time I said 'no' to him. But he got mad and forced me down and began to choke me with his forearm across my throat. I couldn't breathe. I thought I would die. After that, I never said 'no' again." Jasmine made eye contact. "I don't like to talk about it. Choking scares me."

"Thank you for trusting me with your memory. If you wish, I can help you overcome your fear of choking."

"How?"

"I will teach you; just follow my instructions: Sit comfortably. Close your eyes. Breathe deeply in and out. That's right . . . Now, I invite you to imagine the weight of Charles' arm across your throat."

"I'm afraid I'll choke," she said.

"Remember you are safe," I assured her. "What you fear is a memory of what happened a long time ago. Take another deep breath, and listen carefully. Remember what Charles' arm felt like pressing across your throat, but stay calm. Now imagine you grip his arm with your right hand and pull his arm away from your throat. Use all the strength you have . . . that's right . . . and slowly pull it off your throat. You can do this," I coached. "You are brave . . . and strong. Pull his arm away."

With great effort, she did as I had instructed. "As soon as you're ready, Jasmine, please open your eyes." When she was fully aware of her surroundings, I encouraged her to reflect on what had just transpired. "We can practice this as often as you wish until you feel confident that you can cope with this memory by yourself. At night while sleeping, should you feel his arm at your throat, know it's a nightmare. Wake up, get out of bed, turn on the light, and walk around. Tell yourself, 'I'm awake. I'm alright. What I just felt happened in a bad dream.'"

"I heard what you told Jasmine," Joan said upon her return. "You know, I have the same choking memory. Watching me struggle for air while he was raping me seemed to heighten his perverse pleasure. How sick is that, Renate? Do you think Charles was evil?"

"I've struggled with this question for some time, Joan. My understanding of pedophiles is that they use sadistic and depraved practices against children to still their fear of impotence and cowardice and self-loathing. I've wondered what happened to Charles that drove him to become a pedophile. As a child, was he sexually traumatized in the same way he tormented you? Or was he born genetically predisposed to commit such violence, as some clinicians have proposed? Or was he simply born without a conscience? Regardless, I believe his wicked acts robbed him of his humanity and the light in his soul."

Joan cocked her head as though listening to inner voices. "All the Parts paid attention while you spoke," she reported, a bit astonished. "All were in awe of your explanation." After a moment of further reflection, she said sometimes she felt that Charles had "choked" all the life out of her.

I held out my hand and invited Joan to accompany me out to the garden behind my office, where a sickly hackberry tree struggled to survive. For years, a thick vine had wound its way up the trunk, spreading into the branches above. I urged Joan to closely observe how the vine was strangling the life out of the tree.

"Does this vine not remind you of what Charles did? Choking you? Robbing you of life? For me, this crippling vine is like a metaphor for what prevents you from unfolding—the abuse, the lies, the faulty perceptions, and all the other constrictions stifling you."

I retrieved my husband's shears and a spade from the garden shed and directed Joan to cut the vine and free the tree of its stricture. With my encouragement and no little effort on her part, she severed the vine and dug its roots out of the ground. Red-faced and perspiring, she gazed up into the canopy of the tree. "There," she said and patted its trunk.

～

Chapter 45

DISPATCHES

April 4. My telephone rang. "Can I see you for just a few minutes?" asked the melodic voice on the receiver.

"I have an hour later this afternoon. What's on your mind, Joan?"

"I didn't sleep all night. I'll tell you why when I get there."

As she walked in, Joan was cradling a grocery sack in her arms. She placed it within easy reach on the floor beside the couch.

"All night long, way back in my head, I heard a chorus of young voices chanting: 'be good, good is quiet, quiet is safe, safe is invisible'—that old mantra, remember?"

"That was Shadowman's absolute rule to keep you safe. You once told me you had the acronym printed on the inside of your wrist. Now that it's outlived its usefulness, perhaps," I ventured, "Raven can help us find a way to dismantle it."

Joan closed her eyes, and Raven emerged through the stillness of her features.

"I heard, Teacher, and I am in full agreement. Chanting Shadowman's mantra is indeed obsolete. The chorus of voices Joan heard originated in Many Voices' system. I shall meet with her and explain that the old way of protection stifles the young Parts in her care from sharing past experiences among themselves and with Joan and you."

When Joan came back, I informed her that Raven had promised his cooperation. "In the future, when you hear that old mantra, try countering it by chanting: 'I am good. I am visible. I can cry. I can speak out. I will not be punished.'"

"I'll try," she responded, "but you know very well the old way of protecting ourselves is deeply ingrained." *Her noncommittal response made me suspect she was not yet ready to set aside the protective shield of the old mantra.*

Reaching for the brown paper bag, she said, "I've been finding letters and poems hidden all over my house in the strangest places—stuffed in shoes, coat pockets, even under the mattress. Sometimes, I'll find one in a place that even surprises *me*. It appears we've been doing this for a long, long time." She bent close and confided, "I suspect Roger goes through my things whenever I'm not home. Today, I caught him snooping around in my dresser drawer." Tapping the bag, she said, "So I gathered together all these items and brought them here. I hope you'll agree to safeguard them for me."

"I'll be happy to, Joan." *I hoped the writings might hold valuable insights that could hasten her progress in treatment.* Before storing the papers away, we sat on the floor, emptied the contents of the bag onto the carpet, and spread the outpourings wide. There were full-sized sheets of paper, some only half-sized, and some were just thin strips. Many pieces were small and crumpled, yellowed with age, and a few were origami-like packets. There were pages of poems, laments, and essays. Scraps of paper recorded numbers or merely a single word. Some displayed mature penmanship; others were childlike scribbles, calligraphy, or mirrored script; and some were in code. There were also drawings: a knife dripping blood, bleeding hearts, penises, stairs, spiderwebs, and more.

As I handled these amazing traces of bygone torment, carefully unfolding and smoothing and reading them, I observed flashes of emotion on Joan's face—resentment, fear, even anger. A fierce tension enveloped us, which I gathered was the result of the Parts' thoughts and feelings being exposed graphically.

"Oh, my." Joan leaned forward, reached out, and picked up a yellowed sheet of paper torn from a spiral notebook. "I've been looking everywhere for this. It's Diana's letter. She wrote this just before she died in 1994." I strained to hear her reading the letter aloud, her voice a raw murmur.

this is diana. i know i haven't done much to help.
i have been here as a reminder to marjorie of what
happens when all hope is gone. i was the one with
hope. dreams. faith. but the pain and fear became too
much. i'm sorry for what i did. marjorie feels anger
but is doing so much better. i wanted to wait until she
stopped hurting herself. now i can leave. sarah is still
suffering, but i know she is being cared for. i know they
are loved. no one ever listened. no one ever wanted to
be involved. no help. that is what killed me. i think there
is new hope now.

i am ready to go only because my sisters will be
safe. the poem-maker has been a help to me in deciding what to do. i am so very tired. i look terrible. thank
you to the nice lady who gave me a hug. i wish now i
had a kiss, too—i'm almost too awful for anyone to get
close to.

i am sad to leave, but really, i was gone a long time
ago. no one noticed or cared. i love you, my dear sisters. get better. i think you will be safe and loved after
all this time. remember me.

love, diana

"That 'nice lady' was Helen," Joan said. "I remember Diana was a lot like Ana, always helping. She came when I was about twelve—when things were the worst for me. Three years later, after my grandfather died, she went to sleep in grief but woke up when we started seeing Helen. It must have been Ana who told me Diana is buried out behind Elizabeth's House. I miss her. I want to keep this," she said, slipping the paper into her purse.

"Let's put the rest back in the bag," I suggested, and, with care, we replaced the contents into the paper sack. I asked her to pick it up and fol-low me to the storage closet in my office. I opened the double doors, took the bag from her hand, and placed it on a shelf in the farthest corner. "All will be safe here," I said and firmly closed the doors.

"You will not believe this," Joan said, vacillating between annoyance and amusement as she sat back down. She told of a confrontation with Roger, who demanded to know if she was taking all her writings to therapy. She had told him it was none of his business. "You should have seen his face," she said with glee.

Her mood of self-satisfaction changed to one of anxiety. "I'm worried, though, that the company Roger now works for may lay him off soon. Or he may be forced to work out of state if we are to have a decent retirement. And just when we've finally started showing one another consideration and affection." She paused a moment and chuckled. "There might be an upside to his leaving. I certainly won't have to stand at the stove cooking all day." She then recited all the activities she could do in his absence. Last on her agenda was having more time to listen inward to the Parts as they shared new memories—if she felt brave enough.

Joan's intentions to have the Parts disclose new memories directly to her without me present made me uneasy. Would she or any Part become overly distraught or experience a flashback? Act out in harmful ways? Entertain suicidal thoughts? I saw an opportunity now to advance the therapeutic process by encouraging Joan to test her readiness for directly receiving the Parts' disclosures, whatever content they might hold.

"Before you invite the Parts to share at home alone, would you like to practice here?"

"I'm willing."

To help Joan relax, I played a cello adagio on the boombox. I asked her to close her eyes and be receptive to the Parts sharing their memories. She bowed her head and listened inward. Nodding her head frequently as her facial features reflected a kaleidoscope of emotions, Joan suddenly gripped her bodice. A moan escaped her lips, and she began to weep. Concerned, I suggested she thank the Parts for sharing and promise to listen more another time.

Joan opened her eyes. Reaching for a tissue, she sighed, "That was harder than I expected," and wiped at her damp cheeks. Absentmindedly, she tucked the tissue into the cuff of her blouse. A subdued Beth came out to thank her "Oma" for the beautiful music. She recounted what had happened Inside. All the Parts had gone to the Meadow to listen. While assembled there, they gave Joan some of their secrets and hurts. Joan took everything in, and the Parts were thankful to have been heard.

"Oma, there's one more thing. I think Eve and Jasmine want to make trouble again."

"Are they threatening to drink or take pills? Are the helpers and the rest of you being kind to them, as I asked? Are you helping them fit in?"

Through the barrage of my questions, Shadowman's presence replaced an overwhelmed Beth.

"Helper, I'm aware of Eve's and Jasmine's struggle." Thus far, he informed me, they had obeyed his advice not to drink or take pills on impulse. When they wanted to give in, he had reminded them how everyone would be hurt, especially Joan. To keep them from acting out, he said he used my methods and told them to believe in their own goodness to guide their behavior. He encouraged them to accept what Joan had become and to set aside their dislike of Joan's husband. Shadowman frowned, unsure whether Eve and Jasmine could come to terms with their present circumstances. He sensed their strong resistance. I thanked him for mentoring the mischief-makers and expressed my appreciation for his understanding that other Parts had the ability to change, just as he had changed.

"I'm touched by your praise. I'm deeply grateful to have had the opportunity to find the Light within myself. Goodness now guides me in reaching out to the Parts with compassion. But now I must look after my charges, exhausting though they may be."

Joan declared she had heard what Beth and Shadowman said about the twins. She agreed they were worrisome and exhausting and hoped Shadowman could keep them from acting out. Before she left for home, I informed her I had made plans for an extended visit with my relatives in Germany. I would be gone from the end of June to the middle of August and had made arrangements with the therapist she had seen whenever I was away.

"Do you really have to go? Are you coming back? You're not just abandoning me?"

"You needn't fear, Joan. I will not abandon you. When I return, you and I will continue our work. I promise."

~

Chapter 46

ROGER'S CONCERNS

ay 12. Roger came to see me for a private consultation. He expressed anxiety about leaving his wife and the Parts while he worked out of state. Would they drink and drive and have a wreck? Would the animosity between Megan and the twins continue? Could someone get hurt? Would the discord between Joan and Megan continue in his absence? He had followed my advice to reassure the Parts not to be afraid, that he was not Charles and would not harm them. He confided Joan was more receptive to his advances, but he had difficulty coping with her behavior when she regressed and insisted she was a "bad girl." The presence of Ana during intimate moments was a puzzlement and made him uneasy. Lastly, he cautioned that his wife was overworking and on the verge of exhaustion.

Throughout our conversation, Roger would shake his head in exasperation, his fingers combing through his salt-and-pepper hair. I heard skepticism and resignation in his voice. His face reddened in frustration at not knowing what to think or what to do. I encouraged him to remember Joan's and the Parts' behavior and reactions were not about him. Victims of sexual abuse often exhibited the kinds of conduct that were challenging him daily. I praised his sensitivity while interacting with the Parts. Because of Joan's and Ana's interconnectedness, I advised he'd have to get used to her presence, even at inopportune moments, at least until integration. To allay his worries about the drinking, I promised to use every technique at my disposal to oblige Joan and the Parts—specifically Eve and Jasmine—to stay sober.

As he prepared to leave, jangling his keys in one hand, I asked, "Did Joan mention I'll be on vacation for about six weeks? I'm going to Germany to visit my family. I've made arrangements with a substitute therapist to see her while I'm gone."

"I guess we'll manage—somehow," worry in his voice.

Joan's husband's concern for his wife's health persuaded me to encourage Joan to explore appropriate responses to demands on her time and energy.

"I know I'm overworking," Joan admitted three days later in session, "but I've no way of cutting back on my hours. My handicapped boy is just out of the hospital, and his parents can't take any more time off from their jobs. I've asked the agency to send another trained person to share the workload, but there's no one available. Even if there were, they wouldn't see his sweet spirit and love him as I do. I realize being overly responsible for his welfare has exhausted me. And this has created chaos on the Inside and constant switching, which upsets my family. I—"

"Joan," I interrupted, "don't you think you have to first look out for your own well-being? Caring for yourself doesn't mean you care less for the boy."

"Renate, I really don't have a choice."

"What makes you think you haven't a choice?"

"I promised to do all I can for that boy, no matter what. And I *always* keep my promises."

"Even though you're tired to the point you can barely move?"

She sat quietly mulling over my admonition. After some time, Joan reluctantly admitted her willingness to overextend herself was a need rooted in her childhood. As a little girl, she had been a people-pleaser, doing everything for everybody in hopes the adults would notice and love her for it. Sorrowfully, they never had. Joan was about eight when she first became aware of the girl who lived across the street. Grown-ups talked about her in a way that made Joan think she and the girl were alike—lonely and unlovable. *Rejects*, she had thought. So, one day Joan crossed the street and got to know the other girl. She was sweet and loving and happy to be Joan's friend. Though she looked a little strange and was uncoordinated, Joan felt less alone being around her. Her new friend was grateful for every consideration, and Joan felt loved. The neighbors noticed. The more she helped, the more they praised Joan's compassion for the girl with Down syndrome. That had made a deep impression, and ever since, she found extending herself to someone in need—even to the point of exhaustion— made Joan feel worthy of love.

"Perhaps," I offered, "now that *you're* the one in need of care, you can cross that proverbial street to attend to your own well-being and that of the Parts, who are calling for your attention and help. I know your family will love you for it."

Joan squeezed her eyes shut. A single tear found release.

Just after supper the next day, Roger telephoned, his voice a monotone. "Just wanted to let you know, Stephanie and I had to take Joan to the hospital."

"Oh, dear. What happened?"

"When Joan came home late from work again, I saw right away it wasn't her walking through the door. Maybe I shouldn't have, but I got mad, and she flipped out. The next thing I knew, she had a kitchen knife in her hand and threatened if I didn't stay away from her, she'd hurt me."

"Who threatened you with a knife?"

"I think it was either Eve or Jasmine. Anyway, I did my best to reason with her, but she didn't listen. She was furious. I tried to take the knife away from her, but she ran into the garage and crawled under my truck. I got down on my hands and knees to pull her out, but she waved the knife at me and my hand got cut. I'm afraid I handled her pretty rough getting her out and bruised her arm. Stephanie came over, and we rushed her to the hospital. As soon as we got there, the trouble-maker disappeared, and Raven came out for just a minute, and then Bethy."

"That can happen. After an angry Part has caused chaos, she suddenly disappears and leaves it up to others to mollify the situation."

"It's freakin' weird is all I can say."

Joan stayed in the hospital for three days. The doctor reported Joan had prescription drugs and alcohol in her system, which accounted for her unmanageability. From her hospital bed, Joan wrote me a note of apology.

May 17, 2006
Dear Renate, [Abridged]

Again, I've disappointed the people who care for me most—my family and you—and caused everyone pain, fatigue, and feelings of hopelessness. Although I don't remember much of what happened, I know I'm still responsible. I was warned ahead of time by everyone but chose to ignore their good advice. The people I most care for paid the price. My husband, even my daughters, have flat out told me I'm selfish, attention-seeking, obsessive, and stubborn. These were hard words to hear. I don't deny them. How can I? If I don't change, my behavior will destroy my family and lead to my end. I'm sorry, Renate, for what I've caused. I want to earn back everyone's trust . . . and be a blessing, not a burden.

Remorsefully, Joan

May 23. This was Joan's first session since leaving the hospital. I immediately recognized her helpmate was sitting across from me.

"I'm grateful you're back, Ana."

"What choice did I have? Joan's in trouble. She doesn't eat right. She doesn't sleep and doesn't take her anti-depressants. Her ankles are swollen. Her back aches, and her heart works overtime. Plus, she's obsessed with helping that sick boy." Ana sighed with resignation. "I don't take care of other people's sick children. It's too demanding. But when a child is in need, Joan has to help. I couldn't convince her not to work so many hours. What she's doing does her no good. Regardless of how much she gives, she doesn't get what she really wants." Ana dropped her hands heavily into her lap and laced her fingers as if to bring her frustrations under control. "At least, it's never enough."

"What do you think she wants, Ana?"

"She wants to convince everyone she's good and deserves to be loved."

Many victims of extreme trauma, I knew, *needed to prove over and over that they're deserving of love. They willingly sacrifice themselves for others even though it impacts their health, as in Joan's case. To overcome that urgent need would be a challenge for both Joan and me.*

"I tried to warn her," Ana said, "that she was going to have a breakdown and end up you-know-where, permanently. As worn out as Joan is, she's neglecting the Parts, which makes them feel sad and rejected. And a few are just plain mad."

"So I've heard," I replied. "Eve and Jasmine have been especially aggressive."

"Joan had nothing left to give. How could she?" Ana rubbed her forehead as if to smooth away her vexation.

Joan came back.

"You heard Ana, I assume. Remember the commitment you made in your note of apology, Joan?"

"I haven't forgotten, but I still can't cut back my hours until the boy gets better."

"Are you then prepared to take responsibility for what might happen next time you come home from work late and too exhausted to attend to the needs of your family or the internal system? I imagine you must feel grateful that no one was seriously hurt this last time."

Joan's mask of defiance crumpled. Eve appeared.

"It's not Joan's fault. It's mine. No one paid us any attention. So, Jasmine and I drank and took the pills. We wanted to end our misery, but that tall girl with the long black hair told us if we did, all would die, including Joan. So, we asked all the Parts to go to the Safe Place. We thought they wouldn't get hurt there." She hung her head. "Please don't be angry with us for causing all the trouble."

A shift in posture announced Raven's emergence. Unable to hide my disappointment, I asked, "What prevented you or Shadowman or Samantha from doing what you promised?"

"We were too tired, Helper. Joan has been overworking, which depletes the energy of the entire system. This manifests itself in an all-encompassing exhaustion. That's what prevented me from advising and guiding Eve and Jasmine, and weakened Shadowman and Samantha so they could not contain the twins. My apologies; we failed. At this very moment, I lack the energy to continue this conversation. I shall now withdraw and encourage Joan to return to the Outer Edge."

When she reappeared, I reminded Joan of her responsibility to be aware of the twins' concerns, be supportive of their needs, and to stay sober. Before we ended the session, I again gave her a Life Preservation Contract. I asked that she and the Parts read the document with care. During our next session, we would all sign the Contract. That would be our last meeting before I left for Germany, so she and the Parts needed to understand the implications of their commitment.

June 6. Joan pulled the Contract from her purse. She had read it twice and once out loud to make sure the Parts heard and understood. Her voice faltered as she pledged to avoid future crises for her family, and she promised to make time for the ones on the Inside. She also had decided to take everyone's advice and reduce her working hours. With that said, I asked Joan and the Parts to sign the Contract.

Unexpectedly, Raven exited. He reported that all had met earlier at the Meadow to debate what they should do during my absence. Instead of signing my document, they concurred with Shadowman's suggestion that a more binding agreement might be obtained if the ones Inside were to compose their own Contract. They had chosen Joan to be the scribe. After about an hour of contemplative writing, she presented me with a handwritten document defining the responsibilities and commitments of each Part, including Joan and the helpers. Eve and Jasmine were to be sequestered behind a wall of Puppets and remain there under the supervision and guidance of Shadowman, Samantha, and Raven until my return. The mischief-makers would receive compassionate attention from Rose, Sebunome, Beth, and Lisa. Joan would work not more than twenty-five hours per week. She would go to AA meetings regularly and be mindful of nurturing a healthy body, mind, and soul. Everyone would ask for help to avoid a crisis and accept that which was "gladly" given. Lastly, Joan agreed to weekly visits with the substitute therapist throughout my absence.

I signed first, followed by Joan and Ana, the inner self-helpers—Raven, Many Voices, and Elizabeth—and then the helpers, Shadowman and Samantha, followed by the other Parts in attendance.

Signatures:
Therapist: Renate Caldwell, LPC , 6-6-2006
Joan/Ana
rose   ELIZABETH / Beth and Littles too.
Raven   EM
SHADOW +[J +E]   M.V. AND All who listen.
S
(for Sophia) emanueld
Sam

~

264

IV

SOUL SHATTERING

Summer 2006 to Fall 2007

Chapter 47

WRECKED

August 17. After a nine-hour flight returning home from Germany, I barely had unpacked my suitcases when the phone rang. A man's voice I didn't recognize came over the line to report Joan had been involved in a car accident.

"She appears to be drunk, but coherent. She gave me your phone number and asked me to call."

He told me the car was upside down in a ditch. He had found her sitting in the weeds at the side of the road. I asked the Good Samaritan to call 911 while I contacted her family and relayed the information to Roger. After about two hours, Stephanie called to inform me that her father and two policemen had just brought her mother home. Not seriously injured, she had only scratches and bruises but had totaled the car. I heard Joan in the background, ranting. The phone banged against a hard surface. I heard rapid footsteps and furniture scraping across the floor. A few moments later, Stephanie picked up the phone.

"I'm sure you heard. My mother is out of control. She's sitting on the floor, fuming and cussing my sister. I'm going to bring her to your office. You're the only one who can settle her down when she's in this state."

Before I could object, she hung up. Stephanie, escorting Joan, arrived about thirty minutes later. Together, we guided her to the couch in the therapy room. Under her breath, Stephanie told me her mother had fallen asleep in the car driving over. I asked her to wait in my outer office.

I offered Joan a glass of water, which she drank as if parched. She leaned back against the cushions and dozed off. Her short-sleeved blouse was torn at the shoulder, her brown slacks scuffed at the knees. I observed a long superficial laceration on the inside of her right arm, possibly from climbing out of the wrecked car. After only a few moments' rest, she bolted upright.

"Am I still alive?" an unfamiliar voice slurred.

"Yes, you are. Do you know what happened?"

"Some girl screamed at Joan and called her bad names. Accused her of terrible things. It woke me up. I left my hiding place in the Oak Tree and ran out of the Forest to help her."

I assumed Joan must have dissociated at the moment this Part took over and probably knew nothing of what followed. "What's your name?"

"Leaf," she said through a yawn.

Seeing she was low on energy, I told her we could talk more another time. But for now, I would ask a helper to take her back Inside.

Raven appeared. "Samantha will take Leaf to the Meadow. She'll make her comfortable there. She won't be left alone."

"Do you know what precipitated this unfortunate accident?"

"During your long absence, Teacher, Joan and the Parts became dispirited. They feel there is no end to their struggles. It is not in my power to take away their suffering. My calling is to keep them safe and guide them back to the healing path."

"So, was it you who asked the stranger to call me for help?"

Raven smiled graciously and withdrew.

I repeatedly called for Joan to come back. She slowly straightened, rolled her shoulders, and grimaced with the effort. Groggy, she asked for more water. While she drank, I attempted to summarize what I had learned. Joan paid little attention and seemed unable to comprehend what I was saying. *Her emotional outburst probably had spent itself,* I thought. I told her Stephanie would take her home to rest, and we would talk more soon. Joan managed to stand, albeit on unsteady legs. I guided her out of the therapy room and into the outer office, where her daughter was waiting, her gray eyes drained of emotion. I explained that her mother was exhausted but still under the influence. And though she was calm enough now to be taken home, the family should watch over her through the night.

Later, Stephanie phoned to inform me what had persuaded her mother to storm out of the house drunk. Megan had found a half-empty vodka bottle and confronted their mother. They scuffled, but her sister was stronger and poured the vodka down the kitchen sink. According to Stephanie, Megan hurled insults at Joan, who fled her daughter's attack in despair.

"These fights bring out hostile Parts to express your mother's anger," I explained. "This time, I think it was a new Part named 'Leaf.'"

"That must be what happened. Megan has been confronting my mother a lot lately. She hates the crazy stuff Mom does. I've told her to see a therapist to help her understand Mom's problem. But she wants no part of it. She stubbornly insists Mom should change. Period."

"Please ask Megan to be patient. Regardless of setbacks, your mother faithfully comes to therapy and is working hard to get better."

Before Joan arrived the next afternoon, I felt unsure of the direction to take. Should I focus on the potentially fatal auto accident? Or the discord that plagues her relationship with Megan? Or Joan's need to flee to a hiding place in her mind whenever she's unable to face reality? Or her alcoholism? I decided to stay in the not-knowing: Trust my client, allow her to determine what is crucial, and rely on her ability to find solutions.

As Joan entered, clutching her purse protectively, she began apologizing profusely. She confessed to having continued working sixty-hour-weeks while I was in Germany and attributed the cause of the disaster to overworking. She fidgeted in her seat as she told me her husband and Megan, and even Stephanie, distrusted her now. "They monitor my every move. I feel like I'm under a microscope. If I go to the store to buy anything, I'm interrogated. They accuse me of drinking even when I assure them I'm sober."

"What do you think you can do to regain the trust of your family and your self-respect?"

"I know what I have to do," her every word oozing contrition. "We've talked about this many times. First," she began to recite, "my feelings of self-worth are not determined by what other people think but only by how I feel about myself." She stopped. "You know, that is the hardest thing for me." After a moment of further reflection, she resumed her recitation. "Second, keep my promises and make the changes I agreed to before you left. And third, stay sober."

"And that enables you to do what?" I asked.

"Stay in the present and deal with whatever confronts me. Right now, it's Megan. She says she hates me and accuses me of always doing something wrong. She makes me feel guilty about who I've become. I've offered her books to read about MPD. I want her to understand what I'm going through. But she doesn't want to know. She's so hurt and angry that I'm not the same mother she used to have."

"How can you begin to resolve this conflict?"

"I have to accept that I can never be the mother she used to love. Also, I have to learn to accept that I'm not responsible for Megan's reactions to what I've become."

"You actually might do your daughter a favor by allowing her to find a way for getting along with a mother who is now different."

"But she won't," Joan insisted. "She'll continue with her accusations and confrontations."

"What can you do to create some harmony between the two of you?"

There followed a long pause. I waited for her to respond. Instead, she pulled a photograph from her purse. Jabbing her finger at the image of a man standing beside a car, she seethed, "That's him! Megan brought it home after she visited my mother. How could she give Megan *this* photo? When I saw that face and realized who it was, I felt this intense pressure behind my eyes. The Parts started screaming in my head, and I went crazy. I don't remember much after that. I must have gotten drunk. Then Megan and I fought, and the car accident followed."

"Did Megan give you the photo?"

"No, I found it while unpacking her suitcase." She again pointed at the photo and said, "I can't—no, I *won't*—tolerate a picture of Charles in my home!"

"Have you decided what to do with it? Perhaps it would be appropriate to let the Parts also have a say in what should be done with the picture."

Joan closed her eyes. Raven exited to announce the Parts wished the photograph to be destroyed but had asked that Joan complete the task alone, to prove she had the strength of courage.

When Joan re-emerged, her jaw set, she agreed to carry out the Parts' instructions. She asked for a straight pin and scissors as she laid Charles' photo on a small side table. With the pin, she gouged out his eyes and mouth, stabbed his hands and feet, and lastly, his genitals.

"Now you can never look at us, sneak into our room—touch us—or rape us." She reached for the scissors and cut the photo into slivers. "You didn't destroy us. We are free of you, free of your control. We survived in spite of your crimes against us."

I gave her a small, ornamental metal bowl into which she scraped the slivers of paper. She took a lighter out of her purse, lit the pieces on fire, and watched the flame devour the shards of Charles' image.

"Now I need a sheet of paper." She poured the ashes onto the paper I provided and folded it into a small packet. "Will you go outside with me?"

She kept a firm grip on the pouch of ashes as we walked down the street and into an alley. She stopped at a community trash bin. Joan lifted the lid of the rusty dumpster but hesitated. She turned, walked over to a holly bush at the side of the alley, and broke off a short branch with bright green leaves and berries. She gently placed the makeshift boutonnière on the tiny parcel in tribute to the "voiceless Parts in Many Voices' Forest, and those long dead and buried." Opening the heavy lid on tiptoe, she dropped the packet inside. "This is where you belong."

We walked in silence back to my office. "I'm proud of you, Joan. You took your power back."

She squeezed my hand. "I'm ready to go home now."

∽

Chapter 48

LEAF

August 29. "I've heard the Parts talking," Joan began. "Many are in shock since the car accident. They received a tremendous jolt and now realize that, if one Part attempts to harm herself, then all are in jeopardy. I don't think they believed that before. They've decided it's time for the one that caused the car wreck to come out and meet with you."

Joan's breathing became deep and regular. Her body visibly relaxed. After a short time, a Part appeared. "I'm Leaf. I'm the one who drove the car into the ditch."

"Hello, Leaf. We met once before. What caused you to wreck the car?"

"I wanted to help Joan. She was very upset, and I think she had been drinking. So, I came to help. That's what I do."

"Do you know how to drive a car?"

She tilted her head to the side and pulled up one shoulder. "Nooo . . ."

"You gave us quite a scare. But thanks for trying to help. How often do you come out to help Joan?"

"Whenever she needs me. One time I came out when Joan was eight. It was early in the morning. She had to go to the bathroom really bad. The door wouldn't open. She got scared, so I knocked, but no one answered. I had to go so bad I clenched my legs together real tight. But it wouldn't wait, and I wet myself. Then the door opened, and my mother's boyfriend peeked out. His name is Charles. I think he saw the puddle on the floor. He grabbed my arm and pulled me into the bathroom. He took off my nightgown and my wet underwear. He sat on the toilet and pulled something out of his pants. He held me on his lap and pushed me down hard. It hurt awful. He lifted me up and down and started to shake." Leaf drew in a shuddering breath. "Then he whispered in my ear, 'I won't tell your mom that you wet your pants.' I believed he was being nice to me. 'And I'll wipe up the floor, but only if you don't tell. This will be our secret, okay?' Even though he promised not to tell my mother, I knew I deserved to be punished for wetting myself. I thought what he did to me was my punishment.

"I got my school clothes from my bedroom and went back to the bathroom. I wiped the blood off my legs with wet toilet paper and got dressed. Walking to school hurt. When I sat down at my desk, it burned. I could hardly breathe."

"Did this happen when you lived at your grandparents' house?"

"I think so."

"Did you tell your mother or grandmother?"

"No, I was afraid of them. Bad things happen when they're angry."

"Did Charles ever hurt you again?"

"Yes, after Mother married him. He'd sneak into our bedroom . . . Sometimes he'd give me something to drink out of a bottle. I didn't know what it was. It tasted awful. I held my breath and wouldn't swallow, but one of the others must have, 'cause my arms and legs got real heavy, and I sort of got sleepy."

Before she faded, she told me there was another Leaf—her little sister, who was only four and still asleep in the Oak Tree.

Joan blinked her eyes as if becoming accustomed to bright light. Clearing her throat, she stated she had heard Leaf's story. Although painful to hear, she now knew with clarity what had been only a fuzzy and confused memory of when Charles first raped her. She was not surprised to learn he also had been the one who introduced her to alcohol.

"This is one of the important benefits, Joan, of the Parts disclosing their memories. You will gradually have a clearer understanding of the history of the traumatization of your childhood. Perhaps you and Ana and the

Parts may wish to begin recording these stories to create a Lifeline—kind of a timeline of events."

"That would take a lot of convincing. Most of the Parts believe writing down any information about what happened is dangerous. But I'm grateful for what I found out today."

A few hours after I came home from work, I suffered another grand mal seizure. Afterward, I was disoriented and exhausted. My husband helped me to bed where I immediately fell asleep. Sometime after midnight, the ringing of the phone woke me. Mack answered, and I heard him say, "Beth, Oma is sick and can't come to the phone." He hung up without further explanation, and I went back to sleep.

Two days later, my husband received this letter from Beth.

August 31, 2006

Dear Mr. Opa Caldwell,

This is the last time I will call you Opa or even talk to you. Oma said you were diferent (sic). I just asked to talk to you for a second. Just to tell you I will be careful and follow the rules so Oma can keep strong. I wanted to see her today.

But not.

If you were too busy you could say so. But you made me feel like a bad girl like a bothering person and you didn't even say goodby (sic) and just hung up on the phone!! I was trying to be good and didn't even ask to talk to Oma because I know she is tired at night. But I was not good and now I think you are like regular men and don't like me either. You hurt me not like they did but it hurts still. I think I will be afraid of you now. I thought you would listen for a second—but no one but Oma can I guess. I am sorry to have been bad. I am sorry you to (sic) can't love me either. I will be invisible to you now to (sic).

Beth—b.g.g.i.q.q.i.s.s.i.i.! I know and now you do to (sic). I will be quiet and invisible that means good.

274

September 12. This was Joan's first therapy session after my seizure. She commiserated: "I hope you're feeling better. I'm sorry Beth called you that evening you were ill. She told me Elizabeth reprimanded her. I know we've promised many times to call you less frequently, but when the younger Parts feel the need to hear your voice, it seems they call regardless. To respect your privacy in the future, Raven and I decided to implement some new rules. He and the mature Parts gathered the younger ones together in the Meadow to inform them about the new arrangements. I would be their spokesperson and relay their messages and concerns directly to you."

Unlike her usual exuberant and chatty self, Beth came out looking distressed. "Oma, I miss you, and I'm sad. Elizabeth said I can't call you anymore when I need to. I won't be able to tell you what me and Charlotte and Lisa and all the others are doing at Elizabeth's house. And I can't let you know when someone on the Inside needs your help. Or even let you know what they are feeling. If I can't give you their messages, I won't have a job."

"Dear Beth, do you remember what Joan said when she first came to see me? For some time now, I've been doing just as she asked, helping her and all of you to get better and eventually become one person. Now Raven and Joan have decided it's time to take the next step and let Joan be the spokesperson for all of you. That way, she will become more aware of how everyone Inside feels and thinks, and what memories you all share. This is her chance to learn to speak in one voice, which she must do once all of you integrate."

"I know, Oma," Beth replied, sorrow in her voice, "but I want to be just me, my own person, not mixed up with anyone else. I'm afraid to be part of Joan. I'll be lost and won't be able to get hugs anymore. It makes me sad, Oma. Sadder than ever."

"Beth, I'll do my best to help you with your sadness. But try to understand that integrating with Joan will not cause you to lose yourself. You will still be you, only in a different way. This means Joan will have all your memories and feelings, and all the many wonderful qualities you possess—all that you are will still be there."

With that said, I fell silent, waiting to see how Beth might respond.

"I get it, Oma," she said with an impish smile. "You're trying to smush us together like a grilled cheese sandwich."

Her metaphor delighted me. "What a creative way of saying what I just tried to explain with lots of words. Who made you so smart?"

She looked at me, askance. "You know, Omaaaaa . . ."

"Tell me," I pleaded good-naturedly.

"It's God, Oma."

Then her lightheartedness sank. She forcefully pressed her palms together. "Being smushed like this will hurt, I think."

"Sometimes it will," I agreed, "but other times it won't. I imagine when you and the other young Parts integrate with Joan, you will experience the joy of what it means to be part of one mind and one heart and one spirit, just like God intended all along."

As Beth retreated inward with hugs for her and some to share, I decided Raven and I should revisit how best to regulate the Parts' phone calls. Raven immediately came to the forefront and congratulated me on the explanation I had provided Beth. Raven and I were sitting side by side. I placed my hand lightly on his arm. We both sat somewhat stiffly in silence. Looking straight ahead, he announced, "The human touch is quite pleasant. Physical contact is foreign to me. I fly above the physical plane of human interaction."

"From my vantage point," I said, "you bestow Joan and the Parts with a special kind of love that inspires them to continue the process of healing even when doubts and exhaustion overwhelm them."

"Dear Healer, what you call my 'special kind of love,' when combined with your love for the work, your compassion, and the affection you extend to Joan and the Parts, that combination is what inspires them to hope they can overcome the past and develop the strength to believe they are capable of transformation. That is what will enable Joan to reach out for a life free of doubt and fear, a life of self-determination." Raven bowed respectfully and receded.

Joan came forward and thanked me for defusing Beth's anxiety about integration. As she gathered herself to leave, she laughed, "Oh, my—I almost forgot to give you Beth's note for Mr. Opa." I promised to deliver it promptly.

September 10, 2006
Dear Mr. Opa,

   I am sorry about what I wrote. I know the rules are not to call your house to talk to anyone after 7 now. I won't do that again. I'm sorry I got mad. I still love you and hope you will still love me and not be too mad.
Love, Beth

After reading Beth's apology later that day, my husband immediately responded.

September 14, 2006
Dear Beth,
It was OK if you got mad at me because I hurt your feelings. I'm sorry for how I answered the phone, but I'm glad you got mad and dared to write me a note. Your behavior is healthy and mature. That makes me happy for you. I will always love you, even if I make mistakes that hurt your feelings. Never doubt I care for who you are.
Love, Mr. Opa

Chapter 49

THE RESCUE

Regardless of having survived a potentially fatal car accident and the victory she gained by disposing of Charles' photo, Joan did not honor her insights and promises. Over the following five-week period, while continuing to deal with life's challenges using worn-out survival strategies, she drank, suffered debilitating hangovers, spiraled into apathy, and threatened suicide. Empty bottles strewn around the house enraged Megan and led to verbal and physical altercations. This, in turn, further upset Leaf and persuaded other Parts to act out.

Adding to my concern, Roger continued to work out of state as Joan stumbled from one crisis to the next. Stephanie and I did what we could to protect her from any mishaps. During moments of sobriety, Joan agreed that her self-destructiveness not only undermined her health and the patience of her family but also stymied the treatment process. She would offer ways to interrupt the unending cycle of crises, and I would impatiently wave her words away as hollow promises. Like me, the inner self-helpers seemed dispirited and too weary to infuse Joan with energy. Raven informed me Joan had turned a deaf ear to his attempt to advise and guide her. In a missive to me, Many Voices observed that Joan's refusal to reawaken to the task of healing, plus her blatant irreverence for her interdependence with both systems "may lead to the ending of all."

October 19. "I think Raven and the helpers have abandoned me." Joan's affect was flat, her physical movements sluggish when she resumed therapy. "I've failed you, failed my family and the Parts, and failed myself. I have to find my way back, but I don't know how."

"I admit, Joan, I'm at a loss, too. Allow me to consult with Raven. In the meantime, may I suggest you go to the Safe Place. Lock the door, shutter the windows, and suspend your worries for now."

In advance of Raven's appearance, doubt and uncertainty inundated me. The number of crises and Joan's present state of mind made it clear something was amiss. When one crisis was resolved, another followed on its heels. What had I failed to comprehend about the workings of Joan's complex condition? What improvements to my treatment approach could I make to promote growth and healing and interrupt the cycle of maladaptive behavior? Why did Joan and the Parts continue to be overwrought and frightened when they recalled a disturbing memory, experienced painful emotions, or engaged in "crooked thinking"? What persuaded them to ignore or simply forget how to implement the basic principles of self-care and self-protection we had practiced over the past three years?

Nine months ago, I had attempted to persuade Ana to strengthen Joan's resolve by merging, which Ana dismissed outright. Why? Was Ana the birth personality? All along, I had assumed Joan, my client, was. She could be guided into the Inner Realm while Ana stayed only on the Outside or in the White Zone. Joan listened to the Parts' memories and empathized with their feelings, while Ana did not. Joan had disclosed and suffered through many painful childhood memories, while Ana had not. Joan fervently desired integration, and eleven or so Parts had already integrated into her consciousness, but Ana had "no interest" in uniting with the Parts and declared she could "live without them." With such attitudes in opposition to the therapeutic process, I thought Ana could not possibly be the birth personality.

Although Joan voiced her determination to integrate, her persistent disruption of the reunification process made me doubt the veracity of her commitment. Was she simply the caretaker of the Body, acting as the Host functioning on the Outside? If neither Ana nor Joan is the birth personality, who was? Where was she? How could I find her? Could Raven and Many Voices guide me to her? Would they know where and why she had been hidden away?

Could I recover her?

My head was spinning. Were my musings far-fetched? My reading of case studies about MPD, in particular the works of Allison, Bloch, and Putnam, had prepared me to consider the possibility that the child's Self could create a place of safety within the child's mind if the abuse were of such severity and chronicity that the child's sanity, or her very existence, were endangered. If this were so in Joan's case, then had the birth personality taken refuge somewhere? I had to learn more—much more.

Raven emerged. "Helper, I have sensed your concerns."

"I feel something is undermining the Parts' and Joan's resolve whenever a serious disruption occurs. This may sound implausible, but I've begun to entertain the possibility that Joan might not be the birth personality. Rather, I'm wondering if she might have been chosen to act as the Host on the Outside. Do my musings make sense to you?"

Raven smiled, "Your musings are the reality."

Astonished, I asked, "If neither Ana nor Joan, *who* then is the birth personality?"

At birth, Raven revealed, she was named Joanna by her mother and grandmother. A fragile and susceptible infant, she had difficulty thriving in the atmosphere of animosity that existed between the two women. "While living in her grandparents' house . . ." He paused as if to firm his resolve. "Joanna was molested by a babysitter at about ten months of age. As you have been told by Many Voices, this was when Rose split off to endure Joanna's pain. At the age of one, her parents reunited but their marriage was filled with strife and violence. Joan was created to shelter the child before she became too emotionally overwrought by the parents' discord. Joanna's physical abuse started at two, when her enraged and intoxicated father kicked her across the bedroom floor. Joan was there to absorb the shock. The trauma continued . . ." Raven paused again, possibly to allow me to catch my breath.

"The most devastating offense Joanna suffered was at the age of three, when her alcoholic father and his depraved friends sexually defiled the child in a public restroom. As they have confided, Rose and Joan were there, and Beth and Annie, to help Joanna bear the degradation. All this portended dire consequences for the child. And when events in the Outer Realm became too extreme and threatening, what you have called her 'Self' chose Many Voices and me to take her to a region of her mind where she would be protected from suffering and the threat of annihilation. At that time, Joan was deemed most suited to be in charge of the Body and to function as the Host on the Outside. After which, the creation of more Parts continued as the abuses became more relentless and brutal."

I needed a few moments to absorb this dreadful account. "So, Raven, are you saying the child's Self—her life-preserving essence—initiated Joanna's removal from this virulent environment?"

"Exactly, Healer. And Joanna continues to slumber in isolation, where the cruelties and perversities which followed could not harm her."

The confirmation of what I thought were far-fetched musings had my knees trembling and my heart pounding against my ribs. I pressed on. "Where is the birth personality—I mean Joanna? Can we recover her?"

"Joanna can be found in the Abyss located in the Vast Region of Nothingness. It is beyond the most remote features of the Inner Realm and cloaked in complete darkness, impenetrable to human depravities. There, Joanna is entombed within a crevice. She is covered with hardened soot and debris that is the dark decay of early bygone abuse."

Raven looked uneasy. He spoke his thoughts aloud: "Should I attempt a rescue mission alone . . . in darkness . . . across great distances . . . that would be a daunting task."

I emphasized the paramount importance of awakening and rescuing the birth personality. If Joanna were not reunited with Joan and the Parts, I told Raven, integration would be out of reach.

"Then may I request your assistance? Would you consider joining me?"

"I'm honored, Raven," I said, attempting to graciously brush aside his outlandish proposition. "In my opinion, Many Voices would make a much more suitable traveling companion."

Raven gave me an incredulous look. "Helper, since the beginning, Many Voices has been the silent observer, the scribe who records and holds all memories. This being so, it is not her function to come to the aid of anyone. That is *my* purpose. I was the one designated to advise, guide, and protect. It is my duty to bring the birth personality out of Darkness into the Light."

"How can I possibly join you?"

"Your presence in the Inner Realm has been in attendance before. You know full well it is not your concrete physicality that is required."

"But what purpose would my presence serve?"

"As my navigator to guide me through the darkness and across the vast distance to our destination."

"Please give me a moment to consider your proposition."

I closed my eyes. After a few minutes of contemplative meditation, I understood how, by the gift of imagination and using self-directed visualization, I might be able to join Raven's search-and-rescue mission. I haltingly explained to Raven that my presence in the Inner Realm could take on the gestalt of a hummingbird. As this fanciful creature, I could nestle among his black feathers and help him find his way to our destination. *And why not? To rescue the birth personality this way seemed as likely a means as any other therapeutic approach,* I mused inwardly. *Besides, which other mythic creatures were better suited for carrying out such a delicate task? In some mythologies, ravens were revered as "bearers of the Light." And for me, the hummingbird, this tiny "bird of passage" was a symbol of the restoration of life's possibilities.*

With relief in his voice, Raven thanked me. "Before we begin this daunting task, Helper, let me explain my plan for our journey: We shall find our way using the map I drew for you some time ago. To pierce the darkness across Many Voices' Haunted Forest, we shall rely on the luminous glow emanating from our essences and fly on to the Vast Region of Nothingness and beyond, to where Joanna is hidden. Once there, I shall extract the birth personality from the Abyss using the golden ring you hold in your hand."

Taken aback by his prescience, I informed him I had brought the ring to session for a particular purpose. I wanted Joan to wear it to remind her that someone cared. And my hope had been that the ring would help to still her fears, anxieties, and doubts.

"I'm aware of your motives, but there is a higher purpose for the golden ring. It is essential for our rescue of the birth personality and her return to consciousness."

Perhaps as a talisman, the golden ring might invite good fortune and safe passage in our search. Just as likely, I thought it could symbolize rebirth for Joanna and salvation for Joan and the Parts.

I offered Raven the ring.

Inhaling deeply, I envisioned my manifestation of a hummingbird with a long, needle-like bill and sinewy wings adorned with shimmering silver and blue plumage. And so imagined, I joined Raven atop his Perch. As he unfolded his glossy black wings, holding the golden ring in his beak, I clung to the feathers on his back. And thus we began our flight of the imagination. I used his line drawing of the Inner Realm as a guide for our journey across the imaginary landscape. With the aid of his map, I spotted the Safe Place and Elizabeth's House below us. I announced out loud, "There's Rose's Cave on the left . . . We are passing over the Meadow . . . Now we are following along the River of Tears . . . We are crossing the Forest Edge . . . Below is Many Voices' Dark and Haunted Forest." As Raven had promised, our essences became luminous and made it possible to find our way through the Forest's darkness. In my mind's eye, I saw the Forest Girls raise their arms in supplication, begging for acknowledgment of their plight. On the far right, I glimpsed Many Voices' sparkling white cloud. Eventually, I sighted the Vast Region of Nothingness, beyond which lay the Abyss. With avian instinct, Raven located the chasm and, descending swiftly, landed precisely at its edge. I heard his voice thank me for safely navigating us to our destination.

"After awakening the birth personality," Raven said, "I shall seal the Abyss and guide the birth personality to you in the therapy room." He assured me he then would linger awhile at the Outer Edge until Joanna and I initiated our first conversation. I inquired about her present age. In his usual benevolent way, he replied, "Dear Teacher, since I do not measure age by time, I shall leave that evaluation to you."

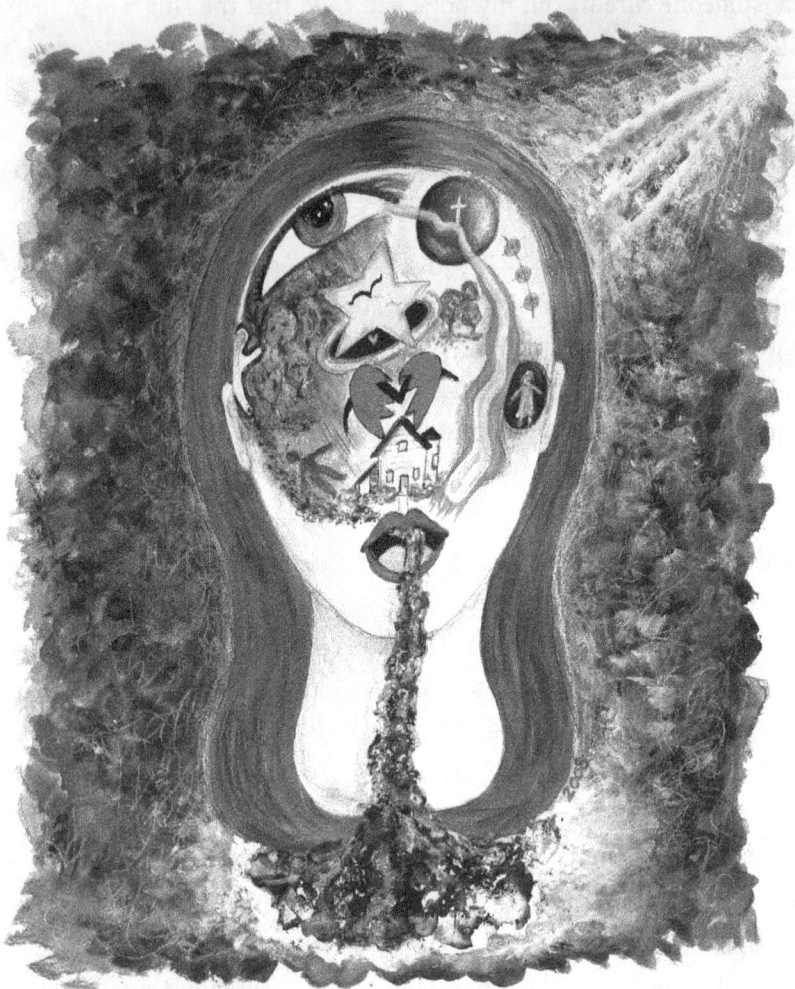

The Inner Realm, Joan 2009.

I withdrew my visualized presence.

As I sat in my rocking chair waiting for the birth personality to emerge from the Inner Realm, my mind's eye saw Raven spread his wings wide and, holding the ring in his beak, descend into the Abyss. With his luminosity dampened to avoid frightening the birth personality, I could picture him clawing away the pulverized decay until he sighted Joanna in a crevice, where she had existed in a state of unknowing for forty-seven years.

"Mama?" An anxious murmur.

Was the birth personality now with me? She sucked her thumb and seemed semi-conscious.

"Mama is all right. You are with me now, and no one will hurt you."

"Daddy?"

"Daddy is gone."

"Daddy gone?" She continued sucking her thumb. "My daddy hurt Mama. Daddy hurt me. I bad." She hung her head. "I go 'way."

I assured her she was a good little girl and encouraged her to open her eyes. "You can look at me. You are safe with me."

Joanna appeared to struggle with what I was saying. She did open her eyes, but instead of looking at me, she looked at her arms and legs. "I dirty."

"I see that," I said, validating her perception. "Don't fret, Joanna. We will wash the 'dirty' off."

She looked up. "I good girl?"

I sat beside her and took her hand in mine. "That's right—you are a good girl."

Her verbal expression and physical behavior suggested her cognitive development to be about that of a three-year-old. She studied my face intently. When she finally spoke again, to my amazement, she sounded like a six- or seven-year-old. *On occasion, I had observed young Parts shifting from an early developmental level to a more advanced one, and then back. Considering the fact that Joanna was a child—not a Part—how could she shift like that?*

"You are here," she said in wonder. "God promised you would come. He said someday a lady with silvery hair and blue eyes would come to make things better."

"I've heard that story before. From another little girl named Beth . . ." *I vowed to ask Raven how the birth personality could know of God's Promise.*

Joanna paid no mind to what I said. Her eyes turned vacant as she stuck her thumb back into her mouth. *How could this young child strengthen Joan's resolve? In their writings, I recalled both Bloch and Putnam had briefly mentioned the birth personality may suddenly appear in the middle of treatment. At such a critical juncture, perhaps I should have allowed the birth personality to come forward on her own "after much of the trauma had* been metabolized by therapeutic abreaction," as Putnam opined. Instead, in my eagerness to halt the unending cycle of crises that Many Voices had warned "may lead to the ending of all," I had forged ahead and brought Joanna out of her bubble of amnesia. How much would she remember, or had she forgotten all about the trauma she had suffered? Although I understood Joanna and Joan had to be reunited eventually, I could not imagine progressing Joanna to Joan's age. How could the birth personality, who possessed only the cognitive and affective capacity of a three-year-old, assimilate all that Joan is? Her brilliance and courage, her resilience and faith, as well as her memories of abuse and betrayal. Her sense of loss and grief, her symptoms of depression and addiction, as well as her experience of life on the Outside. At this moment, when and how their integration could occur mystified me. Until I knew what to do, I decided to give Joanna into the care of Elizabeth, the internal mother. That would afford me time to scour my books on MPD for an instructive or at least an inspiring precedent, which, as it turned out, I would find in Allison's books, Minds in Many Pieces and Memoirs of an Essence.

I spoke through to the Inner Realm and asked Elizabeth to welcome the birth personality into her House and nurture her until I determined how to proceed. I waited for a response. The Body lifted the right forefinger to indicate Elizabeth had agreed.

I softened my voice to ask Joanna to close her eyes and take a big breath. I squeezed her hand and said, "Now go with me to the House where a kind lady lives. Her name is Elizabeth. She has promised to take good care of you until we visit again. Now . . . you will be there with her . . . when you open your eyes."

When Joan returned from the Safe Place, I reoriented her to the present; however, I did not inform her of this new development. I had to formulate a new therapeutic approach to address the implications of this monumental change, for which I had no experience. I had to consider Joan's present physical and psychological fragility, the impact of her changed status within the system, the birth personality's development, and the potential of a new dynamic among the Parts. And do so without doing harm.

"Before I can develop a specific approach that can lead you back onto the healing path, Joan, I have to do further research. Until then, I have something for you." I picked up the ring from the small table beside my chair and handed it to her. "This is a special gift. Whenever you feel anxious or afraid, whenever you are lonely or tempted to drink, wear this ring to remind yourself that you are *not* alone, someone cares."

"Are you sure? It's so precious . . . I mean, really valuable. It should belong to one of your children."

"No, this is my gift for you to keep."

She hugged the ring to her chest. "I shall treasure it forever." Too large for her slender fingers, she slipped the ring onto her left thumb, where it remained for all the years I knew her.

Two days later, Joan phoned to ask for a short visit. After lunch, as I walked over to my office, I saw her sitting on the front porch, waiting for me. She looked delighted to see me and held out a small, gift-wrapped box with a fanciful bow.

"Happy belated sixty-eighth birthday, Renate," she beamed. "This morning, I woke up knowing you needed truffles. So, I stopped by your favorite candy store."

"You know me too well, Joan." I quickly unwrapped the gift and popped a truffle into my mouth. As I savored the soft chocolate, she looked at me mischievously and said, "Synchronicity."

"Oh, yes," I jokingly responded. "Somehow you knew my heart yearned for something delicious. Carl Jung pointed out that synchronicity occurs when least expected, particularly in the matter of truffles."

After our laughter subsided, Joan announced she felt "absolutely wonderful." Her depression had lifted, her mind was clear, and she had regained some self-confidence. To everyone's surprise, she told me, her daughter was making efforts not to be hostile toward the Parts she disliked. She was treating her mother with more respect and even was considering seeing a therapist to learn more about Joan's condition. *And, hopefully,* I thought, *begin to help herself. For my part, I was delighted my client was feeling so high-spirited.*

Later that evening on the telephone, Beth told me how she, Charlotte, Maria, Lisa, and "whiney Annie" had earlier been looking out the window in her purple room upstairs and saw my "golden sparkles" flying into the darkness with Raven. She happily announced Joanna now lived with them in Elizabeth's house and wore a golden ring on her thumb.

I encouraged Beth to teach the new arrival what she knew, but not to worry her with the "bad stuff." As accommodating as ever, Beth promised, "I will, Oma. You know I like to help."

~

Chapter 50

THE SEED OF KNOWING

October 26. Joan's auburn hair framed her face attractively, and her soulful brown eyes were bright and untroubled. She shrugged out of her fall jacket and hung it on the antique coat hook on the back of the office door.

"There's something . . . It's probably not very important. Maybe I shouldn't even bring it up." She paused as if searching for the right words. "For a few days now, I've heard unfamiliar voices. I can't make out what they're saying. They seem far away, not like when I hear the Parts talking. In fact, it doesn't really sound much like talking at all, more like crying or wailing."

Had the clamoring she heard come from Many Voices' Realm? Perhaps the flight Raven and I made across that haunted landscape had raised the Forest Girls' hopes for rescue, too.

"There's another thing I should tell you," Joan continued. "The celestial music, which gives us such indescribable joy, has changed to discordant noise that grates on my nerves." She opened her palms to the ceiling. "What do you suppose is going on?"

"I might have an inkling of what it is," I offered. "But before we explore my hunch, I'd like to talk it over with Raven first."

As I prepared to guide her to the Safe Place, she surprised me. "It's all right, Renate, save your energy. I can get there by myself."

"Please be sure to close the shutters and lock the doors," I cautioned, wanting to speak privately with Raven.

When Raven emerged, I repeated what I had been thinking. "When we flew over Many Voices' domain, I sensed a number of upturned faces beseeching us for deliverance. In light of their despair, is the time right for them to cross over into your system?"

"Helper, when Many Voices determines the time is right for their exodus from her domain, then the Parts in my Realm and I shall give our consent wholeheartedly."

Some time ago, I told him, Elizabeth informed me that Many Voices' system contained more than thirty young Parts that held memory fragments of neglect, mistreatment, and abuse. By my count, that number had been reduced, but if I were to work with them individually to abreact their memories, doing that would be all-consuming. Perhaps as an alternative, I suggested, one of the more mature Parts—one with sufficient cognitive and affective capacity—could speak for them in disclosing their sorrowful tales. From my perspective, that would be a more manageable way to move forward. And if that were possible, then I thought the Forest Girls could integrate into Joan's consciousness as a group without my help.

"Many Voices and I have contemplated these ideas for some time," Raven responded. *I was pleased the inner self-helpers were thinking along the same lines.* "However, before we pursue such a course of action," Raven said, "I shall consult further with Many Voices."

I redirected our deliberations. "Since the birth personality's rescue, I've given serious thought to how Joan and Joanna could be reunited." Inspired by Ralph Allison's work, I believed the internal mother could best help Joanna grow up. I explained to Raven that, in Elizabeth's care, Joanna could absorb the abreacted memories of the younger Parts and their unique attributes. When Elizabeth deemed it appropriate, she could guide Joanna to the Outside to observe Joan's family. And as Joanna matured, she could be co-present with Joan while she went about her daily routine. Many Voices would be best suited for infusing Joanna with what I hoped would be a mercifully selective biographical history. Then, at final integration, Joan would pass on her abreacted memories, adult experiences, and acquired knowledge. Thus preparing Joanna, I concluded, to live an informed, singular life.

"Teacher, as always, future events will unfold as they are meant to be realized." Raven then told me he had observed that the birth personality was already adjusting. To enhance her cognitive and verbal development, Elizabeth was reading to Joanna at every opportunity. Beth, Charlotte, Maria, and even Sophia and Rose were teaching her social skills. "Now and then, Helper, with the guidance of Many Voices, the internal mother hints about events that happened in the past and tells Joanna stories about what she might encounter once she lives in the Outer Realm."

"That's exactly what I had in mind, Raven. And speaking of unfolding events, I was astounded by Joanna's knowledge of one specific event that took place while she was slumbering in the Abyss. How is that possible in her deep state of amnesia?"

Raven cocked his head as if confused. "Helper, to which specific memory are you referring?"

"God's promise to send a 'Helper'. From the beginning, Joan and Beth both proclaimed God spoke to them when they were *seven*. So how could Joanna know of that promise?"

"The seed of knowing was planted by the Sower from the beginning," Raven intoned.

I wasn't prepared to challenge such a metaphysical response. After all, I told myself, who am I not to take to heart their "knowing"? Initially, I interpreted Joan's and the Parts' sweet imaginings as the transference of affection they once held for the "kind German lady" I was thought to resemble. But even Parts from Many Voices' system had alluded to "knowing." Angelina addressed me as "the shining lady," and little Amber identified me as "the Helper." They all seemed to have known me "forever."

Before I could voice my approbation, Raven gave me one of his benevolent smiles. "Dear Helper, God's ways surpass human understanding."

Or more likely, I thought, hearing God's promise may have been an auditory hallucination, like some traumatized children experience. However, what Joan described as the reaction to seeing me for the first time may just as correctly be attributed to a transcendental phenomenon.

After a long silence, the faintest smile crossed Raven's face. "Then as now," his voice fading to nearly a whisper, "Joan, Many Voices and I, and all the Parts are held together by a tender thread of hope spun of God's mercy."

"Which was first extended to Joan as a tormented three-year-old sitting in church enveloped in His grace," I replied softly. "Much later, she credits His mercy for the angels sent to cradle her after being abused. Not to mention the celestial music."

"These were authentic encounters with the Absolute," Raven avowed. "They form the foundation of Joan's unwavering faith in His love and protection."

Raven withdrew. Joan came forward to ask what Raven and I thought was going on. I responded we had concluded that the lamentations and cacophony she heard were being made by the Forest Girls' desperate longing to leave the Darkness of Many Voices' Forest. In a voice rasping with emotion, Joan inquired if Raven and the Parts were in agreement to let them cross over. I asked if *she* was prepared to welcome them. A feeble smile signaled her uncertainty.

At the close of my day, I sat a long while among the early-evening shadows and ruminated on the meaning of Joan's mystical encounters granted by the Sacred. What are those rare moments of grace—what Evelyn Underhill called a "transient unitive state" with God? No other mystic, Underhill declared, had captured that numinous moment better than the sixteenth-century Carmelite, John of the Cross:

> All things I then forgot,
> My cheek on Him Who for my coming came;
> All ceased, and I was not,
> Leaving my cares and shame
> Among the Lilies, and forgetting them.

~

Chapter 51

A FOREST GIRL

October 30. My husband and I were eating supper when Joan appeared uninvited at my front door. I immediately saw she was not well.

"Let's go to my office," I urged.

She flopped listlessly onto the couch in my therapy room.

Unexpectedly, a Part whom I'd never met was sitting before me. Her hand shielded her eyes from the light of a table lamp just to her left.

"We exist in the Darkness. We cry out, but no one hears us—no one sees us."

"I hear you. I see you."

Her eyes would not meet mine. "I'm a Forest Girl. I'm one of many. We are lonely. We hurt. We are unlovable . . . We are tired and wish to die." She began to shiver.

"May I wrap you in a warm blanket?" I retrieved a soft blue shawl I kept for just such occasions. I cautiously draped it around her shoulders, pulled up a chair, and sat directly in front of her. I extended my hands, palms up, in a nonverbal invitation. She didn't pull back and placed her hands in mine.

"You are safe with me," I consoled her. "I am a Helper. Here you are free to tell all you wish me to know. Telling is what we do in this room . . . without being punished."

I could see uncertainty in her eyes. I felt her hands close around mine and begin to squeeze . . . hard. "Go ahead. Press your hurt and sadness into my hands." The pressure increased.

"We slept a long time, and when we woke up, we waited for someone to find us. But no one did."

"So, you came out. To be heard. To be seen. And you found me."

"We want to stop being afraid of Mama and Daddy and Grandmother . . . and that bad man who came to live with us. We want it to stop," her voice rising in desperation. "Stop the hurt. Stop being alone. It has to be, so all can live." The Forest Girl pulled back her hands, wrapped her arms about her abdomen, and bent forward as if experiencing stomach cramps. She moaned like the seams of her heart were coming apart.

In my gentlest voice, I said, "I hear your anguish—and I see your hopelessness. I promise to help you. We will talk another time and get to know one another so you can begin to trust me. We can talk about how you came to feel this bad. But for now, please go back and tell the ones waiting in the Darkness that there is hope."

Her moaning stopped. She straightened, shrugged off the shawl, looked about the room as if committing its features to memory, and vanished.

Beth slipped out. "Oma, I saw the Forest Girl run back. She talked to a few girls that were waiting for her at the Forest Edge. But the others were doing what they always do—they hid behind the trees. And guess what, Oma? The crying stopped a little, and now the Forest isn't so dark. And two or three branches have started to leaf out. And the blue and white flowers—you know, the ones that only grow Inside—a few have popped out underneath some of the trees." She leaned forward to confide, "I know why all of this is happening, Oma. It's because that Forest Girl came to see you. They want you to help them like you're helping us. I think they're planning to cross over to our side really, really soon."

"Let's hope you're right, Beth. Once they do, I trust you and the Parts will be brave and listen to what they have to tell. Remember to be sweet to them."

"I'll try, Oma," Beth's brow furrowed, "but I'm not sure I want to be brave." She was gone in an instant.

"I opened all the shutters in the Safe Place," Joan announced, "so I could listen to what was being said. The changes taking place in Many Voices' Forest must be something to see." Joan laid her hand above her heart. "I think it's a miracle, Renate, that one of the Forest Girls dared to come forward. Like Beth, though, I'm not sure I'm brave enough to hear what they have to tell. If the Forest Girls do cross over, then I suppose they will cause me and the Parts a great deal of anguish." Fear skittered across her face. "And having to sift through those stories and acknowledge the truth in them . . . I'm not sure my heart can take all that pain."

"There's no injury more painful than the betrayal of those who are supposed to love us," I empathized. *I, too, had known, firsthand, that kind of treachery.* "However, right now, it's unclear when the Forest Girls will leave Many Voices' area. Once they begin to cross the Forest Edge, we can hope Raven will advise Samantha and Shadowman to assist. And I'll be here to guide you through the hard times. Meanwhile, gather your strength, and remind yourself that finding the truth was what originally brought you to this room. I wish we could change your past, but the only way to bear its dreadful truth is to embrace the suffering it holds. A wise woman wrote, 'Fear lives in the head, but courage lives in the heart.' The task for every human being, Joan, is to learn when to travel from one to the other. You and I can take comfort in knowing the many times you have successfully navigated that arduous journey."

Opening her purse, she withdrew a sealed envelope. "This is addressed to you, Renate."

After she left, I slit open the envelope and withdrew a poem. These last several lines aptly described the plight of the young Parts residing in Many Voices' Dark and Haunted Forest.

Forever marred, marked unclean, hiding far, far inside
Shadowed figures in perpetual night
Many silent voices now wait
In the solitude of all lost souls
We reach high to the light
Never to hold it close

Many Voices, written for Many

Chapter 52

INTIMACY

November 21. "We want to live," the Forest Girl had pleaded three weeks ago. "And so you shall," I had assured her. *Today, I expected Joan would announce the Forest Girls' emigration and lament the woe they had spread throughout Raven's domain and her own heart. However, I should have known better. Experience had taught me that therapy was not a step-by-step forward progression, but rather more like spiraling around heart-wrenching themes that tie the victim to her childhood past.*

This afternoon, Joan chose to open with a concern that continued to fester unresolved since her earliest days in treatment: her and Roger's intimacy as wife and husband. She expressed anxiety about Roger coming home for Thanksgiving and his expectation of having sex. He had tried to be more considerate but had been unable to sustain the effort. Their sex life had gradually returned to the old ways of demand and submit. That was not the kind of intimacy she desired. Her words came out in a rush as she described how she wanted Roger to approach her. Being tender with words of affection, sweet kisses, and gentle caresses were what she longed for. This was the only way she thought she could possibly find the emotional strength to be responsive.

"I guess I'm a romantic," she said, blushing a bit.

"Can you describe Roger's physical attributes that you find particularly attractive?"

"His hands," she replied. "They are beautiful—sensitive, I'd say. But he never uses them to caress me in a way that awakens tender feelings." She pulled her sweater more closely about her as if for protection against her loneliness. We spoke at length about her and Roger's intimate relationship.

After gaining Joan's approval to conduct a brief directed visualization, I lowered my voice and asked Joan to close her eyes, relax, and imagine Roger's sensitive hands caressing her in ways that aroused her tender feelings while he expressed endearments that were pleasing and nurturing. After a while, Joan opened her eyes, reached for a tissue, and used both hands to press it to her tear-filled eyes. "I'm willing to try," she said from behind the paper veil. "Maybe he'll be willing, too, so we can find some kind of happiness."

"Remember, Joan, intimacy requires trust and practice."

As she walked toward the door, Joan turned to face me. "I know what keeps me from getting what I yearn for. It's my need to never offend or disappoint. Especially my husband. I'm beginning to accept that my self-sacrifice leads to self-denial and loneliness."

I felt encouraged by the clarity of her self-assessment.

The following week, Joan's eyes sparkled as she proudly reported what had occurred during her husband's four-day visit. She had expected some sort of resistance when she explained that his kind of sexual demands made her feel uncared for. Instead of an angry outburst, Roger seemed saddened and had assured her that he was willing to adjust his behavior. At first, she had been skeptical until she saw how he struggled to be more considerate.

"Imagine, Renate, at my age, finally having real intimacy with my husband. When we lay together, and he put his arms around me ever so gently, I didn't pull away—I felt cared for. I felt safe." Her tone bordering on disbelief, Joan marveled that Roger had sincerely attempted to please her. The dam of pent-up feelings broke. She struggled to contain them, but they would not be denied. She fumbled in her purse for a handkerchief.

"Tears are powerful, Joan. They can dissolve the walled-off places where we hold our aching sadness and create a place for hope to reside."

After this emotional release, Joan spoke about the special relationship her husband has with Beth. "When he's home, Roger calls her out frequently. He considers Beth a lovable child instead of accepting her as part of me. I don't resent Roger's affinity for Beth, but I fear he wants me to remain fragmented so their special relationship won't be lost. Last week, he took her to the museum to look at dinosaurs. When we got back home, he kept calling Beth out to ask if she had enjoyed herself. My husband even asked *me* if I thought Beth had enjoyed the outing. How should I respond to such a question?"

"Well, how *did* you respond?"

"I told him I thought Beth had a wonderful time." With a hand over her mouth, Joan bent forward, laughing.

When her mirth was spent, I asked, "How might you respond next time?"

"I'll tell him Beth, like all the other Parts, is not a person. She's part of me. That lovable child is a facet of my personality. As you know, my husband loves my cooking more than anything. Perhaps I can make him understand that Beth and the other Parts are like the separate ingredients that make up my vegetable soup. Each has a distinct flavor. When simmered over a low flame, they begin to blend into a delicious, aromatic soup." Expanding her metaphor, Joan said, "Beth is a perky pearl onion; Rose and Sebunome are shy, humble sweet peas; Elizabeth is a nourishing russet potato; Samantha a self-contained, responsible carrot; and Shadowman . . ." She paused, "Oh yes, he's a tall, stiff-but-moist-inside stick of celery."

I held up my hand, palm out. "Stop! You're making me hungry." With tongue in cheek, I added, "Let's suppose that Eve, Jasmine, and the Furies are like jalapeños, tangy tomatoes, garlic, salt, and pepper—all the spices that add zing to your soup. And don't forget Raven and me. We are gently stirring the pot to make sure all the ingredients are blending well. And Many Voices, that nosy scribe, will record the recipe."

Turning serious, I told Joan even those of us whose minds were not fragmented had personalities made up of different character traits. For our various parts to blend and mellow in a way that made us unique individuals could take a lifetime.

Joan listened inward a moment. "Okay, Beth. I'll go to the Safe Place."

Beth slipped out. Motioning for me to sit beside her, she whispered in my ear, "Oma, do you remember when I told you about whiney Annie? No matter how we tried, she just wouldn't stop crying? Well, she doesn't cry anymore since Joanna came to live with us. At bedtime, when Elizabeth reads to us downstairs in the big room, they sit side by side. I think they like each other—a lot." She gave me her most beguiling smile. "I just wanted you to know.

"Oh, I almost forgot, Oma. I wanted to tell you that Leaf's little sister, the four-year-old, who sleeps inside the trunk of the big Oak Tree, she's awake."

Joan returned, yawning. "I had a short nap. I think it's time for me to go home. See you next time." But three weeks would pass before Joan came back to treatment, an unexpected and ominous absence.

~

Chapter 53

THEY'VE CROSSED OVER

December 12. Grimy strands of hair fell across Joan's face as she slumped onto the couch. Purplish smudges buttressed her eyes, and red blotches mottled her skin. She absentmindedly rotated the gold ring on her left thumb—the ring I had given her after Joanna's rescue. With a skittish feeling in my stomach, I waited.

"They've crossed over," she rasped.

"The Forest Girls?"

"Yes." Her next words came out in a gush of anguish. "I've been having flashbacks. One after the other. Day after day. Night after night." The flashbacks had started with whisperings, she told me. Tiny distant voices. Impossible to make sense of it all, like listening to a crowd. She had been bombarded with images. A flickering kaleidoscope of scenes and sounds, emotions and pain, from which she could not escape. She shook her head. "There are no words to describe the chaos." All the more terrifying, she said, because she saw and heard and felt only snippets: her grandmother's mouth distorted in anger; a slap across her cheek; cold light reflected off filthy restroom tiles; a penis down her throat; a doorknob slowly turning; the sound of a zipper; yellow eyes like daggers; a braying sheep; dry leaves crackling underfoot; bloody legs; a slamming door; cobwebs in her hair; dancing in the attic; fingers groping; young legs running to the woods; a girl's terrified face in a mirror; a wailing infant lying in a crib with outstretched arms; a voice hissing, "Don't you tell."

300

The Forest Girls Crossing, Joan 2006.

"What took me to the very edge of sanity was the outpouring of the Forest Girls' misery, spilling over me like acid. Their scalding despair was so intense—so profound—it could have raised blisters on my soul."

Joan's lips refused to say more. She buried her face in her hands.

"Take a deep breath, Joan, and rest a moment. Breathe in the Golden Light. Invite it to help you think rationally about the outpourings from the Forest Girls. Acknowledge the images, the sounds, and yes, even the pain and longings. Are they truly new to you, Joan?"

A slight compression of her lips was the only indication that she had heard me. She stared with the watchful, empty expression she must have used to hide behind as a young girl. She dropped her chin to her chest and was gone.

Raven emerged. "Helper, I must inform you that Joan has not gone to the Safe Place, as she usually does. Instead, she has fled to the White Zone. What Joan can't face are the wrongdoings and loveless acts of the Mother, the Father, the Grandmother, and all those in whose care she had been entrusted. These are the memories of the Forest Girls. And once Joan faces them and the countless wounds are laid bare, compassion is the necessary balm."

Raven then withdrew. In his place, I recognized Samantha by her posture. With one hand shielding her eyes, she said, "The light is much too bright out here." I had to strain to hear her. "I've been at the Forest Edge, watching the Forest Girls emerge through a small opening. I attempted to organize their exodus, but they pushed through in a stampede. I'm grateful the influx has slowed down." Her voice grew even fainter. "But now, I must rest. I'm too exhausted to do any more."

"Thank you, Samantha. As the Sentinel, you have done your duty."

Again Raven emerged. "There is another matter I wish to bring to your attention. I have heard the ones Inside talking among themselves about the rescue of Joanna. May I advise you to inform Joan of this event before she hears about this shift in her status from the Parts. I fear knowledge of the birth personality will cause her to question the value of her very existence. She must be assured of the pivotal role she will continue to play in the process of treatment and in support of Joanna's maturation."

"You and I understand, Raven, that Joan and the Parts, including the Fragment Parts, are *all* pivotal for the restoration of Joanna's mind." I pointed out that Joan's forty-seven years of firsthand experience and knowledge acquired in the Outer Realm were of paramount importance. Without Joan's contribution, Joanna alone would be incomplete and would not be able to function effectively. To illustrate my point, I led Raven into my outer office to view the large print of Pavel Tchelitchew's painting, *Hide and Seek*.

"I've stood many times in front of this reproduction," I said. "It gives me a glimpse of the painter's struggle toward self-actualization. He chose to portray—in fascinating detail—his struggle through the transformational processes we, as human beings, must endure if we desire to be whole."

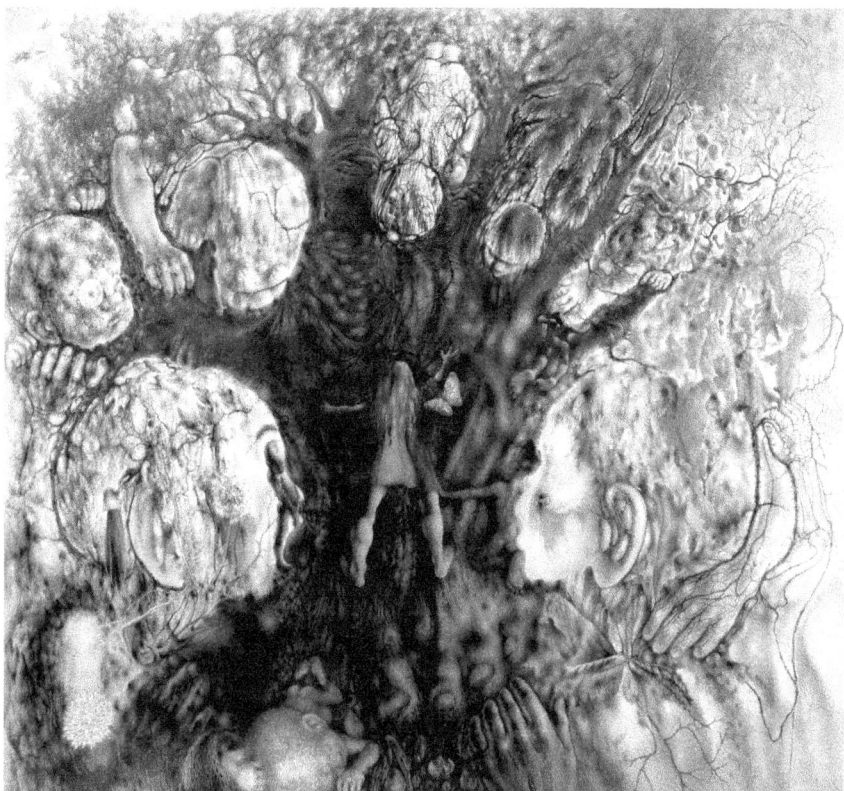

Hide and Seek, Pavel Tchelitchew 1942.

I took my finger and traced the ring of gestalts representing various stages of human development. Turning to Raven, I explained the painting was a visual depiction of what we were trying to accomplish. This entailed creating an autobiographical narrative of each Part—usually a long, iterative process. When complete, I said, when Joan and the Parts are fully aware of what had happened to them, had worked through their suffering and reframed their faulty perceptions—*and* embraced what cannot be undone—then they will be able to transcend the past and integrate with Joanna.

From the corner of my eye, I saw Raven study the many configurations— the Newborn, the Infant, the Toddler, the Child, the Teenager, the Young Adult, and finally a mature gestalt awash in the Golden Light of transcendence. Turning to face me, he said, "I greatly appreciate your vision, Teacher."

303

"About informing Joan," I said, "as soon as she has regained some semblance of stability, I shall tell her of the ramifications of the Rescue and her changed status."

"As you see fit, Helper." He bowed formally and withdrew.

Joan returned from the White Zone without my encouragement. "I can't accept what you've asked me to face. I just can't embrace the Forest Girls' memories. At least not yet."

She gathered up her coat and handbag, and headed for the door.

I called after her, "Make sure to phone me at the first inkling of an approaching flashback. I'll talk you through it before those past memories and the present intertwine."

~

Chapter 54

A DELICATE MATTER

December 19. Doubts racked my mind since promising Raven to inform Joan about the birth personality. By the time she again sat before me, I still had not resolved my dilemma: I feared telling Joan of Joanna's recovery might strip Joan of her hard-won identity; but if I didn't, my circumspection might rob her of the opportunity to become the unified individual she was so desperately seeking.

I felt my heart rattle with anxiety as I cautiously began my explication. I told Joan the frequent crises and her inability to resolve them had, to my mind, become a roadblock to her progress in therapy. But when I sought to shore up her vulnerability with Ana's practicality, Ana had rejected my invitations to merge with Joan. Her and Ana's interdependence raised questions in my mind as to who was the birth personality. In addition, with the emergence of the Forest Girls, the number of Parts and Fragment Parts had dramatically increased to about fifty, which convinced me that the trauma suffered had been more severe and pervasive than I had at first thought. Taking these variables into consideration, plus the conversations I'd had with Many Voices and Raven, especially the one concerning her father's soul-shattering wrongdoing when she was three, had led me to re-evaluate my perception of her role and function.

Joan sat preternaturally still. "What are you trying to say, Renate?"

I first described the magical journey Raven and I had made to the Vast Region of Nothingness and the rescue of Joanna from the Abyss. Then as compassionately as I knew how, I explained what the reawakening of the birth personality meant for her.

Color drained from Joan's face. Her breath came in ragged gasps. "All this time, I thought *I* was the birth personality. But now I've been relegated to being only a *Part? The Host?*" She pressed her fist against her mouth.

"I understand this is an unsettling revelation. It was for me as well. But the paramount fact is you've been the Host, in charge since the age of three. Without your presence on the Outside, none of you, including Joanna, probably would have survived. You are the one that has kept everyone alive and functioning. And be comforted that you and Joanna and the others will continue to be guided and protected by the Self."

"But what will happen to *me?*"

Struggling with my own uncertainty, I assured her she would go on with her life as she always had until the time of her reunification with Joanna. She would love and care for her family. Do what she enjoyed most—paint and write and bake—and, with Ana as her helpmate, she would go on documenting and assembling her autobiography. Just like we had done for more than three years in session, she and I would go on with our work together. The treatment goals and processes would be the same. Undoubtedly, we would have crises to resolve. As we worked toward full integration, I supposed some Parts would accept their interdependence more quickly than others. I anticipated some Parts would need encouragement and assurances to integrate, while others might do so on their own. And while I was unsure how the process of integration would unfold, I was convinced it would take place. We had to trust that the Self, which had set the splitting process in motion, would guide the course of reintegration and thus assure the restoration of oneness. "As these alchemical processes—sorry, Joan, I mean, as these *transformational* processes continue, and as changes manifest themselves, I believe you will feel more complete, more energized, more knowing."

"And in the meantime, what will happen to Joanna?"

Inspired by Allison's case studies, I explained that Elizabeth and Many Voices would be responsible for Joanna's development until final integration. At present, she was in the care of Elizabeth, whose young charges were helping Joanna feel comfortable in her new surroundings, and were sharing some of their memories with her. I told Joan I thought rescuing Joanna already had an impact on both systems. I suspected this had precipitated the emergence of the Forest Girls. As her flashbacks attested, they were already infusing her with their memories of the emotional and physical pain. In time, those memories would be acknowledged and worked through by all.

Even with my lengthy explanation and reassurances, Joan looked wounded. A high-pitched "I'm scared" issued from her throat. "All of this is too confusing. I wish I could go away forever. What would happen if I just stopped therapy?"

"Before you do, ask yourself what the consequence might be."

A long silence ensued as a multitude of emotions flashed across her face. *Knowing I could not protect her from her pain, all I could do was listen and empathize.* She tilted her head back, a vein pulsing in the hollow at her throat as she spoke to the ceiling. "I . . ." She stopped, as if contemplating any number of responses. "We would be lost. All of us. We'd feel alone. Defeated. Depressed, even suicidal. If I stop therapy, my family would be devastated after standing by me all these years, hoping I would get better. No . . . Why should I give up what we've worked so hard for—the sacrifice . . . the tears . . . and all that time?"

"That's right," I said, "why should you give up what you and the Parts have accomplished?"

"But if I did decide to terminate, final integration would be impossible. Right? Then *they* would win—my mother and father, Charles and all the others. Well, that's not going to happen. As soon as I've sorted things out—and that certainly will take awhile—I'm going to have a heart-to-heart conversation with my mother. I want *her* to tell me about my father and what he did that was so horrific that I—I mean, *we* were never the same afterward."

The fight in her voice was encouraging. I waited, hoping for the resolve to set.

After a few minutes, Joan said quietly, "I won't give up."

Nor shall I, I thought. *Joan was my client and would remain uppermost in my efforts to help her accomplish what she had set out to do when she first crossed my threshold. In the end, however, Joanna would be the beneficiary of what Joan was to become.*

~

Chapter 55

THE MOTHER WOUND

December 21. Joan sat with her purse held close against her body, her hands trembling. She was bleary-eyed. "I called my mother last night. When I asked her about what my so-called father had done to me, she was vague. 'Too long ago,' she'd said. That's what she always does. Pretends to remember nothing."

"Joan, I believe you know a great deal about those early years. Plus, Rose and Beth and some others have disclosed how your father abused you."

"But I want to know why Joanna was taken away," she insisted.

Notwithstanding my experience with the birth personality's level of cognitive skill, I offered to request Elizabeth to have Samantha bring Joanna to the Outer Edge. Joan went to the Safe Place to listen, and I spoke through to the system with my request. A Part exited looking forlorn. Instead of Joanna, I recognized the whiney, three-year-old Annie. She pointed to a teddy bear atop my bookcase and begged to hold it.

"May I ask you something, Annie?"

"Uh-huh," she responded, cradling the teddy bear.

"Can you tell me about your daddy?"

She began without a bit of hesitation, and with a surprisingly mature vocabulary. *Was Elizabeth coaching her, like she often did with Beth*, I wondered. "My daddy was sometimes good, and sometimes he was bad. When he was good, he sang songs to me. Sometimes, he gave me a lollypop.

Daddy got mean when he drank beer. He'd yell and hit Mama. And he hurt me sometimes, too. Once my daddy took me to a dark place with his friends, and I got to sit on a tall stool and they drank beer, and I got a sip. It tickled my nose. Then Daddy took me with him to the bathroom and I saw his man-thing. He asked me if I wanted to touch it, and I shook my head. His man-thing got big, and he put it in my mouth. After that, Daddy and his friends were all in the bathroom with me. They did what my daddy did . . ." She hugged the stuffed animal tighter against her chest. "One of Daddy's friends pushed his man-thing in my peenee. It hurt bad. Made me cry. That's when I went Inside, and Elizabeth found me."

Annie buried her face in the teddy bear and murmured, "I miss my mama. I want to hear her voice." *How could this mother fail to notice her child had been sexually traumatized? Did she not see the tell-tale signs? Ruined panties? Bruised genitals? Unprovoked fearfulness? This was beyond my comprehension, both as a therapist and a mother.*

Unexpectedly, I heard another young voice say, "I'm coming," and Joanna emerged.

"You are the shining lady who helped Raven rescue me," she said, a smile on her lips. "He pulled me out of a dark place where I was sleeping."

Listening to her speak and observing her mannerisms, I was surprised by how much she had matured. I asked her to write her name and age on a sheet of paper.

The corners of her mouth turned down. "I can't write so good," she said, setting the teddy bear aside. "Maybe Elizabeth can help me."

She bent over the paper, her tongue curled over her upper lip, and with large block letters printed her name and a number.

"Your name is Joan? And you are five years old?"

She nodded her head. "I know my real name is Joanna, but when I was little, my mama and my grandmother called me 'Joan.' When I grow up, I'm going to be a baby-nurse," she volunteered, "but I will be nice to the babies. I will never yell at them or hit them or make them cry."

On a sheet of paper, she drew a stick figure with a big smile on its face and holding a "baby" stick figure in its arms.

Studying the drawing, I said, "You sure look happy."

Her eyes brightened. "Elizabeth lets us sit at the big round table in her kitchen. We hold hands and pretend we are a big pizza. Beth told me I'm a slice, and she's a slice, and so are all the others. She said we need lots and lots of cheese to melt us all together."

"You like being part of a big cheese pizza?"

"Yesss," she said giggling. Visualizing the scene she described, I couldn't help but laugh with her.

She looked down and discovered the pale-pink polish on Joan's fingernails. She examined them with curiosity. "They're pretty. I like them. Can I go back Inside and ask Elizabeth if I can paint my fingernails pink?"

"What a good idea. Just close your eyes . . . take a big breath . . ."

Joan re-emerged, but with no light in her eyes. "I heard what whiney Annie said. And you were right. I remember telling you about that abhorrent memory. Plus, during Rose's regression, I recall Beth telling about that same ugly scene in the public restroom."

I reminded Joan that, as early as two months into treatment, Beth had mentioned "icky stuff" in her throat. At that time, there was no reason to think that this appalling event had had such a life-changing impact, precipitating Joanna's removal to the Abyss. "Even for me, Joan, it's astounding that the Self initiated such a remarkable phenomenon."

"It's surreal," Joan said, shaking her head.

Two days later, Joan told me she "couldn't let it go." She wondered why Joanna had not talked about the bathroom incident. I surmised that the sodomy and rape and pain had terrorized the child to the point she dissociated and had erected an amnesia barrier that was absolute.

"Do you think she'll ever remember?"

"I hope not until you, Annie, Beth, and Rose have abreacted the emotional distress associated with that event."

Joan said she had again called her mother and pressed her to be more forthcoming. But all she did was confirm that Joan's biological father had been a brutal alcoholic. When Joan asked specifically how her father had treated her, her mother changed the subject. She spoke about having seen him years ago in a grocery store. He had told her about being arrested for sexually molesting a little girl. He claimed he was innocent but had pleaded guilty in return for a reduced sentence. Her mother insisted he was incapable of doing such a thing. "I'm still aghast at the depth of my mother's denial."

"Did you confront her with the public-restroom incident?"

"I wanted to, Renate, but the words just wouldn't come out."

"Did you talk about Charles?"

"I've tried," she bristled. "To this day, my mother has no idea how long and how often he sexually abused me. She didn't want to know then, and she doesn't want to know now. Don't you recall, I wrote her a note when I was ten? Remember what happened? Charles found the note and punished me for it."

"Yes, I remember. He followed you to the woods—"

Joan held up her hand, palm out, to stop me and changed the subject. "My mother is too timid, too scared, to face what happened to me. Still . . . she should have rescued me. But once I realized she never would, I stopped wanting her to mother me."

"Joan, I hear your anguish. All children yearn to be loved and know they belong, to feel safe and have their physical and emotional needs met."

"Not me. Sure, I had food and something to wear, but otherwise, she failed me. I'll always love my mother, but I don't expect her to comfort me. That chapter of hope closed decades ago."

"No matter how old we are," I countered, "we all yearn for our mother to love and nurture us. But those whose mother can't—"

"I know, I know," Joan interrupted. "You've taught me I have to become my own mother. Unconditionally embrace who and what I am. Comfort myself and be responsible for my own welfare."

"That's the choice you have, Joan."

She blinked and fell silent. She pressed her fingers against her eyes. "I have such pressure here. I think one of them wants to come out."

Leaf was out immediately. She had listened while Joan talked to the Mother. How she had weaseled out of admitting anything made Leaf want to "scream and lash out." I offered her the opportunity to yell and punch the couch pillows, but she preferred instead to write a letter to the Mother. I provided pen and paper, and she began writing furiously. At intervals, she would strike the paper forcefully with the pen while hissing angry words. When she was done, I complimented her for the way she chose to externalize her emotions. She admitted the Parts Inside had dictated what she wrote; then she handed me the letter.

Dear Mother, [Abridged]

The morning after you found out he was molesting us, you came into our room and tried to hug us and say you were sorry. We pushed you away. Don't want your hugs or kisses now. The Furies RAGE—I rage in a simmer, breathing out gasps of steam like comes from a [teakettle]. Inside we scream, inside we ache for some kind of good—some kind of love that doesn't hurt. Because your love hurts, too—denial gets in the way—your fear gets in the way. We see you like fragile glass and try not to knock you down with cruelty or criticism.

When we pushed you away, you knew—because [we] knew you could see all of our sad, angry, and yes, some dead eyes, too. We were lost to you then—forever.

So, take the girl's body and tell her to get dressed. Feels like walking to an execution—but really not much left to execute anymore. Walk down the hall into the front room—such flat-out Bullshit—why? Because who is waiting? Who else but Charles with tears in his dead eyes? And this part just absolutely blows our minds clean out of the universe—that son of a bitch with you as a witness pulled us down on his lap and fuckin' guess what, Mama?! He had a hard on—let's all have a good laugh for the obedient little lamb that fuckin' volunteers for slaughter . . . The pitiful (NOT) tears and totally insincere

"I'm sorry, I'll NEVER DO THIS AGAIN!" Did you fuckin'
believe that, Mama?!! Did you really? You sentenced me
to all that happened [after] the day you ran off without
saying anything to marry him. [That] day if there was a
sparkle & hope in our eyes—it died.

> You were a Zombie—
> Some of us became Zombies, too.

"The Parts were terribly upset as they told Leaf what to write," Joan said
when she re-emerged. "There was so much that she couldn't write it all down.
But everything I heard was distressing. Most disturbing was learning that
before my mother ran off to marry Charles, she had been warned—maybe
by his aunt or his mother—that he was a child molester."

Joan stared into space, perhaps fighting off the memory of her mother's
incomprehensible recklessness with her only weapon, a frozen silence. I did
not intrude. *For the greatest grief,* I told myself, *there are no words.*

After a long while, she shook away the paralysis. With leaden arms,
she gathered her belongings and managed to wish me a Merry Christmas.

Shortly after Christmas, my phone started ringing. Most calls came during the middle of the night. When I answered, all I could make out were
slurred syllables, or a faint "help me" or "pleeease, Mama," or screams of
"she lies" and "you self-serving bitch" and "she's a heartless coward." The
disjointed outpourings continued for nights and days. Even Stephanie and
Megan each phoned complaining of their mother's intoxication with alcohol and sedatives. They informed me the chaos started on Christmas Day
after Joan and Leaf took turns making frenzied long-distance telephone
calls to Joan's mother.

*Was I surprised or disappointed? No. Had I expected Joan to consciously
face her mother's betrayal? I had hoped. But the mother wound had finally
burst open,* I reasoned. *What had festered for decades was now spewing
forth, searing and splitting open each small self, permitting the release of a*

multitude of hurts which had accumulated since the Mother had given birth to the infant girl, Joanna, who grew up as many.

January 19, 2007. Her complexion ashen, Joan lumbered on swollen feet toward the couch. The outpouring of the mother wound had taken its toll. I helped her to be seated, and, sensing her need to settle in, I waited.

"I'm grateful to be here," she said after taking a deep breath and exhaling slowly. She had been "out of it" for weeks, had barely hung on, but thought her mind was less scattered now. Without Roger and her children's help, she couldn't have made it through the crisis. Her heart had felt like it might explode. Her mind had been on fire. On the Inside, the Parts had been in an uproar over Leaf's letter and the Mother's denials. She said the turmoil had been further inflamed by the Forest Girls finally and completely letting go of their aching misery. Joan remembered making angry phone calls to her mother, but according to Stephanie, Leaf had done most of the talking and had accused her mother of terrible things.

Since therapy began, Joan and the Parts couldn't find the fortitude to confront Joan's mother with their long-held grievances. But now, desperate to be heard, I thought they had used Leaf as a channel to speak.

"My mother should have been racked with guilt and regret," Joan continued. "She should have called to ask for forgiveness. But not one word. Instead, she called Roger and told him I shouldn't call anymore until I felt better. She knew I was drunk but pretended I was ill."

Joan dropped her eyes. "Anyway," shifting back to the crisis, "most of the time my mind was in pieces. I think Ana was there. I vaguely remember begging her not to leave me. I couldn't sleep. My mind raced with thoughts I couldn't comprehend. When I could snatch a few moments of sleep, I had violent nightmares. I'd wake up gagging, bathed in a cold sweat . . ."

Gazing out the window beyond winter's gray and merciless grip, her eyes tracked some distant memory. Inside her silence, Joan absentmindedly turned the gold ring on her thumb.

Freeing her mind, she placed her purse on her lap. With an unsteady hand, she jerked at the zipper, opened wide the pouch, and retrieved a thick packet of papers. She lifted off the top page and leaned forward, our knees almost touching. "Here." She passed the handwritten sheet over to me. "I found this one on my nightstand after I got up. It's from Many Voices. She describes the audio and visual hallucinations I've been having. Please read it."

Chaos [Abridged]

As we merge tentatively, disjointed cognition [is] accompanied by flashing visions of unrelated black-and-white pictures. Such confusion. Not awake, nor aware, yet not asleep, the mind takes on a life of its own, neither here nor there, past or present. Fear devours the last of consciousness, consuming every bit of control, paralyzing. Reality is gone swiftly, nothing and no one remains. Enmeshed in a living nightmare until insanity seems the safest course. Not a word or sentence to call out, nothing that would bear any semblance to the chaos of being trapped alone in the travails of a past that holds hostage those awakened in a foreign place in time.

—Many Voices

"When the phone-calling stopped," Joan continued, "Roger told me I spent days sitting in a chair alone in the kitchen, holding this bunch of papers in my lap. From time to time, I would look at them, read a few words, and then drag myself to the bedroom and lock the door. Roger said he could hear me pacing, talking to myself, accusing someone of something. When I came back out, still holding the papers, he said he could tell I had been drinking."

Joan again leaned forward and handed me the sheaf of papers, which were letters written to her mother by the Tree Girls and Rose in August 2003, the month before she started therapy with me. Why she had never seen them mystified her.

"Perhaps, whoever left you these letters thought you were not ready to read them until now. Have you read them?" *I was convinced she needed to acknowledge and avow her mother's failures, which had crippled Joan for the greater part of her life.*

"I tried but couldn't make myself. I was afraid of how I'd react. So, I've waited to read them here with you."

In a thin voice, she began to read aloud the letter Samantha, Sarah [Christine], and Sebunome had written to "the Mother" with help from Many Voices and Raven. In it they questioned their mother's failure to protect them from Charles' abuse, which they decried in strong language. Nowhere had been safe, they declared. He accosted them day in and day out—"awake, asleep, in and out of the house, the car, anywhere, everywhere, even in the back row of the movie house." The torture was endless and unmerciful and left only "emptiness inside." The three wanted "to bleed or starve themselves away" but never could.

Joan stopped, visibly depleted. She rested a moment and then labored on.

The Tree Girls condemned, in vehement terms, their mother's denial of the truth as the "worst hurt." They became convinced that something must be very wrong with *them*, and bemoaned feeling "like trash, dirty and used, not good enough to ever be loved in a good and right way." In truth, they simply wanted to be seen as they were, without being "ashamed and disgraced and guilty," to be loved and "kept in someone's heart forever."

The sheaf of papers dropped into Joan's lap. Tears rushed out in spasms of anguish. Blindly, she grabbed a handful of tissues, blew her nose, caught her breath, and asked, "Before I read Rose's letter, do you mind if we get some fresh air?"

We trudged around the barren garden, her cold hand in mine. "If you are not up to reading any more, Joan, we can wait until next time."

"No, I need to finish this. I'm afraid if I don't today, I probably never will." Respecting her wish, we returned to my office and resumed the fearsome task at hand.

With help from Elizabeth, Rose had written in her letter that she felt like never belonging to anyone, like she was a "bad seed," and now lived in sadness. She did not understand why her mother cared so little. Why threats and yelling and embarrassment mattered so much. Why her need for love and safety were never validated. She lamented Charles' theft of her childhood, her mother's betrayal, her loss of a chance for happiness, and her confusion over the contradictions in her existence. Rose professed to hold no anger toward her mother but vowed to care for the feelings of those who "hurt in their heart and body." She did not want to remember the specifics of Charles' abuse, but neither could she forget them. She wanted to feel clean but asked, "How do you clean out your insides?" Her letter ended with the poignant observation, "In the garden of life, I'm the one with the thorns."

"Poor, sweet Rose," Joan said, her eyes swimming. "I identify with her the most. Sad, scared, the bad seed never belonging." Joan leaned back against the cushions and wept softly, one hand shielding her eyes from the sorrow of all she had read.

After some time, Joan seemed to relax, and Samantha crept out. "I'm the one who left the letters for Joan. I didn't mean to cause her all that turmoil, but I was furious at the Mother for not answering Leaf's and Joan's questions. Insisted she couldn't remember. Claimed she didn't know. How pathetic! Now Sebunome, Rose, and I are worried you might think we were too harsh with our indictment of the Mother. We are ashamed of the ugly feelings and mean words you heard us use. We fear we have lost your respect and affection and that you might abandon us."

"How brave you are, dear Samantha, for accepting responsibility. It's never easy to admit that one's behavior might have caused pain to another. I have no intention of abandoning you or any of the others. I promise."

"As Joan read your letters," I continued, "I listened intently. As you know, I've heard about your mother's wrongdoings numerous times, and likely will again, and again. And with every telling, all the inhabitants of the Inner Realm will let go a bit more of the grievances and anger you all hold against her."

"We want you to know we never sent the letters," said Samantha.

"I think it's important to ask yourselves why."

"Sending them would have upset Joan a great deal. She *never* wants to hurt the Mother."

After Samantha faded, I gently touched Joan's arm to bring her back. She opened her eyes and, with a feeble smile, said, "I want to go home now. I need to go to bed."

Standing at the office door, wrapping a sizable woolen scarf about her shoulders, she said, "Even after reading those letters, I'm not sure I'll ever be ready to give up completely the illusions I fabricated about my mother. Accepting who she actually is, Renate—that will take me a lifetime to sort out."

"Maybe." I gentled my voice to say, "One never knows how long it takes to come to terms with our tragedies. Healing our wounds can't be measured by time."

Aware of how much Joan coveted her mother's love, I understood why she resisted surrendering her faulty perceptions. Yet I hoped her desperate need had not brought her to a point where believing she was "a nothing" was the only possible justification for her mother's failures.

~

Chapter 56

BABY DONALD

January 23. After our difficult session the previous week, I was relieved to see a faint smile of satisfaction on Joan's face. "From what I can tell, things have settled down Inside," Joan began. "I've been sober since we last met. I'm working hard to get back to normal. Like they say in AA, one day at a time. Beth has told me the four-year-old Leaf has awakened, left the Oak Tree, and is now in the care of Elizabeth. Eve and Jasmine seduced Leaf to drink, for which Shadowman has taken them to task. He had the twins apologize and confined them in a soundproof Puppet Dome to keep them from making more mischief. After I crossed my heart and promised not to tell, that tattletale Beth said rumors were flying around that Shadowman was going to invite Eve and Jasmine to merge with him. Beth also said you fused Leaf with Raven."

"And did little Miss Gossip tell you Leaf separated from Raven after only two days?" I asked with tongue in cheek.

"No, she didn't tell me *that*."

I explained Leaf's merging with Raven had been premature. Although Raven thought it would allay her anguish and end the system-wide rage, I considered his plan therapeutically unwise. Leaf had not yet worked through her feelings about Charles' exploitation and the Mother's duplicity. However, I had put aside my misgivings after Leaf assured me merging would ease the "tornado" inside her, and Raven proclaimed the merging would grant

320

him greater insight into the Parts' suffering and enable him to facilitate their healing with more empathy and compassion. When, two days later, Leaf re-emerged, I suspected she had been motivated by her wish to reunite with Little Leaf. I told Joan this would require the two Leafs to explore their origin and work through their separate realities.

Unexpectedly, Raven came forward. He apologized for his sudden appearance and said Many Voices deemed it essential to inform me that the story of the creation of the two Leafs was deeply buried in Joan's consciousness.

"You mean she repressed the story? It's not held by the two Leafs?"

"Correct. To facilitate their reunification, Joan has to recover her memory of the death of her infant brother, Donald, and the emotional suffering afterward. Many Voices and I believe only you can guide Joan back in time to recover that memory. We shall stand by to assist. I've asked the Parts to assemble at the Meadow in a Circle of Truth to listen and observe. At its center, both Leafs will be waiting with Elizabeth. Because Eve and Jasmine have expressed deep regret, Shadowman has instructed his Puppets to open the Dome sufficiently that they, too, may have limited participation."

Raven bowed respectfully and withdrew.

I called for Joan, who reappeared, bewildered. "One moment I'm speaking with you, and the next I'm in some kind of silent limbo."

"Raven interrupted our conversation," I explained, "to bestow an unusual task. He asked me to help you remember the circumstances surrounding the death of your baby brother, Donald."

"I was very young when it happened—barely four. We were still living in my grandmother's house. I know I loved him and tried to help my mother take care of him. He was a happy baby, and then one day, he was taken away. That's all I recall . . ." Her fingers trembled as she lightly patted her upper lip.

"May I help you remember what occurred on the day he was 'taken away'?"

She looked stricken. "Do I have to?"

My heart ached for Joan.

~

Many years before, my infant daughter, Sandra Ellen, had died suddenly under mystifying circumstances. Until an autopsy determined the unavoidable physical cause of her death, I suffered terribly not knowing why or how this could have happened. My firstborn asked where her baby sister had gone. When was she coming back? My heart mourned for my daughter's loss and my torment of self-doubt and guilt.

~

Differences in little Joan's situation notwithstanding, her inability to cope with the confusion and her hurt-drenched feelings led, I reasoned, *to the repression of the incident. Putting aside the associated emotional distress she might suffer, I believed bringing to consciousness the uncertainties surrounding Donald's death was essential for Joan's psychological well-being. And according to the inner self-helpers, it was the prerequisite for resolving the dilemma of the two Leafs' reunification.*

"What must I do?" she asked.

"I shall guide you into a meditative trance, and my voice will lead you back to that fateful time."

"All right," she said, resigned.

"Please make yourself comfortable. Close your eyes . . . relax. Take a deep breath . . . and visualize returning to your grandmother's house. Let go of any tension you may be experiencing . . . you are now beginning the journey back to the old neighborhood you loved as a child. You take in the beautiful, tree-lined street. You hear familiar sounds of children playing, laughing. Heavily accented voices of their immigrant parents call out to them. From across the street, your eyes fasten on your grandmother's house. You may feel some unease . . . even feelings of dread. Acknowledge these feelings . . . take a deep, comforting breath, exhale . . . and cross the street. Now standing before the front door, you turn the handle . . . push open the door . . . and enter. There in the living room, you see your grandfather's cane leaning against his armchair . . . and your grandmother's phonograph is playing . . . classical music fills the air. You move about the house . . . your eyes touching this, touching that. Now you are walking down a narrow hallway . . . and approach the door, behind which baby Donald sleeps. You may hesitate. You may experience anxiety. Inhale deeply . . . and open the door . . . and step inside. As you draw near Donald's crib, you are becoming once again the four-year-old Joan."

"Shhhh. Mama is sleeping," a little girl's voice lisped. "She's tired. Donald is sleeping in his crib. He's my baby brother, and I love him. I want him to wake up. He needs to drink his bottle. I pat his little hand, but he doesn't move. His lips are blue. I put his passy [pacifier] in his mouth. He likes it best. But he doesn't want to wake up. I push his passy in some more. He won't open his eyes. I run to tell Mama. She looks at Donald and yells for Grandma. Grandma comes in and pushes me back. They are shaking Donald. Then Grandma hurries out and talks on the telephone. Some men wearing funny hats come in our house. One picks up Donald. He says, 'Everyone out.' I peek in. It looks like he's kissing Donald. One man tells me to go to the living room. He's nice. He calls me 'honey.' They take Donald away. Grandma is crying in the kitchen. Mama sits by the window. She's crying, too. I hug her knees and say, 'Don't cry, Mama. I'm here.' Mama cries more, and I'm sad, too.

"I want to know what happened to my baby brother. But they don't hear me. Grandma and Mama tell me to go outside and play. I sit in the grass, but I don't play. Why won't Donald wake up? Why did the men take him away? When will they bring him back? I'm afraid I hurt Donald. Maybe I pushed his passy in too hard and made him stop breathing." A gasping sob rents the air. "I'm scared. I go away."

A long silence ensued. I stood, stepped forward, and tapped Joan's forehead to bring her back. She opened her eyes, looked at me, and said, "Now I remember," her voice hoarse with emotion. "Being that four-year-old child again, feeling the worry and the confusion, it was anguishing. Sitting by myself in the grass, not understanding. With no one to explain, no one to reassure me I wasn't to blame. I was ignored. Unimportant. Abandoned. That's why I wanted to forget." Her eyes filmed. "I remember when my mother first brought baby Donald home, all bundled up. She bent down to let me look at him. He was so tiny, so delicate, with a reddish-brown wisp of hair. And unlike Lillian and me, he had blue eyes, sort of. Sometimes my mother let me hold him. I remember feeling so grown-up. When I stretched out my forefinger, he would wrap his tiny hand around it and hold tight.

That made me feel all warm inside. I asked my mother if I could help take care of him." Joan wiped at her eyes with the back of her hand.

Sharing her anguish, I said, "Now you understand your actions didn't cause little Donald's death?"

"Of course. But how could I back then? I was only four."

That's when Raven came forward. "Helper, Many Voices has instructed me to inform you that the guilt and sense of abandonment surrounding the circumstances of Donald's death became unbearable for little Joan. Unable to cope alone with these emotions, Leaf was created. However, the burden was too great, so Leaf split in two: One Leaf—known to us as 'Leaf 14'—internalized the feelings of guilt and climbed up into the Oak Tree, entered a large hollow in a top branch, and fell asleep. The other Leaf—known to us as 'Leaf 4'—internalized the feelings of abandonment. She stayed near the bottom of the Oak Tree, found a cavity in its trunk, slipped in, and went to sleep. She slept there for forty-four years, awakening only recently. And as you have heard before, Leaf 14 came to Joan's rescue three other times—once when Charles kissed her inappropriately at the kitchen table; another time when he molested her in the bathroom; and most recently, at the time of the car accident."

This might explain Leaf 14's cognitive and affective development while Leaf 4, asleep in the Oak Tree, remained at the level of a four-year-old.

Joan came forward. "I certainly owe the two Leafs my gratitude. I would like to thank them and ask them to let go of the emotional burden they've carried for me."

"I'm sure such a gesture would help them reunite and eventually integrate. Raven had the foresight to prepare for such an eventuality. You are invited to join the Parts in the Circle of Truth in the Meadow."

"Oh, I couldn't, Renate. Being that close to the Parts would make me too uneasy. I'd rather go to the Safe Place to listen and observe."

"Standing in the Circle of Truth among the Parts is the most fitting place for the fear in your mind and the courage in your heart to converge. How else can you thank them appropriately and ask to receive the emotions that are rightfully yours to hold?"

Joan reluctantly acquiesced and closed her eyes. I asked Samantha and Shadowman to come to the Edge and escort Joan to the Meadow. Some time passed before Beth slipped out and motioned for me to sit beside her. Her voice was thin with exhaustion as she told me Elizabeth had wanted me to know that Joan had thanked the two Leafs, and they had given their feelings back to her. After that, Elizabeth had wrapped her arms around the two Leafs as they "sort of melted together" and became one. With Raven flying ahead, all of them—Beth, Rose, Sebunome, Samantha, Shadowman, Sophia, Elizabeth, with the little ones, Leaf, Joanna, and Annie, and even the few Forest Girls who still lived in Elizabeth's House—all walked to the River to show Joan where their tears had gone while they listened to little Joan's story about baby Donald's death. Beth thought Shadowman had been the one who pointed out a beautiful rainbow in the sky. They all looked up and "*oohed* and *aahed*."

"I wish you could have been there, Oma. Elizabeth said the rainbow was a sign of another promise fulfilled."

"Where was Joan all that time, Beth?"

"I think she stood sort of behind us somewhere."

"And Leaf?"

"First she was with us, Oma, but when we looked back down from the rainbow, she was gone."

Leaf had integrated, I thought. I thanked Beth for being such a reliable messenger.

Stifling a yawn, Beth mumbled, "That's my job, Oma."

I sat a few quiet moments to rest my mind before asking to hear Joan's version of the event. I felt the delicate touch of the Blessing Lady tracing three crosses on my palm.

"What Beth told you is exactly what took place," Joan said upon returning. "After the merging, I followed the procession to the River of Tears, where I, too, mourned for little Donald—and myself." She thanked me for encouraging her to be a participant in the reunification ceremony. "I cannot tell you how privileged I feel to have witnessed my own mind's wondrous complexity and the magical reality it creates. That was an awesome experience."

Suddenly aware of the blanket of fatigue across my shoulders, I brought this marathon session to an end. My body felt stiff from having barely moved in three hours of concentration. I stretched and rolled my shoulders to ease the dull ache in the middle of my back. The three candles had guttered out. I turned off the lights, locked my office door, and trudged home.

Near midnight, the phone rang. An angelic voice intoned, "This is Lisa. I have never spoken to you before. Raven thinks you would like to know that Maria, Charlotte, and I are planning to merge and wish to integrate with Joan. As you know, I'm the one who provides the celestial music Inside. My melodies comfort the others and help them cope when times are troubled. However, now may be the right time to withdraw this comfort, or else some of them may choose to rely on the music to avoid integrating."

Although elated that the integration process was progressing, I felt a twinge of disappointment. Considering what Joan and the Parts might soon face, I thought withdrawing the celestial music was untimely. Regardless of my misgivings, I thanked Lisa for the gift of music she had provided over the years and praised her for the courage to decide to integrate.

"What do you think will become of the celestial music once we are part of Joan?" she asked. "Its beauty has never been heard by people on the Outside."

I assured Lisa the memory of that wondrous sound would reverberate throughout Joan's being for all her life. And she, Lisa, would be that part of Joan's consciousness that remembered.

The following afternoon, as Joan settled on the couch, she complained of feeling blue. She and the Parts felt a significant loss since Lisa had crossed over. The celestial music Lisa provided had been a blessing and so ethereal that words could not convey its heavenly enchantment. As a consolation, I offered to play a violin adagio on the boombox. Rose, who most loves music, came out, and, as the music played, tears clung to her lashes. Her face reflected sheer bliss. Her body relaxed in utter contentment.

Careful not to interrupt, I spoke softly through to the system to remind them that, although this music did not compare to Lisa's, I hoped it would be of comfort when any of them needed solace. As the music ended, Rose came out of her reverie. She took a moment to reorient herself before speaking. "Now that some of us have dared to integrate, Sebunome and I are making plans to fuse, so that, together, we can integrate with Joan. We haven't made any specific plans for the ceremony yet, but we wondered if you could be there with us."

"I would be honored to attend such an important event."

There was a knock at the door. My husband came into the treatment room, thinking me to be alone.

"I heard the music—" he began but stopped short when he saw me with a client.

To my surprise, Rose condoned his intrusion. She appeared unfazed as my husband and I engaged in a brief conversation. While we spoke, I noticed Rose sitting very still, as if deciding what to do. I held my breath when she stood, walked the short distance to where my husband was standing, and put out her hand.

"Happy New Year, Mr. Opa Caldwell."

I couldn't deny my gratification at seeing one of the shiest in the system interacting with a man—and doing so without inhibition.

As soon as my husband left, Rose faded, and Joan came forward. She had witnessed all the events from her vantage point Inside. "I think the Parts realize now," she said with a positive ring to her voice, "that they can take some comfort in the music of the Outer Realm. Your husband's unexpected visit was a bit of a shock," amusement in her voice, "but I guess Rose's reaction is proof her general fear of men has decreased."

I hoped that was so—for the others as well as for Joan.

~

Chapter 57

A LETTER OF TRUTH

February 6. "My family is beginning to recognize the progress I'm making in therapy," Joan beamed. She had told them of Leaf's integration, followed by that of Lisa, Maria, and Charlotte. Plus, Eve and Jasmine were contemplating merging soon with Shadowman. Megan had been quick to say she certainly wouldn't miss "those troubling teenagers." To Joan's surprise, however, Megan said she *would* regret the integration of the younger Parts—the gentler ones like Beth and Rose. Roger, too, had spoken of his reservations about letting go of Beth.

"You're smart to keep your family abreast of your achievements."

"I didn't mention the integration of the twenty or more Forest Girls." Raising a tentative smile, she said, "They couldn't have imagined such a thing. Visualizing that would be like a scene from *Lord of the Rings*."

Joanna, the birth personality, emerged to take Joan's place. Looking me straight in the eye, she rotated the ring on her thumb as she said, "I know I need to learn a lot before I grow up. Elizabeth told me. Like how to read and write, and how to say my prayers, and how to get along with the other girls. At bedtime, Elizabeth reads us stories in the big room downstairs. One girl—her name is Beth—she tells me lots of stories. There is another girl—her name is Rose. She is sad a lot, but she's very kind to me. Sometimes, I hear a grown-up voice in my head telling me things."

"What kind of things?"

"Things that happened after I went to sleep. Things that make me sad."

I was grateful Many Voices was communicating with Joanna.

"Do you want to talk about the sad things?"

"Not now," she shook her head. "I want to go back to Elizabeth's House and play."

A familiar Part emerged but did not speak. She sat in silence, her shoulders hunched, eyes fixed on the carpet. Deciding to take the initiative, I smiled and said, "Hello, Sebunome."

She raised her head and gestured for pen and paper. Bending over, her nose nearly touching the clipboard, she wrote in block letters. When she had filled the page, she looked up with a desperate plea in her eyes. With measured movements, I sat beside her and took the sheet of paper from her hand. I glanced at the mirror-image words. *What a remarkable survival skill,* I thought. I led Sebunome to the mirror above the sink in the restroom and read aloud what was reflected in the glass.

I'm not scared—not of you. Soon I will be leaving into Rose. I want to be ok before I go. Am I dirty? I don't want to take anything bad into Rose. I look back too much—but Rose has learned to look forward. Will you help me get ready?

This is my truth.

He always was watching and touching all the time! Nowhere to hide, always scared. I hate the basement. I hate my bed, I hate the house. I hate always, always being afraid. Not allowed to tell, not allowed to cry and always in trouble because I don't talk enough—sometimes not at all. I'm afraid of people especially men but ladies can do those things too. At the school library. Ruined school feeling safe.

I don't like things stuck inside of me. What if he gets all the kids? I want to die all the time. Once he gave me money and you know what that makes me.

Not allowed to talk about it—the Mother didn't talk about it—the sister said I lied.

When the Mother was in the hospital having a baby he got me up at night and took me in their bedroom. I was bad to my mother.

I don't want to grow up. I went away instead.

We always took turns.

Can I come back and see you again? Maybe one more time?

There are some things I need or need to learn or feel.

   Sebunome

When I finished reading the note, I wrote beneath her name: Yes, sweet Sebunome, I will help you get ready. I signed it Oma, Helper, Healer, Teacher—all the names with which the Parts addressed me. "I understand what you suffered, Sebunome, and believe what you've written here is true. Please accept that you were never bad. Charles was bad." I held Sebunome's hand until she retreated to the Inner Realm and Joan reappeared.

"I remember that shameful incident when Charles abused me in my mother's bed while she was in the hospital giving birth to my little brother, Samuel. I could never tell my mother. It would hurt her too much. Anyway, what would be the point now?"

Being defiled in her mother's bed must have felt like the ultimate betrayal— so overwhelming to a young girl that Joan dissociated and allowed Sebunome to hold the shame and guilt. Eventually, I knew Joan and I would need to work through these onerous feelings. For the time being, I accepted how important protecting her mother was for Joan.

That evening, Beth phoned to tell me that, according to Shadowman, Eve and Jasmine had merged with him. *This was excellent news.*

⁓

Chapter 58

SNAPSHOT: NOW AND THEN

Two days later, Joan came to my office to draw a map of the Inner Realm's present state. This imaginary landscape, the product of Joan's creative mind, had existed long before I became Joan's therapist. During the last three and a half years of treatment, many changes to its geographical character and functions had taken place. Many Voices' Forest had expanded and divided into three different areas. Beth had defined one as "not so scary," another as "very scary," and the third she labeled "haunted and dangerous." Existing buildings in Raven's Realm had been added onto and new ones created. Elizabeth's House had been enlarged to provide a separate cave-like room for Rose and additional bedrooms for other Parts who had moved in. The Safe Place had been erected and expanded. Rose's Cave stood abandoned. The White Zone beyond the Inner Realm had been marked with an "X" to identify Ana and Joan's retreat from all-knowing. The Meadow, once merely a patch of grass, had grown into a field of blue wildflowers and had become the place the Parts met in the Circle of Truth to ponder solutions and celebrate healing. The River of Tears had become a sacred place for cleansing and transformation. Only Raven's Perch remained unchanged atop the tallest Tree, which, unlike the other trees in the Forest, had always been green. Where Many Voices resided continued to be a topic of debate: Beth said she hovered beyond the Vast Region of Nothingness in a sparkling cloud of white mist, while others knew her as being like the wind. *I reasoned what Beth saw as a glittering entity was more likely a manifestation of Many Voices' extraordinary cerebral and spiritual capacity.*

After Joan set her sketch pad aside, she talked about visiting her mother. *Was Joan psychologically ready and physically able to make the trip*, I wondered. Keeping my voice steady, despite my uncertainties, I inquired if she was prepared to face her mother, for whom she and many of the Parts held such intense and conflicted emotions.

Joan listed several practical reasons why she should go: Her elderly mother was getting frail, her house needed repairs, and she had complained of being lonely. However, in the end, Joan admitted the real reason was to prove to herself that she could return to that house of frightful memories, face her mother, and talk about the past.

While I acknowledged Joan's motives, I raised concern for the reactions of the Parts on seeing the Mother.

"I'm scared." I recognized the trembling voice as Sebunome's. She sat with her eyes closed tightly. "I don't want to go back there," she whimpered. "It makes me sick to my stomach. I get shaky and can't breathe." With urging from me, she began reminiscing about what life was like "back there." Her words flowed with an uncharacteristic fluency of speech, offering up details about Joan's early family life under her grandparents' roof.

"After Daddy and Mama divorced, we—I mean Mama, Joan, and Lillie, plus Beth, Annie, and Rose—we all moved in with our grandparents. I was four years old. They had a big basement, where we could play when it was raining outside. Grandmother and Mama yelled and fought a lot. Grandfather was strict, but not scary or mean." She lowered her voice. "We had to be very, very quiet. No yelling. No slamming doors. Marjorie—she liked to slam doors. She got us in a lot of trouble with Grandmother, who would yell, and Mama would get mad. Her eyes would turn yellow, and to teach us a lesson, she'd make us close the door a hundred times without a sound.

"When I was around six, Grandmother told Mama we were too noisy, and she was getting tired of watching us when Mama was at work. She wanted us to move out. Mama told her we didn't have enough money to rent our own place. And there would be no one to look after us. Grandmother said Mama should find a husband. Mama knew only three men who might want to marry her. One was an old man. The second one was not so old, but he drank too much. And the third one was Charles."

I was astounded by the historical knowledge this unassuming Part held. Were other Parts lingering behind her, coaching Sebunome to reveal what they knew about those early years? Was Many Voices infusing her with this knowledge? And had that emboldened Sebunome to speak up as she never had before? Or perhaps when Joan was four, Sebunome had been created to listen and remember until Joan was ready to remember on her own.

"Who do you think she chose?" she asked, looking directly at me now. "Charles. When we asked Mama why she chose him, she told us he was the best-looking. He scared me right away. His eyes were dead and so cold. Almost from the start, he began touching me when no one was looking. And he made me sit on his lap. I didn't like that. And I didn't like him. So, I just sat still and said nothing so I wouldn't get in trouble.

"When my grandparents visited relatives out of town, Charles would stay overnight. That's when he started doing a lot of bad things. He'd rub against me and put his fingers in my private parts. It hurt. I was so scared, I'd shake. The basement was not a nice place to play anymore, not when he was around.

"Before Mama and Charles got married, Charles' mother came to visit. Or maybe it was his aunt. Anyway, she warned Mama that Charles had molested young girls before. I don't know what Mama thought about that. But because Grandmother kept pestering Mama to move out, Mama decided to marry Charles. Without us knowing why, they went on a trip together for about a week. When they came back, they told us they got married. I was eight then.

"We moved to our new house in the country near the woods. That's when what we feared most came true. Charles hurt us all the time. And when he did, afterwards there would be more of us."

"You mean more Parts?"

"Yes," Sebunome sighed, "Eve, Jasmine, Sophia, and some others whose names I don't know. When it was really bad, more pushed out. Samantha, Sarah [Christine], Rose, and the Furies came out to help. Beth was there but got so scared that, after a while, she went to sleep. Anyway, what I remember is when he was around, we pushed each other out one after the other to deal with him. Sarah and Fury 1 absorbed the anger. I absorbed the sadness and distrust. Rose was very brave. She took most of the pain . . . you know, down there. We didn't know about Raven then, or Many Voices, not even Elizabeth and the Blessing Lady. I suppose they were still sleeping.

"One night, Charles and Mama wanted to go out to the movies, but they needed a babysitter. Charles called Aunt Marcy to ask if her daughter, Jolene, could come and look after us. Jolene, I think, was eighteen. We played games, but after a while, she asked if Charles was doing bad things to us. She pointed, you know, down there. We were too scared to say anything, but I nodded my head a tiny bit. When we went to bed, she tucked us in and gave us a sweet kiss.

"We couldn't sleep. We were kind of scared about what would happen when Mama and Charles came home. We heard the car in the driveway and slipped out of bed. Jolene met them at the door and asked Mama if she could talk to her in private. That must have been when she told Mama that Charles was molesting us. Mama and Charles got into a big fight. Later, when Mama came to our room and sat on the edge of the bed, she told us to stop misbehaving, or she would send us away someplace where it was much worse. We all started crying. Mama made us promise not to tell stories to anyone. Then she wanted to hug Joan, but we all pushed her away."

Sebunome held her breath while her eyes explored my face. I encouraged her to continue.

She exhaled. "Some of us pretended to be happy, no matter what. But I never lied about my feelings. I just stopped talking. I got in trouble for that."

"But you were true to your feelings, Sebunome, and found a way to remove yourself from what was happening. Do you know why some pretended to be happy?"

"They didn't want Mama to send them away. They wanted her to love them. And they hoped Charles would stop hurting us. But I knew pretending wouldn't change how they treated us."

This shy Part, I thought, *was making significant strides.* I praised her for daring to be forthcoming. She listened without avoiding my eyes. "What else can I do, Helper Oma, to get better?"

I suggested she interact with other Parts more often. And dare to look around the house where Joan lives, possibly even take a peek at Joan's family—Roger, Stephanie, and Megan.

"I'll try to do all that," she responded, "but I'm not ready to look at Mr. Roger yet. I think I'll take a peek at Stephanie, though. She's nice."

To my surprise, she asked to visit again with the man the others called "Mr. Opa." She wanted to be in the presence of a man without being frightened. I promised we would arrange a meeting. She looked satisfied and left me with a hint of a smile.

I called for Joan, who admitted the rush of memories from Sebunome's disclosures had triggered a great deal of anxiety, fear, and shame. She realized now she wasn't yet ready to go back and face her mother. *A wise decision,* I thought, and told her so.

~

Chapter 59

SACRIFICIAL LAMB

February 15. On this gray and chilly afternoon, I asked Joan if she was aware while growing up that her mind functioned differently than her siblings' or other children's. She vaguely remembered her mother and grandmother accusing her of being the most forgetful child. When asked about some specific occurrence, or if she had done her chores, or even what she learned in school that day, she often drew a blank. When she was older, she noticed gaps in her memory, which she couldn't explain. She began to suspect her mind had tucked away some of the terrible wrongs that went on in her home, her family's cruel and shameful behavior. After she left home and got married, Joan tried to forget everything about her childhood past and avoided feeling anything that wasn't positive. Looking back, she thought she ran on autopilot much of the time but was thankful to be alive and away from what seemed like someone else's hazy, bad dream. If a memory slipped out somehow, she pushed it right back in.

"My life had finally gotten good, but I sort of knew I had to keep my emotions fiercely in check."

"That must have taken a lot of effort."

"I suppose, but I thought my 'good life' was worth every ounce of energy I had to make it so." Her voice strained to continue. "And then—just a few months before my thirty-second birthday—the life I willed myself to have, came crashing down."

I held my breath. *After nearly four years of listening to Joan, was I finally going to hear about the crisis which convinced her to first seek therapy so many years ago?*

"My family and I went to visit my mother and my eighteen-year-old half-brother, Samuel. We were going to celebrate my mother's third husband's birthday. She married Harold after divorcing Charles while Sammy was still a young boy. When we first got there, I immediately sensed something wasn't right. My mother was beyond anger. I sent the kids to play outdoors. When we were alone, she said that very morning Samuel had told her Harold had been sexually abusing him from the time he was eight. My heart dropped. I knew he had been cruel to my brother at times but never thought he was a pedophile.

"While she told me this, Sammy was on the front porch and refused to come into the house. When I approached him, he waved me away. He was so angry and ashamed he couldn't tell me what had happened to him. I wanted to put my arms around him and say I understood his pain." She placed her hand upon her chest as if to hold together the pieces of her broken heart. "I wish we had turned right around and gone back home. But we stayed. I guess I was in shock at the horror of it all, but my mother was more annoyed with the *timing* of Sammy's revelation than outraged at what had happened to her son."

Joan faltered a moment, unable to find the words to describe her distress. She had loved her little brother from the moment he'd been born. She took care of him like a second mother. Fed and diapered him. Held him when he cried and comforted him the best she knew how. And when he got older, she showed him how to brush his teeth, comb his hair, and tie his shoes. "He was such a darling child. I thought my love would protect him, but I was wrong." Joan shook her head in defeat.

A long silence followed before Joan picked up the thread of her account. "While I listened with dismay to my mother's revelation, I felt my brain shake—like an earthquake in my head—and my mind broke open."

"That's when the walls of denial began to crumble," I interjected cautiously, "and the Parts began to reawaken."

Paying no mind to my comment, Joan recalled the insanity that followed later that afternoon. Her mother had prepared a birthday party for the "degenerate" who had sodomized Joan's "sweet little brother." The stepfather had fled the house right before Joan and her family arrived. When the "coward" finally came home three hours later, her mother insisted they all pretend everything was fine. She then orchestrated and directed the "whole, pathetic party." They gave Harold gifts, ate cake, and "celebrated" the birthday of that "monster," the kind Joan had known all too well. The whole affair had been a cruel "black comedy." From that day forward, Joan recalled, her sense of reality changed. She behaved in unpredictable ways her family couldn't understand. Nor could she. Her "good life" was replaced with fear and the dread of losing her mind. She began to lose time. And along with it, herself.

Taking an abrupt turn from her recollections, Joan reported, "Last week, we all worked more on the Lifeline. Once completed, Renate, we'll be able to see how my life unfolded. You and I can trace events and memories, and all the pain they hold. Won't that be amazing?" Satisfaction danced around the corners of her mouth.

Sebunome came out. At first, she appeared shy and timid, though, as I watched, her newly acquired self-confidence began to transform her appearance. She sat up straight, lifted her head, and made eye contact.

"I'm delighted to see how assured you're becoming."

With a slow nod of her head, she acknowledged my compliment. She presented an unexpected request to practice lying on a bed without becoming "shaky all over." I held out my hand and led her to the adjoining guest bedroom. When she stood before the bed, her body began to tremble. I allowed her to cope with her emotional discomfort. She reached out and touched the bed with her fingertips. With a grimace, she lifted herself onto the bed and lay there, her body rigid. Gradually, her breathing became regular, her apprehension draining away. She motioned for me to come close. I drew up a chair to sit beside her. Holding my hand, she began to cry. When her tears subsided, she said with a lopsided smile, "Helper Oma, that was scary, but I did it."

"You were very brave, Sebunome."

Her next request was no less surprising. She asked me to leave the room and shut the door. I did as asked but was reluctant to leave her unsupervised. I left the door slightly ajar and stood nearby, at the ready. After a few minutes, the door swung open; she walked past me into the therapy room and sat on the couch. I sat beside her.

"I did it again, all by myself," she said with pride.

She laid her head on my shoulder, took my hand, and placed it above her heart. "This is where I hurt," she murmured into my shoulder. "Raven believes that you also must have been hurt like us because you understand our sorrow so well."

"We all get hurt sometimes," I responded, careful not to disturb the delicate poignancy of the situation, "and have to find ways—perhaps with a helper like me—to come to terms with what happened to us."

"It's been hard," Sebunome said, "and it hurt a lot. But we believe we are getting better. I think maybe next time, I'd like to tell you why I'm afraid of water."

Without a moment for me to respond, Beth found her way out.

"Oma, we all peeked out and saw Sebunome practice lying on the bed. You know, going to bed was always really scary for us."

"Beth, how can you and the others 'peek out' to see what's happening on the Outside?"

"Sometimes, only one of us is behind Joan's eyes and looks through. Sometimes, a few of us go there, and we take turns looking out. Other times," she giggled, "we all try to look out at the same time. That's what happened the first time we saw you. And, guess what? We saw Raven touch your shoulder, but you brushed him away. Then he remained behind you for a while, and I think you sensed he was there."

She asked for paper and pencil and proceeded to draw what she had just described. But when she lifted her head, I realized it was Rose meeting my eyes.

"Oma, I just want you to know that Sebunome and I are growing together more and more. But I'm still worried about all the things that are coming up—what we still have to tell before we are clean."

"When you do, Rose, I'll be at your side."

Joan re-emerged and indicated she had "sort of" been attentive while at the Safe Place. However, she did not acknowledge Sebunome's brave effort to overcome her fear of lying on the bed, a fear I knew Joan shared with other Parts. Frustrated with her avoidance, I pointed out Sebunome's accomplishment would, in time, prove to be of great benefit.

Joan's face tightened. "I witnessed what Sebunome did," she admitted. "I know how hard it was. But I'm not ready to share with you the dread I felt every night when I climbed into bed. To this day, I still dread it."

Shrugging into her coat, Joan left like a petulant child and ran through a freezing drizzle to reach her car.

February 22. "Roger is getting in touch with his feelings more and more," Joan's mood upbeat. "I think it's Beth's influence." *Joan's recommitment to their marriage a year ago, and her acknowledgment of his kindnesses also may have had something to do with Roger's change in affect.* "He's become more affectionate toward Stephanie and Megan, which he didn't know how to do when they were growing up. Megan and I are getting along much better, too," she boasted. "I'm beginning to enjoy being with her. She has a wicked sense of humor. She can describe something upsetting in a way that makes us both laugh. She's encouraging me not to take everything so seriously. So, you see, Renate, some things at home are improving."

Joan's high spirits gradually faded. "When I was around eleven, my mother took me to the doctor. She had noticed I was bleeding from my vagina. I don't know if she had become suspicious of the abuse, or just wanted to know if I was entering menstruation early. When I was alone with the doctor, I told him about the abuse at the hands of my stepfather. I had hoped he would tell my mother. However, afterward, nothing changed at home. Charles' abuse went on for another seven long years. My mother did not take any steps to stop it. In a way, I understand why she allowed it to go on. She believed getting rid of him meant she would have to move back in again with her mother. I guess that frightened her more than letting Charles have his way with me. I was the sacrificial lamb on the altar of her hopeless dilemma."

Then her thoughts wandered elsewhere. "Would it surprise anyone that Charles abandoned my mother after I left home? He took up with a younger woman who had two little girls and a boy. Charles is only interested in women with children he can sexually exploit."

I let her sit with that abhorrent disclosure before redirecting our conversation.

"During our last session, Sebunome mentioned her fear of water. Do you know what that's about?"

"If you don't mind, I'd rather not talk about that today."

Rose appeared. She announced with uncharacteristic conviction, "Oma, not all of us are ready yet to tell you why we're afraid of water. We went swimming once in a lake and almost drowned." She quickly changed the subject. "When Sebunome and I grow together, I shall move backward, and she will move forward until we are fused. When that happens," she queried, "will my hopes and dreams fuse with Sebunome, too?"

"That's right," I confirmed, "and the two of you will share gifts of character as well. Because both of you are gentle and kind, you will enhance those traits in one another. And I believe fusing could happen soon. But first, Sebunome wants to cleanse herself. She doesn't wish to burden you with the distrust she holds. And once the pain in your vagina has healed, sweet Rose, you'll be ready to merge."

Sebunome came forward through Rose's smile. She asked to go to my outer office to look in the full-length mirror hanging behind the entry door. "I've never seen what the Body looks like," she explained.

"This is nice," she said to the reflection as she curled a coil of auburn hair behind an ear. Touching both ear lobes, she was surprised to find them pierced with dangling earrings. "These are pretty," she said, turning her head side to side. She took a few steps back to examine the Body more fully. "This is what it looks like now, at forty-nine?" There was no mistaking a touch of sadness in her voice.

Unlike the Parts who had fiercely rejected the Body's physical appearance, I thought Sebunome's positive response might indicate a shift away from Joan's disdain for her corporal self.

"Forty-nine is not *so* old, Sebunome."

Her eyes seemed full of questions as she disappeared.

"I tried to listen," Joan said upon her return, "but when Rose started talking about going to the lake, I couldn't breathe. My heart started to pound. I still can't seem to catch my breath."

"Would you like to do some deep breathing before we end this session?"

"No, no." She anxiously looked at her watch. "I have to go home and cook dinner for Roger."

"Maybe between now and our next appointment, you might wish to explore what created your apprehension about the lake. Remember, working through your past is the way forward."

Joan scurried out the door.

Feeling my bones, I made myself a much-needed cup of tea. With mug in hand, I settled into my rocking chair, took a couple of deep breaths, and allowed myself to sink into the positive feelings I had about the considerable progress Sebunome had made in overcoming her inhibitions. Reveling in her accomplishments, I dared to consider the possibility of the other Parts following Sebunome's and Rose's example. I took a quick inventory of the advances made within the system as a whole. According to Shadowman, as reported by Beth, Eve and Jasmine had merged with him. The two Leafs had been reunited and integrated. Lisa, Maria, and Charlotte had voluntarily integrated with Joan. She and the Parts were continuing to process the anguish and longing of the Forest Girls, while Shadowman and Samantha continued mentoring and discouraging discontent. The Forest Edge between Many Voices' and Raven's systems was slowly disappearing. Light was penetrating Many Voices' Dark Forest, and individual trees had begun to leaf out.

My optimism dampened somewhat as I pondered the work yet to be done. How many more Parts would emerge? How many more memories of abuse would come to the fore? How long would it take to work through the remaining anger and shame and despair that continued to fester? When would Elizabeth complete her task of nurturing the young ones in her care, and would they integrate spontaneously? Joanna, also in Elizabeth's care,

had much growing up to do before she would be able to absorb all the Parts'
memories imparted by Many Voices. What would happen to the internal
self-helpers—Many Voices, Raven, and Elizabeth? And there was Beth . . .
Could she surrender the joy of going on outings with Joan's husband, or tea
parties with her "beloved Oma"?

I reminded myself to trust the inner wisdom of the system for guidance.
Of course, I had to remain vigilant to recognize opportunities that would
facilitate the healing process. I felt a great responsibility bear down on me as
I walked the short distance home.

Rose called late that night.

"They're back, Oma," she whispered, sounding frightened.

"Who, Rose?"

"The Dangerous Ones—Fury 1 and Fury 2 and Marjorie," her whisper
barely audible. "We all thought they had gone away. They are mean. We
don't know what to do about them. We're very scared."

I suggested she and the others could meet at the Meadow to discuss ways
to deal with the "Dangerous Ones." Because it was very late, I told Rose we
would talk about this further when Joan came to treatment.

As I crawled back into bed, I mumbled to myself, "So much for celebrating early. Now we have the Three Furies to contend with."

～

Chapter 60

FURY 1

As I walked back to my office after lunch, I saw Joan waiting for me on the porch. She was sitting on the edge of a white plastic chair, clutching her purse, knees tightly pressed together. Her defensive posture reminded me of our earliest meetings. I unlocked the office door and invited her in. Without removing her coat, she sat on the blue couch and, with a sudden forcefulness, told me she hadn't slept "a wink." The previous evening, while having dinner with a friend at a restaurant, a woman at the next table slapped the face of a little boy. Joan had felt her cheek burn as if *she'd* been the one slapped. She claimed something in her head cracked.

"Did something like that happen to you when you were a young girl?"

Joan ignored me. "I think they're back," she said, wringing her hands, her eyes dilated. I thought she might faint. Instead, a Part began to speak in a matter-of-fact voice I did not recognize.

"We *are* back—in an evil, mean place we tried to forget."

I asked her what had brought them back. She didn't answer but started tugging at the sleeve of Joan's coat. The heat under her skin was unbearable, she told me. It burned like "fire" and itched like "mad." She flung the coat aside and vigorously scratched and pulled at the skin of her forearms.

I suggested I could help her soothe what tormented her. To my surprise, she didn't reject my offer. With caution, I escorted her to the restroom. We stood at the sink. I turned on the cold water tap and urged her to cool her arms in the basin. I opened the medicine cabinet, took out the hand lotion, and offered to apply some on her arms. She pulled away, saying she feared the internal fire burning her would blister my hands. I asked if she knew what was torturing her. The Part said it was a red-hot fury burning inside her. "It started when we realized we were helpless and had no voice. If we tried to say anything, my grandmother would get mad and slap us across the face so hard our skin burned like blazes."

Walking back to the therapy room, she complained, "I don't like to talk about any of this." She glared at me. "I don't know you. Where am I, anyway?"

The Part aimlessly paced about the room, picking up various objects and placing them back. I asked if she would like to go outside so I could show her the neighborhood. Without a word, she followed me through the door and off the porch into the front yard. She looked with disinterest at the empty flower beds. We walked beneath the leafless trees and stopped beside the stone wall that separates my property from a neighbor's. She lifted herself onto its flat top surface and sat there. I did the same. We rested for some time, the sun warming our backs, not saying a word. Eventually, I guided her back into my office.

Sitting on the couch once more, the Part confided, "I'm not alone, you know. My sisters are here with me, listening and watching."

"How many are there?"

"Two," she said. "Their names are Fury 2 and Marjorie. I'm Fury 1. We are filled with red-hot rage. Don't touch Marjorie like you tried to touch me. She'll hit you across the face."

"Thanks for the warning, Fury 1. Actually, I'm looking forward to meeting them. I want you and your sisters to know that I understand why you're so angry. Should you choose to see me again, I might be able to help you overcome your red-hot fury."

With a sudden movement, Fury 1 stood, opened the door, and walked into my front office. She canvassed the walls and then stood motionless before *Hide and Seek*, which the artist had painted when he felt death held more promise than life. I watched her eyes wander over the mandala-esque painting—its menacing tree leafed with faces and human forms reflecting the painter's loss, social alienation, and deep melancholy at various stages of his life. I told Fury 1 that when the painter was forty-six years old, he chose to end his suffering by working through and accepting the tragedies that had caused him so much heartache.

"May I look at the picture a little closer?"

I lifted the large poster off the wall and laid it on the floor. We knelt with the picture between us. Lightly tapping her forefinger on first one image then another, she traced Tchelitchew's circle of torment around the composition. She laid her hand on the tree's trunk, as if its darkness reflected what she felt within. Then her attention moved to near the zenith of the tree's canopy, her fingers lingering on a gestalt emitting golden energy.

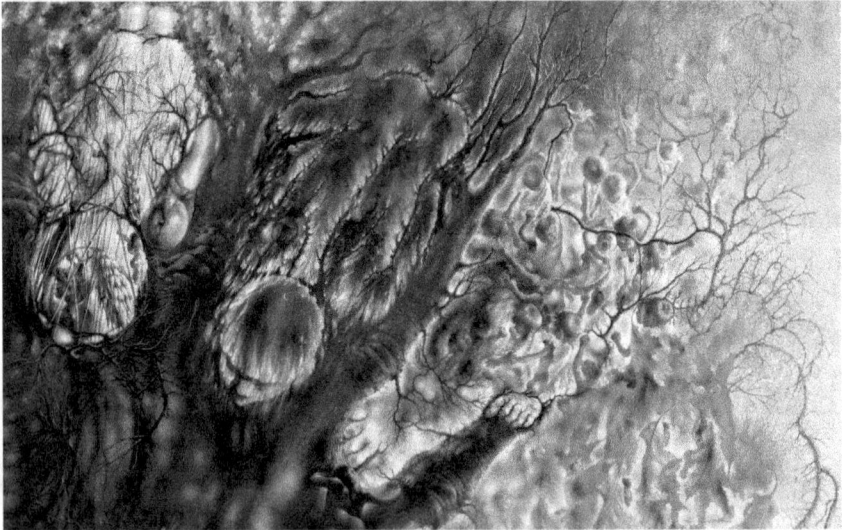

Hide and Seek (detail), Pavel Tchelitchew 1942.

Until this moment, I had not interrupted her exploration, but now I saw an opportunity. I pointed to the figure which was holding her attention. "See how he shimmers and emanates resolve. His knee is bent, his back straight and strong, indicating he's ready to stand and embrace life. You see, Fury 1, this is what Joan and the Parts have decided to do. Instead of remaining apathetic, they have chosen to stand, to work through their sorrow, and mourn their losses. I hope you will choose to do the same."

When we returned to the treatment room, I offered her the ceramic bowl filled with small, polished stones on which Joan and the Parts had inscribed meaningful words or images. She sorted through the black and gray stones, turning them over in her hands, scrutinizing each one. She hastily discarded one marked "Mother" and another marked "Home." When she found one imprinted "Helper" with three red hearts, she held it tightly in her fist.

"May I keep this one?"

I told her the stone had the capacity to absorb her "red-hot fury." I suggested that, when she felt the fury rising, she should hold the talisman in her hand, close her eyes, take a deep breath, and allow the emotion to melt into the stone.

Holding the gift close to her heart, she asked if touching her had burned me. When I replied it had not, she looked incredulous but asked if she could visit me again. I assured her that was possible. I called for Samantha to guide Fury 1 back to the Inner Realm, but she did not respond straightaway. *I thought the delay might be due to her being wary of exposure to Fury 1's volatility. Eventually, when Fury 1 did depart, I assumed Samantha had overcome her uneasiness. The re-emergence of the Three Furies, I was convinced, offered additional opportunities for Joan's growth.*

Before Joan left, I spoke through to the system, asked for the Parts' tolerance, and encouraged them to make the Dangerous Ones welcome.

~

Chapter 61

DEPARTURE

*M*arch 1. In the early morning hours, my nephew in Germany called to inform me that his mother's pancreatic cancer had become grave. I immediately began making travel arrangements to be at the side of my beloved older sister, the daughter of my foster mother.

~

Elsbeth had loved me from first sight, as Mama entered the kitchen with me cradled in her arms. Then and there she appointed herself my big sister, the only one who could sweet-talk me through my frequent outbursts of anger. The one who proudly showed me off to the neighbors. The one who taught me how to feed the chickens and care for the rabbits without my fingers being nibbled. And when the village siren screeched to run for our lives, she was the one who hurried my arms into the sleeves of my robin's-egg-blue coat. Later, if I was bullied in the schoolyard, Elsbeth, her black braids flying and her Magyar eyes blazing, rushed to my defense. As I grew into a rebellious teen, she scolded and coaxed me into doing better. As adults, though we were separated by an ocean, our relationship never frayed, our love never dimmed. And now, I had been called to her bedside to help Elsbeth live into death.

~

Around noon, I called Joan and asked her to see me as soon as possible. She arrived about thirty minutes later. As gently as I could, I informed her

348

about my situation, told her I was uncertain how long I would be away, and assured her I would make arrangements for my trusted colleague to watch over her during my absence.

Tears spilled down Joan's cheeks. Concerned for her safety, I told her she and the Parts had to think about what they would do in an emergency while I was away. I spoke through to the system, explaining the need to write out a safety plan as quickly as possible. I asked all to remember while I was away to use their coping strategies to avoid becoming overwhelmed by anxiety and fear, or by unexpected challenges and disturbing situations on the Outside.

"The most important thing for me," Joan stressed through her snuffling, "is to do my breathing exercises and not lose time. When are you scheduled to fly out?"

"The day after tomorrow, at noon."

"That will give us enough time to figure out a safety plan. We'll work on it tonight and present it to you tomorrow. I'm sure Raven and Elizabeth will help. About the other therapist—I'll tell you how I feel about that when I see you."

I expressed concern about the Furies creating chaos and asked what steps she and the Parts could take to pacify them.

"I suppose we can invite them to the Meadow to join us in the Circle of Truth, where we can tell them they are valued and belong. We could encourage them to share the miseries they've suffered. We'll empathize with the grief that fuels their rage." Joan thought she and the Parts could inform the Dangerous Ones about what had been learned since Helen tried to put them to sleep; the events that had occurred since then; how Roger had changed for the better; and how grown-up Stephanie and Megan had become.

Even though they might try to intimidate Joan and the others, I was confident she could handle the Dangerous Ones. I reminded her that aggressive Parts usually were scared and hurt but surrendered their angry posturing when kindness was extended to them. "When you write out your plan," I coached, "you may want to ask Fury 1 what she and her sisters would be willing to do to keep the peace while I'm in Germany."

The next morning, Joan presented a detailed plan to help her, the Parts, and even the Furies stay calm, avoid a crisis, and remain healthy and safe. The Furies promised to hurt no one Inside and Outside, keep Marjorie close, talk and listen and learn from the others, assuage their rage with cold water, and be mindful of Raven's guidance. Joan and the Parts promised to maintain communication and not isolate; practice coping skills to avoid panic attacks and flashbacks; and engage in activities that nurture the body, soul, and spirit. As arranged, Joan agreed to see the substitute therapist.

The Parts exited in a solemn procession to sign their safety plan and express their compassion for my ill-fated circumstance. Beth came first. She cried over what she called "Oma's pain." Rose exited and put her arms around my shoulders in a timid embrace. Sebunome came out and gave me a sweet smile. Even Sophia, who I had not seen for some time, appeared and gently held my hand. Ana patted my shoulder and matter-of-factly said, "Be safe." Shadowman, looking dignified and confident when he presented himself, assured me of his steadfastness during my absence. Then in a complete turnabout, he laughed bawdily and informed me Elizabeth had developed "boobs." *Taken aback but gratified, I realized this ancient symbol of the maternal signified Elizabeth had taken to heart her long-ago promise to become more physically demonstrative and affectionate toward the young charges in her care.*

Next, a somber Elizabeth, ignoring Shadowman's rude comment, made a rare appearance to wish me "good health." Raven was last to appear. "My dear Teacher, may I ask you to allow the warmth of affection shown by all to soothe some of your heartache. On behalf of Many Voices and myself, we extend our good wishes for your safe return."

I thanked each of them and expressed my gratitude for their empathy. *I was deeply moved by their demonstration of devotion and support not only for me but also for one another. The experience infused me with hope and the promise of a future of cooperation and progress.*

≈

Chapter 62

UPDATES

When I arrived home from Germany the third week in April, I found this letter in my mailbox:

April 19, 2007 [Abridged]

> *Dear Helper, Healer, Therapist, Teacher, and all you are to our system,*
>
> *My very deepest sympathy and compassion to you in the loss of your sister, one who knew you in the deepest sense. I know your heart grieves. To have had such a great love is a gift . . .*
>
> *I believe without love there is no true joy, hope or living—just existence. I imagine you DO get weary of the questions about love from the Parts and of their need for reassurance. You do understand on many levels why this is so, I believe. "Love" often came disguised or required such strict and painful rules. Love was not the pure love for love's sake . . . and never, it seems, unconditional.*
>
> *Changes continue as ever throughout the system, and as typically happens, growth occurs at a more*

rapid rate after adversity and crisis. No one wishes to dwell on the topic of the last crisis . . .

Sebunome is wishing to completely merge with Rose. There is discussion about when [and] what is needed . . . and how it will occur. The Elders agree that any talents and abilities harbored by Sebunome would serve well to be blended into our Rose, who has grown much with nurturing and care over the past years.

Fury 1 has freedom to move about the Inner Realm and gather information as she chooses. [B]efore attempting to participate in the Outer Edge, she's encouraged to consult with the Elders to determine if it will be in the best interest of all. At this time, she is most content to spend time exploring outwardly while no one is in [Joan's] home . . . Fury 2 and Marjorie . . . will remain with Samantha and listen to Fury 1's experiences.

Beth misses you greatly . . . Rose is quite content that spring is here and enjoys the flowers and plants on the Outer Edge . . . Shadowman continues to be a strong and positive presence for all Inside . . . Many Voices chooses to continue writing. Elizabeth, a wise Earth Mother, is there for the young ones [and] talks [to them] about the changes in simple terms [so] that all may understand and accept what will be.

Many thanks and praises to you for your dedication and devotion to all . . .

Raven

I was happy to learn that Joan had managed well during my absence, as had the Parts. No upsets was good news.

∽

Chapter 63

THE BLACK SPIDER

April 21. With jet lag still heavy upon me, I heard the doorbell ring late Saturday afternoon. To my surprise, Raven stood at my front door.

"Dear Helper," he said, "I apologize for the intrusion. Fury 1 and Roger have been embroiled in an argument since Friday night. Before the crisis escalates further, I thought I'd best guide Fury 1 to you. For allowing us to come unannounced," said Raven, "I'm very grateful. But now that Fury 1 is safe with you, I ask your permission to excuse myself."

As we walked to my office next door, Fury 1 came charging out. She began telling me about the shouting match she'd had with Joan's husband. I encouraged her to breathe deeply and calm down. She ignored me, saying she had seen "a huge black spider" on the living room wall, but Joan's husband, "the jerk," insisted it wasn't there.

"I do believe you saw that spider, Fury 1. And I also believe that Roger did not see what you saw. For the sake of argument, let's accept the possibility that what both of you saw was real and true."

"I can't stand him," she blurted out as she sat down. "I know he doesn't like me and insists that my sisters and I don't even belong to Joan."

At just that moment, Roger telephoned to ask if his wife was with me. She had left in a "huff." Frustration straining his voice, he stated he was tired of the "whole freaking mess." When I tried to tell him that he was welcome to talk with me any time, he abruptly hung up with an epithet.

I returned my attention to Fury 1. "Do you recall what precipitated the crisis other than the black spider you saw on the wall?"

"The two of them are planning a trip up north. Staying at the Mother's house. If we are forced to enter that house, Fury 2, Marjorie, and I have decided to hang ourselves under the basement stairs."

"Now I understand why you're upset. Their conversation triggered a flashback. And you saw a spider on the living room wall."

My acceptance of what she'd seen surprised her. I asked if she remembered the time she first saw that spider. Her uncertainty prompted me to suggest putting her in a trance to help her remember. With her tepid agreement, I suggested she close her eyes and allow my voice to guide her back to that moment. As I progressed the trance, she shuddered and with a dry throat said, "I see it. It's crawling up the wall."

"Where are you?"

"In the basement . . . under the stairs."

"Is anyone with you?"

"Charles. He's hurting me . . . His hand is over my mouth . . . I can't scream. I can't get away . . . All I can do is watch that ugly black thing crawl up the wall . . ."

"I understand you're frightened . . . What you are experiencing happened long ago . . . Take a deep breath . . . and exhale your fear. Now return to this room, where you are safe . . . safe with me."

She opened her eyes. "Now I remember."

I told Fury 1 of Sophia's and Beth's disclosures of the same incident and assured her Roger had no idea what she was experiencing.

"So, Joan's husband really *didn't* see the spider?"

"He really didn't. But you know and I know you saw it *in your mind's eye*."

I paused to let that sink in before continuing.

"Next time you're overcome with fear and about to be pulled back into the past, do what other Parts have learned to do. Reach out to Raven for help. He will call the others to gather in the Meadow to listen, empathize, and comfort you."

When a bewildered Joan regained full awareness, I informed her that Raven had brought Fury 1 to me over an argument with Roger. "Do you recall what brought on the uproar?"

"All I know is Roger and I were talking about going back home. He wants to visit his mother, who's getting up in years. And Beth yearns to go back to see her grandmother's house and her elementary school once more. While we were talking, Fury 1 pushed me aside and barged out, I guess."

What happened was a consequence of her conversation with Roger, I explained. The Parts heard them talking and were alarmed by what was said. The Furies and Sebunome had recently expressed their determination not to return to her mother's house. I cautioned that, until these Parts worked through their traumatic experiences, a trip to see her mother was not in her best interest.

"I wish Roger could be dissuaded," Joan said, "from getting embroiled in senseless arguments with Parts like Fury 1. It's difficult for him to tolerate the volatile and destructive ones. *I* even have trouble sometimes admitting they are a part of me. I guess we both have to accept the 'bossy and mouthy' ones are indeed a part of me."

"Please understand that when one of your 'mouthy' Parts has a flashback, the content of the flashback is part of your history of abuse. Moments ago, Fury 1 disclosed watching a spider crawl up a wall while being raped under the basement stairs. Do you recall that incident?"

She quickly masked a flicker of remembrance in her eyes. "Not really. But I've told you several times I always had an aversion to going down to the basement. And as long as I can remember, I've been terrified of spiders."

Knowing this particular memory had been brought to light a third time, I had no doubt it would eventually come forward in Joan's consciousness. I probed no further.

"Anyway," Joan said, flipping her long, wavy hair behind her shoulder, "considering what you said about the Parts' resistance, I'll speak to Roger about postponing our trip."

"That's a sensible thing to do, Joan."

Close to bedtime, Raven phoned to apologize again for the earlier "intrusion." He went on to express grave concern about Fury 1's behavior. Her ability to cross the Edge with such speed made her difficult to contain. She defied learning to behave in a less disruptive fashion or to share her troubling memories with the others. To rein in her independent and impulsive nature, Raven had arranged for her to spend time in the tranquil environs of the Blessing Lady. Furthermore, he had appointed Samantha and Shadowman to instruct Fury 1 in the protocols that inspire consideration and cooperation from the other Parts. He asked for my patience as he continued efforts to tame Fury 1's willful behavior.

~

Chapter 64

THE LAKE

M*ay 1.* "I'm not up to working on anything right away," Joan began. "What I need is just a few moments of peace."

"Let's have a cup of tea and sit out on the porch for a while. It's spring. The trees have leafed out. The first flowers are in bloom. So, come on—it will do us both good." ·

I watched Joan limp stiff-legged out to the porch on ankles more swollen than usual. "I packed my husband off this morning to see his mother." Carefully, she lowered herself onto a garden chair. I sat beside her, poured the tea, but didn't speak. Joan closed her eyes and turned her face to the soft rays of the afternoon sun. *I smiled to myself thinking that people passing by see two women sitting outside enjoying the warmth of the spring day unaware of what we were about. With no idea how we struggle, as Beth might say, to "glue" the pieces of the younger woman's mind together with all the fortitude and care we could find between us.*

She struggled out of the chair. "I left something in the car." She returned with a medium-sized painting entitled *The Lake*, written in pencil on the back of the canvas.

"Several weeks ago, after Rose mentioned the lake, I began having flashbacks—I couldn't breathe. I felt like I was drowning—then I found myself painting this. It's about the time one summer I went swimming with my mother, Lillian, and Charles. School was out, and it was hot. My mother and sister went into the water first; Charles and I followed. He'd pretend to play with me, push me under the water, hold me down, and when I struggled desperately for air, pretend to rescue me like it was a game. But every time Charles pushed me under, he'd press me close to his body and rub me against his genitals. At some point, he reached down and pulled my swimsuit aside and entered me. I held on to him, desperately afraid I'd be pushed under again and drown. I remember he teased, 'You like this, don't you?' Of course, I didn't, but I was too frightened to let go of him."

"And your mother?"

"She was playing with my sister and probably thought we were having fun splashing around in the water."

Joan's face contorted. Fury 1 pushed out. "I was there. We all were," her voice tremulous, "Sebunome and Rose, Samantha, Sarah [Christine], and Marjorie." Fury 1's hands balled into fists. She bent forward and pummeled her thighs. "I felt so goddamn helpless. We all did."

I took her hands in mine. "There's no need to punish yourself. Turn your anger toward the one who took advantage of your helplessness."

The Lake, Joan and Fury 1 2007.

To the ones on the Inside, who also held outrage over this event, I explained that they needed to release that anger to heal the trauma they had suffered. After listening inward for a moment, Fury 1 reported that all wished to participate as a group.

"Then if everyone is ready ... close your eyes ... take a deep breath ... and remember, you are all safe here with me. Now ... I invite you to re-experience your panic in the lake. That's right . . . Stay with the terror . . . keep breathing in and out . . . that's right. Without resisting, let the terror rise . . ."

Her chest heaved. Her breathing became erratic. I paused a few moments before continuing. "Take a long, deep breath . . . and as you exhale, allow the disturbing emotion to slowly subside. Once more, inhale . . . and as you exhale . . . let it go."

Silence eddied about us.

Fury 1's eyes snapped open. "How long do I have to sit here before I feel better? I've endured enough of this," and she disappeared.

"I suffered through that horrible summer outing along with the others." Joan's voice sounded weary. "Now, I guess Ana and I can add the lake episode to the Lifeline."

Beth called around ten p.m. "Oma, Raven told me to call you for help. Fury 1 wants to cut."

"Does she have a knife?"

"I think so."

"Is it possible to speak with Fury 1?"

I waited until I heard a muffled, "Hi."

"I understand you're very upset."

"We're having flashbacks about the lake. We're all hurting. That's why I want to cut. Joan wants to cut, too. She wants to see the blood. She said cutting releases the tension. But Raven said if I cut, I would hurt everyone, even the ones who don't want to see the blood."

"Most of you would feel the cut," I agreed, "and even though cutting may give you momentary relief, after a while, the emotional pain returns and hurts even more."

"Raven told me, if I hurt the Body, then Charles would win. What does that mean?"

"I think Raven is trying to tell you it would undo what Joan and the others have accomplished so far—you know, coming to terms with what Charles did."

Silence.

"I have an idea. When any of you have the urge to cut tonight, instead of using a knife, find a red marker and pretend you're cutting the Body with it. You'll see lots of red that looks like blood, but you won't actually harm the Body. Ask Samantha to help you find a marker. And be sure to return the knife to where you found it so everyone will be safe tonight."

Joan telephoned the next morning to inform me that the psychological turmoil of the night before had passed. Fortunately, no cutting occurred while she had been dissociated. However, she was puzzled over finding red markings all over her body. I smiled to myself, visualizing all the Parts cooperating in wielding the red marker.

Chapter 65

THE TRUTH SEEKER

M*ay 24.* This was our first session in three weeks. Illness had kept Joan from coming to therapy.

"I still don't have much stamina," she said and asked to go to the Safe Place, where she could rest. "I promise to listen, but I'll leave it up to Raven to choose what we work on today."

Sebunome emerged.

"I came to see you, Helper Oma, because I have to get clean before I become one with Rose. I want to wash away the poison stuff he put inside me."

"I'll be glad to help," I responded. "Let me explain what we have to do. I'll guide you back into the past to a time of your choosing so you may re-remember the traumatic events which make you feel unclean. Doing so will not make the memories go away, but it will cleanse the toxins from your emotional wounds."

Reaching for my hand, she said in measured words, "I'm ready. I want to go back to when I was eight. That's when the dread started."

"Then let's begin there. For your safety and my peace of mind, may I suggest we tie a silk ribbon around your wrist? I shall hold the other end in my hand. As you revisit the past, should your feelings become too severe to bear, pull on the ribbon, and my voice will guide you back to the security of this room."

She squeezed my hand in thanks.

"Now, close your eyes, take a deep breath, and allow your body to relax . . . you are beginning to feel yourself getting younger . . . back to thirteen . . . back to twelve . . . you're eleven . . . nine . . . and now you're eight . . ."

"There's Charles . . . and my grandmother's boyfriend," she said in a monotone. "Both abuse me . . . My mother seems not to notice, and that makes me sad . . . I have no one to turn to." She moved forward in time. "I'm nine . . . The abuse gets worse . . . My mother pretends she doesn't know . . . My sadness and dread increase. The librarian touches me . . . What she did makes me think no one can be trusted." There was a long pause, her breathing shallow. The ribbon tightened in my grip. "I'm ten . . . We write a note to the Mother . . . but she doesn't save us . . . and did nothing to protect me. Dread and sadness and distrust are the only feelings I have."

Thus far, Sebunome's re-remembering was unlike how others had reacted. She had not re-experienced the pain of the traumatic events. There had been no expression of terror, no outcry of despair, no tears. Just a rational recitation of what had occurred and the conclusions she made.

"Now I'm eleven . . ." her voice broke with a sob, her stoic demeanor dissolved. "I'm . . . not ready to tell. The others aren't, either."

The tension on the silk ribbon increased to the point that I thought bringing her forward to the present was prudent.

"Helper Oma, I needed to come back to be with you while I emptied myself of the hatred I have for Charles."

Her teeth clamped down on her lower lip as she struggled to maintain her composure. Finally, she spoke: "You raped me. Choked me. Threatened me. You lied. You buried me. Cut me. Used my body. Gave me money. You shamed me," her words steeped in contempt.

Sebunome seemed to stop breathing. I gently touched her arm. She came back speaking with uncharacteristic fierceness. "I never kept your money! I gave it away."

I suggested we step outside for a breath of fresh air. We stood on the porch a few moments in the late May sun. She turned to me and asked to blow the remnants of her revulsion into a plastic bottle, as others had. I fetched a large soda bottle. Sebunome exhaled the residue of her contempt into the plastic jug, capped it, threw it to the floor, and kicked it off the porch. Her eyes flat with disgust, she retrieved the container and discarded it in the garbage bin behind my office. She returned with luminous satisfaction in her eyes.

"That should do it, Sebunome," I said in approval.

As we re-entered the therapy room, I gently squeezed her hand and thanked her for trusting me to guide her into the past. I emphasized how important trust was to the healing process. "You see, Sebunome, through trust, we gain confidence in ourselves and our ability to differentiate who is authentic and who is not. Trust allows us to accept the fact that not all people are bad—that most are good."

Joan re-emerged. I inquired if she and the other Parts had heard what Sebunome disclosed during her regression. Had they co-experienced Sebunome's emotional discharge of hatred for Charles? Joan confirmed she and some of the Parts had, indeed, participated while gathered in the Safe Place. I encouraged her and the others to observe a moment of respectful silence to reflect on Sebunome's truth.

Sometime before midnight, Fury 1 phoned. She reported Sebunome's telling had triggered painful memories among those who had listened. She said the Parts had assembled in the Meadow and together recalled all the abusers who had ever molested or raped them. There had been five perpetrators: Daddy, Charles, the man with black hair, Charles' brother-in-law, and the school librarian. I didn't mention that there had been others but thanked her for letting me know that the Parts were sharing what they remembered. Fury 1 said they again had used the red marker to ease their distress.

June 12. Sophia, the shy outsider, had matured over the two years since suffering through being raped under the basement stairs. Today, she informed me of her intentions to fuse with Sebunome and Rose. However, she felt insecure about what she could offer the union. And she was anxious about merging should afterward it prove to be a mistake. I told her she was smart to evaluate such a big decision beforehand and assured her she had much to offer: her bravery, like when she escaped Many Voices' Dark Forest;

her agility, like how she dodged Shadowman's Puppets; and her speed, as evidenced by running "like the wind" through the Outer Edge. When I extolled her fluency with sign language and how finding her voice enabled her to express her inherent sweetness, she smiled and went back Inside.

Sebunome came forward, her face pinched. She was worried that her mistrust of people would "pollute" Rose once they merged. I comforted her that prudence would be a valuable gift to their union. Ever the Doubting Thomas, Sebunome said she needed to think about that. She reminded me there was one more thing she had to do and asked when "Mr. Caldwell" could meet with her to practice being in the presence of a man without being frightened. If successful, she then could free herself of the pervasive distrust she held for all men, and cleanse herself of the remaining toxins she thought made her unworthy of becoming one with Rose.

With Joan's consent, we agreed on an appointment with my husband during the following week's session.

On the day of the meeting, Joan voiced optimism at Sebunome's maturation. She had heard that Sebunome planned to sit beside my husband to test if he might take advantage of her when given the opportunity. And to test herself if she could overcome her aversion to being touched by a man. Sebunome had agreed to be observed by Joan and the Parts who wished to witness what was about to take place.

When my husband knocked on my office door, I invited him into the therapy room and suggested he sit in my rocking chair across from Sebunome. Taking a chair off to one side, I observed both to be somewhat nervous. I was surprised when Sebunome looked straight into my husband's eyes and asked, "What do you think about men who abuse and hurt young girls?"

"I believe they are confused," he replied, "and perhaps were themselves hurt when they were young boys. Regardless, abusing and hurting girls is wrong and inappropriate. Knowing it has happened to many young girls makes me sad."

Sebunome nodded with approval. "Would you do something bad if you had the opportunity to be alone with a young girl?"

"No."

"Even if she offered to let you do anything you wanted to?"

"No. Doing something to her, even if she would invite it, would be just as inappropriate and hurtful. That would hurt my heart."

Sebunome looked my way with satisfaction in her eyes. Then to my surprise, she asked me to leave the therapy room. She wanted to be alone with my husband to test him further. I left the door ajar and positioned myself in my outer office so I could monitor their interaction. They talked softly and occasionally actually laughed. After about ten minutes, my husband exited to tell me Sebunome wanted me to join them. With a smile, she reported that Mr. Caldwell had passed the test with an "A+." When she had asked him to sit beside her, he left an appropriate space between them. She also asked him to touch her hand—twice, in fact—and he had done so with gentleness, not a "bad touch."

My husband stood, formally shook Sebunome's hand, and left my office.

"I tested Mr. Caldwell . . . It was hard, especially when I asked him if he ever had dark thoughts about girls. He said, 'Yes,' but told me not about babies or young girls, but sometimes about teenagers. Then he explained to me when dark thoughts came into his mind, he listened to his conscience, which told him it was wrong to think that way. I thanked him for being honest. I appreciated he didn't lie and told me the truth."

"Being alone with a man, sitting beside him, asking him uncomfortable questions, even touching his hand, took fortitude, Sebunome."

"I wasn't alone," she corrected. "Samantha, Shadowman, Rose, Fury 1, and some others were close by. They supported me. When Mr. Caldwell spoke his truth," she added, "my heart started to ache."

"When truth is spoken, lies are shattered. Truth changes how one thinks and feels. And change often hurts, even when it's for the better. The truth Mr. Caldwell spoke changed your reality, Sebunome."

"So, it was a bad thing," she asserted, "when Charles acted on his dark thoughts. Now we know he didn't listen to his conscience. Charles lied when he told us we were bad and tried to make us believe we deserved being hurt. If he had listened to his conscience, he never could have hurt any of us. Do you listen to your conscience, Helper Oma?"

"Usually, but when I don't listen to that voice inside me, I sometimes fail to do the right thing. How about you?"

"Most of the time," Sebunome confirmed hesitantly. "Usually we listen to Raven, but sometimes we don't. That's when we get into trouble."

Sebunome bowed her head for a moment and then looked at me beseechingly. "Do you think I did well?"

"You did *very* well, Sebunome."

"Mr. Caldwell said I was smart and good. I hope Raven will be proud of me. I want to go back Inside now and talk with the others."

Without being invited, Beth exited. She asked to take a walk around the neighborhood. As we strolled beneath the trees, she talked of her worries about having to integrate with Joan.

"Oma, I want everything to stay the same. I want to spend time with you, visit with Mr. Opa, and have fun. I don't want to talk about the things that happened, especially the secrets that hurt us. I don't want to be sad. I just want to stay a seven-year-old girl and be happy forever."

Empathizing with her unattainable yearnings, I said, "Remember, Beth, what Raven always says: 'Everything will be as it's meant to be.'"

When we returned to my office, I invited Joan back. She had listened to Sebunome's conversation with "Mr. Caldwell" and believed it had gone well. She was proud of Sebunome and pleased that my husband had been honest with her. "Who would have thought that the shiest, most introverted Part would have that kind of courage? That's truly astounding."

To counter her tendency to experience a Part as separate from herself, I bent Joan's admiration for Sebunome back onto her by praising Sebunome's courage as a reflection of her determination to set aside the distrust she harbored against men.

That evening, sitting on our deck, enjoying the balmy weather and a glass of wine, I thanked my husband for participating in Joan's treatment, as unorthodox as it was. Just after dinner, Sebunome called to report smelling smoke. She believed Many Voices' Dark Forest had been set afire. When I inquired about the cause and received no reply, I suggested, "Is it possible the Forest started to burn when Mr. Caldwell sat beside you and gave his assurance that men who abuse girls are bad? Men who act on their dark thoughts are the bad ones, not the young girls. Men who take advantage when given the opportunity to violate innocence are the bad ones. Perhaps the truth of Mr. Caldwell's statements has ignited the Forest, Sebunome. Perhaps the truth is burning the lies you've been taught to believe. And this is the source of the smoke you and the others smell."

"Maybe," her response tentative.

The truth, I thought, *is like a white, hot flame that incinerates lies and deception. The truth consumes the faulty beliefs children internalize when they are taught they are bad and deserve to be cruelly punished. The truth burns away their negative self-perceptions and false judgments instilled by the wrongful behavior of adults.* "I believe, Sebunome, the truth you have learned from Mr. Caldwell ignited the fire, and what you smell are the lies smoldering. Once the truth burns away the deceptions, you can begin to heal the wounds in your heart and mind."

"Will the truth scar my heart and mind, Helper Oma?"

With less of the schoolmistress in my voice, I answered, "Yes, but those will be healthy scars and will have paled before you integrate with Joan."

Sebunome said nothing further.

The mention of fire and truth triggered a memory from my childhood.

~

Night after night through a tiny attic window, I witnessed the world's condemnation fall from the sky and explode in a fiery fury that purged the murderous lies of the Third Reich. Those same forces of justice freed my birth mother from incarceration. She stood before me in the open attic door. Prison had tarnished her shimmer. Her fur coat ratty now. Her strawberry-blonde hair limp. Her front teeth in decay. The blare of a high-pitched siren warned the village was under attack. With the weight of my little suitcase pulling at my arm, I ran alongside my mother across a field of winter wheat. A handful of villagers sheltered in a tight cluster beneath a stone bridge. Standing in the cold stream, a rheumy-eyed man, chewing his tongue with toothless gums, made room for us. A woman held her young son in an iron grip, refusing to let the war have her last child. When the wail of the siren faded, an eerie silence followed. A sick woman with a racking cough said, "Maybe the war is over." The old man pointed a boney finger at me, "Go see what's going on."

I crawled up the embankment, flat against the damp earth. I saw a line of polished brown boots stepping high, advancing toward us, the ground vibrating. From below me, a voice said, "I hope it's the Americans." As I watched those beautiful, unbroken men from a universe far removed from mine, my six-year-old mind raced into the future. I imagined leaving my ill-fated country to live in the land of these shining warriors. Looking toward the village from my vantage point, I saw a man bent with age, a half-grown boy at his elbow, wave a white handkerchief tied to a stick. My mother grabbed my hand and pulled me toward the crowd gathering around the soldiers. The rheumy-eyed man tugged at her sleeve, pointed toward the burning village, and yelled above the swelling roar that if his house still stood, we could come home with him. In anger, I jerked my hand from my mother's grasp. I didn't want to live in that old man's house. I wanted to go back home—to my foster mother's house—where I felt safe and loved. But it wasn't to be.

~

Chapter 66

LEAVES AND KNIVES

June 21. "For the last few nights, I've heard the Parts talking. No—more like debating."

"Do you know what their conversation was about?"

"They kept their voices too low for me to hear."

"Shall we try to find out? However, should what is being revealed become too upsetting, please lift your forefinger, and my voice will guide you back to the safety of this room."

Joan closed her eyes. Her head inclined to her right shoulder . . . and Sebunome exited, her manner somber. "Thank you, Helper Oma, for seeing me. The older ones and I have been meeting in the Meadow to share what each of us knows. We have reached a consensus that now is the time to reveal the whole truth about Charles' worst deeds—the ones Joan refuses to remember and we desperately avoid speaking about outside the Inner Realm. You've heard some of it already from me and Rose and Shadowman, but they chose me to speak for all and tell you everything." *I was perplexed by this meek Part's rising importance within the system, evolving from Truth Seeker to Truth Teller. Had she been chosen to function in this role because of her stoicism and self-discipline? One who could "tell" without being undone by the horror of the abuses?*

She took a steadying breath and stood. "Can we lie on the floor? Having you beside me will make it easier for me to tell."

We stretched out on the carpet as her mind turned to the past. "We've already told you that Charles molested us from the start, and you know that, after he and Mama married, it got worse." By the time Joan was ten, Sebunome told me, Charles was obsessed with her, and the abuse never let up. That's when Joan and some of the mature Parts wrote the Mother a note and put it in the top drawer of her dresser, where she kept her personal things—earrings and scarves and the like. They waited for her to say something, but she never did. Several days later, Joan and a few of the older ones finished the lunch dishes quickly because they wanted to go to the woods out behind the house. It was their haven, a peaceful place among the trees. Away from the Mother. Away from Charles. Sometimes they would sit on a stump there in the woods and write poems.

"That day, Joan and I rushed out the back door and through Mama's garden. It was fall, and her white mums were in bloom. We thought Charles was rummaging around in the basement. We carefully closed the garden gate so he wouldn't hear it creak. But he must have heard anyway, because he followed us. When we heard the dry leaves crunch under his footsteps," Sebunome shuddered, "we started to shake inside something fierce. Charles had a rope. He grabbed us by the arm and tied us to a tree. He stripped off our underwear and pushed himself into us. 'Guess who found your little note?' he hissed in my ear. When he was done, we watched him pile twigs and small branches around the base of the tree. Then he lit a match and held it up close to our eyes. With an evil sort of grin, he said he was going to burn us alive and asked if I was ready to die. We nodded 'Yes,' Helper Oma. Dying by fire was terrifying—but living at home was worse. He lit one match after the other, holding each little flame close to our cheek while he fondled us. I remember his strange, squeaky voice: 'You had to tell, didn't you? You just won't learn.' Then he lit the twigs around our feet and watched us squirm in the smoke. That's when Joan went away."

Sebunome winced, her brown eyes shiny with terror. She fumbled for my hand and placed it over her pounding heart. "This is where we hurt."

She regained her focus and turned her head to face me. "You see, throughout the torture and rape, others came out, one by one. I could not have survived without their help."

"Thank goodness the Parts came to your rescue, Sebunome." I spoke into her silence, "Is there more to the story?"

"Yes . . ." Charles stomped out the fire and walked away, she said, leaving them there for a time that seemed endless. When he finally came back, he had a shovel and, without a word, dug a long, shallow hole. He untied them from the tree, pointed to the hole, and told them to lie down in the pit. He shoveled dirt in their eyes and mouth, piled dry leaves over them, and threatened to set their "grave" on fire.

"We just laid there, switching and switching and switching, one after the other. After the longest time, he sneered, 'Have you learned your lesson? Now get up. Go home and clean up and look good. Finish folding the clothes before your mother comes home. And keep your mouth shut!'

"We crawled out, barely able to stand on wobbly legs. We got home as best we could."

Sebunome was panting. With my throat constricted in anguish, I somehow managed to say, "You are here with me, Sebunome. You are safe."

"I know I'm safe with you, Helper Oma, but let me tell you the rest."

"When I got home, I was bleeding down there. My wrists were chafed, and I had bruises on my thighs. But I washed up and said nothing to no one. Not ever." This was when many of the Parts went away, she told me. Others hid in the closet or under the bed—any place they thought Charles couldn't find them. Hidden away like that, they would chant softly: "We are invisible. We can't feel. We can't see. We have no name. Quiet is good. Being good is safe. Safe is invisible. We are nothing."

Thinking her story at an end, I started to get up from the floor, but Sebunome implored me to lie back down. "There's something else . . ."

My stomach lurched. I wanted to put my hands over my ears. I didn't want to hear about one more atrocity. "Are you sure you want to go on?" I asked.

"I want to get empty. I want to get clean. So do the others. I have to tell you *all* our truth."

"Very well," I said, "if you're strong enough . . ."

"Do you remember when our cousin, Jolene, told Mama about Charles?"

"Yes, Rose and Joan told me. That's when the Mother took Joan to Aunt Marcy and Uncle David's house."

Sebunome paused. Her next words were leaden, as if the memory she carried was a terrible burden. She told me that the whole time they stayed at Aunt Marcy's house, the uncle sexually mistreated Joan and the Parts. That was when Sebunome and Fury 1 started to believe that all men were bad and couldn't be trusted. When Joan's mother came to pick them up, neither Joan nor a Part told her what the uncle had done because they didn't want their mother to get upset. As soon as they were home, Charles resumed molesting them. One day, their mother went shopping at the mall and left Joan behind to watch little Samuel. Joan didn't mind because she loved the baby. Charles stayed home, too. As soon as their mother was gone, Charles took Joan to her bedroom, pushed her on the bed, pulled off all her clothes, and raped her. "I remember when he was on top of us," Sebunome said, "he was sweating. It smelled bad and made me sick to my stomach. After he finished, he told me, 'Stay put.'

"Charles went someplace, maybe down to the basement, and came back with a knife in his hand. When Joan saw the knife, she got very scared and went away. But me and Rose, Samantha and Sarah Christine, and the Furies—we stayed and took turns while he tortured us with that knife and watched us with those dead eyes."

A chill iced my spine as Sebunome described the torture and mutilation in a voice choked with agony. When she finished her dismal reverie, she and I lay there side by side on the floor, bleak and desolate.

"Did you scream, Sebunome?" my voice wispy with shock.

She shook her head, "No, I didn't scream. I had to be quiet. I had to be a good girl. I could feel the blood trickling out of me. My stomach cramped. My legs trembled. It felt like I was on fire down there. But I didn't cry out. I didn't make a sound."

At some point, Sebunome and the others went away. She didn't remember exactly where, except that it was a white place where they couldn't feel anything, where they didn't hurt. They came to with Charles' hand gripping their jaw and moving their head back and forth. "I heard him saying, 'Don't you play dead now. If you die, it will kill your mother.'"

Sebunome looked at me with dogged grief. "That was true. Mama had not been very strong ever since Samuel was born. So, we didn't die, and we never told. We wanted to protect Mama."

White in the face, Sebunome curled into a fetal position. "All of us are soiled and tainted," she uttered. "We can never get rid of the slimy stuff he put inside us. The scars will never go away. We're branded for life."

After some time, she straightened and matter-of-factly stated, "For the record, Helper Oma, we were only eleven years old."

I turned my face to hers. "Are you ready to get up, Sebunome?" I carefully helped her stand. She leaned against me as she took unsteady steps to the couch. I sat beside her, and we held hands. *How brave,* I thought, *to have trusted me with her excruciating truth.*

She seemed to be listening inward. "All of us want to cleanse ourselves of Charles. And wash off our shame."

I assured her I would arrange a cleansing ritual with Elizabeth. Without another word, Sebunome returned to the Inner Realm.

My energy flagged. I closed my eyes to marshal the strength to complete the last phase of this afternoon's grueling work—for Joan to divulge what she had heard and possibly experienced. I called for Joan. Her voice came to me as if from a great distance.

"I'm afraid I'm stuck Inside. I can't cross the Edge. It's like a strong wind is holding me back. I can see you from behind my eyes, but the view is blurred. The chaos here is overwhelming." In a rush, she said, "I heard all that Sebunome disclosed, and I was there again. With Rose, Samantha, Sarah Christine, Sebunome, two closet girls, Jasmine and Eve, and the three sisters—Marjorie, Fury 1, and Fury 2—even Diana, who I thought was dead and buried. We all were terrified. Like with one mouth, we screamed out the gory details—being tied to a tree, raped, threatened with fire and buried alive . . . even the cutting. We all saw it and felt it and suffered it. Their emotions enveloped me. No, not 'enveloped' . . . *infused* me with their rage and despair, helplessness and shame. The Inner Realm was like a ball of red energy filled with the intensity of all we felt. For the first time as one being, we experienced the trauma of these two ghastly events from beginning to end. Now that I know . . . I feel . . . broken."

Keeping my inner turmoil in check, I spoke through to the system. I urged Joan and the Parts to go to the Meadow, sit in the Circle of Truth, and invite the Golden Light to restore them. When Joan's body language indicated she and the others had achieved homeostasis, I implored the Parts to assist Joan across the Outer Edge so she could return to the therapy room.

When she was fully present, she wept. I allowed her to sit with her grief.

"This was hard," sobbed Joan.

"Yes, this was hard."

Wretchedness had etched furrows around the corners of Joan's mouth. Her cheeks still wet, she reached for her purse and stood. "Don't worry about me, Renate, I'll be all right. But now, I need to be alone. I'll drive to the nearest parking lot and just sit and grieve."

As I walked her to the door, I put my arm around her shoulders and praised her for staying present throughout the ordeal. "Please don't hesitate to call if you need to talk. Day or night."

As soon as Joan's car pulled out of the driveway, I rushed to open the windows to rid the therapy room of the stench of barbarity that had accumulated during Sebunome's disclosures. *Never before had I heard firsthand of such savagery committed against a helpless child. My soul shuddered.*

I was emotionally unable to go home and resume any semblance of my regular life. Instead, I walked two blocks to the university to sit on the bench my husband and I had donated in dedication to the matriarchs in our lives. I poured out my despair to my beloved foster mother, my Mama. In time, I managed to quiet my heart. Student voices chattering as they passed by brought me back to my surroundings. The University clock tower showed five minutes shy of nine. The day was turning to dusk. *Time to go home*, I thought. From half a block away, I saw my husband kneeling in the flower bed at the front of our house. Sensing my approach, he rose, spade in hand, dirt crusted to the knees of his khakis, and walked toward me. My steps quickened. He wrapped one arm around my shoulders.

"Glad you're home," he said. "Are you hungry?"

"Famished," I answered against his cheek.

Raven telephoned late that night to assure me that he had watched over Joan while she listened to Sebunome's grim tales. As Joan learned of Charles' brutality, becoming fully cognizant of his spiritual malignancy, he said his "heart hurt" and then corrected himself to say his "spirit hurt." This had been beyond his ken and had left him adrift.

~

Chapter 67

CLEANSING THE VAGINA

W*hen Joan walked through my office door*, her face was void of emotion. Once seated, however, the restless twisting of her laced fingers told of her inner turmoil.

"I'm not the same, Renate. I might look and act the same, but I'm not. Last session, when I couldn't escape the agonizing chaos, something deep inside me shattered. I feel like Humpty Dumpty," she said through lips that barely moved. "All week, I've tried and tried to put myself together again, but I couldn't."

The nursery rhyme was a perfect analogy, I thought, *for how she seemed to experience herself just now.* "With my guidance, Joan, once you work through Charles' transgressions and move through the terrible knowledge that Sebunome laid bare, then unlike all the King's men, you *will* be able to put yourself together again. And where you were broken, you will be stronger."

"Stronger?" sounding incredulous.

"In time, Joan. In time."

Joan reported that the Parts who'd experienced last week's "ball of red energy" were now in the doldrums. "They feel they've failed to protect me. Failed to keep secret Charles' worst deeds."

"They thought," I explained, "their responsibility was to keep those memories secret from each other, secret from you, and secret from outsiders like me. Now they are dismayed for having forsaken their calling and divulged what they knew." Furthermore, I continued, they had begun to realize they were part of her—not separate. This had left them confused about their identities, individual roles, and functions. Hence, the doldrums. But letting go of their secrets was a positive development that offered her the opportunity to make the memories they held her own.

She heard what I said but was still struggling to embrace that what Sebunome had revealed had actually happened to her. I told Joan that before she and the Parts could relieve the agony those memories held and begin to heal, I believed a cleansing ritual would be beneficial. Last week I had promised to arrange such a cleansing to rid the Parts of Charles' contamination and attend to the scars his torture had left. When I inquired if she wanted to participate, Joan declined and went to the Safe Place. I welcomed her decision. *I thought attending the ritual would have been traumatizing. Besides, any relief the Parts experienced would simultaneously relieve some of that shame in Joan.*

I called for Elizabeth and described what I needed: a room with a large bathtub and a hand spray; plenty of hot water and washcloths and towels; plus soap, lotions, and a medicinal salve. Elizabeth offered the yellow room that Maria, Lisa, and Charlotte had occupied before they integrated. I expressed my gratitude and spoke through to Sebunome, Rose, Samantha, Fury 1, and the others who knew of the abuse in the woods and the cutting. I instructed the Parts to go to Elizabeth's House. She would lead them to the room where the cleansing ritual was to take place. I asked that they put aside their unease and assured them my voice would guide them through the rite.

"Once you're there, please fill the bathtub with warm water," I told them. "Disrobe, and, one at a time, climb into the tub. Immerse yourselves in the soothing water. Reach for the shampoo and wash out the leaves still clinging to your hair. Use a soapy washcloth to lather your entire body. And wash away the grime. Take your time. Be gentle at the raw places, your chafed wrists and bruised thighs.

"Now, what I'm going to ask you to do will be difficult. Give support and encouragement to one another. Remember, you are good. You are strong. And you are safe."

I invited them to take a long, comforting breath and gingerly place a hand on the vagina. "Now, with a finger, lightly trace the scars left by Charles' mutilation. Take heart. What I shall ask of you next may provoke revulsion, even self-loathing. Try to stay calm . . . Be strong. With care, reach deep inside, as deeply as possible, and remove the abuser's 'slimy' discharge . . . When you have completed this necessary task, stand and drain the tub of its dirty water. Use the hand-spray to run clean, warm water over the entire Body. Start at the neck and shoulders . . . down the back . . . and over the stomach. Use the spray to rinse off the last traces of shame.

Innocence Restored, Joan and the Parts 2007.

"When this is done, step out of the tub, dry yourselves with the soft towels Elizabeth has provided . . . and lotion the whole Body. Dip your fingers in Elizabeth's medicinal salve, and gently massage the cream into the vaginal scars."

I paused a few moments. "You have all been brave. You have cleansed yourselves of Charles' degradation. It is done."

The ticking of my watch filled the stillness that followed. I hoped everything had gone well. When Sebunome emerged, she motioned for me to sit beside her. She laid her head on my shoulder. "Touching the scars made the Furies rage but the rest of us were very sad. We wanted to cry. Only our tears didn't flow."

I lightly stroked her hair. "Be patient, sweet Sebunome. In time, the tears will flow."

"Thank you, Helper Oma. We are clean now."

I asked Joan to return, and, after providing a cautionary account of what had taken place, I suggested whenever she found the emotional strength, she could rely on my help to rid herself of the shame of "Charles' worst deeds."

Rose called around eleven that night. After taking a warm shower, she had applied lotion "down there."

"It felt good, Oma. I didn't want to stop. Is that bad?"

I assured her it wasn't.

"Oma, I don't think Joan touches herself there."

"We have to be patient," I said, "and give her time."

Near midnight, the telephone rang again. It was Raven. He sounded unusually distant and reserved.

"Teacher, I am not sure it is wise to teach the Parts about the Body. Beth and Sebunome heard your conversation with Rose. May I advise that what you are trying to teach them is best left unmentioned."

"I apologize if I have displeased you, Raven. I do understand your apprehension." Nevertheless, I told him our objective was to help Joan grow into a fully functioning human being. Part of the process included learning to embrace—in fact, *celebrate*—every aspect of her womanhood. To achieve that goal, Joan would have to heal the disconnect between her mind and body. I was teaching Rose to overcome her inhibitions, so, in turn, Joan would learn that touching and experiencing pleasant feelings "down there" was not disgusting and shameful, but normal and healthy. "My hope, Raven, is to help Joan heal the schism so that, on the day of Joan's and

Joanna's reunification, a positive attitude toward her womanhood will be Joanna's inheritance."

"Very well, Teacher. I shall yield. But I'm not entirely convinced of the correctness of your methods."

~

Chapter 68

THE ONLY MEDICINE

July 31. The first rays of sunlight plated the sky copper. My husband and I were sitting on our deck, drinking our first cup of English tea, when the telephone rang. I could barely hear Beth's lisp. "Oma, a lot of drinking's going on. I'm scared."

"Where is Joan?" I asked, my heart sinking.

Beth whispered that Joan could not be found. I asked if anyone had called for Raven's help. "He just sits way up there on his Perch with his eyes half-open. I don't think he likes drinking, Oma. He says it causes lots of problems. Can you help?"

I told her I would phone Stephanie to help. When Joan's daughter answered, I apologized for calling so early and told her of Beth's warning. "Do you know anything about this?" She replied that Megan had come over to her apartment the previous night. Her sister had been beside herself as she reported their mother had been drunk for the past few days. Like many times before, father and daughter had found empty bottles in the utility room hidden under Joan's art supplies and in the garage among her garden tools. "The family can't tolerate my mother's abuse of alcohol any longer."

"The last few sessions have been challenging for your mother, Stephanie."

"That may be, but we're tired of her lies."

Deny and deceive are what addicts do, but I kept that thought to myself. Instead, I explained that her mother drank to numb her pain. And hid her drinking in fear of the family's scorn and the loss of their love. "Your mother is at a pivotal point in her therapy, Stephanie. I'll do all I can to help her through this challenging time, and I know she desperately needs her family's support."

I didn't hear from Joan for another eight days. When she eventually made it to my office, she sat looking like a schoolgirl expecting a scolding. Several times she struggled for words that seemed to stick in her throat. Usually, I would reach out, meet her halfway, and encourage her to speak about what was lying on her heart. But not today. I had grown weary of alcohol hobbling her treatment.

For years, I'd taught her how to cope with newly emerging memories. Even though what Sebunome had brought to light was devastating, I had hoped that Joan and I could have mourned the tragedy and talked through the emotional repercussions of those heinous acts. Instead of calling for my help, she again chose to use alcohol to escape her pain, even though she knew drinking was detrimental to her psychological and physical health, sowed strife within her family, and undermined her capacity to manage her past constructively. I chastised myself for having been too tolerant in allowing this maladaptive behavior to go on. The time had come, I thought, for Joan to take responsibility for addressing her addiction.

"I believed I had the strength to do what the others had done," Joan finally said. "I went into the bathroom to cleanse myself. I turned on the shower, took a deep breath, and stepped in. As soon as I felt the first drops on my shoulders, I must have lost time."

"Do you remember going to the liquor store?"

"That was probably Fury 1."

"Do you know what persuaded her to do that?"

"Maybe she felt like I did after Sebunome revealed what Charles had done."

"More likely," I said, "when you braced yourself to cleanse your vagina, Fury 1 must have been co-present and felt your terror and your subsequent need to numb out. That's what I think persuaded her to take over the Body and go to the liquor store."

"I don't remember any of that. All I know is she's ruining my life, and I want you to get rid of her."

"Perform an exorcism? It's not the Middle Ages, Joan."

"Could you at least put her back to sleep?" *What a misfortune that would be after all the effort to win her trust.*

"I can't do that either, Joan. Fury 1 would have to be retraumatized and *choose* to go back to sleep. If she did, then you, Joan, would have to experience the anger you are too frightened to express."

Recoiling from my statement, Joan wrapped her arms about her. "But Fury 1 causes so much trouble. No one likes her, not even Raven."

"Instead of shunning her, I suggest you and the Parts embrace her, share her burden. And Joan, please communicate this to Raven as well."

"I don't know where Raven is. I called for Samantha's help, but she didn't respond either."

"They are probably exhausted," I speculated, "and have withdrawn to renew their energies."

A lull in our conversation provided the opportunity for me to refocus Joan's attention on her addiction. I asked if she had considered how much power she had over her family when she drank. She contended no one knew about her drinking except Roger. I pointed out that her children knew. I was sure her employer suspected, and probably her neighbors and friends at church as well. "All that chaos your drinking causes—the arguments, the worry, the burden your inebriation places on those you care for—someday, Joan, they will lose their patience and turn away."

She looked shocked. "Are you trying to make me feel guilty?"

Many times, I had asked Joan to enter a substance-abuse program but had failed to convince her. Now, all I could do was urge her to once again recommit to Alcoholics Anonymous and seek the support of her sponsor. I considered it imperative for Fury 1 to be co-present. Both of them needed to hear firsthand from those in AA how abusing alcohol had cost them their jobs, their families, and eventually their health. The attendees, I explained, hoped sharing their stories and accepting responsibility for their drinking would help them stay sober so they could rebuild their lives. Trusting in a Higher Power, they believed if one asked for help in a prayerful manner, one would receive it.

"I've given your predicament serious thought, Joan. I think you should take some time off from therapy to focus solely on getting help with your drinking problem. If AA is not right for you, I again urge you to enter a substance-abuse program."

"But I don't want to stop coming to therapy. I'm sober now."

"Yes, you are today. How about tomorrow? Or the day after? Or the next time you encounter something difficult to deal with? If you hope to make progress in therapy, you can't continue to drink. Otherwise, integration will elude you. To afford you the opportunity to achieve sobriety, I've decided to suspend your treatment for the next three weeks."

I handed Joan a contract with terms reflecting my expressed expectations. Also, I stipulated we meet weekly to review her progress. She looked glum as she penned her signature to paper.

"I'm still sober!" Joan proclaimed at the end of the first week. However, she admitted family obligations had prevented her from going to AA meetings. She and Fury 1 had been reading *The Big Book* together. Suppressing my exasperation, I reiterated the difficulty of overcoming her addiction in isolation—and stressed the importance of attending regular meetings, even several times a day, if necessary. Joan responded by losing time, unable to acknowledge her "drinking problem." *How impregnable was Joan's denial.*

A week later, Joan rummaged in her purse to present me with signed attendance slips from several AA meetings and announced she had admitted to being an alcoholic but only to herself. Although I encouraged her to take the next step, she was "not ready yet" to stand and admit her alcoholism publicly. Fury 1 slipped out to tell of discovering "good people" at AA meetings and assured me she'd "pester" Joan to go there if trouble arose that might lead to drinking. Then Joan again came forward and promised to be ever mindful of what drives her to drink. If tempted, she would immediately call her sponsor and go to AA. But if her sponsor was unavailable, I agreed that Joan could call me.

Addiction, Joan 2009.

At the end of the third week, Joan reported, with considerable pride, to having stood up at the last meeting and, in front of all those people, admitted to being an alcoholic. She told them if she didn't stop drinking, she would lose everything dear to her—her family, her health, and her mind. A couple of hours before going to that decisive meeting, Joan had met with her sponsor and shared her intention. They prayed together, and her sponsor assured her she was taking a critical step toward recovery.

"Driving me to the meeting, my sponsor noticed how nervous I was. She squeezed my hand and told me she had my back. I relaxed and closed my eyes. I silently spoke to Fury 1 and explained what I intended to do. She and her sisters had to cooperate if we were going to stop drinking. Fury 1 agreed to look through my eyes and listen.

"So, I stood up—for me *and* for Fury 1—despite my shame and fear of rejection. I told the members I realized they could not stop me from drinking. I had to do that for myself. Still, I asked for their prayers. I told them I wanted to get sober. I wanted to live. No one interrupted while I spoke, they just listened. When I sat back down, everyone applauded. I saw a woman dab at her eyes. A distinguished-looking man in a suit walked over and shook my hand. Someone else patted me on the shoulder.

"I wasn't comfortable disclosing to them when and why I began drinking. But I need to tell *you*. You already know that Charles started it all when I was about eight. From then on, alcohol was the only medicine to ease the onslaught of his relentless assaults. When I was around ten, I discovered my mother kept vodka in the basement. Whenever she sent me down there to do the laundry, I'd drink some. After a while, I spent lots of time in the basement pretending to do other chores while I drank. I'd add water to the bottle so my mother wouldn't notice. When the bottles were empty, I'd smuggle them out of the house and claim ignorance when my mother wondered what had happened to her vodka. By the time I was twelve, I was going to school drunk. By fourteen, I started experiencing blackouts. And by seventeen or eighteen, I suspected I was addicted to alcohol.

"After I got married, I thought I could be a social drinker. However, you and I know I was fooling myself. In my late twenties, Roger had a near-fatal car accident. The concussion and other injuries changed him. About that time, Stephanie had pneumonia twice, and Megan had one childhood illness after another. Nursing everyone around the clock was exhausting. My drinking increased. After six months, when I thought life was returning to normal, my back blew out. The pain from the surgery was agonizing. When my insurance denied a morphine pump, I became a closet drinker.

"That went on for many years." Joan grew still as if dredging up some crushing memory. Pulling her purse tightly against her body, she said, "There's another reason why I drink. Since I've been sober these last three weeks, I've seen fragments of a memory flash before my eyes. I've been pushing them aside because they make me feel ashamed. The snippets are so vivid and come so often now that I can't ignore them anymore." She took a sip of water to steady her voice. "I've figured out that they are about Samuel and the time I lived at home after high school."

Joan worried the corner of her lower lip. "That's when I began to suspect my little brother was being . . . molested by my mother's third husband. I didn't confront the pedophile. Even more disgusting, I didn't tell my mother. I stayed quiet and did nothing, like I was paralyzed, and buried my suspicion . . . allowing the atrocity to continue. I could have rescued little Sammy . . . but I didn't. Then I moved away when Roger found a job here."

She sank into herself. "How can I ever forgive myself for being such a coward, so negligent? When I think about what became of Samuel . . . He was brilliant but dropped out of school at fifteen and worked menial jobs all his life. He's obese now. An addict . . . and married to an addict. They have two children and live on food stamps. Although he loves them, his kids are malnourished and live in squalor. He's also a thief and has talked my mother out of her life's savings. He's exploited her until she has nothing more to give. I understand why he punishes her for not saving him from that horrible man. In part, I'm guilty, too, for not having protected Samuel. Loving him had not been enough," she said, her eyes welling. *I hoped she would cry to soften her despair. In my mind's eye, I saw the River of Tears rising. Could I ever persuade Joan to accept the fact that the conditioned responses she'd used to protect herself all her life were the causes of her inaction?*

"I no longer can ignore—no, *deny*—that I knew early on about this tragedy and could have prevented it."

Joan fell silent and stared out the window at the trees thrashing in a sudden summer gale. When she turned her attention to me, I asked, "So, what are you feeling, Joan?"

"Guilt and regret," she said, as sorrow spread across her face. "And I have to accept what I cannot change."

"That's right," I affirmed and said nothing more. *Submitting to reality like this, so uncharacteristic of the woman I had come to know, suggested a*

long-repressed burden had been lifted from her soul and that the healing pro-
cess was back on track. I decided Joan and I were ready to resume treatment.

Not long after, Joan suffered a mild heart attack. *Heart-sick,* I thought.
She remained hospitalized through the middle of August. When I visited,
the Parts confided their fear of the "men in white coats." After her discharge, Joan needed a period of convalescence. Then, during the evening of
August 21, I had another grand mal seizure. My doctor immediately started
a series of trials to find appropriate medication for my "late-onset epilepsy."

The intensive therapy and dire revelations of the last four years had taxed
both Joan's and my physical and psychological endurance.

~

Chapter 69

LIVING IS TOO HARD
WITHOUT LOVE

September 7. About three in the afternoon Joan telephoned, sounding on edge. She was upset with Roger and generally fed up with life. I felt a tension headache rise from the base of my skull as I wondered what had provoked her exasperation this time. In a voice without affect, she asked if she could sit on the porch in front of my office for a little while until she regained a semblance of "sanity." I agreed and busied myself catching up with administrative chores left undone in the wake of my illness. As the afternoon drug on and my headache intensified into a migraine, I became concerned about Joan's delayed arrival.

Finally, near five o'clock, she called to say she was on her way. I sat on the porch to wait as the late-afternoon shadows lengthened. After twenty minutes, to my dismay, I saw her car approaching on the wrong side of the street. My heart sank. To my relief, she managed to pull into the driveway without hitting the corner of the building. She got out and lurched toward me hugging a white plastic shopping bag. I rushed to meet her and guided her to a chair on the porch. She sat motionless, staring straight ahead with indifference. I waited about ten minutes for her to speak, but nothing was forthcoming.

I went into my office to call her family. No one answered, so I returned to the porch to cope alone with Joan. As if thinking out loud, she muttered,

389

"I've had it with him. I'm done." By the intonation of her voice, I realized it wasn't Joan but some other Part. I asked who was speaking.

"It's me, Fury 1," she slurred. "I'm drunk, and I've come here to kill myself."

"Can you tell me what's making you feel so desperate?"

"What I want I can never have."

"What do you want?"

"To stop the hurt in my heart."

"What is hurting your heart?"

"Telling won't change it. The only way to end my misery is to kill myself."

"On the contrary, Fury 1, telling may very well help to change whatever *it* is. But if you kill yourself, you'll kill the Body. What do you think will happen to Joan and the other Parts?"

"I'm my own person. If I kill myself, that won't affect the others."

With a sweeping gesture, Fury 1 held up the bag she had brought with her. It was full of Joan's prescription drugs. "I don't need these anymore. I'm going to throw 'em in the trash."

On uncertain legs, she made her way around the corner of the building. Approaching a large green garbage container, she struggled to lift the lid but managed to heave the bag inside. Abruptly, she turned and ran out into the middle of the street and stood there, looking confused. I held my breath as an oncoming car swerved to miss her. She whirled about, ran to a neighbor's yard, and cowered behind their hedge. I pleaded for her to return to the porch. Instead, she scuttled back across the street, darted into my side yard, and disappeared from view.

My husband joined me in searching for the runaway, and together we eventually found her wedged beneath my husband's old Cadillac parked in the carport next door. I fell to my knees, held out my hand, and coaxed her to come out of her hiding place. She timidly grasped my hand as I helped her to awkwardly stand. I brushed the grime from her slacks and wiped her tear-stained cheeks with the hem of my blouse.

Fury 1 searched my eyes. "Living is too hard without love . . . but dying is even harder," her voice desolate. I wrapped my arms around her. She pressed her face into my shoulder and let go a pitiable sound. I asked if she wanted to retrieve the bag of Joan's medications. Standing on tiptoe, she reached into the dark, smelly recesses of the dumpster, retrieved the filthy bag, and pressed it to her chest as if clinging to life itself.

As we made our way back to my office, I recalled her assertion awhile back that she had never been loved. *Could unrequited love be the source of her determination to self-destruct? She needed more than the comfort of my acceptance and caring. But from whom?*

Settling Fury 1 on the couch, I attempted to bring Joan forward. After repeated tries, I suspected Fury 1 had closed off the Outer Edge to bar communication. Resigned to being unable to explore the issue at this time, I phoned Stephanie to collect her mother. When she arrived, we managed to convince Fury 1 to get into the car. As Stephanie drove off, she promised to call as soon as her mother was home safe. About thirty minutes later, she telephoned to report they had made it home despite several attempts by Fury 1 to jump out of the car. In frustration, Stephanie told her it was her choice to jump or not.

Thank God she didn't, I thought and urged Stephanie to convince the entire family to meet with me as soon as possible to develop a strategy for ensuring her mother's future safety.

~

Chapter 70

THE FAMILY

September 13. Joan and Roger and their children, Stephanie and Megan, sat in a semi-circle before me in my now-crowded therapy room. I thanked them for coming and gave an account of what had happened the previous week. I described how Fury 1's intention to kill herself had endangered Joan's life and had put my husband and me in a precarious position. I suggested we explore what each of them could do to help prevent such a crisis from recurring.

Roger ignored my suggestion and spat out, "When I came home that day, Fury 1 was running around drunk and screaming she was going to kill herself." His jaw muscles flexed. "I'm just plain tired of coming home to find Joan, or a Part, drunk. I want Joan to know this cannot go on."

"I hear your weariness, Roger," I said, meeting his angry gray eyes, "but can we explore what precipitated last week's crisis?"

Joan interjected, "I want you all to know I don't have any memory of what occurred. I was told that Fury 1 got drunk, drove over here, and created a real scene."

"Think back, Joan. What happened just before you lost time?"

"I was upset with Roger. When I was released from the hospital—after my heart attack—my doctor gave him written instructions on how to care for me. Somehow, he misplaced them, and I didn't get the care I needed."

I looked at Roger. His lanky frame shrugged away her complaint. "When Joan had her heart attack, I asked for a few days off from work. I went to see her every day in the hospital. And after she came home, I did all the household chores. I washed the dishes, cleaned up the house, did the laundry, went shopping, and whenever she needed something, I got it for her. I sure as hell don't recall the doctor giving me any instructions."

"I appreciate you doing the chores, Roger, but after my heart attack, you showed no compassion or empathy for what I was going through."

I opened my mouth to mention that his perceived inattentiveness might explain Fury 1's desperate behavior, but Joan was not to be denied.

"There's another thing that upset me. When we came home from the hospital, you turned on the TV to watch your car races. You turned up the volume so loud I couldn't get away from the noise. It showed me how little you cared."

Roger retorted in anger, and the bickering escalated.

I held up my palm. "I'm not in a position to resolve your dispute over the television. You're adults. I'm sure you can work out a compromise. Now, what else happened that afternoon?"

This time *Joan* ignored my question, continuing to focus her ire on Roger. "Whenever something annoys you, all you do is get mad and yell. If a Part comes out you don't like, you argue with her or tease her, and it usually ends in a fight."

"Most of the time, I get along just fine with the Parts. But when one like Fury 1 gets drunk and creates a ruckus, I get mad. And you're right—that usually leads to a fight."

I broke in. "Is this what happened last week?"

"Yeah." Roger's cheeks reddened as if embarrassed. His long fingers raked through his hair.

"I've observed whenever one of the Parts acts out, she's upset about something—something which hurts her. A reasonable response," I suggested, "is to approach her calmly and ask what is troubling her. If she becomes hostile, you can call me. I'll find out what's on her mind and try to reframe whatever is the cause of her discontent. If that doesn't work, I'll ask you to bring her to my office."

He yielded without protest, all the heat gone out of him.

I turned my attention to Megan, who was sitting between her mother and father in a teenage funk. Resembling her father, his narrow face and dark-brown hair, she wore jeans and a sequin-trimmed T-shirt. "Your mother speaks fondly of you, Megan. She appreciates you helping whenever she's not well."

"I don't mind helping when she's having a hard time," Megan replied. "But I don't like her drinking."

"And was she drinking that afternoon?"

"No, Fury 1 was. I told her to go back Inside so my mother could come out, but she refused. Said she didn't have to. She could do whatever she wanted, and there was nothing I could do about it. That's when I got furious and tried to take the bottle away from her to pour it down the sink. It turned into a wrestling match. Fury 1 got so upset she hit me with the bottle and pushed me down. She sat on me!" Her voice was shrill as she blinked her eyes, stemming hot tears.

"I appreciate you wanting to help your mother, Megan. Next time, though, before getting embroiled in a verbal or physical altercation, remind yourself that fighting with Fury 1 will only inflame an already volatile situation."

"I just want her to stop drinking. What makes her . . . what makes Mom want to get drunk all the time?"

"Why don't you ask her?"

All eyes turned to Joan, fidgeting in her seat. "I've spent four years in therapy with Renate," she began. "Once or twice a week for three hours at a stretch, working to get well. And every time I come here, the Parts reveal more and more abuses. Some I remember, or only vaguely. Some I don't. But when I hear what was done to me, I feel like a knife is being pushed through my heart. I want to scream and lash out. With each revelation, Renate helps me work through my emotional pain. She teaches me to reframe my perceptions to soothe my heart and mind. But sometimes in the car, after I leave this room, my heartache and abhorrence and shame engulf me. I often break down in tears. I pray to God to help me understand how people who were supposed to care for me could willfully scar my body and mind forever. That's when I lose hope that I'll ever get right. Every cell in my body screams for a drink. Like a sleepwalker, I end up at the liquor store and buy the cheapest vodka on the shelf. Believe me, I don't like the taste. I just don't want to think anymore. Or be ashamed. Or feel guilty. I just want to numb out—pass out and fall into a dark hole where I can forget who I am or what I am."

Joan searched for understanding in the eyes of her family.

"I know it's hard to believe, but it's not always me that gets drunk. Sometimes, when I lose time, a Part takes over my body and goes to the liquor store. Fury 1 does it. Samantha used to do it. So did Sarah Christine and Eve—remember? Some of us are alcoholics. We all have the same need. But when I come to and climb out of the hole, I'm confronted with the chaos and uproar that occurred while I was dissociated—like what Fury 1 caused the other day."

"However," I said, "you don't go to the liquor store after every painful session. For the benefit of your family, please explain the other ways you cope besides drinking."

"You've taught me I have choices . . . Well," she tilted her head back to focus on the ceiling as if instructions were imprinted there, "I start by breathing deeply. I summon all the energies I possess to stay in the present and identify what has set me off. I tell myself I have value and deserve a better life. But if I feel my resolve waning, I call on Raven and God to guide me through this difficult time."

"And instead of reaching for the bottle . . ." I prompted.

"I call my sponsor and ask for her help. Often, we just talk or go to an AA meeting. At home, I read *The Big Book* and ask the Parts who drink to read along. The most important thing for me is to admit I am an alcoholic, and that drinking is destroying my life and the lives of my family."

"Are you prepared to promise your family—?"

Interrupting, Roger scoffed, "Joan has made lots of promises before. Nothing's changed."

"You have a right to be skeptical—"

Stephanie broke in, attempting to placate her father. Pushing back the curly red hair from her forehead, she said, "Dad, please ease up on Mom. She just explained what makes her drink. When Mom's integrated, things will be different. We have to be patient and trust Mom and her therapist."

"I can't promise," Joan conceded. "And I can't promise Fury 1 will never get drunk again. I can't promise she won't try to commit suicide, either."

"Mom," Stephanie, now exasperated, rasped, "if that's the case, then go right ahead. I'm tired of trying to prevent a tragedy when you refuse to prevent it yourself."

She swiveled away from her mother and spoke directly to me. "I have been my mother's 'keeper' since I was about ten. I remember how she was before the alters came out. She was the best mom. Did everything for us. Participated in all kinds of activities at school. But after the alters came out, everything changed."

Stephanie's voice caught in her throat, her gray eyes brimming. She struggled a moment for composure and then declared that her obligations to keep her mother safe, manage her father's impatience, and alleviate her sister's distress were becoming too much of a burden. She wanted to focus on her job, spend more time with her husband, and perhaps have children one day.

While listening to her daughter, Joan started to quietly cry. Sniffling into a tissue, she apologized for being a "burden." She told Stephanie she had been her best friend and only confidante since the Parts' reawakening. She acknowledged how unfair that had been. Henceforth, she declared, she would stop relying on her when something went wrong. "I want you to be free to enjoy your life."

Stephanie, wiping at her eyes, choked out, "It's okay, Mom. I know you didn't mean to burden me. You and Dad can still depend on me whenever something goes wrong. I hope all of us will find ways to cope with the hard times our family's going through."

Sensing an opportunity, I asked the family what changes could ease the situation at home.

In unison, Joan and Roger faced Megan and said, "Clean up your messy room."

Megan's face crumpled.

"Helping with chores without being asked," Joan added, "would stop a lot of arguments. I know it's my fault that you don't clean up after yourself. I've spoiled you. I thought it would make up for all you went through—putting up with my drinking and never knowing what Part would be out when you came home from school."

With emotion-laden words, Megan confessed she was ashamed to bring friends home. She accused her mother of having ruined her life by being a "hopeless drunk."

Joan's shoulders heaved. Tears came in a torrent. She pressed her fists against her eyes as if to dam the flood.

Speaking over the sound of her mother's shame, Megan asserted she was done trying to control her mother's drinking and dealing with Fury 1's escapades. She, too, insisted the burden of responsibility was more than she wanted to carry.

"Your efforts, Megan, have been well-meant. However, keeping your mother sober and safe was never your responsibility." I explained that her mother was the only one responsible for her and the Parts' actions. She alone was accountable for seeking help to achieve sobriety. I sought out Joan's red-rimmed eyes. "Perhaps I should have made this clear earlier that your mother and Fury 1 have made great strides in their attempt to achieve lasting sobriety. Before this latest debacle, your mother was diligently attending meetings and had been sober for nine weeks. I'm certain her commitment to sobriety will continue."

"Dear Megan," Joan's voice soft with compassion for her daughter, "I want you to know how much I appreciate you looking after me when I was drunk. What I've put you through! For that, I'm very sorry. But from now on, you don't need to do that for me. I want you to understand I'm not angry only at you for not picking up after yourself. I'm upset because *no one* asks to help around the house. What I don't appreciate is having to do everything for everyone."

"But Mom," Stephanie countered, "you always did everything for us, so we never had to help."

"Well, it would help a lot now if everyone would pitch in and do their fair share. I have to go to therapy and AA meetings. And besides chores, I want to paint and write and bake cakes for my clients. But all that takes time, and that means I cannot and will not continue doing everything for everyone."

Joan looked at her family, her expression a mixture of sorrow and hope. "All my life, I've taken care of others. As a girl, I took care of my younger sister and brother. I did the household chores while my mother was at work. I took special care of you all. Made sure you had what you needed. I've looked after handicapped children, seeing to their special needs. Now at forty-eight, giving up what I thought was my responsibility to each of you, to just focus on myself . . . Well, that will take some adjustments by everyone." *She inevitably will encounter challenges in making that adjustment,* I thought. *She may feel guilty and unworthy when she focuses primarily on what she likes to do. Since early childhood, she'd internalized that sacrifice-for-others made her a "good girl." I suspected this belief continued to echo within, directing her choices. Freeing herself from this stricture would allow her to unfurl her potential.*

Turning to face her husband, Joan asked, "Do you think focusing on my talents will give me a sense of pride I never had before?"

"I hope so," Roger answered. "Everyone admires your talents. All of us want you to do what makes you happy. We love you and want you to get well." *His tenderness,* I thought, *enhanced his natural good looks.* He praised his wife for having raised their two "wonderful" children, and acknowledged her high moral standards and her readiness to be of help to others. He smiled disarmingly. "It's all right with me if you do your own thing, but please don't stop cooking your pasta dishes. And you know how much we enjoy your cannoli. You wouldn't deny us that, would you?"

Joan made eye contact with each member of her family as she thanked her husband for his support. "What do you think about me fixing up the storeroom beside the garage as my little studio? I'd like to paint it blue."

Roger smiled in silent approval as he stretched out his long legs and crossed them at the ankles. I praised Joan and her family for their candor, and for allowing me to witness their love and devotion. I hoped they were better equipped now to respond to troubling situations at home. The encouraging progress Joan and the Parts were making had convinced me that, as soon as Fury 1 came to terms with what was ailing her, the destructive behavior would cease.

The exhausted family filed out, except for Joan, who stayed behind for a quick word. Concern furrowed her brow. "I don't see how I could have promised to stay sober, Renate. Fury 1 may come out at any moment and take over the Body. She can close off the Edge so the Parts and I can't move back and forth. She can then do anything she wants on the Outside."

"At the first opportunity," I promised, "we'll explore what empowers Fury 1's ability to block the opening at the Outer Edge and hold hostage everyone Inside."

"I just wanted you to know if that happens, there's not much I can do. And remember," Joan cautioned, "this has happened twice before."

After Joan left, I felt too tired to reflect on this puzzling phenomenon. I gathered my notes, blew out the candles, turned off the lights, locked the door, and slowly walked the fifty paces or so home. My husband was waiting, anxious to know why I was so late. "You look so tired," he said. "I'm worried about your health. You continue to work these long hours, even though you're still recovering from the seizure."

"Be patient, my sweet man. Joan and I are making substantial progress. We're getting closer and closer to our goal." *And Joan,* I thought, not without a sense of pride, *had found her voice.* In European fashion, I kissed both his cheeks; then I went to the kitchen and poured myself a glass of red wine.

To my surprise, Joan brought Roger along to our next session. She moved with confidence to her usual place on the couch. Roger moved with less assurance to the seat he had occupied the previous week. I welcomed them both and asked what had motivated Roger's unexpected presence. Joan explained he continued mistreating Fury 1. She thought his name-calling and accusations immature and his scolding demeaning. All of which continued to incense Fury 1. *It seemed the accomplishments achieved last session were for naught, and the discord had continued, if not worsened.*

"On occasion, Joan and the Parts have talked about how much your anger offends and hurts them," I said to Roger. "You might not be aware that they co-experience the discomfort you inflict. That means when you hurt a Part, you also hurt your wife. I hope this understanding may give you pause."

With an edge in my voice, I suggested he consider apologizing to Fury 1.

"I doubt apologizing will change anything," Roger retorted.

"This might be so, but should you choose to treat her with respect, assure her she deserves being cared for, and show regard for her feelings, she just might discontinue her oppositional behavior."

I invited Fury 1 out to visit with us. She avoided making eye contact. Roger somewhat clumsily apologized. I asked her to consider Roger's words of goodwill. She looked at me with leaden eyes and abruptly disappeared. *I realized a constructive dialogue between the two was unlikely at this time.* For Roger's benefit, I described my understanding of Fury 1's cold rejection. "She's testing you. She wants you to accept her as she is, regardless of her behavior. Find the goodness in your heart to reach out to her and treat her kindly. I think you'll be surprised that, over time, she'll learn to trust you and set aside her ill-mannered ways."

"The other day," he said, "Fury 1 told me she wanted to do what Sarah Christine had done. Remember that?"

The sudden reference to Sarah Christine made my head swim with vertigo for a moment. In my mind's eye, I visualized Sarah Christine's deliverance from her sorrow of love unattained. I couldn't help but wonder what persuaded Fury 1 to choose Roger as a confidante. Could the one she espoused detesting be the one she hoped would love her?

I remembered too well and was grateful that Roger had alerted me to Fury 1's most recent suicidal ideations. Should Fury 1 choose to emulate Sarah Christine's fate, I explained, I would first encourage her to examine her motivation. If Raven and the helpers validated her reasoning, I would invite Fury 1 to go to the Meadow to face the Parts in the Circle of Truth, there to convey her feelings. After the Parts expressed their empathy, Shadowman would escort her to the River of Tears. Her mentor, Samantha, would dress Fury 1 in a white gown. Raven would crown her with a wreath of wildflowers, and all would bid her farewell. Samantha then would lead her into the River of Tears to dissolve, her essence becoming a positive force within Joan.

Roger's eyes were wide with amazement. "I had no idea that's what you do in here."

Joan sat up a bit straighter. "What did you think we do here?" a hint of pride in her voice. "What we do is tell our stories. We endure the suffering of our losses, our regrets, our grief. This helps us get well. Sometimes Renate puts me in a trance, talks to the Parts, and performs a ritual like she just described."

Just two hours after our session, Roger telephoned, sounding frustrated. As soon as he and Joan had arrived home, Fury 1 had burst out, hurling verbal abuse his way. She accused him of not having meant a word of his apology, that he was a fake, like all men. I asked to speak with Fury 1, but she refused to come on the line. I requested Roger to keep me informed. To assuage his weary sigh, I told him of my admiration for his support and loyalty throughout all the years of Joan's affliction. His emotion-choked voice and unpretentious, "I appreciate that," confirmed the decency in this man's character I was growing to respect.

Chapter 71

THE FURIES

For the past few weeks, I had become increasingly alarmed by Fury 1's control over the Body. Her ability to dominate the Parts and keep the system closed off from the Outside gave her the freedom to ignore the safety precautions against endangering Joan's life. Her control thwarted Raven's guidance as well as Shadowman's and Samantha's duties to mentor and protect. I was most concerned that her hegemony would make it impossible even for me to intervene. To keep Joan safe, I had to re-establish the balance of power inside the system. To understand Fury 1's ability to wield her dominance, I needed to know which Parts were equally in despair and supportive of Fury 1's deadly intentions. Fortunately, I wasn't completely unaware of which ones were her silent co-conspirators.

At the close of our previous session, Joan and Roger had agreed to a follow-up meeting. I met the couple in front of my office. The fall afternoon was inviting, so I asked Roger to sit with my husband on the deck in the backyard of my home next door while I spent time alone with Joan. I told Roger I would call his cell phone as soon as Joan and I were ready for him to join us.

Joan sat facing me with a quizzical look in her eyes. I explained I wanted to meet with Fury 2 and Marjorie to determine their involvement with Fury 1's intentions and their contribution to her empowerment. I invited Marjorie and Fury 2 to exit.

A Part emerged, her mouth a white line, her eyes behind narrow slits. "I am the sister of the two Furies," she snarled. "I'm the one who hates him the most."

"You mean Charles?"

Rage, Fury 1 2008.

"Yes. I hated his hands touching me. He forced me to know what I should never have known. I hated him more than any words can say. I wanted to step on him and grind him into the floor like a cockroach. I wanted to break his bones to hear him scream in agony. I wanted to cut him, slit his throat, and see him lying on a cold, hard floor bleeding to death. Just once, I wanted him to fear *me* instead of me fearing him. This is how I felt about him then, and I feel the same now. The only solace I've had throughout the years is that I have never cried. Never shall I give him that satisfaction. When he lies on his deathbed, old and weak, I pray unending nightmares of us will taunt him. I hope our silent screams tear at his ears. I want him to feel the burn of our scars. I want him to choke on the blood and filth gushing from our vaginas."

After I recovered from her barrage of hate, I said, "You must be Marjorie."

"Yes, I am."

"I hear your fierce hatred for Charles."

"And my sister—the one you haven't met yet—feels the same. Her hatred is like powerful waves relentlessly crushing boulders to sand."

"You speak like a poet, Marjorie."

"All of us are poets. All of us have written about our suffering. Our hatred and our helplessness."

Her focus shifted as though listening inward. "Fury 2 wants you to hear a poem she wrote. May I recite it for you?"

RAGE
I want to cut and bleed.
Break all the glass and walk through it,
Swallow it, cut deep, cut deep.
Set a fire and lie in it,
Scream till my throat bleeds.
Watch myself go down the drain,
Away, far away from here.
To become quiet, cold and still,
To not know, or feel, or even be,
I want to disappear.
—Fury 2

"Can you grasp now why we are resigned to our fate? We can't unleash our rage and vengeance on Charles. So, the sweet reward of our undoing will deliver us from grief's dark embrace that has held us captive for as long as we can remember. Regardless of the fatal consequences for Joan and the others, we are ready to wreak our unrequited wrath on ourselves and perish."

With my worry veiled, I asked, "Does Fury 1 feel like you and your sister?"

"Ha! Fury 1 never could feel the rage and hatred we felt. She always thought herself more like damaged goods. A throwaway, a nothing. She tried to be a goody-two-shoes amongst all the lies and torment. She wanted to be loved, but no one ever did. When she's on the Outside, she tries to fit in. But she can't get along with Joan's bossy daughter and fights with Joan's husband, who is blind to what she wants most."

"And what is that?"

"Like pathetic Joan, all Fury 1 wants is to be loved, even by Roger, as absurd as that is." *Not so absurd,* I thought. *Fury 1's longing for love may be reflective of Joan's long-ago yearning for her father's love.* "But all of Fury 1's hopes have been dashed. She's deeply depressed and drinks and gets angry and lashes out."

"Are you and Fury 2 helping her to kill herself?"

"Yes—we are sisters. We support her and want her to succeed. We give her all our energy, which makes her strong. Stronger than any of the others. She can overpower them, lock the opening to the Outer Edge, take control of the Body, and find some meds or a razor blade or anything else that will do the trick."

"I appreciate your . . ." I searched for an appropriate response, "loyalty to your sister. And I respect the emotions that motivate such a drastic solution. However, death is irreversible. Committing suicide will rob Fury 1 of the opportunity to put aside her distrust of men and gain Roger's affection." *Until Fury 1 took to heart the truth Sebunome had uncovered in her conversation with "Mr. Caldwell," I was convinced her faulty perception of men would perpetuate her distrust of Roger.*

Marjorie shrugged.

Instead of pursuing her deadly intentions, I asked if she and her sister would consider joining the others to complete the work of healing. I assured her I was prepared to listen to the causes of their outrage and would teach them positive ways to deal with their torment.

Marjorie slipped away. *I hoped she intended to discuss my offer with Fury 2.*

I got out of my chair and stretched, walked over to Joan, and gently touched her forehead. When she re-emerged, I asked if she had heard Marjorie.

"Every angry word."

"What Marjorie revealed should give us pause. We must be vigilant."

Joan nodded.

I called Roger to join us. He sat beside his wife and said, "I know Fury 1's mad about something that happened fifteen years ago. She accuses me of hurting Joan for selfish reasons. She won't let up, just goes on and on. I've apologized a hundred times for what I did." He turned sideways to address his wife. "I'm not the same man now, Joan. You know I've changed."

Joan's face purpled as Fury 1 pushed out. "How would you like to be forced to have sex right out of the hospital? Joan begged you to wait until she felt stronger. But oh, no! You insisted on getting what you wanted, no matter how much it hurt us."

"I'm sorry! How many more times do I have to apologize?"

"I don't care how sorry you are," Fury 1 yelled. "I don't trust you. You're just like all the rest."

"And what do you do?" his voice rising. "You nag and yell. You get drunk and risk Joan's life."

Their squabbling went on. I could see Fury 1 and Roger's antipathy was not to be appeased. A wave of weariness and futility spread through me. I snapped, "Stop it! The both of you! You disregard the tools I've encouraged you to use to get along. Neither of you is concerned that we need to prevent a crisis, possibly a suicide. That should be our focus here."

I realized I was practically shouting. I could see Roger was white with shock. A whiney voice lisped, "Mr. Roger isn't always mean, Oma. Most of the time, he's nice."

Beth's timid intervention brought me to my senses. I apologized for my unprofessional outburst and failure to intercede before the discussion went awry. Roger stiffly accepted my apology, while Beth's eyes were wide with confusion. Uncertain how to deal with the situation, Roger stretched out both hands and said, "Come on, Bethy—let's get outta here and get some ice cream."

Never before had I allowed Joan to leave my office in a state of dissociation, but I was too exhausted to think rationally. My patience depleted, I had nothing left to give. I didn't gather up my notes as I usually did. I left everything and walked home empty-handed. My husband immediately knew something was amiss.

"You look dog-tired," he said. "And why shouldn't you be? Taking care of Joan demands so much of you. You're on call day and night."

"That's my job, dear man," I responded. *Frankly, I thought I should be working at a residential clinic, where I would have the assistance of support staff. I longed for such a luxury.*

"Anyway, you should be proud," he said. "While you and Joan worked together, Roger and I visited. He's grateful for what you've done for his wife and family. Joan's improved so much that he thinks she'll be well soon."

I appreciated my husband's words of comfort. But where would I find the energy to go on? I admonished myself for neglecting my own welfare for too long. To overcome my mental and physical fatigue, I knew I needed to seek counseling for myself. But tonight, I was too tired to talk or think.

I dragged my body off to bed.

Samantha called to matter-of-factly report that Marjorie and Fury 2 were considering setting aside their hostility, and had sought sanctuary with Shadowman. He had committed to mentoring the two sisters in surrendering their hatred and would instruct them on how to cooperate with the others. *Surprised by the sisters' decision, I was nevertheless relieved and grateful for Shadowman's help.* I asked to speak with Raven. Like a polite telephone operator, Samantha said, "One moment, please."

Raven spoke without his usual vigor. "Dear Healer, I am fully aware of your physical and spiritual depletion. May I say: this, too, shall pass. For the present, consider taking care of yourself so you may regain your former vitality. Be hopeful. As soon as the Furies and Joan are ready to continue the treatment process, let me assure you we shall reconnect."

That night, I suffered another seizure. According to my husband, my body thrashed about in the bed until I regained consciousness. He took me to the Emergency Room, where I was tested for a stroke. Fortunately, the test proved negative. However, my blood pressure remained alarmingly high. I was admitted to the hospital for further observation. After two days, I was released and advised to rest for at least two weeks.

During my convalescence, Joan baked me a cake. When she brought it by, along with homemade chocolate truffles, her eyes glowed. I could not help imagining the Parts on the Inside pressing against her pupils, jostling one another for a peek out. I told her, without exaggeration, that I had never seen such an exquisite layer cake. *I thought Joan to be the most accomplished person I'd ever had as a client—painter, poet, baker, and chocolatier par excellence.*

October 11. After regaining my health, I returned to seeing clients. Roger called requesting a brief meeting. It was nearly dark when he and Joan arrived in his green truck. As they took their seats across from one another in my therapy room, I could not help but notice Joan's movements were lethargic. Despondency weighed heavily on her shoulders. Roger looked apprehensive or angry; I couldn't tell which until he jumped right in.

"I'm worried about Joan," he said with uncustomary urgency. "For the last few days, she's been getting more and more depressed. She just sits around the house and doesn't do much of anything. Fury 1's out a lot. She continues to dominate everything. And when I tell her she isn't in charge and should go back Inside, she bad-mouths me and says she's tired of being told what to do. When I ask Joan to come back, she doesn't."

"The last few days," Joan mumbled, "my mind hasn't functioned well, and Fury 1 takes advantage."

"Several days ago on the phone, you told me you were depressed. I urged you to keep taking your antidepressants. Have you been taking them?"

"I'm not sure . . ."

"Would you like me to make an appointment for you with your psychiatrist? Perhaps she can determine if your prescription needs adjusting."

Joan shook her head.

"Then you and I have to find out what is making you feel so sad."

I thought the cause of Joan's extreme depression might be exhaustion after four years of intensive therapy. Another likely factor could be her shock at Sebunome's disclosures of Charles' worst deeds. Not to mention the demands on her fragile ego to have publicly admitted she was an alcoholic. Plus, her feelings of regret and guilt over her failure to protect "little Samuel." And, of course, Fury 1's dark mood could have exacerbated Joan's emotional distress.

I assured her we would work on the cause of her symptoms and also address Fury 1's troubling behavior at our next session. In the meantime, I advised Roger to watch over Joan and proposed putting a few safety precautions in place. First, Joan and Fury 1 should stay home for the next few days, even forgoing AA meetings. Second, Roger and Megan should be responsible for Joan taking her antidepressants regularly. And third, Joan should take care of her health, eat and sleep as well as she could, and be mindful of negative ruminations. If her emotions became distressing, I suggested she work in the garden, perhaps prepare the flower beds for winter, or rake leaves to release tension. Looking pointedly at Joan, I stressed she was to remain co-present with Fury 1 to monitor her mood and behavior.

To Roger, I emphasized the importance of preventing Joan and Fury 1 from getting drunk and harming themselves in ways we would all regret. I suggested he be responsible for securing Joan's car keys, her money, and medicines; be doubly vigilant in making sure no alcohol was in the house; and most of all, be patient and kind. Roger pointed out that his job prohibited him from "babysitting" Joan and Fury 1 for several days. I suggested he and Megan share the responsibility and ended the session with my promise to call regularly for a status update.

Early the next morning, I went to a colloquium on bipolar disorder. During the morning break, I telephoned Joan, but no one answered, leaving me uneasy. At noon I called again. Megan answered.

"May I speak to your mother, please?"

"She's not here."

My heart jumped. "Where did she go?"

"She went to her AA women's group."

I struggled to keep my voice calm. "Did your father drive her there?"

"No, he went to work early this morning. She drove herself."

"Before your father left for work, did he tell you your mother was to stay home?"

"He told me to watch over Mom, but he said it was okay if she wanted to go to an AA meeting."

I could barely contain my consternation. "How did your mother seem this morning?"

"We hardly talked. She spent the morning in the backyard raking leaves and digging a hole."

I kept my alarm in check. "I'll try to reach your mother on her cell phone." But before I hung up, I couldn't help asking, "Do you know how big the hole is?"

"Let me check." Returning a few moments later, "It's not really big," she said.

Joan didn't answer her cell. I called Megan back. "Do you know the name and phone number of your mother's sponsor?"

"Not a clue."

Irritated by this irresponsibility, I said, "I shall attempt *again* to reach her in about one hour. Call me if you hear from her."

"You don't have to use that tone with me," Megan snipped and disconnected.

Between noon and two o'clock, I repeatedly called Joan's cell phone. Unable to reach her, I decided to err on the side of caution and called 911. I identified myself as a therapist and stated my reason for calling. The police assured me their patrols would be on the lookout.

However, with my trepidation growing, I excused myself early from the seminar. From my car, I called Joan's home phone again. Roger answered.

"I thought we had agreed that Joan should stay home," I said, exasperated.

"There's nothing wrong with her going to an AA meeting. In case you don't know, that's what people do when they have a drinking problem."

Ignoring his dismissiveness, I said, "Last night you asked me for my help, and I gave you my best advice. The very next day, you disregarded my instructions. This morning, Megan told me Joan had dug a hole in your backyard. Please humor me—would you go and check the size of that hole?"

The phone clonked down. When he came back on the line, Roger's voice had a hollow ring. "It's pretty big."

I felt as if a rusty saw had abraded my nerves. I reproached myself for failing to foresee how advising Joan and Fury 1 to work in the garden might trigger a flashback taking them to that terrifying autumn afternoon in the woods where Charles had tortured them.

"Use your imagination," I said. "What might that size of a hole mean considering Joan and Fury 1's depressed state of mind?"

I informed Roger I had called the police and would contact him as soon as I heard from them. At dusk, the police telephoned to notify me my client was home and safe. Roger called confirming their report and told me Joan had not gone to AA but instead had decided to visit her sponsor and that they had gone out for a cup of tea. I was greatly relieved. Joan's safety was paramount. But if she and her family wanted me to continue as her therapist, they needed to be more respectful of my advice when it came to my client's safety.

Around eight that evening, Stephanie called. "I just talked to my mother," her words leaden with exhaustion. "She doesn't recall you saying she had to stay home all day."

"Stephanie, my instructions last night were clear."

"I understand you were concerned about my mother's safety. But now, Mom's afraid you'll give up on her."

Being upset didn't mean I planned to discontinue treatment, I explained. To achieve Joan's goal, everyone needed to work together and keep their promises. Stephanie lamented that her mother's disorder had made everyone's life difficult. She knew how "grueling" helping her mother had been for me, adding that, without my help, she was convinced her mother would be dead by now. Despite the current worrisome situation, I told Stephanie I was heartened by Joan's progress and commitment to healing—her courage, resilience, and, most importantly, her faith and trust in a Higher Power made her integration a real possibility.

~

Chapter 72

I'M DONE WITH ALL THAT

October 13. Knowing Joan slept late, I waited until eleven to call. When she answered the phone, I sensed her unease. Nevertheless, I inquired how she was feeling.

"Fine," the word clipped.

"Can we meet some afternoon this week to plan how to move forward?"

"I don't have much to say," she responded. "Besides, after all that happened the other day, why would you still want to work with me?" Without waiting for my answer, she said, "My husband and daughter are upset with you. They feel you were rude and behaved unprofessionally and should apologize."

"Disregarding my advice to keep you safe was negligent as well as disrespectful. Nevertheless, please let Roger and Megan know I'm willing to meet and listen to their grievances."

"They don't want to see you."

"Then let's focus on what *you* want."

Ignoring my offer, Joan said, "Fury 1 wants you to apologize, too, for yelling at her."

Exhaustion swept over me. "Perhaps we *should* take some time off. After we've rested, we can resume treatment, reset our goals, and go forward with new resolve."

"I'm not sure I want to come back."

I felt my patience drain away and asked Joan to consider entering an inpatient program at a well-respected clinic that focused on MPD. Their intensive-care program could be beneficial. I could arrange her admission and promised to write a treatment summary to facilitate her admittance.

"I don't want that. I don't want to go out of town. Anyway, my insurance won't pay for it . . ." Joan's voice trailed off. Then she said with uncharacteristic enmity, "Whether I live or die, I'm not your responsibility anymore."

My fingers felt stiff and cold on the receiver. "Are you terminating my services, Joan? Is that what you're saying? If that's the case, I must accept your decision." I thought a moment. "But until you find a new therapist, I'll be available should you need my counsel."

"That's not going to happen."

"What's not going to happen, Joan?"

"Finding a new therapist. I'm done with all that," and severed the connection.

From a therapist's perspective, Joan's rejection of all I could offer was understandable. Her belief in me had crumbled. The one person who year after year had loved and accepted her unconditionally—the one who she thought would never disapprove, never criticize, or get angry and send her away—had toppled. Her fragile, positive self-regard, so painstakingly acquired, had cracked. And through that crack had wormed the old belief that she was of no value, an object to be discarded on a whim. But before her therapist could dismiss her, her false self had come to the fore to dismiss me instead. My heart constricted. What a loss! The endless hours we had invested, so many hard-won victories, and so much love. Integration had been in sight, but now her choice to terminate treatment pre-empted the best chance to achieve her aspiration to become whole.

~

V

TRANSCENDING THE PAST

Fall 2007 to Spring 2008

Chapter 73

ʀAPPROCHEMENT

November 3. After several weeks without contact, I received a phone call from Beth. She wanted to know if I still loved them. I answered: "Forever and ever." Beth had sneaked out to call even though Joan had the Parts all locked up inside the Inner Realm and only let them out when Mr. Roger was at work and Megan was at school.

Always the messenger, she reported that Fury 2 and Marjorie continued to be under Shadowman's guidance. Their goal was to become like "brave Samantha," always doing what's fair and good for everyone. *I hoped relinquishing their toxic emotions indicated Joan had accepted the sisters' rage as her own. Was she now prepared to work through what she had felt since Charles first laid hands on her?*

"We all want to come to see you, Oma. Even Joan does. But she's too stubborn to call."

"Joan and I need a time out, Beth, to recover from all that's happened."

November 20. My health continued to improve with rest. Carefully examining both my mental and feeling states, I believed I had regained sufficient equilibrium to initiate contact with Joan. I felt a need to know how she was getting along. Besides, I missed her. So, I telephoned. When Joan recognized my voice, she became teary.

"I've been depressed," she confided and blew her nose. A shaky silence stretched between us. "Beth misses you terribly. She doesn't understand why she can't come to see you. Would it be okay for her to visit you some afternoon?"

"How do *you* feel about that?" I probed.

"I'd do it to please Beth. It's hard to listen to her constant begging. So, if it's all right with you, I'll bring her to your office."

Knowing it was Joan's way to reconnect, I said, "How about on the twenty-seventh around three o'clock?"

I greeted Joan at my office door. Her auburn hair had been brushed to a high gloss. Her winter coat looked new, as did the paisley scarf at her neck. Her brown eyes avoided mine as I invited her in. She stepped across the threshold and stopped, as if unsure what to do next. I motioned for her to follow me to the therapy room, where I had set a small table for tea. I pointed to a chair. Clutching her purse like a shield, Joan moved forward on wooden legs and sat with a sigh. She closed her eyes, and Beth emerged with an angelic smile.

"Hi, Oma," she chirped. "I've missed you," and stretched out her arms for a hug.

She looked at the table I had arranged with cups, saucers, and a plate of butter cookies. "How nice, Oma."

I smiled and asked if she would like to pour the tea. She did so with the utmost care. Staring at the cookies, she announced, "Those are my favorites." I held out the plate for her to take one. Like she had done at other tea parties, Beth bit off a tiny bite, making sure the cookie did not touch her lips. As she began to chew, her eyes dulled, her face flattened. *I thought she might be experiencing a flashback to the time when her biological father and his "friends" had forced the "icky stuff" down her throat. Or to the time when Charles had pressed his forearm across her neck, choking off her breath. An uncommon hatred rushed through me. I wanted to reach back into the past, seize her father and Charles by their throats and throttle them. I struggled for composure.*

"Beth," I whispered, and, to my relief, her eyes refocused. Her throat must have relaxed because she swallowed. With unexpected maturity, Beth announced that Raven and the older ones had decided to return the ring to me. After the events of October, they felt unworthy to keep it. I explained the ring's purpose was to remind them that they were not alone, that someone cared. It symbolized the rescue of the birth personality and held the promise of healing and wholeness. It had been bestowed as a token of the trust and love we felt for one another.

"We know the ring means love, Oma, and how precious that is. And that's why Raven and all of us feel it should belong to your children."

"Love is not dependent on biology, Beth, but solely on the heart, and can be just as precious as the love between a mother and her own children."

Beth put her hand over her heart, her eyes liquid. "Oma, you really do love us—all of us."

"That's why the ring is yours. Forever."

We were both quiet as we sipped our tea and ate cookies. After a while, Beth confided she had heard Joan's family talking. They hoped Joan would return to therapy. But Beth thought Joan was too frightened to call me, afraid I would refuse to take her back. I told Beth I was sure Joan would, in time, find a way to reach out.

December 19. Joan telephoned to say putting Beth in charge of making contact with me had been unfair. She recognized that initiating the resumption of therapy would have to be her responsibility. "I want to have back what you and I had before we became upset with one another."

"Nothing ever stays the same, Joan. Events happen, hurtful words are spoken, and we behave in ways that reveal our flaws. I suppose when you saw me angry and frustrated, I fell off the pedestal which you and the Parts had put me on. I apologize for the mistakes I made during those difficult days. Should we resume treatment, Joan, I shall listen respectfully to all that has upset you and the Parts."

"I still don't know . . ." she said. "I just don't want to be a burden. You've already done so much for all of us."

I didn't respond to her veiled expression of unworthiness.

"I'll leave it up to God," she said. "Perhaps eventually, the trust we've lost can be restored."

"Your uncertainty is understandable, Joan. When all is right, we'll know how to proceed."

~

Chapter 74

Adversity Transforms Us

S*hortly after the New Year,* Joan called to request a meeting to share "something important." She brought along a painting which she leaned facedown against the side of the blue couch before taking her seat. It had been three months since Joan had terminated treatment.

"I was anxious about coming to see you," she said, her large brown eyes taking in the familiar furnishings of the therapy room.

"I'm glad you came despite your apprehension."

She picked up the painting and turned it around so I could view it. The artwork was a clear departure from Joan's usual artistic expression. The dominant color was various shades of red applied with forceful, emotion-driven brushstrokes that created a layered surface. The composition included five human figures and a raven. The upper right corner was in gold, with a sprinkling of green leaves and three tiny red hearts. In the lower left corner was a teetering bottle, out of which a devilish gestalt spewed forth.

"At the end of December," she explained, "the painting just poured out of me. I suppose it represents my response to what was happening during those tumultuous sessions in October."

She pointed to the most prominent element, a black figure wrapped in forest greens behind which rose a black sun. "This is Shadowman. He's standing guard to protect us from harm."

Joan had placed Shadowman's head on a soft, full-figured female form. I pointed to the white sickle of a waxing moon which cupped the back of his head. "What do you suppose this represents?"

"Three or four years ago, you mentioned the moon symbolizes the feminine side of our psyche."

Adversity Transforms Us, Joan 2007.

But behind the moon was that black, radiating sun, the symbol usually associated with the masculine, I thought. *Could the symbolism represent the fusing of the feminine attributes he had been nurturing as a helper with the masculine attributes he possessed as the protector? Had Joan begun to embrace Shadowman's masculinity as a complementing aspect of her feminine self?*

"He doesn't seem angry or threatening," I observed, "but he may have been aggrieved." I pointed to the bleeding heart on his chest. "How upset he must have felt when we had our falling out," I said, looking her full in the face.

"I know Shadowman watched during our . . . heated exchange," Joan said. "But he's not hurt or angry and hasn't gone back to his old ways."

Lightly tapping a red female form just to the right of Shadowman, I said, "I suppose that's me. Even though the face is featureless, I recognize the blonde hair."

Joan pointed to a prostrate figure in black. "This is you, too."

"Looks like I've fallen off the pedestal."

"How you spoke to us in that last session forced us to see you as a flawed human being like everyone else."

"I'm relieved you've recognized that fact." *I was uncomfortable being idealized. If we were to resume our working relationship, Joan could be more frank and honest with her therapist "off the pedestal." And,* I thought, *unburden herself of the need to please me.*

Joan next pointed again to the lower left corner of the painting. Rendered in pale grays, a female figure knelt in front of the bottle out of which poured the darkness that had persuaded her and the Parts to betray themselves, that poisonous substance which had stifled their growth for such a long time.

"I imagine the kneeling figure is Fury 1," I offered. From the upper right corner, a golden ray streamed diagonally down to where a humbled Fury 1 knelt. I placed my finger where the ray touched her head. *Did I dare to hope the beam of Golden Light symbolized redemption? Did it hold* the promise that Joan and Fury 1 would at last set aside their addiction to alcohol, freeing the treatment process to proceed unhindered?

"What does this mean?" I pointed at the white swirls which divided the painting into upper and lower panels. "It looks like frothy waves."

"Perhaps it represents God's promise to send a Helper. You are floating on the white 'froth' like an angel from on high. Your hand is resting atop my head in a gesture of healing."

"So that transparent figure of a young girl at the edge of the painting is you?"

"Maybe the girl I used to be. You see that sheet of paper in your hand? It holds the record of her truth—that much I know."

I directed her attention to the intense yellow color in the upper right corner. "Throughout the turmoil, I can see the Sacred was with you. The crimson presence of the Trinity, the three red hearts bathed in a golden light, was an inspired vision."

Joan smiled. "I never thought of the tiny red hearts in that way, but I did feel God was always with me. After I poured all of my disappointment and anguish onto the canvas, the Parts and I were at peace. We understood that if someone we loved was upset with us, that didn't mean we were unworthy or unlovable. Or that we had to run away and hide. In the past, whenever someone was angry at us or had hurt us, our feelings for that person died, and we pretended they had never existed."

"Sometimes, Joan, adversity transforms us."

With a bittersweet smile, she said, "It certainly has transformed me."

As soon as Joan closed my office door, I picked up the red painting she left for me to study. *Her insightful analysis impressed me. My actions a few months ago had wounded her soul. Her creative genius had captured the moment she chose to suffer through my betrayal. The picture signified the ending of her unconditional, childlike trust in her beloved therapist.*

With a growing sense of hope, I blew out the candles, turned off the lights, locked the door, and made my way along the narrow stone path toward the warm glow from the windows of my home, confident her visit held the promise that we would resume our work together.

A few days after my meeting with Joan, I found a letter of apology from Fury 1 in my mailbox. She wrote "with a humble heart" that she had come to realize her actions had "harmed others" and not just herself. She expressed a desire "to make restitution" for her transgressions. And promised with "brutal and painful honesty" to untangle her "twisted thinking" so she could learn to make positive choices. I was grateful to read she had stopped craving alcohol and wished to face the past and future without seeking solace in drink.

Near the end of her letter, she stated her "pride and stubbornness" had robbed her of the opportunity to "transform herself through love" as other Parts had done. I wrote back that her sincere expression of remorse had touched my heart and assured her that the opportunity for transformation was still open. Should she choose to return to therapy and resume the process of healing, I would welcome her decision.

∼

Chapter 75

RECOMMITMENT

January 17. Whether or not my exchange with Fury 1 had any bearing, Joan and I resumed treatment with remarkable ease. She appeared composed as she sat upright on the couch, her purse placed to one side on the carpeted floor. As usual, I sat opposite in my rocking chair, notepad and pen in my lap.

Joan began what sounded like a carefully rehearsed apology. "Fury 1 is not solely responsible for the chaotic and hurtful events of last fall. Ana and I are certainly guilty of not working harder to care for the system. I'm saddened that you and your husband got caught up in all the turmoil. Your kindness seems to have mattered little. That you gave and gave until you became ill breaks my heart. There isn't anything I wouldn't do to change that, if I could. I am so sorry."

"What's important now, Joan, is that you are here." I affirmed my commitment to continuing our work. In turn, she pledged her dedication to work toward a "positive ending."

Rose emerged, her voice soft with affection. "I missed you, Oma. I'm so sorry Fury 1 upset you. She upsets everybody. When you stopped seeing Joan, we felt abandoned. But instead of going away, going to sleep like we used to do, we tried to be brave and feel our hurt feelings like you taught us. We're all happy you didn't send us away forever. Now God's promise can be fulfilled."

Rose's hopefulness gave way. She stammered, "I—I don't want you to get upset again, but do you remember when Fury 1 got in trouble because she had been drinking? You asked her to stay home and help Joan clean out the flower beds and—and rake the leaves. We think she was remembering the time Charles buried us in the woods out behind Mama's house, and that's why she dug the hole. Remember, Sebunome told you?"

Again, I silently reproached myself for my lack of foresight. For Fury 1 to re-experience the trauma of that autumn afternoon must have been ghastly. I told Rose it had been my mistake and apologized.

She tilted her head to one side as if listening inward. "Oma, everyone heard what you just said, even Joan. After I go back Inside, Sebunome wants to talk to you."

A mere sliver of a smile was Sebunome's greeting. "Helper Oma, when you were putting angry words on top of angry words, I want you to know I didn't go back to my hiding place at the Forest Edge 'cause I know now that angry words do not hurt like bad touches. You could have left us forever, but you didn't. Thank you for that."

"I never planned to leave you, or Joan, or the others after the crisis. I promise that we will not part until that 'happy day' when all the secrets are let go and all of you are integrated."

"But not before, right?"

"That's a promise, Sebunome."

Then I heard a deep voice say, "I'm here, Helper. I wish to speak to you as well."

Shadowman's eyes were serious but kind, his posture imposing but non-threatening. "I hold no grievances against you. I'm aware Joan painted a picture of that fateful session last fall. It depicts me as a formidable presence that could be interpreted as menacing. You must know I never intended to harm anyone. I was simply standing watch. Had it been necessary, I would have offered my assistance to defuse the situation."

"I appreciate your protective presence that evening, Shadowman. Thank you for your devotion to the system and to me."

Shadowman dipped his head in acknowledgment of my compliment. "I'm grateful there are no misunderstandings or misgivings between us."

He hesitated as if gathering his thoughts. "I would like to thank you—formally. You were instrumental in my transformation. I'm grateful you did not give up on me even though I struggled against your help and advice. I must admit," he chuckled in self-deprecation, "I was a handful. Full of rage. Full of revenge. Always ready to harm the Parts whenever they failed to abide by my rules."

"Your intentions were noble," I reminded him.

Shadowman stood, spread his arms wide, and pivoted around. "Notice I have sparkles now and do not need the threatening razzle-dazzle of my Puppets. Nor do I need my deep, imposing voice any longer. I have become 'see-through' as Beth says—emptied of the terrible knowledge which shaped my original purpose."

Shadowman's words filled me with tenderness. I told him witnessing his transformation to a helper had been a privilege.

Joan returned. "Your conversation with Shadowman . . . What can I say? You two were like a mutual-respect-and-admiration society. Thank you for speaking with Sebunome and allaying her worries. Poor Fury 1," Joan empathized. "Listening to Rose, I now understand clearly why Fury 1 dug that hole. How dreadful it must have been to relive that hideous event in the woods. The terror she must have felt makes me shudder."

Walking home after our session, I felt gratified by this good start to the resumption of Joan's therapy. She and the Parts had found the ability to rise above conflict instead of withdrawing. They had chosen to hold on to our hard-won trust. And at last, had realized anger did not have to destroy a relationship. Altogether, they had demonstrated a rekindling of commitment to our work.

January 18, 2008
Dear Renate, [Abridged]

My heart is filled with such joy that not only has our relationship survived quite intact but seems to have evolved and strengthened to a new level. I have learned so much with and through you these past years; and although this newest lesson was extremely painful and truthfully, quite frightening in its intensity, I have seen how honesty, trust, and love must be the foundation for a genuine human relationship to survive. I do thank God that we both (and also the Parts) valued the hard work and hours spent together enough to have walked through the fire, so to speak. Again, thank you for all you have done . . .

In ending, in my own awareness, I want to say that I am so very happy that you are feeling better and have your sparkle back! With much affection and care,

Joan/Ana

During the last two weeks of January, Joan canceled her appointments one after the other. On the eve of the thirtieth, we agreed to meet the next day. She canceled that appointment as well, telling me she felt poorly but couldn't explain why. I reminded her that in times like this, attending therapy would be beneficial. She excused herself by saying she had prayed, asking God to take away her "burden." Thus far, she hadn't received "a sign" but insisted He soon would answer her prayer.

When the call ended, I made a note to address Joan's literal reliance on God.

Two days later, Joan called in despair around five in the afternoon. She had prayed but still felt hopeless and lost. She had no one with whom she could unburden herself. I offered to see her that evening. Before Joan could respond, Fury 1 interrupted to accuse me of having verbally mistreated her during the October crisis. I reminded her that the events of last fall had been addressed. But I was willing to continue this conversation—but only face-to-face.

Around six-thirty, Joan appeared at my office door, her hair in disarray, her mascara smudged. I invited her in. Taking her usual seat, she immediately dissociated. Fury 1 burst out, accusing me of not expressing regret for shouting at her. She had written a letter of apology and expected the same in return. She fumed, "All the people I've known have betrayed me, including you. I was just beginning to trust you, maybe even love you."

I reminded her of her actions before the crisis—the broken promises and the destructive behavior that endangered Joan and the Parts—which she had admitted to in her letter of apology.

Red-faced, she leaped off the couch, took a threatening step toward me, asked if I had intentionally tried to hurt her feelings, and blurted out, "Were you so uncaring?"

"My actions were fueled by frustration and exhaustion, but I never intended to hurt your feelings, and I never stopped caring for you."

"But you shouted at me! You were just like *them*." Her tears started to flow.

"In your heart, Fury 1, you know I'm not like Charles and your mother. If it will restore your trust in me, I apologize for shouting at you. I hope you can forgive me."

"I do," she sniffled into a tear-dampened tissue.

Joan re-emerged and, without conscious thought, crumpled the tissue. She examined her fingernails with exaggerated intent. After peeling off a few remnants of polish, she finally looked up. "In my mind, I know you will be as committed to our work as you always have been, but my heart tells me that you may not love—I mean, care for me and the Parts as you did before." She stifled a sob. "I know you're disappointed. You feel we've let you down. And that makes me feel like I've always felt—flawed and unlovable."

I wanted to reach out and comfort her but refrained. Instead, I allowed her to stay with those feelings authored by her fear of losing my affection and losing my belief in her as a worthy human being.

As she readied herself to leave, I tentatively put my hand on her shoulder. She gave me a wan smile and thanked me for seeing her at this late hour.

I knew before Joan could surrender the intense attachment she had developed for me, she would have to accept that the "Good Mother" she adored, the one who accepted her unconditionally, would eventually leave her. At that moment, her heart would break. This wounding would create the space where her internal mother could unfold—a mother that would never leave her, always love her, comfort, and guide her. I remained convinced that her resilience and faith, which had made her long-term survival possible, would help her through the dark tunnel of loss, where she now found herself.

~

Chapter 76

MANY VOICES

February 6. A litany of physical complaints spilled from Joan's mouth. I empathized and suggested her ailments might be psychosomatic triggered by the emotional distress she experienced in our previous session.

What occurred next was unprecedented.

Her eyes rolled back in her head. Her lips struggled to form words. With outstretched arms, palms up, she tilted back her head and pulled her spine erect. I held my breath. A voice with a priestess-like intonation began to chant: "I am us. We are us. All are one. Each Part is one light. All make up a great light in the image of God. I am Many Voices. I speak for all. I am the observer, the one who holds the complete history. I channel the details through Raven, who guides, protects, and advises. His task is to convey my knowledge to the Parts and to you, Healer."

"I understand," I said. "You are reason, and he is love."

A faint smile softened the impenetrable veil of her countenance. She slowly lowered her arms. Her voice continued in a monotone. "I have come from far away. I have struggled through Forests, gathering up the remaining Parts and Fragments. A powerful wind made coming forward difficult. My stay shall be brief."

This was a rare opportunity, I thought, *to elicit her wisdom for hastening integration.* I asked if there was something she could impart to help

432

me see more clearly additional opportunities for healing or ways to work more effectively.

"I have given you blessings since the work began. Almost all pieces of the puzzle have been put into place. To complete the task, the un-evolved shall be encouraged to evolve, so all can merge into a whole."

Again I asked if there was anything specific she could impart.

"You have already done what was needed," she said. "You listened, you believed, you interpreted, and most of all, you loved. There is one thing I wish to convey: The last remaining delusions must be redirected, cleansed, and transformed so all the Parts may embrace the truth—the total truth— and can live into the now, unafraid of becoming one."

Many Voices' features brightened. "I observed you and Raven flying across the Realm to rescue the one who is the birth personality, without whom integration cannot be attained."

As she spoke, her energy ebbed. In a fading voice, she announced she was returning to her seat beyond the Vast Region of Nothingness.

I called Joan's name. She moaned, moving her head from side to side. When she finally was present, she said, "It was difficult to get through the Outer Edge because of the wind. I've never felt anything quite like that before. The Parts and I seem to have been caught in a windstorm that compressed us together to speak as one. I never imagined so much effort would be required." Joan paused a moment to reflect. "Speaking in one voice was extraordinary. I shall never forget it."

"Speaking in one voice, Joan, foreshadows what is to come."

While gathering up her belongings, she muttered that she could never share this bizarre experience with anyone. "If I did, I'd be hauled off to an asylum."

"It's a rare privilege," I offered, "to be in touch with your highest level of consciousness. For those of us whose minds are not fragmented, we have to strain to tease out the wisdom in this way of knowing. All we hear is distorted noise, a syllable here, a word there. It's like listening to the news on an old radio with waves of static interrupting the vital message."

"I suppose hearing that voice," she said, "is the *only* 'privilege' in being a multiple."

A week later, Joan came through my office door exhilarated. "Yesterday, the Parts and I had horrific flashbacks throughout the afternoon. We survived them without dissociating. It was like I was in two realities, the past *and* the present, simultaneously. I kept telling myself and the Parts the terror we were experiencing had happened a long time ago. I gathered the Parts in my arms and took us all to safety."

"Where did you go?"

"The blue room where I paint and write, where I'm the happiest. The memories washed over us as we huddled there in a corner. We did a lot of deep breathing and praying until the flashbacks subsided. I could hardly wait to tell you. I want you to be proud of us. This is the first time we were able to keep from falling into Hell without depending on your help to survive."

"Joan," I said in jubilation, "you and the Parts did more than survive. You stayed co-present with the Parts, cooperating and supporting one another. What a significant accomplishment."

"I have something else to tell you." With a girlish giggle, she confided, "I've been making new friends."

She had found a website where women with MPD talked to one another about living a roller-coaster life. She recounted her conversations on the internet and how proud she felt of our work in comparison to so many other stories of failed therapies or ineffective treatments.

"I've also been corresponding with a multiple living in England who has a good therapist like I have in you. Only her approach is not as innovative. What impresses my new friend is that you honor the individuality of each Part and utilize their talents and creativity to achieve my goals. She's surprised how respectful you are of my faith, especially how you encourage me to rely on it when I'm feeling disheartened. She was amazed to hear that, on occasion, you direct healing rituals inside the Inner Realm. I also mentioned that we meditate before we start our work and that you sometimes guide me into a trance so I can recover memories. What contributes most to our treatment, I told her, is your unwavering belief in our inherent goodness and your willingness to express love."

After listening to Joan's report without interruption, I told her of my delight that she had found a friend with whom she had so much in common. I appreciated her assurance to the women on the internet that they could get better. I hoped she also shared information about books and journals but cautioned her not to take on the role of therapist.

"Don't worry. I just tell them what I know about myself, what I've learned from you, and how grateful I am to have found you after so many years of waiting."

~

Chapter 77

THE DARK FORCE

February 20. Joan was elated I was back from attending an out-of-town conference. She felt a part of her was missing whenever I was away. I chose not to address her statement of dependency. Joan began to fidget. She licked her lips as if they were dry or chapped. I waited.

"For the past few days, I've again been thinking about going to visit my mother."

After a moment's reflection, I said, "For safety's sake, I wish you would wait until after integration. You'll be more confident and less vulnerable."

"My mother needs me," Joan countered. "She's sick. I need to take care of her."

"Couldn't your sister go in your place?"

"She and my mother have been estranged for many years. Besides, Lillian's husband is an invalid, and she can't leave him alone."

"How about your younger brother then? He lives close by, doesn't he?"

Joan shook her head. "Samuel hardly ever goes to see her unless he wants money. So, I have to go. I have no choice."

Her gaze drifted out the window to the light snow dusting the barren branches of the trees next door. She admitted every time she thought about returning to "that house," she shook inside, became nauseous, and couldn't breathe. She feared the memories and images and sounds of her abuse would assault her from every corner. How could she possibly enter "the Room" and lie on the bed?

Joan began hyperventilating. I sat beside her and held her hand. I encouraged her to stay in the present and reminded her, "You're an adult—strong, resilient. You are your own person."

She squeezed my hand. "I've crawled through Hell and out the other side into the Light. When I'm having a hard time at my mother's, I'll remember to turn the ring on my thumb and know I'm not alone."

I asked Joan what the Parts thought about going back. The contours of her face distorted into a grimace. With uncharacteristic menace, a voice growled, "I can do horrible things to the Body. I can hurt you and destroy this room."

Prickly heat irritated the nape of my neck. I was perplexed. *Had some unknown Part forced Joan aside? Was it an undiscovered persecutor like Shadowman once was? Or something else embedded in the matrix of the system?*

Uncertain how to proceed, I gently called for Samantha to take Joan to the Safe Place. I heard her voice say, "Helper, what you ask will be difficult. A Dark Force is encircling us."

I spoke through to the system asking the Parts to rely on their strength and remain calm. I suggested they assemble on the Meadow in the Circle of Truth and visualize the "Dark Force" materializing there at the center of the circle. I instructed them to hold hands and fasten their eyes on that Force. "Summon your courage, and examine what it may represent. Perhaps it is something you recognize as being within you. Address this Dark Force. Invite it to enter into a conversation with you. Can you bring yourselves to accept it, embrace it, as part of you?"

Raven exited. "Teacher, I recognize your good intentions. Please exercise caution. This Dark Force is not a Part to be transformed. I shall advise the Parts *not* to embrace it, but rather *expel* the malevolent presence from their midst before it poisons all we have become."

"So, what are the Parts to do?" I asked.

"They must stay united and unafraid," he instructed. "They shall cover their hearts with their right hand and defeat it with chants of affirmation. And thus banish this intrusion from the Inner Realm."

To honor the Parts' initiative, I yielded to Raven's directive. I observed Joan's body convulse. The mouth spewed forth odious words of hatred: "Bad, worthless, defiled, disposable, damaged, outcast, dirty, untouchable . . ." *I recalled Shadowman's list of sixty words describing Joan and the Parts' negative self-perceptions.* I urged the Parts to uplift their arms and invite the Golden Light to watch over them while chanting self-affirmations to drive out the Dark Force. I monitored the situation for any indicators of distress. As I sat watching, the tension and strain drained from Joan's face, and the Body collapsed to one side.

Malevolence, Joan 2008.

Careful not to frighten Joan, I eased the Body upright and softly called her name. She shook her head, as if shaking off the trance, and opened her eyes.

"Were you able to hear and see what happened, Joan?"

"I saw a darkness enveloping everyone. But it didn't succeed, because the Parts remained unafraid and did as Raven instructed, which caused the venomous thing to pale and shrivel."

"Do you understand what the Dark Force represents?"

"It's all too familiar." Her eyes again drifted to the window and the ice-encrusted limbs of the trees outside. She folded her arms across her chest and pushed back into the cushions. Her voice dropped to a chilly whisper. "The Dark Force is my self-hatred. It's who I think I am: worthless, dirty, defective. All my life, I tried so hard to be perfect. I turned myself inside out to create a false self while the real me withered. I blamed myself for everything—the abuses, the rejection, the neglect, even the humiliation. When I was old enough to comprehend that the evil was *outside* of me, my self-loathing did not diminish. It had permeated the pores of my being. To this day, it gnaws on me, threatening to devour me, literally."

Her lips looked parched. She took a sip of water. Looking at me over the rim of the glass, she confessed, "I never realized until now that this hatred for myself was what drove me many times to attempt suicide." She bowed her head and, with a finger, rubbed the deep creases across her forehead. "Before I go back to see my mother, I have to let go of all of that. Otherwise, I'll fall victim to the negative chatter in my head that I've heard all my life."

"That's when you must pause, Joan, and affirm who you truly are—a deserving, worthy human being."

I could hear the urgency in Joan's voice when she called to request one last session before her departure. When she arrived, her resolve of the previous session seemed to have dissipated.

"I feel panicky about visiting my mother."

Joan stopped abruptly. She focused inward, listening intently. She shook her head as if frustrated. "It's hard to understand what's going on. The Parts are all clamoring. Emotions are running high. If this chaos continues, what then?"

"Do you want to explore this with the Parts?"

"Absolutely."

"Then I propose you meet with them at the Meadow and listen to their concerns. If you're ready, I shall ask Fury 1 to meet you at the Edge to guide you there."

"Why ask Fury 1 to take me? I'm not comfortable with her."

"And why is that?" *By pairing the two, I had hoped Joan would learn to tolerate being in Fury 1's presence.*

"Her anger disturbs me . . ." Reluctantly, she went Inside.

I spoke through to the system to propose they sit in silence a moment and then take turns to voice their apprehension about the pending visit to the Mother. The Body's right hand gestured impatiently. I handed over a sheet of paper and a pen. A kind of furious automatic writing in rapid strokes covered the page with capital letters:

FURY 1 YELLING: I'M MAD, I'M MAD. NOTHING BUT LIES, LIES, LIES!!!
MARJORIE AND FURY 2 SCREAMING: WE ARE OUTRAGED.
JOAN TREMBLING: I'M ANXIOUS.
SOPHIA WHIMPERING: I'M AFRAID, I'M AFRAID TO GO BACK.
ROSE: I'M SAD, I'M SO SAD.
SEBUNOME: DON'T TRUST, DON'T TRUST.
BETH WISTFULLY: I WANT TO GO SEE MY SCHOOL, MY
GRANDMOTHER'S HOUSE.
SHADOWMAN: I STAND GUARD.
THE FURIES AND SOPHIA: NEVER FORGIVE, NEVER FORGET.

"Now I know how you feel," I said upon reading the message. "Is there anyone that can entertain the idea of tolerating the Mother?"

The hand wrote:

MOST ARE UNSURE. JOAN WILL TRY . . .

Once they were in the presence of the Mother, I advised them to be supportive whenever one of the Parts became distraught. "Stay calm. Stay strong and united, as Raven would instruct. Stay in the present. Use your coping skills. You can do this."

Raven emerged. "Blessings to you, Teacher. Many Voices and I witnessed what just transpired. May I assure you nothing will strangle the goodness and courage held within each Part. Be confident the Parts and Joan will hold steadfast during the tribulations that lie ahead. Remember, the seeds have been sown. Have faith they will unfold and bloom." Raven withdrew.

The hand began to write again, this time with calm determination:

We Believe in our Goodness. We Believe in Ourselves and Trust in God. Shame, Guilt, and Self-hatred will not Darken our new-found Reality. We Believe there is Love which Heals. We are Willing to Believe in the Goodness of Others. We Trust in our own Power and Strength because we are One and One is All. And most Meaningful for Us is We know the Truth about the Past and what We Truly are.
—Many Voices

Joan stood. Still in a trance, she stretched out her arms, palms to the ceiling. With eyes closed, she began walking *backward* out of the therapy room toward the front door of my office. I opened the door. Unaware of me, she halted at the threshold. As the rays of the late-afternoon sun caressed the back of her head, she stated with conviction, "Lies can't survive the Light." In a soft voice, I affirmed her truth and then led her back to the couch.

She opened her eyes. I asked if she knew what had occurred.

"I'm aware now of the Parts' misgivings. I heard Raven's statement, and felt the Light extinguish the lies of the past."

After a pause to again listen inward, Joan said, "Fury 1 wants you to know that when the Parts become afraid or angry because of what they hear and see at the Mother's house, they promise not to switch. They will cry only on the Inside and abide by the guidance of Raven and Many Voices. And not forget to go to the Safe Place to read and listen to music. If they feel threatened, they will assemble in the Circle of Truth on the Meadow to chant self-affirmations." With palms uplifted, she said, "You see, Renate, the Parts have ways to cope."

"But my concern is for *your* psychological and physical well-being."

"Don't worry," Joan replied. "If I feel the need to get away, I'll take a walk or go to the library or visit my mother-in-law. I plan to keep a journal. Each day, the Parts and I will record an entry. I hope to write some poetry, and I'll send you letters about what's going on. If all that fails to keep me going, I can always call you. But if I can't endure another moment in that house with my mother, I'll pack my things, catch the earliest available bus, and come home."

"Keep in mind, Joan, should you lose your confidence before you leave tomorrow, you can always choose to postpone your visit."

"My mind's made up."

I helped her slip into her jacket and walked her to my office door. I wished her a safe journey as we embraced in farewell.

Before I closed my office for the night, I reviewed our work of the last week. *I hoped Raven and I had done enough to strengthen Joan's and the*

Parts' egos to face Joan's mother with confidence and feelings of self-worth. I believed we had pacified the Furies. However, I could not help being concerned for the younger ones in Elizabeth's care. How would they react at the first sight of Joan's mother? Would they come out crying and beg her to hold them? Or would they be afraid and hide?

As I walked home, alternating between hope and apprehension, a poignant childhood memory emerged, one I had folded away long ago, about *my* return home after the war.

~

It was the fourth summer I had knelt in the blueberry patch under pine trees so tall I had to crane my neck to see their crowns. We were a small group of displaced girls, wards of a rural religious order, picking berries to earn our keep—berries in the summer, apples in the fall, potatoes and kindling come winter—all to be sold in the village market.

I have no memory of how I came to live with the nuns in their convent, a graceless building wrapped in dingy plaster that once had been daffodil yellow. I suppose I was traumatized after my birth mother deposited me there at the close of the war. I recall a click of a light switch jolting me into awareness of my new surroundings. I was lying on a thin mattress in a large room with girls of various ages. A voice shouted, "Get up. Time for Mass." Frightened, I lunged for my little suitcase under the bed and pressed it to my chest for protection.

I soon learned to avoid the ire of the nuns and adapted to a life of measured steps and hushed voices. I adhered to rules that were absolute: Mass before daybreak, black bread with a smear of jam for breakfast, household chores before a few hours of school in the village, afternoon chores in the kitchen and laundry, vespers at four, a starchy evening meal with no meat, butter, or milk, then darning socks and mending clothes in the evening, and bedtime prayers kneeling before an iron-rod bed.

Living for years in ritualized monotony hollowed out my longing for reuniting with my foster mother. Yet on that summer day, while kneeling in the blueberry patch, my life turned about. I heard my name called from a distance. "Mother Superior wants you to come to her office. A woman is here asking for you." Over my shoulder, I yelled back, "What color is her hair? Red or brown?" The messenger ran up to me and, with hands on her knees, panted out, "Sort of brown."

The world fell away. With my heart thudding, I found my legs, stumbled over my pail scattering the berries, and pounded down the dirt path toward the convent. As I rounded the corner of the building, I saw her standing in the middle of the courtyard. She had aged. Silver threaded her dark-brown hair. Incised worry lines ran from the sides of her nose to the corners of her mouth. A raw cry rose from deep within me. Struggling for air, I choked out, "Mama. Mama." Tears flooded down my cheeks. In my haste to reach her, my feet tangled, and I stumbled. On hands and knees, I crawled toward her. She rushed to my side and knelt, her beautiful, plain face bent to mine, her soft brown eyes taking me in. I heard her say, "My precious little girl. I found you."

My foster mother had come to rescue me from the loveless and cloistered existence of the convent. I felt a tearing in my chest as if the strictures that trussed my heart were ripping apart. She helped me stand, but my legs found no purchase. I heard my voice repeat, "Don't leave me. Don't leave me, Mama." With her arm across my back for support, we hobbled inside to meet with Mother Superior.

It took weeks to clear the bureaucratic requirements. On the day of my departure, a young nun tied a small placard around my neck inscribed with my name, age, and destination. With my little suitcase in hand, I climbed onto the local milk truck which delivered me to the railway station. The station master escorted me to the train and settled me in. A whistle blew, the cabin lurched, wheels bit into the steel rails, and the train rolled forward. Steam hissed and swirled past my window. The countryside flew by at an accelerating pace. At last, after six years of waiting, I was going home.

~

Chapter 78

THE VISIT

February 26—April 12

During Joan's six-week visit with her mother, my mailbox overflowed with her letters and notes and copies of her journal entries. Joan wrote that a blizzard had delayed her flight five hours. She arrived exhausted and anxious but was welcomed with "hugs and kisses" by her mother and brother in a teary homecoming.

Her mother tried her best to be considerate, even sweet, and had gone out of her way to make the house comfortable for Joan. Unfortunately, she *had* to sleep in "the room" as other bedrooms were "not suitable," in her mother's estimation. Joan vowed to do the best she could under the circumstances with a night-light burning and the closet doors open.

Snowed in and feeling caged for weeks on end, Joan and the Parts recorded, usually late at night, their daily thoughts and feelings and observations in a journal. She noted her mother rarely left the house. A blaring television was her sole connection to the outside world. She had no friends. The only living creature in her life was a big, unruly dog which her mother disciplined with a wooden spoon, causing Joan and the Parts to "zone out." Seeing what her mother had become and how she lived, Joan couldn't help pitying her.

After listening to her mother's stories about her childhood and sorting through old photographs, Joan was amazed at how much of her life she had missed—dissociated, she thought, lost somewhere in her mind.

The whole time there, Joan felt herself "vibrating," tolerable most of the time but always "on edge." She avoided the attic and only went to the basement out of barest necessity. Coping with her mother's "negativity and ever-increasing criticism" was especially trying. She experienced periods of "blankness," moments of internal disarray; but when the noise and tension threatened to overwhelm the Parts, she would gather them to safety sitting in a rocking chair. The young Parts never came out, wanting nothing to do with Joan's mother. Fury 1, bound by her desire for Renate's trust, had not broken her promise to stay sober. Some days, horrid memories would "pop up here and there," causing moments of panic where she felt like "breaking down." But with reliance on her creative talents, plus Ana's practical support and my letters and phone calls, Joan managed to maintain the outward appearance of calm even in the face of her mother's intense scrutiny—those "yellow eyes" following her every move.

The Parts and Joan ached to get out of the house, and one afternoon, they broke free. Joan took them to a beautiful park with snow-laden trees, and allowed the Parts the opportunity to come out. This enabled Joan to decompress. Another day, she managed to get away and drove her mother's car over icy roads to take Beth and the others to see the grandparents' house and the elementary school.

Most days she thought she'd been able to take "pretty good" care of herself. But at night in that room, she was filled with feelings of vulnerability and memories of "mind-splitting and sorrowful wretchedness." She had felt "his presence" and was sure the Parts did as well. Surrounded by that evil, she had faced the "demons of the past" that tested her strength and spirit. But, she wrote, she had "not cracked."

All in all, Joan thought the visit had been productive. She loved her mother, always had, and would work on forgiving her for the "time and effort" it would take to get over the "damage" her mother had inflicted. After spending six weeks under the same roof, though, Joan came to the realization that she could not save her mother from a barren and isolated existence. She vowed their many troubled yesterdays would not overshadow her life's purpose and joy.

April 23. The afternoon was dreary, clouds heavy, advertising rain. The foul weather didn't dampen my spirits. I was excited. Joan was coming to session for the first time since her trip to see her mother. Unlocking my office door, I caught myself humming an old German folk song. I placed a new box of tissues on the side table along with a bottle of water. I lit three candles and set out two mugs with spoons and sugar and milk. At the sound of her car in the driveway, I plugged in the electric tea kettle. As Joan walked through the door, she smiled widely, the light in her eyes signaling she was glad to be back in "our room."

Over a cup of steaming English tea, we talked and let the flow of our conversation determine the pace of therapy. She thanked me for my calls and letters. They had uplifted her spirit during the dark moments when she felt most vulnerable. In return, I expressed my appreciation for being kept well informed.

Four years before, when her mother came to visit, Joan said she noticed her mother had aged. This time, Joan saw how frail her mother had become and how much older she looked: tired and worn, her auburn hair now gray, her hands wrinkled and red from a lifetime of hard work. Seeing her in this way made Joan feel selfish for having not visited more often.

"There's not much more to tell you about my trip, Renate. As I wrote you, my mother hardly let me out of her sight. I had little free time, but the day before my flight back home, I was overpowered by curiosity." Joan excitedly told me how she had walked through the snow on that wintry afternoon to the "woods" behind her mother's house. To her astonishment, the "forest" was a modest stand of trees. "I couldn't believe that grove of oaks was the inspiration for Many Voices' Haunted Forest." *I could,* I thought, *a "peaceful place among the trees." Where the young Fragment Parts had fled to suffer their injuries in frozen silence until reawakened, and Joan had to remember.*

"Amazing how my mind works," Joan said.

Tucking a loose strand of hair behind her ear, she went on to recount how sweet and considerate her mother had been at first. "But it didn't take long for her negativity and criticism of everybody and everything to resurface. Pretty soon, that included me. Whatever I did to help out around the house never met with her approval. She even told me how I should dress." With a dismissive flick of her hand, she said, "I didn't let it touch me. I reminded myself I was in charge of my life, no longer a helpless victim of my mother's intimidation and Charles' abuse. That's when my fears fell away." Refusing to be demoralized by the past, she had felt herself unfold, liberated from the power of her dread—free of her mother, free of Charles, and free of all that had taken place so long ago in that house.

I was heartened by her resolve and strength of character. The long hours of hard work over four years had come to fruition.

"Since my return home, Renate, I've noticed I seem to have fewer flashbacks. Also, I'm less apprehensive about going to bed, and, thank God, my nightmares aren't so frightening." She reported remarkable changes also were taking place in the Inner Realm. Samantha and Shadowman had dismantled the Puppets' net. Although the young Parts—Beth and two toddlers—still lived under Elizabeth's care, the mature Parts, except for Rose and Sophia, had taken up residence on the Meadow. Joan told me they had begun to come together in the Circle of Truth to discuss how best to respond to what upset them, even encouraging Beth and Sophia to voice their opinions. Best of all, going Inside to participate in the Parts' discussions now aroused less anxiety in Joan.

I was delighted to hear that the Parts were coming together as a group to find solutions for their concerns without my guidance. Were they beginning to surrender their separateness?

"What's more," Joan rolled her eyes, "since Fury 1 achieved sobriety, Samantha wants to go to AA to find out what goes on there. And Beth wants to go, too, to meet Fury 1's new friends."

Joan's eyes went wide with discovery. "Did you know, Renate, there are Parts you've not met? Who have no name, never speak, and will never come through the Edge to the Outer Realm?"

447

"From what I've read, Joan, these are Fragment Parts that hold merely a sensory detail of a memory. Most integrate spontaneously without the help of a therapist. No one seems to know exactly how that happens."

"What goes on in my mind is such a mystery," Joan remarked, shaking her head. "But I guess I just have to trust that whatever goes on in there serves a purpose."

With pride, Joan went on to describe her newfound ability to tolerate disturbing thoughts and uncomfortable emotions that the Parts, like Fury 1 and her sisters, held for her. She had accepted that her way of thinking, feeling, and acting could be flawed. And like every other human being, she wasn't perfect and didn't have to be. This newfound freedom and the positive responses from people around her gave her hope in finding a purpose in life. Joan had been daydreaming about formally studying art education and thought this would make her "feel more complete."

I mentioned James Hillman, a transpersonal psychologist, who posits that within every human being is an "acorn of potential" which holds our talents, gifts, and innate aptitudes. He believes if we consciously seek out and nurture our potential, then we can attain what we imagine we want to be. I assured Joan she could achieve her dreams once she fully accepted her worth and honored her gifts as a creative human being.

"Late at night, when I wrote in my journal," Joan said, "I entertained the idea of writing a book about my life, getting my story out to others who have been victimized like me. Perhaps it would serve to inspire them to get well. What do you think?"

"A noble aspiration, Joan."

"Would you help me write my story, Renate? After all, you have the vocabulary," she said with a wicked smile, "and hundreds of pages of notes. Plus, my poetry and paintings. We could use my Lifeline as a guide."

"I'd be honored to collaborate with you, Joan. But I must warn you, I have no clue how to write a book."

Joan groaned in mock theatrics, "Just my luck."

As our amusement subsided, Joan said, "Beth and Fury 1 insist on seeing you."

Without further invitation, Beth exited, making a long face. "Oma, it's true—the Inside is changing," she lisped. "It's getting smaller. Almost all the Trees in Many Voices' Forest are gone, but Shadowman's Tree is still there. It has completely leafed out, and morning glories are climbing up its trunk. It's so pretty, Oma. I saw Shadowman leaning against it, resting. But he looks like he's getting thinner and thinner. I can almost see right through him," she said with awe.

"Is Raven's Tree still there?"

"Yes, he sits up there on his Perch and watches over us. But the River of Tears is drying up, and Rose's Cave has gotten really small. Elizabeth's House is nearly empty. Lisa, Maria, Charlotte, Annie, some of the babies, and several of the Forest Girls who came to live with us—Amber, Angelina, and Maggie—they've all crossed over to the Outside. Elizabeth tells me to be brave. She says I'll be crossing over soon." *The imaginary landscape, that refuge Joan's creative mind conjured up, had served its purpose, and I thought it would soon be no more.*

"Oma," she whined, "I don't want to be brave. I don't want to be old, like Joan. I want to stay like I am now, just a happy seven-year-old girl with blue eyes and red hair in a ponytail."

"I'll help you to be brave when it's your turn to come to the Edge and cross over."

Beth wasn't to be mollified. "What worries me most is when I'm Outside, I'll never see you again. I'll never be able to hug you. I'll never be able to tell you how much I love you." Her bottom lip protruded in a child's pout.

"Somehow, I think you will always know me, Beth. Instead of looking at me through your eyes, you'll see me through Joan's eyes. Instead of hugging me with your arms, you'll hug me with Joan's arms. After integration, you and all the others will love with one heart, think with one mind, speak with one voice, and, when you talk to God, you'll do so as one soul."

"But will *you* see me? How will you know it's *me?*"

"When Joan is happy or mischievous, I shall think of you. And when the sun shines on Joan's hair and I see the red highlights, I shall think of you."

"Thanks for trying to make me feel better, but I don't think I'll be getting brave real soon. Anyway, Oma, I have to tell you something very, very important. The crooked rules and lies and twisted thoughts which confuse us—you know what I mean?—we are crushing them. Stomping on them with our feet. Smashing them into tiny, tiny pieces. We'll use them to build a path from the Inner Realm to the Outer Edge. That way, Oma, whoever decides to cross over will have a little trail to follow to the Outside."

"What a splendid thing to do, Beth."

Her face was radiant as she receded, and Fury 1's features pressed through.

"I think we're all beginning to look forward to being Outside with Joan. It still makes us a little scared. When we close down the Inner Realm, can we keep a small portion intact—like the Meadow—where we can go until we feel brave enough to go Outside again?"

"Once you all integrate into Joan's consciousness, there will be no need to go back. The Inner Realm will be no more."

"Then I'll have to think about this integration business some more," she said.

"Perhaps you might talk it over with Samantha and Shadowman," I suggested. "But before you go, I have a surprise for you."

I presented her with a small, royal-blue, crystal heart embedded with a white-and-gold starburst. I explained the heart represented her kept promise to remain sober for six months. Enchanted, she cupped the tiny heart in both hands as I conveyed the meaning of the colors: Blue represented divine knowledge, white represented truth, and gold represented love.

"In the future, when you're tempted to drink, hold this memento in your hand. Allow its presence to help you examine your feelings and acknowledge their cause. Embracing that knowledge will dispel your need to reach for the bottle."

Joan returned without being called, the crystal heart nestled in the palm of her hand, seemingly in full acceptance of the talisman's purpose.

～

Chapter 79

DRIVING OUT ANGER

May 15. "I'm out of patience with my body," Joan complained while seating herself with a groan. "If it's not my heart, it's my back or my ankles. Now it's my right wrist and thumb that hurt. I can't write or paint, and you know how *that* makes me feel."

Something dark washed over her face. "What perturbs me more than anything is that I didn't express the anger I feel toward my mother when I had the chance. I spent six weeks with her in *that house.* We talked about all kinds of stuff, but not once did I tell her how angry I am. Even when I looked right into those yellow eyes. At the time, I thought I had put all my resentments behind me, but here I am today, ranting and raving."

"This should be a day of celebration, Joan. As hard as it may seem, today you could permit yourself to release those angry feelings."

"Little good can come from anger," she objected.

"Anger is a human emotion. We all get angry at times. Letting go of anger can relieve your physical ailments and cleanse your mind of emotional toxins. If expressed constructively, your anger may help heal the injuries inflicted by your mother's betrayal. Consider starting a dialogue with her. Recall the many ways her failings harmed you. Allow her to explain why she failed you."

"But how do I start?"

Raven exited abruptly. "Teacher, it grieves me to disagree with you. Joan is not ready yet to externalize her anger. Our priority must be to cleanse the angry feelings Fury 1 holds against the Mother."

"For years now, Raven, the Parts have worked through the anger they held against the Mother. They've cried, screamed, wrote long letters of accusation, even vented their rage in poems. Now, I believe, it's Joan's turn to do that work. Unvoiced anger will fester within her and feed disharmony and despair throughout the Inner Realm."

"Please trust my judgment in this matter," Raven entreated.

I lifted my right arm, palm out, in a conciliatory gesture and, against my better judgment, yielded to his petition.

Fury 1 emerged through Raven's features. *Would she be hostile,* I wondered, *belligerent, vengeful, or overwrought with emotion?* As I studied her demeanor, I realized my concern was unfounded. Fury 1 sat calmly before me, awaiting my guidance in surrendering her anger. She was not alone. She said if I were to look into her eyes, I would see Samantha, Sebunome, and her two sisters watching and waiting to participate. I assured them of their safety and induced a meditative state. I suggested Fury 1 visualize the Mother sitting in a chair across from her. She covered her face with both hands. "I can't look at her. I won't!"

"Remember, if looking at her is unbearable, then you can make her image go away with just a snap of your fingers."

"No, no," she objected, "Raven advised we have to do this. But before we do, I want to absorb Fury 2 and Marjorie so we can speak of our outrage in one voice. They hate the Mother even more than I do."

With no further discussion, she closed her eyes, took several deep breaths, and, without faltering, declared, "My sisters and I are one." *This unplanned fusing of the Dangerous Ones,* I thought, *might hasten integration. I was grateful for this unexpected gift.*

Fury 1 looked steadily at her visualized image of the Mother sitting before her. Perhaps empowered by her sisters' fusion, she stood, took one step forward, and shouted, "You never believed us when we tried to tell you the truth. You always chose to believe his lies and deceptions. How could you not know when he left your bed and sneaked into our room? Did you put a pillow over your head so you wouldn't have to hear our moans? When he pressed his arm against our throat, we couldn't breathe, or call for help. Do you hear me, Mother? How could you leave us alone with that degenerate when you went to work at night? We all want to know why you didn't rescue us. Why you didn't protect us. Why you chose to marry that pervert. Just to get away from your mother? And when you knew what was happening, you neglected your responsibility. You betrayed us all. We hate you! I hate you! You've never been and never will be our mother. Do you hear me, Mother? Do you?"

Her face a mottled red, she picked up two small pillows from the couch, and, one after the other, threw them at the chair where the imagined Mother was sitting. "Take this, Mother. How does it feel, Mother, to be hurt and unable to defend yourself?"

As Fury 1's energy flagged, I got up and guided her back to the couch. When seated, she sobbed into the crook of her arm, her body quaking.

"She never, never . . ." Her keening faded.

"She never what, Fury 1?"

With a thick tongue, she choked out, "Who cares." She flicked tears from her cheeks. "I'm done for today."

Raven reappeared. "Well done, Teacher."

"Thank you, Raven, but I think Fury 1 and the others are the ones who deserve your praise."

"I am aware of their hard work. Unfortunately, I fear the merciless barrage of accusations hurled at the Mother has scraped off scabs from some wounds that were healing. However, as disturbing as their accusations were, they dispersed much of the Darkness within the Inner Realm, permitting the Light to better embrace us all."

Raven bowed and withdrew.

I stood and gently tugged at the sleeve of Joan's blouse. With her eyes barely open, she began massaging the furrow between her brows. "My forehead is sore, like my brain's been stung by a hornet." She was relieved Fury 1 had absorbed her sisters so that "those two troublemakers" could never again spread fear Inside or Out. If ever she chose to confront her mother, she vowed never to do so in such an unrestrained and violent manner. *I knew whichever way she chose to bare her woundedness would become a transformative experience, shifting her perspective on her mother's behavior and changing the dynamics of their relationship.*

After a long moment gazing out the window, Joan said, "I think I'm fortunate to live at this moment in history, when treatment is available for people like me. In the Dark Ages, I would have been accused of being possessed and burned at the stake. In more enlightened times," Joan's sarcasm pronounced, "I'd have been charged with blasphemy and hung on the rack until I recanted. Not so long ago, I would have been pronounced insane. Locked away and given electroshock treatments. I think I told you, when I was delusional a few years ago, my family took me to the hospital where I was sedated and restrained. It was terrible."

"It pains me that happened to you, Joan." In general, I told her society had become more knowledgeable and accepting of what was currently referred to as dissociative identity disorder (DID), even though I preferred calling the disorder MPD. An increasing number of mental-health professionals now acknowledged that those who suffered this serious disorder could be treated and made whole using the therapeutic approaches that served as the framework upon which I relied in seeking a healing path to her recovery.

"I guess we both have something to be thankful for," she said.

A comfortable silence wrapped around us, but not for long. Joan seemed compelled to again address her troubled relationship with her mother. "My younger sister and I were told to behave like little ladies—always be polite and never draw attention to ourselves. Complaining was not tolerated, and if my mother suspected we had violated one of her rules, she became enraged, yelling and screaming at us. Sometimes my mother became so mad she ignored us for days. Afterward, she would try to be nice, but that never lasted. Her screaming devastated me. But being ignored confirmed I was nothing."

"Did that make you angry?"

Joan ignored my question. "I don't want to excuse my mother's behavior, but she raised us as she had been raised. Both of her parents came from traditional European backgrounds and believed children should do what they were told. And if the children disobeyed, they were punished."

"Not all mothers raised in old-country ways mistreat their children," I countered. "You express understanding for your mother, but I know you hold anger for her, too. Do you suppose expressing that anger might be therapeutic?"

"Letting go of that kind of anger would make me feel ashamed," she said, sitting more erect. "Anyway, I believe expressing anger toward one's mother is immoral."

Having heard Joan repeatedly express this high-minded attitude, I handed her my office copy of the Bible to read Matthew 21:12.

After silently reading the passage, she paraphrased, "Jesus became angry at the people who defiled His Father's temple and drove them out."

"What might this mean for you?"

"If Christ can get angry, why can't I?" she conceded.

I didn't respond, hoping for Joan to voice more insight.

"I have to drive out of my heart—my temple—the anger I hold for my mother, don't I?"

~

Chapter 80

THE COLLEGE GIRL

June 4. Joan trudged to her seat with discouraged steps. "I've been feeling weird the past two days. Like I'm in a fog."

"Have you been Inside to find out why you've been feeling strange?"

She closed her eyes. Confusion spread across her face. Her eyes snapped open and flitted around the room in what looked like startled apprehension.

"Who the fuck are you?"

I rocked back in my chair as I took in this newcomer from out of the blue. "I'm Joan's therapist."

"*I'm Joan!*" she challenged, tapping her chest. "Where am I?"

"You're here with me."

"Where the hell is 'here'?"

"You're in my treatment room."

"Treatment room?" A tremor of alarm in her voice.

"How old are you, Joan?"

"Is this a goddamn inquest, lady?"

"I see you like to swear."

"I can say what I want and do what I want. I'm not afraid of you or anyone else. If you must know, I'm eighteen. But I need to get back."

"Back where, Joan?"

"My dorm, where else? I have to pick up my books and go to class. If I don't get back pretty quick, I'm going to be screwed."

"What classes are you taking?"

"Early Childhood Development and Art."

"You enjoy going to college?"

"I love it," she responded. "And at college, no one bothers me. And I mean no one!"

"I've met another Joan. She's a lot like you. She's artistic and writes poetry."

"I don't know her," she said with a dismissive wave of her hand. "Look, lady, I've told you several times already I have to go back. I've missed two days of classes already because my mother insisted I come home."

"And did you go?"

"Ha! You must be kidding," she scoffed, her right leg jiggling. "When she tells me to do something, I do it or else."

"Why did she want you to come home?"

Her head tilted to meet the shrug of her right shoulder. "She took me to a doctor's appointment. It was weird. He stuck something inside me that hurt like hell. Then I felt like I was being flushed down a toilet. I don't remember anything after that."

"Were you pregnant?"

"What the hell do you think? My mother was afraid it was Charles' kid and wanted to get rid of it before anyone found out. But just because she thinks he made me pregnant doesn't mean he did. Anyway, who cares."

"You mean Charles was not the only man you had sex with?"

"There've been others. Sex is all they want. If they ask, I give." A bitter laugh followed. "Anyway, I don't care, I'm used to it. Now, help me get back."

As I had done with others, I escorted her to the bathroom and placed her in front of the mirror. "This is what you look like now."

She stared aghast. "That's not me," wagging her finger at the reflection. "I'm not fat! And I'm definitely not old." She leaned toward the mirror. "Are those gray hairs?" She sounded incredulous.

"That Body is certainly not young and thin anymore," I said, and then gave her a quick update of Joan's life over the last thirty years. I ended my history lesson by explaining that Joan's mind had been fragmented into Parts and that she was one of those Parts. "When you were in the doctor's office and felt like you were being flushed down the toilet, you must have gone to sleep. A special kind of sleep. You stayed that way for more than thirty years. For some reason, you have awakened now and come out to talk to me."

"That's nuts!"

"Your interests in art and children remind me of the Joan I know. May I call you 'Joan 2'?"

"I'm not like her," she snorted, "and frankly," pointing to the face in the mirror, "I don't *want* to be like her. Just let me go back now and forget about all this crap."

"There's no going back," I said as gently as possible. Her former life was gone, I told her. She wasn't in college anymore and was an alternate personality in a fifty-year-old woman's mind. I invited her to take a walk with me to see where Joan and the others like her lived now.

"I'm not going anywhere with you," she said, taking a step back. "You think I'm crazy, don't you? You probably want me locked up!"

I held out my hand. She slapped it away but then sheepishly followed me out the door. We strolled around the neighborhood. Joan 2 pretended she wasn't interested, but I could see her eyes roving here and there. Then with her face turned away, she muttered, "I'm . . . Maybe I do need to be committed. I hear voices talking, and they seem to be inside my head."

"I know that must be odd to you," and explained that other Parts like her resided in Joan's mind. They talked to one another. And now that she was awake, she could hear them, and they could hear her, even though she was with me on the Outside. Her mouth gaped open, her eyes wide in stunned disbelief. She reached for my hand and held it tightly. "So where am I supposed to have come from?"

"Where you 'come from' is what the Parts and I call the Inner Realm— inside Joan's mind. You'll reside there with them."

"How do I get back '*inside*'?"

I assured her a helper Part would come to assist her. "When you get Inside, the Parts will likely share with you their memories and what happened in all the years after you went to sleep."

I felt her hand tremble in mine, and she was gone.

Beth exited. "Hi, Oma. All of us pulled really, really hard to get Joan 2 back Inside. We are going to take good care of her. And when she gets used to us, we'll tell her what we know."

"Thank all the Parts for me, Beth. Tell them I'm proud of how well they are cooperating with one another."

Amusement danced in her eyes. "I don't have to tell them, Oma. They already heard what you just said."

Joan came back, her lips pressed together, her eyes avoiding mine while she fidgeted. I watched patiently until she finally spoke.

"Such foul language. I can't imagine she's part of me—of us. I'm not even sure I can accept her. Mark my word, she'll cause a setback if we have to work through what she knows."

"Let's call her 'Joan 2' so there's no confusion. Perhaps her language was rough, but I wonder if you haven't sometimes thought about telling Charles off—cussing at him. Or telling your mother off." *That might have been liberating*, I thought.

"Well, you know I couldn't," she spit out. "You know what would have happened to us—to me. What she said about the abortion is . . . Having an abortion is shameful. I'm not ready to talk about it."

"A couple of years ago, I recall Ana told me your mother forced you to have such a procedure."

Joan ignored my remark. "Listening to how she talked about men," she fumed, "I cannot imagine having been promiscuous like that. Allowing men to do whatever they wanted." She lapsed into silence.

After some minutes, a faint smile crossed her face. "This Joan 2 dared to leave, though, didn't she? She got away. I wish I could have."

"But Joan," I interjected, "you were the one who got away and dared to go to college. And Joan 2 came to support you in your studies. Now that she's awake again, she'll have difficulty understanding why she can't go back to college, and she'll have problems adapting to her new circumstances. I pray you will embrace Joan 2 as an important part of you."

Joan looked pained and ignored my urging. She pulled a piece of folded paper from her purse, opened it, and burnished the crease flat with her thumbnail. She recalled having felt optimistic while driving home from a recent AA meeting. Words had "floated around" in her head, so she stopped on the side of the road to "scribble" them down before they "evaporated."

I asked her to read what she had written.

RESOLUTION

Out of chaos, that darkness
Where surely no light can be seen
A spirit torn and bruised
Held together precariously
By the glue of love
With dedicated compassion
From the heart of a kindred spirit
Born into chaos and loss.

To survive, and evolve
Into the kinder side of life
A gentle voice beckons
Those lost and frightened to safety
Guided onto a path untrodden
Led by innate wisdom
Held tenderly within
Yet eternal.

Preserved, and from the pain
A purity springs forth
From the darkness
Points of light
The final resurrections
Of the torn soul sacrificed
Now gently brought together
Piece by piece.

Slowly, a picture forms
Nothing lost and parts fusing
Together with promises kept
A spirit ablaze
Reaches toward the brilliant
Infinite light of eternity
All salvaged, reclaimed and reformed
For a purpose yet to be.

Joan for All

When Joan finished reading, she held the poem out to me. "This is for you, Renate," she said through the mist of her tears.

I took her poem and held it to my heart as a splendid expression of the value of love to restore and repurpose the soul.

Joan telephoned mid-morning the next day to say Sebunome needed to speak with me and asked, "Can we meet for coffee?"

"I'm planning to run some errands. Having a coffee would be nice."

The café was packed. A noisy chorus of voices greeted us, so Joan and I decided to sit on the terrace under a Cinzano umbrella. At the table, Joan lightly touched my hand to signal she was about to move aside. Her body seemed to shrink, and her shoulders hunched forward.

"Hello, Sebunome." I kept my voice low. "It's good to see you."

With her head bowed, she addressed the tabletop. "Before Rose and I become one," she murmured, "I want to learn what it's like being Outside in public. I want to learn to look at people—strangers, I mean—without being afraid."

"An excellent goal," I said. "What do you think you should do first?"

She peeked at me from under her eyebrows. "Lift my head, right?"

That made me smile. "Good. Let me suggest what you can do next. Take a deep breath, and look around. Choose one person you believe is safe to look at, and watch what she does. Think you can do that?"

"But I shouldn't stare, right? It's impolite."

461

I further suggested she could go with me inside to order our drinks. She followed me through the bustling cafe, holding the back of my blouse bunched in her fist. At the counter, I ordered a latte and could sense her hesitate. "Go on, Sebunome, you can order whatever you like."

"Water, please," she stuttered, peeking around my shoulder.

On the way back to our table, gripping her glass with both hands, she had to negotiate her way through the crowd on her own. When we were seated again, I murmured, "Well done, Sebunome." A glimmer of a smile suggested she, too, was proud of her achievement.

While we sipped our drinks, Joan 2 pushed Sebunome aside.

"Tell me what *I'm* supposed to do? I don't know where I'm at. I don't know anyone except you. I hear that other person you call 'Joan' talk to her friends sometimes, but *I* have no one to talk to. I want to go back to college and be with my friends. I have nothing here that belongs to me," she said, "not even a purse where I can keep my stuff."

"I know this must be confusing," I said. "I promise I will talk about your situation the next time Joan comes to therapy."

She gave me a bewildered look and disappeared.

"I think Sebunome made a good start. Don't you?" Joan said, now sitting across the table from me.

"Yes, she did. And Joan 2? Her vulnerability is touching. Can you help her adjust, Joan?"

~

Chapter 81

THE LIFELINE

The following afternoon, I learned that the Parts and Raven were making efforts to familiarize Joan 2 with her new life and surroundings. Joan had provided her with a purse and emptied a dresser drawer where Joan 2 could keep her personal items. Apprehensive of Roger's reaction, Joan had not informed him of the emergence of the new Part but did tell Stephanie, who promised to help the family adjust to the newcomer. When asked, I gave my permission for Joan 2 to telephone me at home if she abided by our long-established rules.

Joan reached into her over-sized tote and withdrew a scroll of paper tied with a blue ribbon. "I have a big surprise. I hope it will make you happy." She stood and proudly presented me with her Lifeline. "This chronicles everything we could remember about our life from the very beginning until that fateful day almost five years ago when we first saw you."

She and Ana and the Parts had worked for more than two years preparing her autobiographical chart, all painstakingly written by hand in beautiful cursive. They had recorded dates, names, locations, and abuses from infancy through late-summer 2003—an arduous and often frightening task—and had also identified when the Parts were created.

"Compiling the Lifeline, Renate, has been the most healing project the Parts and I have ever done together. After documenting all the abuse we had kept secret for so long, we knew we could never again deny what happened to us. When we saw it in black and white, we knew it was our truth. For the longest time, we didn't want to do it—you know, write down all the horrible things—but it's finally done."

What Joan and the Parts had accomplished, piecing together compart-mentalized memories into a cohesive history of their experiences, was a significant therapeutic achievement—a breakthrough testifying to the hard-won acceptance of that which could never be undone. I felt humbled by their dedication and commitment to moving forward.

Our celebration was cut short by the appearance of Joan 2. I asked if a Part had helped her come to the Outer Edge.

"Yes, the one with long, black hair and a shiny breastplate. What's with that?"

"Her name's Samantha," I replied. "She's the Sentinel."

"Whatever. Anyway, she's teaching me to come out and go back without help. I came to see you, though, about something weird. I keep hearing a voice, and I wonder if I'm hallucinating."

"What does the voice sound like?"

"It's gentle and kinda . . . preacherly."

"That voice belongs to Raven. He is an inner self-helper. Do you hear him right now?"

"Yeah. He's telling me I should study what Joan and the others have put together."

I rolled out the Lifeline on the floor. "Take your finger, and trace the entries until you come to a familiar event."

"Here it is!" She pointed to the entry noting when Joan went to college. "*I'm* the one who went to college when I was eighteen," she said. "And *I* was the one who Mother brought home to have an abortion." Joan 2 shook her head, puzzled. "How strange," her brow furrowed. "I don't remember telling anyone about this besides you."

"Perhaps I can explain. Another inner self-helper named Many Voices is the system's scribe. She holds all the history—all the memories. She some-how transferred that knowledge about you to the writers of the Lifeline."

"That's bizarre."

Within seconds, Joan returned. I described how Joan 2 had identified her place on the Lifeline. Joan reached for the document, carefully rolled it up, and stated she would add Joan 2's name, the last to be recorded.

June 10. Fury 1 called a few minutes before midnight. Anxiety vibrated in her voice. She complained of picking up fierce tension from another Part. I suggested she might be co-experiencing Joan 2's emotional state. "Have you approached her?"

"I don't like her," Fury 1 replied without hesitation. "She resents me for some reason."

Abruptly, Joan 2 came on the line to tell me how disoriented and confused she felt. Nothing made sense, and she felt like a stranger in Joan's home. I replied I knew a Part who had picked up on her bewilderment. Without telling Joan 2 who I had in mind, I told her I believed this other Part could be persuaded to help her adjust.

"Oh, I know who you're talking about," she said. "She's a troublemaker. I knew about her when I went to college. She was drunk all the time, even had blackouts, and caused me to miss class. I remember beginning to lose confidence and feeling worn out all the time. And like you said, that's when I must have gone to sleep."

More like wrapping herself in a bubble of amnesia, I thought. "But you held on to your college memories, Joan 2, you just remained unaware of what transpired during the long period that followed."

"I don't get it. What's more, I don't want to. Can't you help me go back?"

My job, I explained patiently, was to help her adjust and encourage her to share her memories with me and the other Parts, and to listen to what they had to share with her. Understandably, this would take time and effort and might prove distressing. "Concerning the Part you called a 'troublemaker,' her name is Fury 1. I want you to know she's reformed. She no longer drinks."

A deepening silence followed. It seemed I had failed to engage her. Then, to my astonishment, Raven's voice came through the phone to say Fury 1 had done an about-face and volunteered to escort Joan 2 back to the Inner Realm. With that heartening news, I wished them all goodnight.

June 13. After our usual initial period of relaxation through meditation, I informed Joan about the late-night conversation I'd had with Fury 1 and Joan 2. I summed up: "Both Parts were distraught. Did you overhear what they had to say?"

"Yes, I listened in."

"Do you remember attending college?"

"I remember being excited about going," she said. "I had chosen a college in another town. My mother went with me and helped me find my dorm. I was looking forward to leaving home but anxious about meeting the other students. And frightened about meeting my professors. I prayed they'd all be women. After a few weeks of constant anxiety, I thought about going back home. But I stayed. I enjoyed my classes. Then I began losing time and fell behind. Eventually, I had to drop out. Now that I know Fury 1 was there drinking and having blackouts, I should blame my failure on her." *I suspected Fury 1 drank to ease Joan's anxiety.*

"What was your major?" I asked.

"Fine arts and education. Painting, poetry, and music have always been my favorite subjects in school. I dreamed of becoming an art teacher. I wanted to teach first and second graders to help them express their creativity and have fun making things."

"What did you do after you left college?"

"I went home to nurse my ill grandmother. I enrolled in a junior college there, but that didn't work out either. After that, I met Roger. Sometimes I dream about enrolling again, but now with all my family responsibilities . . . and what if Fury 1 came out and created a scene or Beth slipped out wanting to make friends?"

"Perhaps after integration," I offered.

A glimmer of hope curled around her.

I told Joan I felt obligated to speak with Fury 1 and Joan 2 today. I wanted to persuade Fury 1 to share the memories she holds and convince the "College Girl" to forgo her wish to "go back." But Joan thought their dislike for one another might present an obstacle. I reminded her how Shadowman and Samantha had been adversaries but, over time, became allies. Also, Fury 1's altruistic act of absorbing her two sisters so the treatment process could go forward should give us hope that these two Parts would cooperate. I suggested Joan join the Parts at the Meadow to listen to what Fury 1 and Joan 2 had to say when they came to the Edge to talk with me.

Joan 2 exited first, her eyebrows arched, as if she was unsure what was to come. "Were you ever scared when you tried to do something important?"

"Oh my, yes," I replied. "I was thirty-one when I started night school to get my high school diploma. Boy, was I scared. Being an immigrant, I struggled with the English language. My eleven-year-old daughter tutored me. Eventually, a college accepted me as a provisional student. Despite the age differences, the younger students welcomed me. But the professors were intimidating, and the university library was overwhelming. One particular professor took a special interest in me and encouraged me to persevere. After a while, I became more confident. Especially," I chuckled, "after I learned I didn't have to read every book in the library to earn a degree."

I kept to myself the dire circumstances that motivated me to obtain an education.

~

At twenty, I had arrived in the land of those shining warriors my six-year-old eyes had seen at the end of the war. By then, they had taken off their spit-shined boots and splendid uniforms in exchange for everyday attire. The first ten years in my adopted country proved to be injurious. My spirit was worn raw by poverty and brought low by shame and violence. I was forced to live in isolation—loneliness and depression pressed down on me. Nightly anxiety over the survival of my children and myself would wake me gasping for air. At the age of thirty, I understood I had to save myself from the mental and emotional apathy that characterized my life. I had to become like one of those shining warriors and rescue the remnants of what was left of me. In my struggle, helping hands of strangers reached out. Their kindness spurred me on to take heart and pursue what I had always wanted—an education. And when I was afforded that opportunity and stood at the threshold of a new life, unlike a quarter-century before, no one snickered, no one turned their face away or sent me to the far wall. Instead, I was invited to sit in the front row and fill up with learning that held the promise of independence and a life of purpose.

~

"I could have succeeded, too, if Fury 1 hadn't sabotaged my education with her drinking." Joan 2 sounded peevish.

"She's right behind you," I said. "Would you like to step aside and let her come forward? You can tell her yourself how you feel and why."

"I want you to know," Joan 2 said to Fury 1, "I was scared all the time. And even though I was afraid, I tried hard to do well. But I never knew when you would get drunk and make me black out. I missed too many classes. After a while, I got worn out and lost confidence." Her shoulders sagged in resignation. "I guess I lost my dream."

Her arms raised, palms open, as though begging forgiveness, Fury 1 responded: "I wasn't aware getting an education was your dream. And I didn't know my drinking was undermining your efforts. I drank to numb out my anxiety. It's a shock to learn that I was the culprit who made you fail. I'm truly sorry for what I did and would like to make amends somehow. I want you to know I've changed. If you give me a chance, perhaps we could be friends. I can tell you everything I've learned about what's going on around here."

Congratulating both for their cooperation, I proposed they continue their conversation Inside at the Meadow. After a long while, the Blessing Lady, as mysterious as ever, came out, traced three crosses on my palm, and disappeared. I sat there in my chair, curious about what could have occurred at the Meadow to bring forth this approbation.

Joan slowly re-emerged. She had not joined the gathering at the Meadow, preferring to watch from a short distance away. She had seen the Parts standing in the Circle of Truth to welcome back Fury 1 and Joan 2. All were relieved and gratified that the pair had found understanding. With the approval of those assembled, Joan explained, Samantha stepped forward to ask if Joan 2 would consent to merge with Fury 1. "I saw the two nod in agreement. Then Samantha asked them to press their palms together and allow Joan 2's memories to flow into Fury 1."

Joan paused, her breathing shallow. "I feel drained. Fury 1 wants to speak to you."

"I feel like a grilled cheese sandwich," Fury 1 said with a wry smile.

"You look like a *smart* grilled cheese sandwich," I said, returning her smile.

"Merging with Joan 2 was so different compared to absorbing Marjorie and Fury 2. I welcomed Joan 2's love for learning, even her disappointments. It was a *good* experience."

Beth popped out. "Oma," she gushed, "when Joan 2 and Fury 1 pressed their palms together, a Golden Light shone above them. Now that I've seen how it works, I'm not so afraid anymore." Then she shyly asked, "Who do you suppose I'll become a grilled cheese sandwich with?"

"I can't say, Beth, but we'll know in time."

"I think I'd like to be a peanut butter and jelly sandwich instead."

We both were laughing as Raven exited to tell me the Parts were gratified at the outcome of the day's events. A sense of calm had now settled over the system.

Two years earlier, the Parts had struggled without success to find a solution for ending the disruptive behavior of Eve and Jasmine. This time, the Parts had determined, on their own initiative, what would benefit the system and advance treatment a step closer to integration.

~

Chapter 82

AFTERMATH

June 17. "I've had a terrible week," Joan said, pressing her purse tightly against her body. "I felt anxious and angry. And I don't know exactly why. But the worst of it happened when I picked up the phone to make an appointment with my gynecologist. I had a flashback to when my mother forced me to go to an abortion clinic."

Was she finally ready, I thought, *to come to terms with what had shamed her and burdened her soul?*

"It was so real, Renate. I was sitting on a table in a small operating room, undressed from the waist down. The doctor ordered me to spread my legs and probed around inside me. I felt sharp pain moving up my abdomen and down my thighs. I was nauseated and cramping and struggled not to faint. When I climbed off the table after the doctor pulled the poor thing out of me, I felt like a lamb taken to slaughter. My mother helped me get dressed. I had a hard time lifting my legs as she tried to put my underwear on me. 'Pull yourself together,' she said. 'Act right. Nothing is wrong with you.'"

When she came out of the flashback, Joan said she was curled in a fetal position clutching her abdomen, full of guilt and rage. Even though she forced herself to get up and do meaningless chores to distract herself, the feelings remained.

"Looking back, I should have refused to go to the clinic. But I gave in so my mother's denial could remain intact, and no one would suspect her degenerate husband might have impregnated me."

"Was Charles still abusing you at eighteen?"

"Yes," she sighed. "By then, he considered me his personal property."

"How did you feel about having an abortion?"

"Ending a life . . ." Joan took in a shivery breath, "I thought we were committing murder."

"Joan, you did not commit murder. The abortion was your mother's choice. Aside from wanting to cover up what went on in her home, your mother may have had other motives. What would carrying his child be like for you? Then raising his child—that would remind you every day of what Charles had done."

"I just wish I could have stood up to her."

"If you had been a grown woman. But as a frightened young girl?" I said nothing further and allowed Joan to sit with her feelings.

Unexpectedly, Sophia appeared. I welcomed this shy outsider.

"Don't look at me," she said, "I'm dirty, and my hair is full of cobwebs. I'm still hiding close to the Forest Edge. I feel lonely and lost. And I don't know how to change."

I suggested Elizabeth and the young Parts would eagerly welcome her. As the Mother on the Inside, she had always provided shelter and comfort for any Part in need. I told Sophia I was sure Elizabeth would invite her to stay with them in the House. I gave her an encouraging smile.

She closed her eyes. And went Inside.

After a long interval, Beth rushed out, excited. "Oma, I have to tell you something. Sophia came to the back door. Elizabeth let her in and filled the bathtub with warm water and took off Sophia's dirty clothes and combed out her matted hair. And guess what?" Beth's eyes were aglitter with mirth. "When Sophia climbed into the tub, Elizabeth took all *her* clothes off, too, and got in the tub with her." She clamped her hand over her mouth as if to hide her youthful embarrassment. "Oma," she lisped, "I wish you could have been there. We all saw Elizabeth's breasts."

While Beth chattered on, images of benign, primordial mother-goddesses flitted through my mind. I visualized the once flat-chested Elizabeth sitting in Sophia's baptismal bath with her full bosom exposed to the waif. The internal mother had evolved, in a figurative sense, into an archetypal mother emanating life-affirming sustenance.

Coming out of this reverie, my attention returned to what Beth was reporting. "I took them lots of towels and I brought a clean white nightgown for Sophia. We've all decided she should stay in the yellow room next to mine. It has a canopy bed. Sophia is so short, Oma, she'll have to use a ladder to get up onto the bed. I think after she rests a little, we can read and play and have lots of fun together." Beth bubbled with laughter. "Perhaps my stinky-winkiness will rub off on her."

I thanked Beth for her account.

Joan came forward and reported that crossing through the opening to the Outside had become easier. She described the Edge as having almost melted away. While Inside, she had seen Sophia crawl out of her hovel near the Forest Edge and had watched her bathing in Elizabeth's House.

"What does Sophia's cleansing signify?"

"She's surrendered the shame of what happened under the basement stairs."

I smiled my approval. "And what does that mean for you?"

"I can stop being ashamed, too."

~

Chapter 83

ʙLACK SACREDNESS

June 25. Unlike her usual punctuality, Joan arrived late. "Please give me a moment to get my bearings," she said. "Getting out of bed was difficult today. I lost someone dear to me a few days ago, and ever since, I've not been myself."

She told me they had become friends about the time the Parts first started coming out and creating havoc. People who knew her, including her family, thought she had lost her mind and needed to be "locked up." Although her friend might have been confused by her behavior, he never judged her. Her voice broke. Tears spotted the front of her blouse. I handed her a tissue. Between hiccups, she wondered aloud why good people had to die before their time. She dabbed at her eyes and exhaled deeply. "Beth and Samantha loved him, too. I can feel their grief at his passing."

Joan cocked her head to one side, as if listening inward, and then muttered, "This is strange. I'm being bombarded with some kind of truth rising out of . . . a black sacredness."

Quickly shifting gears, I inquired if this "truth" was about her or about others.

"It's about me," she fretted. "This black sacre—whatever it is—is demanding I acknowledge my flaws and shortcomings."

"This 'black sacredness' assailing you, Joan, might be what Carl Jung called your 'Shadow.'" I explained Jung theorized that the Shadow held what people preferred not to know about themselves and what they didn't want their family and friends to know. They kept this other side of themselves hidden away in the dark, operating without the explicit knowledge of their conscious mind. "No matter how hard they tried, they could not deny or suppress what they believed was unacceptable about themselves. Little by little—or sometimes suddenly, as in your case, Joan—the truth would rise to the surface of their awareness.

"Think of Linus in the *Peanuts* comic strip. His blanket, which he drags along behind him, is like our Shadow that slides along behind us. If we are prepared to discover what is hidden in our personal realm of darkness, if we do as Linus does—bringing his blanket forward and lifting it to his cheek ever so lovingly—if we dare to bring our Shadow forward into the light of consciousness, then we offer ourselves the opportunity to become more complete human beings."

"I know all about my flaws," Joan squirmed. "My perfectionism and stubbornness. My self-loathing. My cowardly fear of confrontation. My distrust and envy of people with normal lives. I can be hateful and vindictive," her words pouring out in a torrent, "and resentful and insincere—a phony. Then there's my reluctance to forgive. My grandiosity—deluding myself that I can be everything for everyone and everybody." She gulped air to continue. "Worst of all is my hatred and murderous rage. That makes me feel I'm evil, like them. To think I harbor evil within me—that I should embrace this black sacredness, this shadow-thing—the thought is intolerable."

She looked away as if staring at old memories. "I've seen evil close up, Renate. It's marked my body. Demeaned me. Touched every aspect of my existence. My distrust of most everyone has its reasons, you know. Even when people are kind, I still doubt their sincerity. Not to doubt is dangerous, even life-threatening."

"Several of your Parts, Joan, are daring to accept positive feelings from others," I countered, "and risk reciprocating those feelings. Beth and Samantha are good examples. They freely share their affection with people on the Outside, like your friend who just died. Rose is another example. She has overcome her fear of people and doesn't shy away from a caring touch.

Could we ever have imagined Fury 1 establishing friendships at AA? She has even learned to trust and care for me."

Joan frowned. "Fury 1 is lost when it comes to *real* relationships. And Sebunome is still struggling with trusting people on the Outside."

"Because they are parts of you, Joan, those are your feelings. They reflect your struggle. Unless you can trust people and have sincere feelings for them without fear of being hurt, your path will be a lonely one. Having a close relationship is one of the joys life provides."

~

Chapter 84

EMPTY

July 1. Her hands lay limp atop her purse as Joan sat silently looking out the window. "I feel worthless. Helpless and just plain tired. No joy. Nothing." She begged me not to tell her family. She was trying to appear "perfectly normal," but she was weary of the struggle. "I'm worn out. Empty."

She sank deeper into the cushions. "I don't like to feel this way," she said. "When I'm in a dark hole like this, it takes too much effort to crawl out."

Softening my voice, I said, "I can see how emptied out you feel." I let her sit with her feelings awhile and then said, "But you *have* managed to crawl out, Joan. You're sitting here in this room with me, where we can explore the cause of your physical and emotional depletion."

Joan looked too despondent to be engaged. She reached into her purse. "Raven asked me to give you this." In a glance, I realized the missive was not from Raven, but from Many Voices. I handed it back to Joan.

"I believe this is meant for you. Are you up to reading it aloud?"

Joan read this abridged version.

You [Joan] are the Outer Edge for a reason. You embody, literally, the assets that would be most acceptable to others in the society at large . . . In order for all the work to come to fruition, new Parts must not be forged. Old ways should be abandoned. This will take much effort to achieve— strength, dedication, and perseverance—especially from you, Joan . . .

476

[Y]ou, who exists in the Outer Realm, [must] take care of worldly matters until all become joined. This situation must be worked on daily in a conscious manner as the Teacher has taught you. Identify trigger situations, fight to stay aware. Raven remains an advisor and will, in the coming days, offer suggestions [for] ways strength [may] be attained for you . . . to move ahead.

[Y]ou must hold on to faith, not lose hope, and create some joy . . . All Parts deserve to play a part in the fulfillment of the purpose of being, not [only] the pain of life, but also the joy . . . There is nothing to fear and a total life to be gained.

Do what you must, you on the Outer Edge. God does not make mistakes. You are not a mistake.

—Many Voices

"These are important words to ponder, Joan," I advised.

To my surprise, she snatched up her purse, stuffed the letter inside, and left with a quick, "See you later."

Joan called the next day around noon to request a meeting. As she walked through my office door in the late afternoon, she pulled Many Voices' letter from her purse and waved it at me. "She wants me to become more responsible and deal with situations and memories, even triggers, without losing time. No matter what happens or how *I* feel, Many Voices wants me to stay in the present and handle everything by myself without depending on the Parts to rescue me. This means I can never get away, never rest."

"Why don't we reread Many Voices' letter? Then together, we'll sort out what she's asking of you."

I listened while she again read the letter out loud.

"I guess I overreacted," she said, subdued. "In her letter, Many Voices states if I continue to refuse accepting responsibility for what she calls 'worldly matters,' then the system will stay fragmented. She thinks coming to my rescue every time depletes the Parts' energies and interrupts our preparations for achieving integration."

I told Joan I interpreted Many Voices' meaning to also suggest that, instead of retreating to the White Zone, she should stay aware, be self-reliant, and use her coping skills to avoid being pulled into the past by some triggering event.

"It's easier to talk about it when I'm with you but much harder when I'm alone—like yesterday, when I was pulled down into a dark place."

To buoy her spirit, I reminded her that the Parts' character traits were her own. And even though not yet integrated, she could draw on their attributes when the need arose: Ana's common sense and self-sufficiency; Samantha's confidence and courage; Shadowman's strength and fidelity; Sebunome's prudence; Fury 1's tenacity; sweet Beth's joy for life; and Rose's altruism. "And, may I add, I believe if you still your thoughts and calm your heart, you will hear Raven's voice advising and guiding you to know what is noble and good."

She thanked me for my assurances and for reminding her of the resources she possessed to alleviate her depression and feelings of helplessness. She asked how I was able to explain all that with such clarity.

"I'm a therapist, Joan, plus I rely on my own Raven to inspire me," mischief in my voice.

"If I would dare tell anyone what you and I talk about in this room," Joan teased right back, "they would scratch their heads and probably think you need help as much as I do."

"I'm so *flattered* by your assessment of my methods."

"Oh, they *do* help," Joan replied in mock concession, "even though they are, shall I say, quite unconventional."

July 9. After our usual meditation, I suggested visiting with Sebunome about their shared distrust of people. Joan consented. I entreated her to be attentive, and then I invited Sebunome to come forward. She exited immediately to ask for my help. She wished to revisit her past one last time to set aside her sadness and distrust before becoming one with Rose. With newfound maturity, Sebunome informed me she remembered how we did this before. I left the choice to her as to which specific events to revisit. Without further prompting, she closed her eyes, exhaled deliberately, and entered a state of self-hypnosis to re-examine what had afflicted her and created such distrust.

A good while later, Sebunome opened her eyes. Revisiting the past had not quite resulted in what she expected. The Mother was not the all-powerful, unloving woman she remembered. Instead, she now looked small, frail, and unsure of herself. When she caught sight of Charles, all she saw was a pathetic creature. Her dread of him was replaced with revulsion. She paused and then asked me if there was a way to rid herself of this disgust. I gave it some thought before inviting her to step outside. I directed her to stand near the edge of the porch. "When you feel the wind touch your face, inhale deeply. Then slowly exhale those wisps of revulsion and allow the wind to carry them away."

As instructed, Sebunome closed her eyes, tilted up her face, stood motionless, and waited. Within moments, the leaves on the maple trees stirred, and I heard her exhale deeply. She took a step back from the edge and faced me. A soft smile parted her lips, her eyes luminous.

Again comfortably seated in the therapy room, Joan reappeared. Like Sebunome, she, too, was in the process of reframing her perception of her mother. "As a child," she recalled, "I was obsessed with earning my mother's love. I so desperately longed for her to hold me. To tell me I was her sweet little girl whom she would shelter and comfort always. I did everything to get her attention. I was good. I was quiet. I never complained. I tried to be the best little helper—I fetched and cleaned and took care of my sister and brother. But she never seemed to notice me. Once in a while, she would unexpectedly hug me, but then just as quickly, her affection would be gone. And despite her indifference, I tried so hard to attach myself to her. But her actions let me know I really didn't matter."

A tremor racked Joan's body. A groan escaped her throat. She began to cry. I sat in silence, watching tissues collect in her lap. *The unfulfilled longing of her inner child and its ensnaring grief had bound her heart and crippled her emotions for most of her life. Although I didn't deceive myself that these were the last tears Joan would shed, nevertheless, I felt immensely gratified as I watched her tears wash away the festering perniciousness of the wounds inflicted by her mother's inability to mirror how precious and lovable she was. Or even to validate her existence by acknowledging the child's eagerness to please and help. Joan's pain had finally opened a fissure in her psyche into which something other than her mother's negligence could take hold and flourish. Perhaps, now she could become what Donald Winnicott termed a "good enough mother" unto herself, a mother who would never leave her, always love and protect her.*

Her sobs eventually subsided. She heaved out a breathy apology. "I'm sorry, Renate, I didn't plan on this outpouring. As you can see, I learned to feel unworthy early on from my mother. Setting that aside will be an ongoing struggle. But thank heaven, you've shown me how deserving I am—deserving of love and praise, even admiration. In a sense, you helped me give birth to myself. I consider you my spiritual mother. To think that soon I will have to leave you makes me sad."

"Once final integration has been achieved, Joan, be assured you and I will always be connected in spirit. And we'll forever remember the valuable work we did together and the commitment to healing we shared." *And I hoped her ego had grown strong enough to process the admissions made this session. I was cautiously optimistic but told myself that the next few days would reveal how well Joan was going to handle this afternoon's "outpouring."*

~

VI

A VIBRANT MANDALA

Summer 2008 to Spring 2009

Chapter 85

THE VERY BEST MEDICINE

July 17. When I heard her car in the driveway, I went outside to greet Joan. Considering the torrent of emotion expressed in our last session, I was grateful to find not a trace of bereavement in her eyes. Hand in hand, we made our way through the shade beneath a majestic maple onto the front porch of my office. Sitting in the swing together, I told her of my phone conversation with Rose a few days before. Rose had complained that her vagina burned like someone had been cutting her "down there." As a stop-gap measure, I had suggested she talk with Elizabeth, but Rose asserted her "job" was to hold the pain for the others. I reminded her she already had accepted that the healing process entailed sharing her physical pain with the other Parts. Rose responded that being a "person of honor" made such an act unconscionable. This regressive behavior had perplexed me. If fear of losing her purpose had motivated Rose to insist again on this faulty self-perception, then, evidently, she was trying to stall her integration. I had told Rose we would address her situation at our next therapy session and until then, to remain patient and brave.

Joan said she also had heard Rose's complaint and shared my concern. When we adjourned to the therapy room, I spoke to Joan of my hope that Rose would have returned to her more evolved self by today. I proposed working with Rose initially, and then, if all went well, I would steer treatment toward integrating Rose and Sebunome. Joan gave me a half-hearted smile of approval. Before directing her to the Meadow to be with the others, I encouraged her to remain attentive and participate in the events as they unfolded.

In the quiet moments that followed, Rose emerged. She looked uneasy and seemed reluctant to meet my eyes.

"Oma, I'm sorry I went back to my old ways. Not knowing what would happen to me and Sebunome once we merged and then crossed over—that terrified me. Will we still *be?* Will we know that we *are*, or will we simply dissolve? Can you explain what will become of us?"

"I'm not sure, Rose, that I have the right words to express how you will continue to be. After you integrate with Joan, my understanding is your memories and all the wonderful attributes you possess will be preserved in Joan's mind. Once everyone, even the youngest Parts, have integrated, I visualize the result to be a vibrant, unified mandala."

Confusion clouded her eyes.

"Perhaps I can explain it better another way. Let's play like you are sitting at Elizabeth's big, round table with a jigsaw puzzle spread out before you. There is a large piece in the center with silver light radiating in all directions. There are many other puzzle pieces of various sizes, colors, and configurations fitting snugly around the centerpiece. Now imagine these puzzle pieces represent the Parts that have already integrated. The centerpiece represents Joan. Another piece represents Jasmine, another Eve, Leaf, and so on. There is a large piece for Sarah Christine and smaller ones for Maria, Charlotte, and Lisa. The many small pieces are the Forest Girls, some of whom you and I have met and know by name. Remember JJ, No Speak, No See, Alice, Slut, Amber, Maggie, and Angelina? Notice that to the side of the puzzle there are pieces that still need to be put in place. And now, make believe it's your time to integrate with Sebunome and become part of the puzzle. Do you see a puzzle piece with colors that reflect you and Sebunome?"

Without hesitation, she pretended to select a piece, one she described as emerald green and cobalt blue with rose-colored veins. "Do you know why I chose those colors, Oma? Green is for me. I care for every living thing without ever harming them. Blue is for Sebunome, who's always honest and loyal to people she cares about; she knows what is right and wrong. And the rose color stands for love and hope."

"All right, then. Are you ready to fit your puzzle piece into its place? Decide where your piece fits best. Study carefully what's before you. Look closely, Rose. See how the colors and patterns are interrelated and interconnected to create a meaningful whole. The completed puzzle represents all of you functioning as one individual—one heart, one mind, one voice."

With eyes closed, Rose took her time to reflect on my metaphor. After several minutes ticked by, her eyes opened and locked on mine. She told me she had placed their piece where she believed it belonged in the puzzle and now was eager to merge with Sebunome. She asked if the ceremony could take place in her Cave.

"If Sebunome is ready, and if the Parts and Raven give their consent, it certainly will be all right with me."

I waited for Rose to report back. Soon she announced all had approved of her wish but cautioned that, after their integration took place, what she and Sebunome had borne would be known to everyone. "Including Joan," she said, making the point. Then in a soft undertone, "Everyone has decided, Oma, to assemble in front of the Cave to say goodbye."

"Thank you for telling me, Rose. Do I see a question in those soulful brown eyes? Be assured I will be there in spirit."

She stood. "Dear Oma, thank you for all you have taught us. Most of all," her voice broke, "thank you for the love you gave us. That was the very best medicine." She bent forward and lightly kissed me on the cheek. "I will move aside now, so Sebunome can speak to you."

Like so many times before, I marveled at the subtle transformation of features as Sebunome's face emerged through Rose. She took my hand and said simply, "Thank you, Helper Oma, for keeping your promise."

Now it was my turn to feel my throat constrict with emotion. I had learned to care deeply for this brave introvert who, to my astonishment, had become the "teller of truth" for Raven's system. As I struggled for composure, Sebunome faded and Rose with her.

Joan returned from the Inner Realm, her breathing shallow and rapid. She knew most of what Rose and Sebunome had disclosed but still resisted acknowledging the terror of being buried in a grave of leaves and the agony of her vagina being mutilated. "If I am to internalize these . . . memories as my own, then I want you sitting beside me holding my hand."

I moved to the couch, took her hand in both of mine, and promised to remain at her side. Joan closed her eyes and went back Inside. I waited for what I knew was to follow. She sat quietly for several minutes before her body began to writhe. Her head moved back and forth. Moans escaped her throat. I held her hand tightly while her consciousness assimilated the full impact of Rose and Sebunome's memories. Eventually, the moans became whimpers, followed by a bruised silence.

Beth slipped out. "Elizabeth told me to tell you about everything that went on Inside. First, all of us, even the Little Ones, helped sweep out the Cave. Then we put green branches on the floor and covered them with blue and white flowers from the Meadow." *At long last, vaginal innocence and purity had been restored, at least metaphorically,* I thought. "But Fury 1 didn't help," Beth tattled. "She was too upset when she heard what was going to happen. Anyway, Raven brought beautiful gowns for Rose and Sebunome to wear. Then Raven flew back to his Perch. Before Rose and Sebunome went to the Cave, they came over to Elizabeth's House to thank her for having been such a good Mother on the Inside. After that, both of them walked to Shadowman's flowering Tree. They thanked him, too, for his help and protection and said goodbye. When they visited Samantha, they told her she had been their role model. Rose and Sebunome told me and Sophia to be brave like them when it's our turn to cross over. Then after they said goodbye to everyone, Rose and Sebunome went into the Cave. We all waited outside. I heard them talking, but I couldn't understand what they were saying. Elizabeth explained they were ready to become one and were thanking each other for being best friends. Then they merged, Oma," awe in her voice. "But when they crossed over into Joan, their memories made me sad. And I think Fury 1 is mad at them for leaving her behind and all alone."

Beth's features subtly changed. Before me sat Samantha, erect and self-assured. Proposing now to cross over, too, she was prepared to lay down her golden breastplate and sword, and surrender her duties as Sentinel. At this juncture, she thought joining the others to add her courage and support would further contribute to Joan's welfare on the Outside. Having paid her respects to Raven and said her goodbyes to Shadowman, Elizabeth, and those who remained, Samantha had taken a last look at her Tree, the River of Tears, the Meadow, and Many Voices' white cloud glittering in the far distance. "I hope, Teacher, you will approve of what I have decided to do."

With that said, Samantha put her arms around me and wept. I thanked her for all her help and released her from her duties as Sentinel. Smiling through her tears, she integrated.

No sooner had Samantha integrated than Joan came back. "What an amazing experience. I'm at a loss for words. So much to take in . . . My head feels so *full*. And my forehead is tingling again. No, that's not it—my brain feels electrified, like an energy rush." She massaged her forehead. "Thank God for Beth. She described the ritual at the Cave perfectly. It was magical, but bittersweet when I realized I'll never hear Rose, Sebunome, and Samantha's voices ever again. I never totally appreciated the sacrifice Rose made on my behalf and the others. What a burden she carried all these years. And now, I'm also fully aware of Sebunome's gift—keeping people away who might have harmed and exploited us. Her mistrust and vigilance kept us safe. Absorbing their memories was overwhelming, Renate. How will I cope if I can never escape them?"

I assured her that we would continue to talk and feel through these memories until she discovered ways to come to terms with them without the need to dissociate.

"Now I want to go home and sit in my blue room and sort all this out."

I believed the task of achieving homeostasis—balance and harmony—in her newly altered state of consciousness would be another truly transformative experience for Joan.

About two the following afternoon, Roger telephoned in a dither. He had come home from work to find Joan lying on the backyard deck, "curled up like a baby," calling for "Mama and Oma." I explained that several recent therapy sessions had been challenging and unsettling. I asked him to take her inside, make her comfortable, and as soon as she regained some semblance of coherence, inquire if she needed to see me.

Near four o'clock, Roger brought his wife to my office. Joan was dressed in a faded floral kimono. She was wearing flip flops, hadn't a trace of makeup, and her hair was in tangles. She slumped onto the couch with a groan.

"How could I let this happen?" she asked, shaking her head. "The first few hours after Rose and Sebunome and Samantha integrated, I felt fine—more complete. In fact, I was proud. Then I began thinking about how our work was coming to a close. I panicked and obsessed about never seeing you again. It even affected my sleep. I remember having a weird dream," she said, embarrassed. "I saw Beth, Sophia, myself, and a few young Parts sitting on your lap, all entwined. Then we started to crawl into your stomach. I guess we were trying to become part of you."

"Sounds like you're experiencing extreme separation anxiety," I said. "After five years of intensive treatment, you're reacting to the realization that, after integration, you will live your life without me."

"But before our final goodbye," Joan said, "we'll continue to work together, won't we? After integration, right?"

"That's the plan," I assured her.

"On top of it all, I heard Fury 1 complaining about having been left behind. Instead of comforting her in some way, I must have regressed. And that's when Roger found me."

"How would you feel," I asked, "if we went ahead and integrated Fury 1 today?"

Joan cringed and reached for a tissue to wipe the perspiration beading her upper lip. "I've already absorbed what Rose, Sebunome, and Samantha knew and felt. Having my mind flooded with Fury 1's memories . . . Do you think I'm ready for that, Renate?"

Hoping to allay her fears, I unveiled the plan I had conceived over the last few days to help Fury 1 suffer through the conflicted emotions she held for the Mother—Joan's mother.

Raven emerged. "Healer, I feel your plan will serve our objective very well. Before you proceed, though, I would like to ask for Many Voices' approval." He listened inward a few moments and then announced, "Many Voices is in full agreement. She thought it appropriate Fury 1 face her conflicting emotions in the Dark Forest, where memories of the Mother's failings had once been held by the Forest Girls."

"Asking Fury 1 to enter that vast Realm alone," I said, upon reflection, "might be too intimidating. I shall ask Shadowman to walk with her to the Forest Edge and wait for her until the letting-go of her painful emotions is complete."

He bowed and withdrew.

"I'm here, Teacher, and honored to serve," Shadowman said upon exiting. "I shall do as you have suggested. Afterward, should Fury 1 decide to become one with Joan, with your consent, I would like to offer my assistance in guiding her out of the Inner Realm. I, myself, am ready to walk toward the Light and join the others. I miss Samantha. Our work together and her friendship brightened my lonely existence."

When I expressed my gratitude for all he had contributed, Shadowman blinked back tears. "It is I who must express my gratitude. It was you who encouraged me to move out from behind my Tree and cleanse myself of all the slime and darkness. You convinced me to surrender my primitive methods for keeping the Parts safe. You made possible the Puppets' release from bondage to become white feathers in Raven's tail. Thank you for trusting me to become a helper."

Shadowman's voice became raspy. "My dear Teacher," he said, "this may be the last time you and I speak. Perhaps this is our goodbye."

My heart missed a beat. "My dear Shadowman, for you and me, there will never be a 'goodbye.' You will live forever in my heart. Your loyalty and courage, and all your positive attributes will not be lost when all are integrated. When that time comes, your essence will live on in Joan's consciousness."

He stood, took my hand in his, and lovingly placed it against his cheek. Without another word, he was gone.

I stole a few moments to compose myself. Joan came out to find herself standing before me. Noticing tears glistening on my cheek, she handed me a tissue in a consoling gesture.

Joan had heard my discussion with Raven and expressed surprise that Fury 1 held conflicted feelings toward her mother similar to her own. She was now ready for Fury 1 to integrate, but only after Fury 1 worked through her sorrow. "I don't think I could withstand being burdened with her raw emotions in addition to my own," she said and returned to her place on the couch.

When Fury 1 came forth, I acknowledged her feelings of having been "left behind." I told her outright that the time had come to integrate. But before that could happen, Raven and I had agreed she had to face and work through the conflicted emotions she held for the Mother. With a catch in her throat, Fury 1 admitted to wanting her mother to love her. But no matter how hard she tried, her mother never did. Unlike Joan, Fury 1 wasn't sad, just mad. However, she hadn't been enraged like her sisters, but only pretended so no one would know how much her mother's behavior hurt her. When I explained the work before us was to take place in Many Voices' Realm, her eyes went wide with surprise. Then with a resigned shrug of her shoulders, she said, "I guess it's my time now."

I sat beside her. She laid her head on my shoulder. "You are the only one who ever loved me. Thank you, Helper."

Fury 1 slid off the couch and sat on the floor in a yoga position. She closed her eyes and raised her arms as if to receive blessings from the Golden Light to sustain her throughout the forthcoming transformation of her beleaguered self.

Returning to my chair, I spoke through to the system and engaged Shadowman to accompany her to the edge of Many Voices' Realm. From there, I asked Fury 1 to proceed alone to the center of the Dark Forest, where the Forest Girls had found refuge.

"Listen to the guidance of my voice . . . hear the echoes of the memory fragments the Forest Girls left behind . . . sense their need to be held and comforted . . . hear their pleas for protection and rescue . . . acknowledge the fears a slamming door elicited, the silence those piercing yellow eyes demanded, and the disregard in the Mother's voice . . . respond to these echoes of suffering caused by unfulfilled yearnings for love . . . embrace your conflicted emotions for the Mother . . . suffer them through . . . accept the facts of your relationship which you cannot change . . . and come to terms with your unanswered longings."

As I said these words, I observed movement behind her eyelids. Her body stiffened. She grimaced and retched as if vomiting up her anger from the chasm of her despair. There followed a stream of guttural sounds and a heart-rending wail. With her eyes shut tight, she buried her face in her hands, whispered "Oh, Mama, Mama," and coughed up great sobs of sorrow.

When the anguished outpouring eventually stopped, I heard Many Voices speak:

Fury 1, you have no more need to hurt. No more need for self-punishment. You have freed yourself of the entanglement with the Mother. Freed yourself of your anger and surrendered your unrequited love.

A shiver rippled through Fury 1's body, drawing out a deep sigh. She fell to one side, curled into a fetal position, and lay motionless. In my mind's eye, I saw Fury 1 and Shadowman, hand in hand, cross the Edge to the Outer Realm to join the others and become one with Joan.

I kneeled beside Joan and called her name. Her eyes fluttered open. She struggled to her feet and eased onto the couch. She began to weep and, through her tears, said, "Fury 1's anger was my anger. Her sorrow was my sorrow. Being loved by my mother—that's what we needed most."

I handed her the box of tissues.

"My head feels strange . . . so full again." In slow motion, she raised her right hand to touch the center of her forehead. Making small circular motions with her middle finger, she murmured, "Ummm. There's that tingling sensation again."

"I'm no neurobiologist, Joan, but I like to believe transformative work can enhance neural growth, change the electrochemical connections in your brain that can activate a physical response—that 'tingling' in your forehead. On the other hand, the mental processes required to absorb what Fury 1 held have expanded your consciousness, that 'full' feeling you've sensed before."

While I spoke, Joan's facial expression turned serene. Many Voices exited. She didn't speak but, with her hand, indicated her wish. With pen and paper, she wrote:

> Part of the healing is to embrace the unseen, both positive and negative, enough that you find joy and peace in the visible. All thanks be to God and to you, our Healer. Well done.

After reading Many Voices' note, Joan and I agreed it was time to end this eventful session. She telephoned her husband to pick her up. As she walked toward the door, purse in hand, she turned and asked, "Once we're all integrated, will we—I mean, will *I* have a normal life, like other people?"

I chose my words with care. "I suppose you will," I responded, "at least, most of the time. Our work has not erased the memories of your childhood trauma. Once in a while, those memories will come forward, causing heartache and feelings of loss and regret. Honor them, and grant them their due."

Joan gave me a long look, a melancholy ache in her eyes, and walked out the door.

After she left, I felt elated by the success of Fury 1's integration, but drained, hardly able to rise from my chair after this demanding four-hour session. I gathered my notes, put them in a folder to be transcribed the next morning, blew out the candles, turned off the lights, locked the door, and shambled home.

~

Chapter 86

TOWARD WHOLENESS

July 21. I stood at my office window waiting for Joan as the sun slid behind a dark cloud. She labored up the front-porch steps just as rain started dropping out of the sky. I had encouraged her to meet me for a follow-up to explore any consequences resulting from our last couple of sessions. *Had she noticed any particular changes in her behavior and affect from integrating Rose, Sebunome, Samantha, Shadowman, and Fury 1? Could I detect nuances in her facial expression, vocal inflection, and body language—anything reminiscent of those five major Parts?*

Her movements were listless as she took her seat, her eyes avoiding mine, her purse lying flat on her lap, her attire an odd mismatch. Sensing her vulnerability, I gentled my voice to ask how she was feeling. Her face scrunched up with uncertainty. "I don't know how I should be feeling. My thoughts are a jumble. I don't hear their voices anymore. But inside," her voice fretful, "my head feels like they are still sort of unsettled." I reminded her of how long Sarah Christine and the Forest Girls took to become fully blended.

She raised a meek smile and then said, "I'm losing less time. It makes the days stretch on and on, and the nights never seem to end. I'm crying a lot. Mourning, I guess. I've noticed I have difficulty telling time and can't seem to remember important dates. Believe it or not, the other day I forgot Megan's birthday. I recall something like this happening after Sarah Christine dissolved. Remember?"

493

Gradually, Joan's mood lifted. "One moment I feel like fifty, old and tired and overwhelmed by my responsibilities. The next moment I feel like a teenager, delighting in my daughter's music, laughing and giggling about the silliest things. Does that make sense to you?"

"Think back, Joan, to our last two sessions. You absorbed five Parts who were all adolescents."

"Am I trying to relive my youth and do all the things I missed as a normal teenager?" She became pensive. Her eyes clouded. "Anyway," shaking her head as if to free her mind from some dark place, "like I said, I'm laughing more now."

Joan went on to describe other changes in her behavior. She seemed to connect with people more easily and admitted to having stopped taking her family's criticism personally. She no longer believed she was the one at fault whenever something went wrong. Her family was having a hard time adjusting to her participating freely in their conversations. And when she offered an independent opinion, they accused her of not being herself anymore. She responded that they were now in the presence of the "whole Joan," she told me with a chuckle of satisfaction. *I thought Joan's newfound confidence and independent attitude, what she felt about herself and how she interacted with her family, were reflective of the character traits that had defined Samantha and Fury 1.*

Her eyes slid away from mine and aimlessly roamed the bookcase as though she needed to calm her emotions. "There's something else . . . Since Rose and Sebunome integrated, I can't stop dwelling on Charles carving his initials on me. It makes my brain cramp."

"Would you like to talk about this memory?" I said, knowing she would benefit from narrating the horrific tale in her own words.

In a voice gripped with appalling bereavement, she began recounting the violence of Charles' depraved act of labial mutilation. Looking inward, handling each word in the palm of her mind, she built each sentence with agonizing acuity. My shoulders ached with tension as I listened. When she finished, a terrible stillness hovered about us. *I knew Joan had now internalized this memory and had to live with it for the rest of her life. In the retelling, comes acceptance and ownership. In the retelling, the painful truth can never be denied.*

"When this memory burdens you, Joan, partner with Ana to help you cope."

Her hands flew up with astonishment. "Oh, don't you know?" she said. "Ana integrated when Fury 1 did."

"I wasn't aware . . . I wish I'd had the chance to say goodbye." I couldn't keep the disappointment from my voice. *I had rarely interacted with Joan's helpmate and never found a plausible explanation for why she existed outside the system. But I knew, henceforth, when Joan faced challenges, Ana's practicality and levelheadedness would balance Joan's extreme sensitivity and strengthen her confidence.*

Joan's face grayed with fatigue. She retreated to the Safe Place.

A somber Raven greeted me with his usual chivalry. "Dear Healer, I am aware this has been a trying afternoon. Nevertheless, I am bound by duty to bring to your attention another matter. As you know, a Part called 'the Girl in the Mirror' splintered off from Beth during a traumatic event. I believe the time has come for them to reunite. This must occur before Beth can integrate." *I appreciated my "co-therapist" bringing forward this unattended issue.*

Beth emerged through Raven's features. I inquired if she remembered the Girl in the Mirror.

"Yes, Oma. She's stuck there in the mirror above the sink in the bathroom. She looks very sad."

"Raven told me that sad girl once came to help you."

Beth nodded. "When my daddy took me to the bathroom and pushed that *icky stuff* down my throat. Remember, Oma? I was very little."

"Are you willing to take her back, even with her sadness?"

"If you want me to, Oma."

"I think it's time, Beth. Please close your eyes and take a deep breath. Open your heart. Thank the Girl in the Mirror for helping when you were being hurt. Invite her to come back to you."

Beth's body tensed. She shuddered. When she opened her eyes, she was on the verge of tears.

"I need to go now, Oma," she said. "I'll ask Elizabeth to take down the mirror." She disappeared, trailing a sad smile.

When Joan came forth, she told me of holding Beth close and wiping her tears, assuring her she was not alone with her sadness. *An act of self healing,* I thought. I was pleased.

Chapter 87

THE GRANDMOTHER

August 25. With dusky circles under her eyes, Joan limped toward her seat on the couch, wincing as she lowered herself onto the cushions. "I've had a rough time." Joan pushed her words out with effort. Lifting the hem of her skirt, she said, "Look at these ankles. I'm retaining so much water I can barely get around." She pulled aside the collar of her blouse to reveal a large lesion and told me several more were at various spots on her body. Stretching out her right arm, she grimaced as she demonstrated the lack of movement in her wrist and thumb. "Plus all my aches and pains have dredged up some not-so-pleasant memories."

Joan leaned forward. "Have I told you my mother wasn't an only child? My grandmother had a son named Gary and another daughter named Linda. My grandmother doted on Linda."

"That must have hurt your mother, being second best. Perhaps that's another reason she grew up so insecure."

"I still don't feel sorry for her. My mother could have chosen to treat me differently," her tone rough with scorn. "Anyway, Gary and Linda both left home as soon as they came of age. They broke off their relationship with my grandmother and never returned. My mother stayed behind. She was only fifteen and pregnant with me. Thinking about her being forced to stay with my grandmother, who could be cruel and pitiless, makes me sad. Makes me want to be kind to her now to make up for what she went through back then."

Her words of compassion made me hopeful Joan was finally setting aside her resentment for her mother. Perhaps she had decided to heed Raven's warning that to harbor an unforgiving heart injured the one who refused to let go.

Leaning back into the cushions as if retreating into herself, Joan recounted a host of troubling memories about her grandmother, who hated that Joan's mother, with her young daughters, came back to live with her after the divorce. The two women fought constantly, screaming and physically threatening one another. Terrified, Joan would hide in a bedroom closet with hands over her ears. Eventually, they would notice Joan's absence, search for her, and when they found her, they would scold her for frightening them. If she and Lillian committed some childish infraction—spilling a drink, cluttering up the living room—her grandmother would become furious and stare at them hatefully. She resented taking care of the children when Joan's mother worked. Sometimes she threatened to give them away. Once, she became so infuriated at them for running through the house laughing that she forced both grandchildren down to the basement, filled the laundry sink with water, and pushed their faces into it until they choked, all the while screaming, "Why do I have to take care of you?"

"When she washed my hair," Joan further recalled, "she would dig her sharp fingernails into my scalp. As she combed the tangles from my hair, she would jerk so hard I cried. One time, she became so irritated that she cut off my long, wavy hair. When my grandfather saw me, he asked what had happened to my 'crown of glory.' All I could do was sob. I hid in my room for days. When I had to come out, I was so embarrassed that I wore a cap. Grandmother would whip it off my head and call me 'silly.'"

Joan sighed and described how her grandmother's mood could change in a flash. Something would cause her to blow up like a volcano, but, in the next instant, she'd be kind. On rare occasions, she'd tuck Joan and Lillian into bed at night and kiss them, the only person who ever did. But more often than she cared to remember, her grandmother simply ignored Joan—just as her mother did.

"On one of my visits back home," Joan continued, "my mother talked about her childhood and let it slip that some strange things went on in her parents' house. Like in the middle of the night, my grandparents would go into my mother's and Linda's bedroom, choose one, and march her to the bathroom, where they would give her a cold enema. She'd be forced to hold the water in for a painfully long time. My mother and her sister were terrified of being chosen for that ordeal."

"During the time you lived with your grandparents," I probed, remembering Beth's bathroom disclosure, "did they do anything like that to you?"

She wrinkled her nose as if smelling an unpleasant odor. "When I was little, my grandparents gave me and Lillian cold-water enemas, too. I suppose it was some kind of old-country obsession with keeping kids' bowels moving. I don't know. Or perhaps they believed enemas would cleanse children of their badness—whatever that means. At some point, I remember my grandfather stopped participating in this nocturnal torment. Instead, my grandmother and her boyfriend continued the nightmare." Joan shuddered. "I wish all of this wasn't true."

I allowed her to sit with her disappointment awhile; then I asked if there was something positive about her grandmother that was of lasting value to her.

She lifted her head. "Sometimes after my mother went to work, my grandmother and I would go downstairs to the basement, where she had a large professional kitchen. She knew how to make truffles from scratch. I stood on a stool watching her. And when we made chocolates and sugar candy, I was in charge of filling the molds and carrying them to the freezer. She sold the candy to the neighbors on holidays. She also baked fancy cakes for social events, like I do now. She'd let me measure the sugar or sift the flour. After the cakes were baked, she'd let me help make the frosting, and best of all, she taught me how to decorate them.

"The thing I most appreciate about my grandmother is she taught me to love classical music. Whenever we were down in the basement cooking, or baking, or making candy, we listened to an opera by Puccini, or Verdi, or Vivaldi. She'd hum or even sing along. Those were happy times."

"Seems to me, Joan, your challenge is to somehow find a way to accept her flaws and treasure her gifts that continue to enrich your life."

Joan nodded and recalled their last visit together. "We shared the most beautiful day, full of gentleness and love." With a tremor in her voice, she ended her story. "I wish I could have been there when she died. That she had to die alone . . ."

Years of repressed regret and grief washed down Joan's cheeks.

~

Chapter 88

DOUBTS PUT TO REST

Joan resumed treatment after a month's absence. Our hard work over the summer had left her physically ill and emotionally depleted. While convalescing, she confided having felt deep compassion for the young girl she once was and, to her surprise, experienced that sentiment as healing. She said her husband had been unusually attentive and kind while she recovered. Only in the last few days had Joan resumed her duties around the house, returning to a life of normalcy.

After a pause, Joan asked if a productive and well-adjusted life would be possible should she decide not to fully integrate. *I suspected fear of losing the familiar and the companionship of the remaining Parts might have caused this question to resurface.* As I had explained in one of our initial meetings, some with MPD choose not to integrate because their Parts had learned to cooperate and satisfactorily deal with life. However, I pointed out a number of possibilities could result in undesirable consequences. "Simply choosing not to integrate," I cautioned, "harbors the temptation to dissociate to avoid dealing with life's challenges and unsettling situations." I reminded her that practically anything could happen while losing time. "New Parts might come into existence. Or a dominant Part like Fury 1 could take over the system with unforeseen repercussions."

"After coming this far," she said, "I wouldn't want to risk such an uncertain future."

With her query seemingly addressed, Joan moved aside to listen as Beth came forward.

"Hi, Oma. Elizabeth told me after Sophia crosses over, it will be my turn. Rules are rules," Beth lisped. "Me and Elizabeth have started a list. I told her I would like to have a lavender gown and a wreath with white blossoms from the Meadow. That's as much as I know so far. I guess when the time comes, you and Elizabeth and Raven will help me say goodbye, and I'll become one with Joan."

I congratulated Beth for making preparations.

She listened inward a moment. "Elizabeth wants to know if you would be willing to talk with Joanna."

"Of course," I replied.

When Joanna came forward, I immediately noted the maturity in her voice. She informed me of having absorbed all the memories of the Parts. Many Voices and Elizabeth had taught her the history of the tragic events that occurred after the inner self-helpers had taken her to safety. The internal mother had on occasion taken the birth personality Outside to observe the activities and routines of Joan and her family. Her teachers now thought she was well prepared to integrate with Joan as soon as Beth and Sophia crossed. With a confident smile, she thanked me for helping them all heal.

Uncertainty crept into my mind. Had I made the right decision putting the inner self-helpers in charge of Joanna's maturation? Should I have played a more active role in that process? Would she remain incomplete, unable to function effectively after reunification? Would she and Joan choose to form a conjoined partnership, undetectable even by me? An inspired adaptation of wholeness. Should I promote such a solution, I wondered, or continue to shepherd Joan and Joanna toward oneness?

I praised her for being a good student under Many Voices' and Elizabeth's tutelage. On the day of final integration, I explained, she would be further enriched by Joan's memories, knowledge, and experiences gathered from living on the Outside. With a nod, Joanna acknowledged my statement and went back Inside.

Joan confirmed she had been attentive throughout my conversation with Joanna. With something akin to awe in her voice, she remarked, "Did you hear how confidently Joanna spoke?" Then mischief twitched at the corners of her mouth. "I hope I'm invited to Beth's celebration."

"I'm sure that can be arranged," I quipped.

"This is exciting, Renate. We're almost there."

"I believe we are, Joan."

On this hopeful note and with final integration approaching, I thought to suggest that Joan consider dismantling the Safe Place, as it had now served its purpose.

"But where shall I go when I need to get away?" Her voice held an edge of panic.

"To the blue room in your home, the place you created for that purpose."

As her mind made the connection, relief lit up her eyes. "Of course," she said. "But taking down our place of refuge, Renate, will be a bittersweet task." Joan went Inside to follow through, I hoped, on my suggestion.

Raven appeared. "Teacher, Many Voices and I have spoken about how our way of being will be transformed by the momentous changes to come. After all the Parts have integrated, both systems and the imaginary landscape will dissolve. Many Voices and I will surrender our separateness but continue to be Joan's inner voice of love and reason." *And what would happen to Elizabeth, the internal mother? I'd like to believe her essence would continue in support of Joan's effort to establish a "good enough mother" within her psyche.*

Raven smiled enigmatically. "You and I, dear Healer, will always be connected. Your essence and mine will continue to communicate but on a different plane of knowing."

Joan returned misty eyed, the corners of her mouth tugging at a tentative smile. She reported the Safe Place had been dismantled with the help of Beth, Sophia, and even Elizabeth, accompanied by the two toddlers that remained. "Before it was taken down, I sat in my easy chair, put my hand in the cool, clear water of the fountain, and gazed through the crystal dome at the stars for the very last time."

With that wistful remark, our session closed.

As I walked home that evening, thoughts and images of Raven's and Many Voices' reunification crowded my mind. *I visualized them dancing joyfully within the vastness of Joan's consciousness. Many Voices' white mist of crystal particles encircling Raven's silvery sparkles. Touching, separating, then pausing to embrace and meld into a seamless union of love and reason, what Jung called "the sacred marriage of soul and spirit."*

~

Chapter 89

THE HAPPY DRUNK

October 21. Shrugging out of her fall jacket, Joan uttered under her breath, "Okay, Okay, Beth," as she sat on the edge of the couch. "Even before I could brush my teeth this morning, Beth started pestering me to be the first to talk to you today. Well, here she is."

Beth emerged, out of breath. "Pushing through the Edge," she announced, "is really, really hard, Oma. The opening has gotten really tiny since almost everybody has left."

"And when you and the others have integrated, the Edge will close completely."

"I don't want the Edge to close," Beth said with uncharacteristic defiance. "I don't want to go Outside. I'm staying Inside. If Joan's body hurts all the time, I don't want to grow up. I'd rather go back to sleep."

"Going Outside doesn't mean you will become part of Joan's body and feel the hurts. Going Outside for you means leaving Elizabeth's House to 'melt like a grilled cheese sandwich' with Joan's mind."

She frowned, as if mulling over my explanation. "Will the love I have for you still feel like purple sparkles? Will you feel it in your heart?"

"Absolutely."

"But before I cross over into Joan, Oma, I have to find my courage, 'cause right now, I don't have any."

"Well, get busy, Beth, and find some," I teased.

Her mouth crimped in what looked like irritation. An unfamiliar Part pushed out. My brow furrowed in surprise and fleeting resentment at this unexpected intrusion. The latecomer sprang off the couch, tittering as she moved on unsteady legs around the room. She pulled out a book from my library, leafed through the pages, and tossed it aside. The Part looked behind a painting and then let it flop back against the wall. With casual indifference, she squeezed between my chair and the window, pulled up the blind with a loud *zip*, and pressed her nose against the glass.

"Where am I?" her breath fogging the windowpane. "Do I know you?"

I attempted to explain, but she quickly lost interest. With a sigh, she slumped onto the couch, her facial features flaccid, her eyes unfocused. Concerned, I called for Joan, but there was no response.

A weak voice lisped, "I'm sorry, Oma. I couldn't stop her. She forced her way out."

"Please ask Raven to see me, Beth," my voice sterner than I intended.

Raven appeared, looking contrite. "Teacher, I hear your annoyance. Allow me to apologize for being unaware of the existence of this Part."

"Who is she?" I asked in consternation, thinking our plan for integration would have to be postponed. "I recall you combed through both systems and reported no other Parts were to be found."

"That is true. The oversight is solely mine. I am as surprised as you. Nevertheless, may I share with you the information Many Voices has just this instant imparted?"

"Go ahead," my annoyance unabated.

Raven explained that the Part had been created at the time of little Donald's birth. Her initial role was to assist four-year-old Joan to care for the infant. After the baby's premature death, she, like other Parts, played a vital role in helping Joan survive the many traumas that marred her tragic childhood. Many Voices had told Raven that this new Part, like Joan, had a close but troubled relationship with the Grandmother and shared Joan's deep love for the Grandfather.

"I noticed her unsteadiness, Raven. Is she another Part addicted to alcohol?"

"Let me assure you this Part is *not* an alcoholic. But, as strange as it may sound, she manifests the effects of alcohol on the Body."

"But you're certain she doesn't drink?"

"Correct. Now, if I may excuse myself, I must return to my Perch."

How could this new Part continue to experience the physical effects of alcohol, I asked myself, *when all the alcoholic Parts had integrated? And Joan had been sober for more than a year. I remembered Leaf describing a similar happenstance. Compartmentalization must account for this phenomenon: One Part holds the memory of an action, while another holds the memory of the consequence of that action. Like one Part remembering an abusive event, another holding the affective consequence, and a third holding the sensate consequences.*

I heard Beth's voice again. "Please, Oma, tell the Happy Drunk to come back Inside so Sophia and I can help Joan come out."

When Joan finally emerged, she looked bewildered. "What happened?"

Listening to my account of what had taken place, she looked shocked. "Oh, no—not another drunk! We're so close to integration."

"Raven has assured me she's not an alcoholic."

"Thank goodness."

After Joan left, I looked around my disheveled office. Without picking up or even writing my progress notes, I went home, where my husband met me at the back door with a glass of red wine. When he asked if the afternoon had been trying, with a wave of my hand, I replied, "Don't ask."

November 11. "The last few weeks have been extremely turbulent, even dangerous," Joan announced. "Without Raven's help, I don't believe I'd be sitting here today."

Joan reported that one day she found herself driving on the freeway without a clue where she was going. Raven had helped her drive to the nearest exit and find her way home. Later, Elizabeth and Beth told her that Sophia and the "Happy Drunk" had become agitated, took several sleeping pills, and left, saying they were "going home to God."

I asked Beth to guide the Happy Drunk out to see me. As before, she sprang off the couch. But before she started her mischief, I insisted she sit back down.

"Do you remember what you and Sophia did a few days ago?"

"We shared some memories we have in common. Like what happened under the basement stairs. And at the movies. And that ugly time in the Mother's bed . . ."

"What happened then?"

"We felt rotten, so Sophia pinched Joan's sleeping pills, and we took some. Then we went back Inside. She took me to some Forest and then wandered off. I had no idea where I was. That kid with the lisp found me, but I still don't have a place to stay."

"How about staying with Sophia and the others at Elizabeth's House? They can take you to the River of Tears, where—"

"Absolutely not," she interrupted. "I won't go near any water. I'm afraid I'll drown. I almost did, you know, when he raped me in the lake."

"I'm sorry, Happy Drunk, that you had that terrible experience, too."

"Stop calling me that. My name is Jane."

Hesitantly, I reached out my hand to comfort her, but she pulled away. "Don't touch me," she said. "All I want is to be left alone."

Regretting my eagerness to console her, I asked Sophia to meet Jane at the Outer Edge and guide her to Elizabeth's House. Sophia exited, her head down, and apologized for taking the pills. I expressed my empathy for their despair and asked her to help Jane fit in.

Then Beth re-emerged, barely able to contain her excitement. "Oma, I have a beautiful surprise for you. I've finished my life story." She withdrew a large yellow envelope from Joan's purse. "This is for you, Oma. It's the story of my life. I call it My Own Story of Love."

The envelope contained a thick stack of papers with a bold, color-ful title page. I carefully leafed through her delightful gift, admiring its creativity.

"There are lots of pictures, Oma."

"So I see, Beth. Your drawings are adorable. And your beautiful cursive handwriting. Would you please read your story to me?"

Like a proud child, she recited: "This is the story of me, the me that was before and the braver me now . . ."

When she finished, I applauded, "Bravo, Beth. What an excellent job."

She beamed, her eyes sparkling joy as she handed her "book" to me. "I want you to have My Own Story of Love so you'll remember me for always.

"You know what, Oma? I think I found my courage, 'cause I'm not as scared as I was before about going to the Outside. But I worry you'll forget me."

My Own Story of Love, Beth 2008.

"How could I, Beth? I have your life's story right here in my hands. Each time I read your book, it will remind me of you." I told her she would always live in my heart. And I would be ever grateful for her bringing messages back and forth; for easing discord among the Parts, even between Joan and Roger; and for calling for my help before a Part got hurt. She brought happiness to everyone, so how could I ever forget her? I bent forward, my face almost touching hers, and whispered, "Once you are on the Outside, every time Joan giggles or is especially happy, I shall know it's you."

She took a deep breath. "Now I'm really, really happy, Oma. I will always love you. Forever and ever."

My eyes touched Beth's with affection as she disappeared. In the quiet that followed, I sat with her book cradled in my arms, awestruck by her innate capacity for joy and love to safeguard the heart from unthinkable torment. I reread the last page:

— The last page —

So this is the end of my book. It is my story the way I wanted to tell it. Just me Beth. Something all my own. I choose to be the happiest I can be, but I can cry and still be o.k. I can have wishes that can't come true but I can still wish and feel happy inside those pretend wishes..

I could write about some really sad stuff but thats for others. I have been the luckiest of all the girls I think.

I know what I know and that's that without love there would be nothing.

So I will look at all the good and pretty things in the world. I will love with all my heart. I will be grateful for miracles, like the one about being found. My heart is filled because of all the love and the inner realm isn't a dark place anymore. Soon I will move on.

Written for myself and for my Oma who was brave enough and loved us enough to stay!
                    xoxo

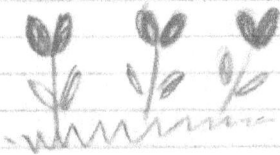

— The End —

⁓

Chapter 90

HOPE

November 24. Joan's mental and emotional states were in turmoil. One moment she was confident, the next, she couldn't make the simplest decision. Her emotions went from one extreme to another. I comforted her by explaining that she continued to feel unsettled because her mind and brain were still sorting, associating, and assimilating the memories and feelings of the integrated Parts. While this might be confusing and upsetting, in time, once the process *was* complete, she would be able to function in a more rational and emotionally coherent way, and with newfound confidence.

Somewhat placated, Joan voiced a cautious commitment to working through the "emotional seesaw." She noted that staying present when her husband and children were home had been exhilarating but exhausting. She doubted her ability to sustain this kind of effort day after day. I assured her that, to stay healthy, she had to find ways to disengage from all the noise of daily living—take a walk, listen to music, read a book, or find a quiet place to sit and daydream, so her mind could wander and her energies recharge. Joan exhaled a puff of air in relief.

Raven emerged to say he had closed off all communication lines to the Inner Realm so he could speak with me in confidence.

"Helper, I'm reluctant to reveal there is a frail, nine-year-old Part you know nothing about."

Dear Lord, another surprise? Will it ever end?

"Her name is Hope. She has been under my protection since I rescued her long ago. At one time, she held fear of the supernatural and believed she was insane."

"How chilling, Raven. What pushed her into such a state?"

"It was Charles' doing," he replied. "When the Mother went to work at night, Charles went outside and stood in front of Joan's bedroom window. He would scratch against the screen and make high-pitched noises pretending to be a ghost. Or climb up to the attic and make eerie sounds through the air vents. Other times, he would go to the basement and growl and screech, pretending to be a monster. Sometimes, Charles manipulated the electrical panel so the lights flickered off and on. Afterward, he would go to Joan's room and pretend to rescue her. Unbeknownst to him, Hope was there, huddled in a corner, trembling and whimpering. He would lift her in his arms, carry her to the bed, and molest her. Over the years as my ward, she has learned to accept what she saw and heard was Charles' malevolent mischief-making. With my guidance, little Hope has been able to work through the emotional and physical trauma."

If that is so, I thought, *then what has persuaded him to reveal her existence at this late date?*

"I have only just realized that this fragile Part is plagued by a darker memory, one which I am unqualified to remedy. That is why she needs your help. I trust you will extend compassion and patience as you have with the others. Like them, she may be shy to speak at first, but you will have my full support."

Joan's features softened, her forehead smooth, her eyes velvet.

"You must be Hope," my voice gentle.

She turned her face aside and spoke to the wall. "I've been hiding under Raven's wing, sleeping there since I was nine. Sometimes I peek out, but not often. Raven told me it was my time to go Outside to meet a lady with silvery hair and blue eyes and talk with her."

"I'm that lady, Hope, and I'm glad you came to see me."

She kneaded her hands fretfully. Then in a rush of words, she told me of the wicked incident in the barn with the sheep, and the depravity of the three men.

"You are very brave to recount this dreadful story, Hope. I have heard others tell of this event. You were not the only one there. I believe you can take some comfort from knowing that."

She faded.

Joan's face looked drawn, the skin taut across her cheekbones. I avoided probing her reaction to Hope's disclosure. *I thought it prudent to wait for a more appropriate time after the Christmas holidays.*

January 8, 2009. "Ever since Hope spoke to you about the barn incident," Joan said, "my mind's been plagued by indelible snapshots of being there, hanging onto a railing, stripped of my underwear. I hear the cackling of those perverts. Their laughter bathes me in a cold sweat. My legs turn to rubber. To keep from falling, I have to hold on to something. The only thing I can do to keep from fainting is to use my breath. I recall that Rose and Sarah Christine abreacted this disgusting event several years ago. I shied away from participating then. I hid behind a tree and watched as they scrubbed themselves clean in the River of Tears."

Her voice thick with contempt, she asked, "Don't you think it's about time to rid myself of this evil deed?"

I heard Hope's small voice say, "I'm here, behind Joan. Raven told me to come out and share this moment with her."

"Are you aware of Hope's presence, Joan?"

She responded with a slight dip of her head.

I asked them both to re-remember all they had experienced in the barn. Joan squinched her eyes shut, her lips compressed. Her hands balled into fists. Struggling not to lose time, she began to breathe rhythmically. I waited. In time, a single tear ran down her cheek. She opened her eyes and said, "Hope and I thank you."

Joan's features morphed into Hope. With surprising sophistication, she said, "Joan and I went to the Meadow and suffered through the most indecent deed men can do to an innocent child. We held one another, and cried and cried until we were able to let go."

~

Chapter 91

UNHINGED

During the four weeks following our therapy session with Hope, Joan seemed to come unhinged, doing everything imaginable to derail our work together. Like an adolescent struggling to come of age, torn between yearning to live on her own terms or remaining dependent on the support and safety of therapy, she canceled sessions, claiming illness or needing to bake a cake for a church function. When she did come, Joan was distracted, unable to focus, or emotionally volatile. Her mood would alternate between being resentful and vindictive or sad and despairing.

During one such session, Joan accused me of hoping to be done with my "little project" and reminded me how I had wanted to "get rid" of her years ago by suggesting a stay at an out-of-state clinic. No sooner were the words out of her mouth than she began chastising herself for being rude and ungrateful: how hard I had worked, how much I had given, how deeply I cared for her and the Parts, how gifted I was as a therapist, how she would be in my debt for the rest of her life.

However, her attempt to restore goodwill didn't last long. "I resent you calling me 'fat,'" her face flushed with anger. "Does my appearance repulse you? You've known since day one how sensitive I am about my weight. You knew how hurtful your comment would be. I can never forgive you for that."

Before I could respond, Joan told me her husband was beginning to grumble about how long her treatment was taking and was resentful of all the money he was spending on her therapy. After venting about the unfair boundaries I had set to keep her from calling me any time of the day or night, she complained the work was too demanding. My expectations were unreasonable. I pushed too hard and required too much of her. In the middle of this rant, she ran out of steam and seemed to deflate. Crestfallen, she accused herself of being unworthy of becoming "a whole person."

"Seeing everything in a negative light twists my thinking," Joan said. "I feel helpless, and that makes me feel hopeless. How can I ever become a person who matters? How can I ever expect my family to forgive me for the hell I've put them through? I feel completely incompetent to face what I know I have to do."

"Leaving the safe haven of therapy and having to plunge into life as a fully functioning individual is a daunting task, I grant you."

Joan cradled her bowed head in cupped hands. "How can you forgive me for hurling all those unfair grievances at you?"

"Some of your grievances were justified, Joan." I reminded her she had been not only a participant but also an equal partner in her treatment. "When two people work together with intensity and focus, as we have for more than five years, disagreements and missteps and hurt feelings are bound to happen. That's just part of the process."

February 9. After spending weeks in the misery of crooked thinking, Joan presented me with two paintings. Picking up the first picture, she explained, "I painted my twisted thoughts to look like a nest of snakes which nibble away at my mind." The second work was in black, white, and red. "These white squares framed in black, with red stripes and blotches, represent the notes you took when the Parts and I disclosed our secrets. Thank God you wrote it all down: the many lies we crushed; the shame and guilt we felt; our mother's betrayal; and Charles' depravities. We all saw you scribbling as fast as you could."

"My notes hold the history of your suffering, Joan, and your efforts to heal."

She leaned over to set the artwork aside. When she sat back up, Sophia had slipped out.

"Helper, I'm ready," she announced. "I'm ready to become one with Joan. I've been sitting on the bank of the River of Tears. The whole time, Raven hovered above me. When I told him of my thoughts, he gently advised, 'Do as all the others have done before you. Enter the River of Tears, and wash away the sorrow.' So, I did. Now I'm free to walk toward the Light. Thank you for your kindness and patience, and for guiding me to Elizabeth, who provided the care and love I needed."

Twisted Thinking, Joan 2009.

Notes and Secrets, Joan 2009.

That said, she disappeared.

Joan, her eyes closed, leaned back against the cushions with a look of contentment on her face. I let her linger in that restful state. After some minutes, I gently tapped her forehead. She let out a deep sigh, opened her eyes, and yawned. "Oh, my goodness. I must have fallen asleep. I had the most enchanting dream. Beth, Sophia, and I sat on the bank of the River of Tears dangling our feet in the trickling stream. We were dressed in beautiful gowns with wreaths on our heads. It was so serene."

I informed her that Sophia, moments ago, had announced her intention to integrate.

"I guess that explains the sweetness I feel right here," her middle finger lightly tracing circles on her forehead.

"I believe that's Sophia's 'sweet' essence blending with yours," I said as a fanciful thought occurred to me. "You also may have been gifted with Sophia's ability to do sign language and run like the wind."

With a quiet laugh, Joan lifted her pant leg a few inches. "Not with these ankles."

~

Chapter 92

OVER THE RAINBOW

February 16. "Jane or Hope?"

Joan and I were trying to determine which of the two should be integrated next. Unable to decide, Joan asked Raven for his advice. At first, we were surprised at his choice of Beth, considering her reluctance to leave the Inner Realm and give up her attachment to Elizabeth, Oma, and Mr. Roger. Upon reflection, however, we accepted his counsel since Beth had already worked through her trauma and fulfilled her purpose as the messenger and goodwill ambassador.

Joan moved aside so Beth could come forward.

"Oma!" She stood up, hands on her hips, pretending to be annoyed. "What you and Joan talked about with Raven, I already know it's my turn. But before I cross over, I want to go with Mr. Roger one more time to the zoo and have ice cream. I need to tell him to practice giving good kisses and hugs for Joan. That will make her feel loved."

She asked if she could say goodbye to "Mr. Opa" and watch him do the African dance I had told her about. Oddly, she also wished for my husband and me to dance to "Over the Rainbow," her favorite song. *Was she expressing Joan's long-forgotten childhood longing to see her feuding parents in a caring embrace?* "I want to take those memories with me forever," Beth said. "After that, I want me and you to finger-paint. Let's make a picture about the journey I'm going to make from the Inside to the Outside. I'll paint Elizabeth at the bottom of the picture watching me walking on the Path of Crushed Lies toward the Outer Realm. And at the top of the picture, I'll show you waiting for me at the Outer Edge."

With Joan's consent, I called my husband to say Beth and I would like to pay him a visit. He waited for us at the back door with a smile. The African music was already playing, and as I had requested on the phone, "Mr. Opa" performed the dance he learned in Ghana many years before. Beth clapped her hands with delight when he took

Over the Rainbow, Beth 2009.

a bow. Fulfilling her other wish, my husband and I danced to Judy Garland's wistful version. Beth's eyes glittered with joy. At the end of our visit, she thanked my husband for allowing her and the others to look into his blue eyes, touch his hand, and learn that not all men hurt young girls.

Making our way back to my office, Beth took off her shoes and walked through the garden, feeling the grass tickling her toes. Here and there, she touched a leaf or picked up a stone to marvel at its uniqueness. She plucked a humble, white-petaled wildflower and held it out to me. "This forget-me-not is for you, Oma." Then, with a last look over her shoulder, she waved goodbye to "Mr. Opa."

As soon as we re-entered the therapy room, Beth and I got out the finger paints and sat on the floor. While painting, she comforted herself by saying she understood integration would not mean she would die. She now believed that, in some magical way, she would always see me through Joan's eyes. Unable to hold back the tears any longer, she sniffled, "You know, Oma, I'm a good helper. You filled me with love, and now I'm going to help fill Joan with love and make her life better."

She gave me a long hug and went Inside.

Beth's big day finally arrived. I spent the morning making preparations and reviewing the step-by-step instructions she had provided for conducting her integration celebration. Upon arrival at the appointed hour, Joan presented me with a bouquet of yellow roses and a box of truffles she had prepared for this special occasion. Beth chose the roses, she said, to reflect the "golden sparkles of Oma's spirit."

"On my way out of the house, Beth told my husband she would integrate today. She thanked 'Mr. Roger' for the fun and affection they had shared. Beth cried, but he just sobbed. I could not console him. Their bond was so strong. She brought out the goodness and the gentleness in him. You know, Renate, Beth affected everyone that way with her charming presence. I shall miss her."

When I raised my eyebrows, she laughed. "What am I talking about? Beth isn't leaving. Her spirit is part of me and will be with me for the rest of my life."

Beth appeared, smiling. "Oma, would you please prepare our tea with milk and honey like the Queen of England drinks? While we eat our truffles, we can sip the tea so we don't get the chocolaty stuff stuck to the roof of our *mouth-esth*."

To cover my amusement, I turned away to prepare our tea as directed, placed two cups on a side table, and put two truffles on a small plate. We clinked our cups, sipped our tea, and nibbled at the heavenly truffles. When done, we licked our fingers with delight, wiped our "mouth-esth" with tiny napkins, and cleared the table for what was to come.

"Oma, it's time to go Inside," Beth's expression serious.

I sat still a few moments; then I took a deep breath and visualized my presence as an observer making the last journey into the magical realism of the Inner Realm.

Beth went ahead, and my "golden sparkles" followed her along the Path of Crushed Lies. Arriving at Elizabeth's doorstep, we were invited to enter. "Wait, Oma. I have to take my shoes off and wash my feet first. Rules are rules."

Climbing the stairs leading to her purple room, Beth found Elizabeth, Joan, Jane, and Joanna already assembled there. Her dress—pale lavender with small pearls at its neckline and a tiny purple flower pattern at the hem—had been laid out beforehand by Elizabeth. Before dressing, Beth declared she wanted to lie on her purple bed once more to voice her appreciation for the comfort it provided. Lying there, she looked around her room one last time. "Thank you," she said, "for sheltering and protecting me for such a long time."

Elizabeth slipped the lavender dress over Beth's shoulders. While she lovingly fastened the bodice with tiny pearl buttons, Beth whispered, "Dear Elizabeth, thank you for caring for me and teaching me to read and write and for helping me feel happy when I was sad. And thank you for showing me how to be a helper." The internal mother placed a flower wreath on Beth's head and thanked her for helping bathe the Parts, who were dirty when they first came to the House. And for sharing her room and making them feel at home. "Thank you, Beth, for all the joy you have given."

Beth hugged Jane and Joanna, who expressed their gratitude for helping them adjust to the Inner Realm, and for sharing her memories and encouraging others to do the same. Then Beth said goodbye to Raven, who was perched on the windowsill, and to Hope, who was peeking out from under his wing.

I withdrew my visualized presence, and prepared myself for the last phase of Beth's integration. When Beth returned, she said Elizabeth had walked with her along the Path of Crushed Lies leading to the Outer Realm. Reaching the Edge, she had gently caressed Beth's cheek and then turned and went back. "Joan followed behind me, Oma. She's now standing by until we are all set to become one. I wrote a poem for today."

IT'S TIME
I'm going but not far away
Crossing over not the reversal way
There is so much to do and see
I'll grow up now and cross over right into me.

From Inside to Outside to stay
It's time now and I'm not really going away
It's a bit sad I'll not be just me
But Raven and Oma say I'll have more being we.

God's plans are coming to pass
We all waited so long now the time's right at last
There is so much to do and see
Today's the day to be brave and cross into a new me.

by Beth

"This is for you, Oma," she said and handed me the poem.

"Are you now prepared to integrate your feelings, your memories, your special gifts—all that you are—with Joan? Are you ready to do this, Beth?"

"Yes," she lisped softly.

"Before you do, would you like to tell Joan how much you have appreciated all she provided?"

Beth began by thanking Joan for taking her to the hobby store to purchase the "colored pencils and paper and paint and stickers and glitter" for her projects. She thanked Joan for watching cartoons with her when Elizabeth was too busy and for permitting her to play with the cat and talk to the bird and for allowing her and the others to have fun when Mr. Roger was at work. I turned to Joan and asked if she was ready to receive Beth. She nodded and closed her eyes, which remained closed for quite some time as sweet murmurs and soft giggles escaped her lips. When she opened her eyes and became fully present, she said, "Beth is with me now. If you don't mind, I want to spend some time alone. That will give me a chance to fully embrace her."

As soon as I heard Joan's car pull out of the driveway, I telephoned her husband that she was on her way home and assured him Beth's integration had gone well.

His voice choked with emotion, Roger managed to force out, "Losing Beth is hard. I'll never hear that sweet, young voice again. Did you know she left me a note telling me how much she loved me? I shall treasure it forever."

"Remember, Roger, Beth's joyful spirit will live on in Joan. If you look closely, you'll see the Beth you cherish in Joan's eyes. Now you have the opportunity to love Joan in much the same way you loved Beth."

February 24. "All the way here today, I felt such joy. Spring has come early. It's so beautiful outside—why don't you and I go for a walk?" The afternoon light accentuated strawberry highlights in Joan's auburn hair as we made our way out of the office into the sun. "I have so much energy since Beth integrated. I feel younger and joyful—a bit giddy," a smile in her voice. "Grocery shopping has become a real adventure. The shapes and colors of fruit arranged in pyramids captivate me. I find myself reading labels on cans and packages with childlike curiosity. It takes twice as long to get my shopping done."

"Have you been to the hobby store since Beth integrated?"

"I don't dare. I might never come out."

We both laughed.

"I've become sort of self-conscious of my new behavior," Joan confessed. "Roger has asked me what's going on. He's been acting sort of weird himself. The other day I figured it out. By being especially kind to me, I think he hopes to get a glimpse of Beth, perhaps even coax her to come out."

"If you wanted, Joan, you could draw on Beth's charm and playfulness to minimize Roger's sense of loss during this period of adjustment."

We approached a bench under a large oak tree and sat comfortably. "There are days," she confided, "when my head fills to overflowing with all kinds of memories. I've noticed this happening more and more as the Parts have integrated. Events and episodes from the past flow through my mind. But I don't see these memories in snippets anymore or experience them as flashbacks. They are more like a movie with scenes rolling on from beginning to end. I can't find a switch to shut it off. Seeing all the craziness this way is taxing, but I hold on. I won't break apart. I've worked too hard to put myself together. But these memories will always be part of me, won't they? They'll always influence who I am and what I become." *As they will be for Joanna after integration*, I thought.

"They can become a positive force in your life if you honor them, Joan, even grieve over them. Speak about them to someone you trust as often as the need arises. Eventually, they will find a resting place in your mind. This doesn't mean they will never rise again, but, hopefully, you will have learned to put them into perspective. They will be less disturbing, less overwhelming. A wise woman once wrote these memories are like stones in a stream, their rough edges rounded and smoothed by the continuous flow of the current. Visualize carrying these 'stones' around with you in a pocket in your slacks. Every time you reach into your pocket, you touch them and remember what they hold. Though you will always carry these memories with you, Joan, in the current of daily activities, they will gradually lose their 'rough edges' and the power to disrupt your life."

Joan stood, and we walked back toward my office. A step ahead of me, she said over her shoulder, "What you say about the future gives me hope, Renate."

~

Chapter 93

JANE

February 28. Having agreed to proceed with Jane's integration, I asked Joan to move aside so Jane could come forward.

"Oh, it's *you* again," her words slightly slurred. She shambled over to my chair and lightly touched my face. "You *are* real, all right. I knew you'd come someday."

"Tell me more about yourself, Jane. Raven said you don't drink, yet you act as if you're intoxicated. Are you aware of how that came about?"

"As I recall," she said, "whenever another of us took a drink, I would start to feel good—sort of relaxed—and pretty soon, I no longer cared what was happening to me." She spoke as if her tongue was swollen. "Many mornings getting ready for school, I felt fuzzy-headed and unsteady on my feet. I'm sure my mother saw the state I was in." She managed a sad smile. "I don't know how she could miss it. At school, the teachers weren't much better. They paid no attention even when I had my head down on my desktop, asleep. Sometimes they sent me to the office, but the school nurse never asked why I was out of it. I really don't blame them. But I do blame my mother for pretending not to notice. I wish I could have told her."

"Perhaps you can tell her now," I suggested. She fixed me with uncomprehending eyes. "Imagine your mother sitting across from you in that white chair. Can you see her, Jane?"

"Sure, if I pretend."

"Tell her whatever it is you wish to say."

She worked the muscles in her jaw before speaking. "Mama, I know you saw how I stumbled around the kitchen and hardly touched my breakfast. Most of the time, I walked around with a hangover. Why did you choose to be blind? That creep you married made sure the others were drunk before he did his nastiness. I just laid there like a piece of meat, numbed out. Why didn't you save me?"

Jane cradled her head in her hands and murmured, "I never, ever want to feel that awful again." I allowed her to sit with her grief.

Joan now spoke up. Although, while growing up, she hadn't been aware of Jane, she recalled feeling drunk in the morning and going to school in that condition. We agreed that, before Jane could integrate, she had to get over the affectation of being intoxicated.

In deep thought, Joan sat on the couch a few moments; then she stood, slipped on her coat, and said an abrupt goodbye. Through the office window, I watched her walk toward her car. To my surprise, she turned back and dashed up the porch steps. Standing in the office door, radiating determination, she declared, "I would like integration to be completed before Easter. I want all of us—my family, you, and, of course, your husband—to attend the Easter service at my church. Celebrating my rebirth on that day will be an appropriate thing to do, don't you think, Renate? We have worked so hard to get me off *my* cross."

Joan stood proud and tall, a work of art cast in suffering, I thought in admiration.

"That will give us only five weeks to integrate Jane and Hope," I cautioned. "And you and Joanna."

"We can do this," she said with confidence. She looked exuberant, but I feared she had asked me to work a miracle.

March 3. "I don't feel well," Joan wheezed. "I think I have bronchitis. I'll just sit here while Jane talks to you."

Within seconds, Jane came forward. She walked over to my chair, bent down, and, with care, touched her palm to the left side of my face. "I can see you've been hurt right here."

"I was injured a long time ago. The wounds healed and left only faint scars."

"Does it still hurt?"

"When the weather gets cold, that side of my face aches."

"I have a lot of pain, too. Not in my face. Right here," she patted her chest. "Do you think my hurt might heal someday and leave only faint scars like yours?"

"That's what we are here to do—to start healing your pain by talking about what happened to you."

"You already know what happened and how I got hurt. Elizabeth said that, before the other Parts integrated, they told you everything. I don't see the need to rehash all that. It's ancient history."

"So, what do you wish to share with me?"

Jane's expression softened. "My most precious memory—my grandfather. He never said much, but I knew he loved me in his quiet way. He always told me how smart and good I was. I can see now how his unwavering love and approval helped me get through the darkest times. He was very handsome, too, but crippled from polio. He was sad and lonely, and he knew my grandmother cheated on him. But he never raised his voice at her, or me. I never was scared of him. I trusted him."

"What a blessing your grandfather must have been for you."

Jane's tone became bittersweet. Her grandfather had died when she was fifteen. A few days before his death, he told her to be strong and that, someday, she would be free. At the time, Jane hadn't understood. She suspected he knew about the abuse but felt helpless to intervene. After his passing, she ran away but was brought back. Knowing her life would continue as it had, with no one to turn to, she went to a place where she could never be found. "But now that I'm awake again," her eyes full of questions, "I'm still lost. I don't know anything that's happened since then."

I proceeded to recount the events in Joan's life over the intervening thirty-five years. I included the Mother eventually divorcing Charles and his remarriage.

"Who would marry *him*?" disbelief in her voice.

"Sadly, a woman with a boy and two young girls. But no one knows what happened to Charles after that. What we do know is he can never hurt you again."

I paused a few moments to let my statement sink in before asking if she was prepared to discuss integrating with Joan.

"I can't imagine what that would be like."

"Think of a large pizza. Picture each slice topped with different ingredients. If these slices represent different Parts, then you are another slice with toppings that reflect your attributes, memories, and feelings. Imagine now, your slice being placed among the others, the whole pizza slipped into the oven and baked until the cheese and all of the toppings have melted together."

Having learned to cook from her Italian grandmother, my metaphor made total sense to her. Jane laughed and, in high spirits, went Inside.

Joan spoke: "I share Jane's sorrow about my grandfather's death. And I'm haunted by guilt," she said as regret stole across her face, "for not having warned that other woman Charles married. I get sick thinking about how he must have tortured those two little girls."

"But hadn't you moved away?"

"Regardless, I should have driven back and warned her. But I didn't."

"Who else had a responsibility to inform her about Charles?"

"My mother. But she didn't, either. You know how she is."

Blameless, I thought.

"I wish you could have been with me the other night." Joan smiled from ear to ear. "When I came home from our last session, Jane put your pizza metaphor to the test. She immediately went to the kitchen and announced her plan to make pizza for supper. She investigated the refrigerator and pantry and gathered several kinds of cheese and other yummy ingredients for toppings. She grated the cheeses, chopped the garlic and bell peppers and mushrooms and onions, and then sautéed the hamburger meat and added tomato sauce. Instead of using ready-made dough, Jane made the crust from scratch, just like our grandmother taught us. She rolled it out

and flattened it into a large pizza pan. Then she etched lines on the dough to make narrow wedges, and carefully placed individual ingredients on each tiny slice, added the sauce, and popped it into the oven.

"My daughter and husband, who both love pizza, were sitting at the table, waiting with mouth-watering anticipation. When Jane pulled the pizza out of the oven, she turned to carry her masterpiece to the table but somehow stumbled. The pizza flew across the kitchen and plopped down right in front of Roger's feet."

Joan put her hand over her mouth, one arm hugging her midriff, heaving with laughter. "You should have seen Roger," she hooted. "He jumped up and started yelling at the top of his lungs. I think he thought she threw it at him. Jane picked up a glass and threw *that* at him." Joan couldn't contain her laughter. "You should have seen his face. To keep the situation from getting out of hand, Raven came out to explain that Jane had accidentally tripped and dropped it. Roger apologized for yelling. That was when I took over, looked at Roger with mischievous satisfaction, and went to bed, leaving him to clean up the mess. To top it all off, no pun intended, he went without supper that night," she crowed.

Joan's features morphed. Jane came out, annoyed. "Being yelled at hurt my feelings. I can't imagine being married to a man who yells like that. I wouldn't put up with it."

"Roger doesn't yell all the time," I said. "If you come out more often and get to know him, you'll find he's a decent man. Who knows, you might have an opportunity to prepare another pizza and get it to the table without dropping it in his lap. That certainly would put you in his good graces."

To ease her vexation, I proposed we take a walk. Like all the Parts, she loved being outside. Chatting as we strolled through the neighborhood, her pronunciation became more distinct and her steps steadied, as if the effects of alcohol were wearing off. *I thought the decrease in her physical symptoms held promise. Was she getting over her affectation?* She slipped her hand into mine and confided in a low voice, "When I'm with you, I don't feel so . . . troubled."

"What do you mean, Jane?"

"I don't have to be on guard every moment. I've grown to trust you."

"And when we trust, Jane, we stop being afraid."

After some time, we returned to the treatment room. When I tried to tell Joan about our conversation, she stopped me with a wave of her hand. She had heard the two of us talking and explained that, most of the time, she and Jane were co-present.

Encouraging progress all around.

"Jane has been spending more time on the Outside with me," Joan said to begin our discussion. "She even had a civil conversation with Roger one night, which convinced her he wasn't so bad after all. She told me she now 'felt okay' in my house. We spent a couple of afternoons running errands and shopping. She enjoys watching people and takes in everything around her." Joan laughed, "Jane certainly likes to drive my car. One evening, we went to AA, and I let her drive. On the way, I explained how these meetings helped me stay sober. At the meeting, she talked with some of the people there and seemed to like them."

"How about Hope?" I asked.

"Hope is shy. Doesn't say much. Wait—Jane wants to talk to you. I'll move aside and listen."

Jane came out immediately, her face set in a pensive frown. "I need to tell you some things that weigh on me. My mother's house was a dark and lonely place." They lived in total isolation, she explained, cut off from the outside world. Her mother and Charles had no friends and had nothing to do with the neighbors. No one ever came over to visit except the grandparents, who came by only during the holidays. The children never were allowed to invite other children over to play, nor could they play with them at their house. Aside from school, they hardly ever went anywhere. Jane pointed out that their isolation created the perfect setting for the awfulness that went on behind closed doors.

"From the first moment I saw Charles—I must have been around seven— my stomach flip-flopped. I knew he was bad. Creepy. He had sickly white skin, orangey hair, and pale-blue eyes which moved constantly. When my mother announced they'd gotten married, in my mind, I screamed, *'Why him? Why him?'* But I didn't say anything. I don't think my mother ever considered if he would be a good father for her two little girls."

Jane fell silent. I waited.

Joan spoke: "You know I have a younger sister. She wasn't like me. Lillian was a fighter. My mother didn't dare scream at her because she would scream right back. She didn't take anything from anybody. Unlike Lillian, I was submissive, did what was expected, and tried never to draw attention to myself. But it didn't matter. I seemed to be a target for everyone. I thought I must be marked. A few times, I went into the bathroom and looked in the mirror to see if I had a black X on my forehead. Do you believe I'm marked?"

"Most certainly not," I replied.

"Then why did Charles choose me?"

"He chose to victimize you because he thought he could control you. He knew you were afraid of your mother and saw she had trained you to keep quiet and not complain. He exploited your submissiveness. You were never to blame."

Jane moved forward. She looked fragile sitting there.

"Do you understand, Jane, what I just said to Joan? Charles chose to prey on your helplessness; but in truth, he was a weak and troubled man, who felt alive only when torturing one of you."

"But what made him so cruel, so callous?" Joan was the one asking.

"I can only imagine he grew up in a house devoid of any kind of humanity, a place where love had no chance to thrive. Charles must have spent his formative years neglected, mistreated, and probably abused. I *can* say for certain that no one ever held out a hand to save him from his dire circumstances. Remember the barn incident? It revealed the sexual deviancy of his father and brother. And so, Charles became like them—a man who preyed on the innocent and helpless."

A thoughtful stillness followed. Then Jane spoke: She described what had happened to keep her and the Parts from becoming like Charles and the other abusers. "My mother didn't believe in God, but when I first stepped inside a church, I felt God wrap me in his embrace and say,

'I am glad you are here.'" Jane had been enchanted, she confided, with the organ music, the singing, and the praying. No one had scolded or demeaned her. Everyone made her feel welcome, like they wanted her to be there with them. Until she went to sleep at fifteen, church had been the only place where she felt completely safe and free.

Leaning back into the comfort of the cushions, Jane looked around the room, as if saying goodbye to the paintings on the wall, the teddy bears above the bookcase, and the talismanic stones in the ceramic tray. Her eyes lingered on a bronze sculpture of a woman without arms sitting in a rickety chair, looking too weary and anguished to rise. I placed the heavy statue carefully in her hands. Cradling this evocative figure on her lap, she observed, "In my mother's house, I felt helpless and hopeless just like her." As Jane handed back the sculpture, her eyes held mine . . . and then she was gone.

Her eyes bright with amusement, Joan said, "As Jane integrated, I heard her say 'It's like pushing through Saran Wrap.'"

I privately marveled at such an expressive way to portray the act of integration.

While preparing to leave, Joan reminded me, "Don't forget, April 7th is our big day." I waved in agreement as she went out the door. As I gathered up my notes, the afternoon's events swept over me in a wave of fatigue and optimism.

~

Chapter 94

A SECOND CHANCE

March refused to give up winter. Slipping out of her woolen jacket and pulling a knitted scarf from her neck, Joan announced, "I have something wonderful to tell you."

"I'm all ears."

"I've befriended an elderly woman who lives across the street," she said, taking her seat. "She was sweeping her front porch and waved. I waved back. For some reason, I felt drawn to her right away and gathered up my courage, crossed the street, and introduced myself. She came down the porch steps, held out her hand, and said, 'I'm Louise.' I could see she was up in years and a bit unsteady on her feet. Since then, we've spent a lot of time together. Most afternoons, we've had coffee. We sit and talk about anything and everything. Her daughter and three grandchildren live out West. She's a retired high school teacher. Taught art and music—how's that for a coincidence? I told her a little about me, but not much. Some afternoons we play cards. She loves gin rummy and usually wins, which tickles her to no end. Her mind is sharp for a ninety-year-old, and Louise has a wicked sense of humor. She's become like a surrogate grandmother." Joan paused and frowned. "Not at all like my real grandmother. Louise is wise and caring. I'm amazed I have such deep affection for her. Not being afraid I'll get hurt is a new experience for me."

I felt gratified Joan drew on prudent Sebunome's gift of recognizing trustworthiness. Joan had intuitively identified a person with whom she felt safe and confident enough to initiate a trusting relationship, one that offers her laughter and joy without the fear of being betrayed.

Joanna appeared unexpectedly. "Many Voices said my time to reunite with Joan will happen soon. Before it does, I want to thank Elizabeth for taking care of me after I was rescued from the Abyss. She tutored me about Joan's life Outside and how to get along with people. I love her, and I've learned that we have a special connection that can never be severed."

Alarms went off in my head, but I didn't interrupt.

"I was told my birth was a difficult one. During labor, my mother was taunted by her mother—my grandmother, who was enraged at my mother for being unmarried. She yelled and demeaned her in front of the doctor and nurse. She accused her of having disgraced the family and called her a slut, who deserved all the pain she was experiencing. I was told my mother went into shock and that I became stuck in the birth canal. Elizabeth came to my rescue and guided me into this world."

I masked my skepticism with caution by asking, "Who gave you this information?"

"Many Voices, of course," Joanna replied.

"Elizabeth was there to facilitate your birth?"

"It's what I've been told."

I thanked Joanna for this astounding revelation, and she withdrew.

Joan immediately spoke up. "I vaguely remember my mother telling a friend about the ordeal she suffered during labor. I believe the doctor had my grandmother removed from the room until after I—I mean Joanna—was born."

Working to help heal a woman with MPD had challenged my objectivity innumerable times. As thought-provoking as Joanna's statement was, my commitment to guiding the integration process to a conclusion before Easter left me neither time nor energy to investigate the implications associated with a maternal inner self-helper responding to the existential fears of an unborn child in utero.

March 23. "As you can see, I'm a real mess," Joan said, ruefully pulling her skirt aside to reveal lesions on her shins. She again complained of upper respiratory congestion.

Symptoms, I thought, *caused by the anxiety over her impending integration.*

Frail Hope slipped out, her neck pulled into her shoulders, her chin clamped to her chest. From beneath her brow, she looked up at me. "Raven says it's my time to cross," a quaver of vulnerability in her voice. "What would happen if . . . if I stay behind?"

"I suppose you would be left all alone."

Her soft brown eyes grew round with alarm.

"On the other hand, if you decide to cross, you will live in the Light and bestow Joan with your promise."

Hope took a quiet, resigned breath and said, "Perhaps before I go, I could make something to leave behind. Something solely of myself."

With that said, she faded.

"Sweet Hope," Joan sympathized, "how torn she feels to leave the safety of Raven's wing."

Turning her gaze out the window at the budding trees, Joan marveled at who she had become through therapy, and what the integrated Parts had bestowed. She was more aware than ever of her talents and gifts and now understood how multifaceted a human being could be. She was filled with feelings she'd never felt before. Expressing them without inhibition took her breath away. Knowing and accepting her personal history were the greatest gifts. And glorious was the fact that her faith in God and His love had not diminished. Although her mind had been shattered, she always trusted that, someday, He would fulfill His promise.

A hush fell over the therapy room. *Admiration for her achievement filled my heart. Shepherding her emergence from Darkness into the Light had been a journey of hard work, mystery, and grace. Now I believed Joan was ready to enter the last phase of treatment—reuniting with Joanna.*

As if she read my thoughts, Joan said, "I know I'm ready, Renate. I'm not afraid."

"Louise has not been feeling well," Joan said a week later. "Considering her age, I suppose our time together will be short. When she passes, I shall miss the laughter and companionship," her voice sounding small and mournful. After some time, a faint smile softened her face—Hope emerged.

"I've decided not to stay behind," she said and presented me with a sheet of paper folded neatly in half. On one side, Hope had drawn what she called "Raven's Feather Heart." On the other side was her self-portrait.

"This feather heart represents Raven's love," she declared. "He told me I had not been a coward when I flew with him up into the sky to escape. He said my purpose was to take everyone's hope to safety."

"When you cross over," I said, reflectively, "you'll be returning that hope to Joan."

Raven's Feather Heart, Hope 2009.

I sat beside her. As so many had done before, she took my hand in hers and murmured a final goodbye. I gently squeezed her hand as my voice guided her back to the Inner Realm.

As I sat waiting, Joan's features gradually softened. She opened her eyes and rubbed her forehead. "No headache," her eyes bright. She reported the ritual had been completed with unusual solemnity. They had all embraced. Raven then tucked Hope under his wing one last time and flew her toward the Light.

Hope's Self-Portrait, Hope 2009.

After Joan left for home, I sat awhile longer in my rocking chair. I felt a profound sense of fulfillment. *Perhaps Hope's bequest was intended for me as well.*

Roger called an hour before Joan's next appointment. He sounded distraught. Joan had been rude and was stumbling around like she had been drinking. Since our appointment was within the hour, I assured him I would explore what had caused such behavior. He professed to already know. Jane had somehow unfused from Joan and was acting out. Joan was upset about the separation. Roger had astutely reminded her that Beth and a few of the others took some time to become "solidly integrated." I praised him for applying what he had learned about the intricacies of MPD. He laughed self-consciously and said the survival of his marriage depended on that understanding.

Joan arrived in a state of agitation. She kept her eyes averted. "I had a conversation with my sister," she began, fiddling with the clasp on her purse. "It got pretty intense when I told her what happened to me growing up. This was the very first time Lillian listened. Before, she always brushed me off. I told her everything—the truth about our mother, our grandmother and her lover, and all about Charles. And she didn't accuse me of making everything up."

Jane came out in a splutter. "All that stuff Joan and her sister talked about is old news. I should know—I was there until I was fifteen. But that's not why I came out again. Joan and Lillian started talking about what to do with the Mother now that she's old and needy. Who would take care of her? Lillian said she couldn't and wouldn't. She can't stand her. She left home early and hasn't had any contact with the Mother since—none to speak of anyway—and has no intention to start now. Let me tell you," wagging her finger in my face, "if Joan decides to invite the Mother to move in with her, I will never integrate. Not now, not ever. If Joan takes her in, life will be unbearable for everyone. And I do mean *unbearable*."

"I can see you're upset, Jane. But I have no knowledge that Joan made such a commitment. What you heard, I suspect, was Joan and her sister talking about *possibilities*."

Joan moved forward. "I dread the thought of having to endure my mother's constant presence. When I thought about her living with us, my blood pressure spiked. I thought I was going to have another heart attack. Sometimes I think I should forgive her, but how can I? Sometimes I feel sorry for her . . . but often, I just don't care. And sometimes I miss her and don't know why. The most surprising thing is that I even love her. How is that possible? I want Jane to know I certainly haven't decided what to do."

Jane spoke up. "Not having made a decision does not mean *never*. It might mean *maybe*. There's still a chance she'll invite the Mother to live with us."

"I suggest you trust Joan to do what's best. However, if you choose to stay unfused, you will put the whole integration process on hold. Is that what you wish to do?"

"Not really. I want what everyone wants—you included."

"So, are you willing to be rejoined with Joan regardless of the uncertainty surrounding the Mother?"

"I guess."

After Jane's reintegration, Joan sat quietly for a few moments before commenting, "I'm certainly glad we're together again."

"So am I," relief in my voice.

At that moment, I sensed the presence of the Blessing Lady. As had often occurred whenever a resolution had been achieved, she traced three crosses on my palm. To my astonishment, she leaned forward and whispered, "Goodbye, dear Healer." In all the years of treatment, the Blessing Lady had never spoken. Her next revelation was no less startling.

"Now that our work is done, I shall reunite with Raven. He is the one who created me to provide a reassuring touch, a comforting caress whenever a Part was in agony or despaired or was confused. When I made the sign of the three crosses on your palm, I did so to express our gratitude—Raven's, Many Voices', Elizabeth's, and mine—for doing all you could to inspire healing."

As she receded, she lifted her right hand in a gesture of farewell.

In early April, Joan called with an urgent request to see me. I worked her into my schedule that afternoon. Upon her arrival, I learned she wanted to understand why Parts become unfused. "Now that I know something like that is possible, I have to be vigilant to avoid such a thing happening again."

Unfusing was not unheard of, I told her. Should a Part become re-traumatized by an outside event—as in Jane's case by Joan's conversation with her sister—then those intense emotions could trigger a separation. Parts also might become unfused, I cautioned, if their concerns had not been fully resolved. Using the example of Leaf 14, I explained she had unfused from Raven because she had not been reunited with her twin. I pointed out Joan should also be mindful of the possibility of a traumatic event reactivating dissociative responses. That old coping mechanism could split off a new Part. Plus, there was one other possibility—an unrecovered Part could make herself known.

"Why wouldn't she come forward during treatment, like all the others?"

"Most likely she was not yet ready to disclose a 'secret' she held. Perhaps some post-integration event triggers her appearance, and only at that time is she prepared to share her memory."

Joan exhaled loudly. "I guess there could be some surprises after integration."

"That's a good reason to continue treatment afterward." The goal, I explained, will be to learn to live in the new reality and adapt to daily life from the perspective of a whole person. This will include developing additional coping skills to meet unforeseen challenges with confidence. I reminded Joan of what Raven taught us: In time, everything will be as it is meant to be.

Raven came forward. "Dear Healer, now that the memories have been beaded into a necklace of the most intricate design, I am confident we may proceed. Elizabeth will dismantle the House and return the material used for its construction to the place from which it has been borrowed. Seeds will be sown at the site where the House stood. They will germinate and blossom into multi-colored wildflowers as soon as Joan and Joanna integrate. Upon their exit from the Inner Realm, the opening at the Outer Edge will be sealed permanently.

"Soon, Healer, you and I shall say goodbye. The work we have been called upon to accomplish has been completed. Allow me to convey my profound respect. It has been a privilege to partner with you as a 'co-therapist.' I'm looking forward to having more opportunities for contemplation and conversing with the One you choose to call 'the Sacred.' There may come a time when you and I shall meet in your dreams, where we shall fly to a Place of Knowing that renews the spirit and nurtures the soul."

"Renewal—what a welcome proposition, dear Raven. So, this is not really 'goodbye.'"

With a gracious smile, he took his leave.

"I can't imagine," Joan quipped, "what post-integration sessions will be like after all this drama. They certainly will be calmer, probably dull in comparison." Joan's eyes dimmed as though the light reflected inward. I honored her silent introspection. Lifting her head to look me square in the face, she said, "Making sense of the future will have its trials. But who would want to mourn the chaos and torment of living with a fragmented mind? Certainly not me."

~

Chapter 95

A PROMISE FULFILLED

April 7. The day of final integration was at hand. I dressed professionally in a pinstripe suit with a white silk blouse, my favorite silver broach with amethyst stones pinned to my lapel. With high anticipation, I went to my office an hour before Joan was scheduled to arrive. I lit three candles, sat in my rocking chair, and remembered how Raven, Elizabeth, Joan, and Joanna envisioned the integration celebration taking place. Then I reviewed my notes from the night before to ready myself for the culminating event. Putting the notes aside, I closed my eyes and visualized the reunification procedure. I practiced the breathing exercise to release my apprehension and invited the Golden Light to impart its wisdom and guide me through what was to unfold.

When Joan opened the office door, I stood to greet her. She was wearing a dark-blue rayon dress and black leather pumps. A tiny cross was hanging from a braided chain of gold around her neck. Her brown eyes beamed with anticipation.

"My goodness, Joan—you look lovely."

She twirled around, exuberant in her good looks. She took her seat among the cushions on the blue couch, placed her purse beside her, and fixed her soulful eyes on me. "Before we start, Renate, I want to thank you for leading me out of Darkness and loving me into life. You helped me and the Parts suffer through so many sorrows. You guided me to find the strength to transform what had crippled me—what made me feel small and dirty and unworthy. You never gave up on me, no matter how difficult or tiring the struggle became. What we have achieved together feels like a miracle."

I felt my throat constrict. *What could I say to this brave and gifted woman whom I had learned to respect and hold dear?* To prevent myself from tearing up, I teased, "You're using *my* vocabulary again."

She arched an eyebrow. "I didn't once use 'alchemical processes.'"

"True, you did manage to avoid *that*."

We both laughed.

"But it's me who must thank you, Joan, for trusting me to be your Helper. Our work together, though lacerating at times, has been the most meaningful and exhilarating learning experience of my life. Responding to your 'struggle' has forced me to acquire a new body of knowledge and skills, which I shall always value. What we faced together called upon my imagination and creativity in ways I could not have envisioned. Despite the tragedies that marred your life, your endurance and determination to overcome them showed me what real courage looks like. Your unshakable faith and capacity for goodness and laughter are the true miracles."

Her manicured hand flew to her chest. "We'd better stop now," she said, "or I'll dissolve in tears." She crossed her legs. "Everything Inside is nearly gone." A hint of melancholy colored her voice. "The River of Tears has dried up. The Meadow has shrunk to a small patch covered with wildflowers in honor of all who assembled there. I shall always remember the Inner Realm, where we learned to share our memories and cleansed ourselves of the abuses and transcended those wrongs. Never to re-enter that imaginary landscape is hard to accept. But now that all the Parts have integrated, there's no longer a need for that place of refuge."

"I, too, shall never forget the Inner Realm and all the inhabitants and wondrous features your genius created. May I now have the honor to guide you Inside one last time to where Elizabeth and Joanna and Raven are waiting?"

I began as I had so many times in the past: "Make yourself comfortable . . ." Soon, Joan was breathing slowly, rhythmically, her facial expression serene as she joined the others Inside.

Keenly aware this would be my last opportunity to speak through to the Inner Realm, I thanked Raven, Elizabeth, Joanna, and Joan for their presence. I praised their fortitude for partaking in this event, which would culminate in full integration, thus ending Joan's years of multiplicity, and restoring Joanna's psychological cohesion. Before continuing, I encouraged Joan and Joanna to honor the myriad contributions of Raven and Many Voices, and to always treasure their wisdom. To Elizabeth, I conveyed my appreciation for her reliability and kindness which contributed so much to the success of our work. I thanked Many Voices for her epistolary chronicle of the past. Finally, I commended Raven for his unwavering fidelity to our work—even in the bleakest hours—and for serving, in the words of Ralph Allison, "as the conduit for God's healing power and love." I then invited Joan and Elizabeth to express their gratitude to one another for what each had provided. Joan's fingers were laced reverently, her brow knitted in earnest affection as her lips moved soundlessly.

In the quiet moments that followed, I leaned back in my rocking chair, alert to any troubling facial expressions and body agitation suggesting distress.

After a considerable time, Joan exited. "Joanna is right beside me," she said. "I wish you could have been there, Renate, to see all of us gathered among the wildflowers." I listened with delight as Joan conjured up the magical realism of the last event to take place in the Inner Realm. "Elizabeth looked very dignified," she said. "I had never seen her without her apron and keys. She was dressed in a black lace gown with a beautiful white rose on her right shoulder. Joanna wore a white satin gown with a gorgeous red rose pinned to her left shoulder." Joan had expressed her gratitude to Elizabeth for providing the young Parts a haven—a place to be and rest and learn—and for offering them comfort. In turn, Elizabeth praised Joan for functioning as the Host on the Outer Edge, ensuring the welfare of the Body, and for providing the Parts the chance to gain insight into home and family life.

Now Joanna spoke up to say she, too, had gratefully acknowledged the care, nurturing, and many lessons Elizabeth had bestowed. All of which facilitated her maturing into a woman with strength of character. After that, she and Elizabeth had embraced in farewell.

Again Joan spoke: "Raven led Joanna and me to the tiniest pinprick of light, through which we exited the Inner Realm. I didn't look back," her voice somber with finality, "but I know Raven sealed the Outer Edge immediately after we passed through."

At this time, I asked if both were ready to take the final step. With their affirmation, I directed them to close their eyes so that we might proceed.

"Invite the Golden Light to descend upon you . . . welcome its blessings and feel it infuse you with hope and joy for what is to come. Humbly ask its guidance that you may discover any remaining apprehensions. As you breathe in . . . and breathe out . . . slowly release these wisps of concern . . . allow them to vaporize one by one . . . Now that you are prepared for what's before you, open your heart and soul . . . your mind and spirit . . . to receive one another, so as to commence blending and joining. Reach out, and embrace all that you are. Fill yourselves with vitality and confidence . . . with hope and clarity of purpose. Grow in the knowledge that you matter and are of value . . . and understand you have all it takes to live your singular life. And as you become one, be cognizant of your freedom to live in balance and harmony . . . and to choose your response to any challenge. Let your mind fill with the sense that you are never alone but are always in a protective and loving Presence. When the reunification process is complete, open your eyes."

The familiar Body shifted slightly as though having to become comfortable within itself. Large brown eyes opened. "I'm whole," a melodic voice announced. "We are one." The voice grew resonant. "Joan and I are permanently intertwined from this moment forward."

"Congratulations, Joanna," I said in joyous relief.

"Please call me 'Joan.' We both thought it best that way. Otherwise, my family and friends will be confused."

I asked how she felt.

"It's difficult to describe." A furrow creased her brow. "I feel victorious and vulnerable at the same time." She lowered her voice, "It's kind of unsettling. All this newness . . . But I'm whole now. My mind and heart are full—thanks to Joan for all she's given, for what she's been, and in every way always will be."

Playfully flinging her arms wide in a mischievous fashion, which I recognized with delight, she teased, "I feel like rejoicing. Where are the trumpets and the drum roll?"

I got up from my rocking chair and sat on the couch beside the integrated Joan. Like so many times during our five-year sojourn, she reached for my hand and laid her head on my shoulder. She thanked me for guiding her back to herself—the person she always was meant to be.

"With what I've learned from Many Voices and Elizabeth," she said, with conviction, "combined with the wealth of Joan's life experiences, knowledge, and skills, I'll be able to pursue a purposeful life that reflects who I am. I'll be free to express my feelings without fear. Free to use my intelligence. Free to utilize my talents any way I choose. Now, with control over my body, no one has the power to defile me. I can trust my judgment and not rely on the opinions of others. I'm a person of substance, not an object to be thrown away. I know I deserve to be loved, and I can choose whom to love." With profound humility, she said, "I shall live a life that belongs to me."

A new way of being for Joan, I thought. *She knows what matters to the heart, not just to the mind.* I felt a sublime contentment envelop us, a golden moment in an atmosphere of sacred beauty. We sat like that in peace until she withdrew her hand from mine. Joan retrieved her purse and, avowing her affection, tapped her chest above her heart while murmuring, "I'll see you soon." And with care, she closed the office door behind her.

I sat alone in the gathering twilight thinking of the triumph of Light over Darkness. A testament to the connection with the Sacred embodied in us all. *And what of love?* I mused. *Only love can transmute suffering and fear, self-loathing and anger, and usher in a pathway to recovery from a past that cannot be undone.*

When the candles guttered out, I stood up from my rocking chair and stretched what seemed like every fiber of my being. I turned off the office lights, locked the door, and slowly made my way through the garden, and to home.

～

THE INHABITANTS
OF THE INNER REALM

Joan's Parts
Listed according to their first appearance during treatment

Beth, the Messenger, is seven. Created at two and a half to endure the grand-parents' maltreatment. Her role is to preserve harmony and maintain communication.

Rose, the Altruist, is thirteen. Created at the age of ten months to endure sexual molestation. She holds the physical and emotional pain of sexual abuse.

Samantha, the Sentinel and one of the three Tree Girls, is eighteen. Created at age five to infuse Joan with confidence.

Maria, the Pollyanna, is six. Sees the world through rose-colored glasses.

Lisa, the conduit for celestial music, was created at seven to provide solace.

Fury 1, one of the three Furies, is twelve. Created at age six. Holds Joan's anger and longing for love. She is alcoholic and suicidal.

Annie, the Whiner, is three. Created during a violent confrontation between Joan's parents.

Sarah Christine, the Fatalist and one of the Tree Girls, is sixteen. Created at six to cope with the sexual abuse of the stepfather. Holds Joan's anger, longing for love, and is alcoholic and suicidal.

Charlotte, the Ballerina, is ten. Appeared at the age of four to endure being sexually molested by the grandmother's boyfriend.

Sebunome, the Truth Teller, is twelve and one of the Tree Girls. Created at four by the violent conflict between Joan's parents. She holds Joan's fear and distrust of both men and women.

Shadowman, the Persecutor, is an eighteen-year-old male. Created at two by the father's violent behavior. Holds rage against all abusers and outsiders. He controls **eighteen Puppets,** who serve as his minions. Their ages range from four to seventeen.

JJ is eight. Created to hold Joan's confusion caused by her mother's mixed messages.

Sophia, the Outsider, is nine. Holds the terror and shame of rape.

Cannotlook is seven. Holds rage against the stepfather's cruelties.

Amber is three. Holds the fear of the Mother's yellow eyes.

Angelina, a Protectress, is three. Created to protect Joan's sister, Lillian, from her father's violence.

Slut, a streetwise adolescent, is promiscuous and alcoholic.

Eve and **Jasmine,** the Mischief-Makers, are thirteen-year-old twins. Created to hold the terror of choking.

Alice, a pre-adolescent, perceives herself as a surface reflection.

Maggie, a Protectress, is seven. Created to protect Lillian from the wrath of the grandmother and the abuse of the stepfather.

Ana, the Helpmate, is forty-five. She came forward at age ten to provide Joan with strength and stability.

Fat and Ugly, the Bulimic, and **Thin and Bad,** the Anorexic, are eight-year-old twins. Respectively, they hold anger for the Mother's betrayal and sorrow for her indifference.

Leaf 14 and **Leaf 4,** the Oak Tree Dwellers, are fourteen and four years old, respectively. The former holds feelings of guilt and the latter holds feelings of abandonment.

Joanna, the Birth Personality, is not a Part. At the age of three, she was sexually assaulted, during which she entered a state of amnesia. She reawakened after forty-three years. Under Elizabeth's care and Many Voices' tutelage, she matured to a fifty-year-old by the time of her reunification with Joan.

The Forest Girl, a mature Part from Many Voices' system, speaks for the other Forest Girls' desperation and wish for being saved.

Marjorie, one of the Three Furies, is eleven. Created at five, she is filled with murderous hostility for the stepfather.

Fury 2, another of the Three Furies, is eleven. She holds rage and is suicidal.

Joan 2, the College Girl, is eighteen. Created at seventeen to endure an abortion and support Joan's collegiate experience.

Jane, the Happy Drunk, is fifteen. Appeared at the age of four to assist Joan in the care of baby Donald.

Hope, Raven's Ward, is nine. She holds terror of the occult, the shame of the stepfather's depravity, and the expectation of hope.

Diana, the corpse buried behind Elizabeth's House, was created at twelve to help Joan through the worst times. Died at fifteen.

Fragment Parts: The Girl in the Mirror, Feather, Three, Five, Tiny Baby, Biger [sic] Baby, two toddlers, Six, Nine, No See, No Talk, No Name, Bad, and another eight or more unnamed Forrest Girls.

The Inner Self-Helpers

Many Voices, the Observer and Scribe, holds biographical information and provides a refuge for those Parts in her system. She is imagined encapsulated in a sparkling cloud of white mist.

Raven, the Light Bearer, advises, guides, and protects Joan and the Parts in his system. He manifests the gestalt of a dignified black bird.

Elizabeth, the Internal Mother, is the fifty-year-old caretaker of infant and pre-adolescent Parts residing in her House.

The Blessing Lady, the Comforter, bestows the ceremonial sign of the three crosses.

THE IMAGINARY LANDSCAPE

The Outer Realm, Joan's geographical and social environment.

The Outer Edge, the passageway through which Joan and the Parts exit and return.

The Inner Realm, the imaginary environment created by Joan's mind as a place of refuge where the Parts exist in various stages of awareness. Divided into two separate systems, each is guided and protected by an inner self-helper: Raven and Many Voices.

Raven's Perch, located atop the tallest leafed-out tree.

Elizabeth's House, a two-story structure consisting of bedrooms, living room, kitchen, and bathroom. Behind the House is a small garden with two graves—Diana and Baby Donald.

Rose's Cave, a dark place of solitude and safety.

The Meadow, a patch of green that evolved into a meadow covered with wildflowers. A place of rest, contemplation, and regeneration where the Parts congregate in the Circle of Truth.

The Waterfall, a cascade from the crying of inward tears.

The River of Tears, a place of transformation and cleansing of psychic wounds.

The Path of Crushed Lies, the pathway leading to the light of consciousness.

The Safe Place, inspired by the therapist and created by Joan as a fully furnished, soundproof place of security and observation, with bolted doors and shuttered windows.

The Forest Edge, the border between the two systems.

The Tree Girls' Tree, a barren tree located near the edge of the Dark and Haunted Forest.

Shadowman's Tree, a large gnarled, leafless tree at the edge of the Dark and Haunted Forest.

The Seat of Many Voices, a sparkling cloud of white mist.

The Dark and Haunted Forest, an area of lifeless trees inhabited by the Forest Girls.

The Vast Region of Nothingness, a barren plain with sharp-edged cliffs and deep valleys.

The Abyss, a crevasse where the birth personality is entombed.

The White Zone, an area of Joan's mind devoid of consciousness.

IN GRATITUDE

Writing Joan's story was among the most challenging learning experiences of my career. After I voice-recorded my handwritten treatment notes, Marcy McCurdy, my trusted assistant, transcribed the audio files with laser focus and brought Joan's story to life on the computer screen. She attended to every task, large and small, with fierce determination and infectious enthusiasm. During our long hours together, I learned to respect and love my young friend. I am deeply thankful.

Mack, my husband and partner of almost fifty years, made the most constructive offerings. As my in-house editor, he cajoled and coaxed me to add to, cut from, and improve on those portions of the manuscript most dear to me. Trampling ever so gently on my pride, he insisted on "straightening" my German-English sentences and finding the "better" word. His infinite devotion and unwavering support for me and Joan's story sustained me. Without his contributions, this book would not have come into being. He is a blessing.

In my long life, I have learned "Helpers" appear when most needed. Kathleen Baker Blease is such a helper. Her editing suggestions and comments were insightful, wise, and sensitive, leading me to where I needed to go. I shall be ever grateful.

Many thanks to Frank Kresen, Sarah Cortez, and Bob Gookin for their perceptive writing acumen, generosity, and editorial professionalism. I am in their debt.

My heartfelt gratitude goes to Gina Dittmer for her dedication and professionalism in photographing Joan's art work.

To my early readers, and to those who listened and answered and advised, thank you: Sabine, Rebecca W., Chandler, Leah and Richard, Carla, Alisa, Rebecca F., Betty, Marca, Chris, Cassie, McKenzie, Michal, and Ashley.

～

RESOURCES

I owe a debt of gratitude to those distinguished authors and prominent mental-health professionals whose wisdom and knowledge persuaded me that healing a fragmented mind was possible. In particular, I wish to express heartfelt thanks to Ralph Allison, Colin Ross, and Terri Clark whose books were my constant companions in guiding me to find a healing path.

Alcoholics Anonymous. (1994). New York: A.A. World Services, Inc.

Allison, R. B. (2003). *Memories of an Essence.* www.sacaaa.org/occasional_papers/memories_of_an_essence_synopsis.htm. Date referenced 1/29/2007.

Allison, R. B. and Schwartz, T. (1980). *Minds in Many Pieces: The Making of a Very Special Doctor.* New York: Rawson Wade Publishing.

Baer, R. (2007). *Switching Time: A Doctor's Harrowing Story of Treating a Woman with 17 Personalities.* New York: Crown Publishers.

Beauregard, M., and O'Leary, D. (2007). The Spiritual Brain: A Neuroscientist's Case for the Existence of the Soul. New York: HarperCollins Publishers.

Beck, A. T. (1976). *Cognitive Therapy and the Emotional Disorders.* New York: Penguin Books.

Bliss, E. L. (1986). *Multiple Personality, Allied Disorders, and Hypnosis.* New York: Oxford University Press.

Bloch, J. P. (1991). *Assessment and Treatment of Multiple Personality and Dissociative Disorders.* Sarasota, FL: Professional Resource.

Bowlby, J. (1988). *A Secure Base: Parent-Child Attachment and Healthy Human Development.* New York: Basic Books Publications.

Borysenko, J. (1990). *Guilt Is the Teacher, Love Is the Lesson.* New York: Warner Books.

Braun, B. G. (Ed.). (1986). *Treatment of Multiple Personality Disorder.* Washington, D.C.: American Psychiatric Press, Inc.

Breuer, J. and Freud, S. (1957). *Studies on Hysteria.* New York: Basic Books.

Brinson, J. (1994). *Murderous Memories: One Woman's Hellish Battle to Save Herself.* Far Hills, NJ: New Horizon Publishing.

Campbell, J. (1968). *The Hero with a Thousand Faces.* New Jersey: Princeton University Press.

Chase, T. and Phillips, R. A. (1987). *When Rabbit Howls.* New York: E.P. Dutton Publishing.

Chernin, K. (1985). *The Hungry Self: Women, Eating, and Identity.* New York: Harper Perennial.

Chu, J. A. (1998). *Rebuilding Shattered Lives: The Responsible Treatment of Complex Post-Traumatic and Dissociative Disorders.* New York: John Wiley & Sons.

Clark, T. A. (1993). *More Than One.* Nashville: Thomas Nelson Publishers.

Coelho, P. (2006). *The Alchemist.* San Francisco: Harper San Francisco.

Cohen, B., Giller, E., and Lynn W. (1991). *Multiple Personality Disorder from the Inside Out.* Baltimore: Sidran Press.

Courtois, C. A. (1998). *Healing the Incest Wound: Adult Survivors in Therapy.* New York: Norton.

Damasio, A. R. (1999). *The Feeling of What Happens: Body and Emotion in the Making of Consciousness.* New York: Harcourt Brace Publications.

Damgaard, J. (1987). *The Inner Self Helper: Transcendent Life within Life?* Petaluma, CA: *Noetic Sciences Review.*

Diagnostic and Statistical Manual of Mental Disorders: DSM-IV (1994). Washington, DC: American Psychiatric Association.

Erickson, M. H. and Rosen, S. (1982). *My Voice Will Go with You: The Teaching Tales of Milton H. Erickson, M.D.* New York: Norton.

Frankl, V. E. (1984). *Man's Search for Meaning.* Boston: Washington Square Press.

Freud, S. (1962). *Aetiology of Hysteria.* London: Hogarth Press.

Gardner, M. (1960). *The Annotated Alice.* New York: Bramhall House.

Greenspan, S. I. (1992). *Infancy and Early Childhood: The Practice of Clinical Assessment and Intervention with Emotional and Developmental Challenges.* Madison, CT: International Universities.

Haddock, D. (2001). *The Dissociative Identity Disorder Sourcebook.* Chicago: Contemporary Publishing.

Herman-Lewis, J. (1992). *Trauma and Recovery: The Aftermath of Violence— from Domestic Abuse to Political Terror.* New York: Basic Publishing.

Hillman, J. (1996). *The Soul's Code: In Search of Character and Calling.* New York: Random House.

James, W. (1898). *The Varieties of Religious Experience: A Study in Human Nature.* New American Library.

Jamison, K. (1999). *Night Falls Fast: Understanding Suicide.* New York: Vintage Books.

Janet, P. (1890). *The Major Symptoms of Hysteria.* New York: Macmillan.

Johnson, R. A. (1991). *Owning Your Own Shadow: Understanding the Dark Side of the Psyche.* CA: Harper San Francisco.

Jung, C. G. (1969). *Aion: Researches into the Phenomenology of the Self* (Bollingen Series XX). Vol. 9, Part 2. Trans. R. F. C. Hull. Ed. H. Reed, M. Fordham, G. Adler, and W. McGuire. Princeton: Princeton University Press.

Jung, C. G. (1968). *Psychology and Alchemy* (Bollingen Series XX). Vol. 12. Trans. R. F. C. Hull. Ed. H. Reed, M. Fordham, G. Adler, and W. McGuire. Princeton: Princeton University Press.

Kabat-Zinn, J. (1990). *Full Catastrophe Living: Using the Wisdom of Your Body and Mind to Face Stress, Pain, and Illness.* New York: Bantam Doubleday Dell Publishing Group.

Kalsched, D. (1996). *The Inner World of Trauma: Archetypal Defenses of the Personal Spirit.* London: Routledge.

Kasl, C. D. (1992). *Many Roads, One Journey: Moving Beyond the 12 Steps.* NY: Harper Perennial.

Keyes, D. (1981). *The Minds of Billy Milligan.* New York: Random House Publications.

Kidd, S. M. (2002). *The Secret Life of Bees.* London: Penguin Publishing Group.

Kohut, H. (1977). *The Restoration of the Self.* New York: International Universities Press.

Kopp, S. B. (1974). *The Hanged Man: Psychotherapy and the Forces of Darkness.* Palo Alto, CA: Science and Behavior.

Krakauer, S. Y. (2001). *Treating Dissociative Identity Disorder: The Power of the Collective Heart.* Philadelphia: Brunner-Routledge Publications.

Kubetin, C. A. and Mallory, J. D. (1992). *Beyond the Darkness.* Houston, TX: Rapha Publishing.

Lerner, H. G. (1985). *The Dance of Anger: A Woman's Guide to Changing the Patterns of Intimate Relationships.* New York: Harper & Row.

Maslow, A. H. (1968). *Toward a Psychology of Being.* New York: Van Nostrand Reinhold.

Miller, A. (1983). *For Your Own Good.* New York: Farrar, Straus and Giroux.

Myss, C. (1996). *Anatomy of the Spirit.* New York: Harmony Books.

Olson, S. E. (1997). *Becoming One: A Story of Triumph Over Multiple Personality Disorder.* Pasadena, CA: Trilogy Books.

Oxnam, R. B. (2005). *A Fractured Mind: My Life with Multiple Personality Disorder.* New York: Hyperion Publishing.

Peck, M. S. (1983). *People of the Lie: The Hope for Healing Human Evil.* New York: Simon and Schuster.

Perry, B. (1997). *Childhood Trauma and Neurological and Physical Development.* Workshop: Mental Health Authority. Oklahoma City, OK.

Post, B. (2004). *Touch in Psychotherapy: Exploring One of the Most Taboo Subjects in Mental Health Today.* Workshop: Post Institute for Family Centered Therapy. Oklahoma City, OK.

Prince, M. (1906). *Dissociation of a Personality.* New York: Longman, Green.

Putnam, F. W. (1989). *Diagnosis and Treatment of Multiple Personality Disorder.* New York: Guilford Press.

Rogers, C. R. (1951). *Client-Centered Therapy: Its Current Practice, Implications, and Theory.* Boston: Houghton Mifflin.

Ross, C. A. (1994). *The Osiris Complex: Case-studies in Multiple Personality Disorder.* Toronto: University of Toronto.

Ross, C. A. (1989). *Multiple Personality Disorder: Diagnosis, Clinical Features, and Treatment.* New York: Wiley Publishing.

Russell, D. E. H. (1986). *The Secret Trauma: Incest in the Lives of Girls and Women.* New York: Basic Publishing.

Scarf, M. (1980). *Unfinished Business: Pressure Points in the Lives of Women.* New York: Ballantine Books.

Schreiber, F. (1973). *Sybil.* Chicago: Henry Regnery Publishing.

Schwartz, R. (2014). *Healing Trauma from the Inside: An Internal Family System Approach.* Workshop: Oklahoma Association for Marriage and Family Therapy.

Schwartz, R. (2001). *Introduction to the Internal Family System Model.* Oak Park, IL: Trailheads Publication.

Tavris, C. (1982). *Anger: The Misunderstood Emotion.* New York: Simon and Schuster.

Thigpen, C. H. and Cleckley, H. M. (1957). *The Three Faces of Eve.* McGraw-Hill, New York.

Trujillo, O. R. (2011). *The Sum of My Parts: A Survivor's Story of Dissociative Identity Disorder.* New Harbinger Publications, Inc.

Tyler, P. (1967). *The Divine Comedy of Pavel Tchelitchew.* New York: Fleet Publishing Corp.

Underhill, E. (1915). *Mysticism: The Preeminent Study in the Nature and Development of Spiritual Consciousness.* New York: Doubleday.

van der Kolk, B. (2014). *The Body Keeps the Score: Brain, Mind, and Body in the Healing of Trauma.* New York: Viking.

Walsh, R. N. and Vaughan, F. E. Eds. (1993). *Paths Beyond Ego: The Transpersonal Vision.* Los Angeles: J. P. Tarcher/Perigee Publishing.

Walsh, R. N. (1990). *The Spirit of Shamanism.* Los Angeles: Jeremy P. Tarcher, Inc.

West, C. (1999). *First Person Plural: My Life as a Multiple.* New York: Hyperion Publications.

Westerheide, J. (2004). *Clinical Hypnosis and Healing from Abuse.* Workshop: A Chance to Change Foundation. Oklahoma City.

Westerheide, J. (2003). *Training in Clinical Hypnosis.* Workshop: A Chance to Change Foundation. Oklahoma City.

Wilber, K. (2000). *Integral Psychology: Consciousness, Spirit, Psychology, Therapy.* Boston: Shambhala Publications.

Winnicott, D. W. (1965). *The Maturational Processes and the Facilitating Environment: Studies in the Theory of Emotional Development.* New York: International Universities.

Youritzin, V. K. (2002). *Pavel Tchelitchew* (Monograph). University of Oklahoma: Fred Jones Jr. Museum of Art.

ABOUT THE AUTHOR

R*enate F. Caldwell* is a WWII and domestic violence survivor. She came to America to get "educated," received her GED at thirty-two, and was accepted into university as a provisional student. She earned degrees in Education and Journalism, a master's degree in Human Relations, and has completed two years of postgraduate study in Transpersonal Psychology and Mysticism. Ms. Caldwell received recognition and awards for her work as an educator, journalist, and video documentarian—all of which contributed in useful ways to her more than twenty years of practice as a Licensed Professional Counselor. Her experience as a therapist includes attending to clients suffering from multiple personality disorder, post-traumatic stress, domestic violence, and schizophrenia. Ms. Caldwell worked with FEMA to provide crisis counseling for victims of terrorism. She is a member of the International Society for the Study of Trauma and Dissociation.

www.ingramcontent.com/pod-product-compliance
Lightning Source LLC
Chambersburg PA
CBHW050231270326
41914CB00033BA/1873/J